LEGAL PLURALISM AND EFFICIENCY IN MARRIAGE LAW

LEGAL PLURALISM AND EFFICIENCY IN MARRIAGE LAW

Rorick Tovar Galván

INTERSENTIA
Cambridge – Antwerp – Chicago

Intersentia Ltd
8 Wellington Mews
Wellington Street | Cambridge
CB1 1HW | United Kingdom
Tel: +44 1223 736 170
Email: mail@intersentia.co.uk
www.intersentia.com | www.intersentia.co.uk

Distribution for the UK and
Rest of the World (incl. Eastern Europe)
NBN International
1 Deltic Avenue, Rooksley
Milton Keynes MK13 8LD
United Kingdom
Tel: +44 1752 202 301 | Fax: +44 1752 202 331
Email: orders@nbninternational.com

Distribution for Europe
Lefebvre Sarrut Belgium NV
Hoogstraat 139/6
1000 Brussels
Belgium
Tel: +32 (0)800 39 067
Email: mail@intersentia.be

Distribution for the USA and Canada
Independent Publishers Group
Order Department
814 North Franklin Street
Chicago, IL 60610
USA
Tel: +1 800 888 4741 (toll free) | Fax: +1 312 337 5985
Email: orders@ipgbook.com

Artwork on cover: clivewa / Shutterstock

ISBN 978-1-83970-229-7
D/2022/7849/26
NUR 822

British Library Cataloguing in Publication Data. A catalogue record for this book is available from the British Library.

Eine neue wissenschaftliche Wahrheit pflegt sich nicht in der Weise durchzusetzen, daß ihre Gegner überzeugt werden und sich als belehrt erklären, sondern vielmehr dadurch, daß ihre Gegner allmählich aussterben und daß die heranwachsende Generation von vornherein mit der Wahrheit vertraut gemacht ist.

A new scientific truth does not triumph by convincing its opponents and making them see the light, but rather because its opponents eventually die, and a new generation grows up that is familiar with it.

Max Planck
Wissenschaftliche Selbstbiographie (1948) 22

[English translation in: Gerd Gigerenzer. *Gut Feelings*. (2007) 105]

Regulatory Competition and the Law Market for Matrimonial Issues

Source: Cartoon drawn entirely by Clive Goddard and reproduced with his kind permission. The book's author wants to thank Sophia de Groot for her input in developing the cartoon concept.

FOREWORD

This book is dealing with a very interesting and important topic: the law applicable to a marriage with cross-border elements. The relevant international (including European) instruments as well domestic private international law rules dealing with specific aspects of a marriage (matrimonial property/maintenance/divorce) often lead to the applicability of different laws to different elements of the relationship. This *dépeçage* (splitting up the choice of law/*Zersplitterung*) sometimes causes legal problems and nearly always causes practical problems. This is very irritating for the (ex)spouses concerned and is highly problematic in light of legal certainty. (Ex)spouses will need highly specialized legal assistance in order to know precisely which legal system governs which area of their relationship. These difficulties are very well described and illustrated in this book. From my own experience, I can also say that even professors of private international law married with a foreign spouse have difficulties to determine precisely which law applies to which elements of their own marital relationship. The author of this book, Rorick Tovar Galván, who moved from Peru to Spain and later to Switzerland and got married in Switzerland before being naturalized there, has his own experiences with the uncertainty caused by splitting up the law applicable to the various aspects of his marriage.

It is a good decision that the book focuses on the three mentioned aspects of a marital relationship (matrimonial property/maintenance/divorce) and excludes, for example, the validity of the marriage as such, the effects on family names or the personal effects of the marital relationship. The three issues chosen are governed by instruments developed by, respectively relevant for Member States of European Union (the Hague Protocol of 23 November 2007 on the Law Applicable to Maintenance Obligations; Council Regulation (EU) No 1259/2010 of 20 December 2010 implementing enhanced cooperation in the area of the law applicable to divorce and legal separation; Council Regulation (EU) 2016/1103 of 24 June 2016 implementing enhanced cooperation in the area of jurisdiction, applicable law and the recognition and enforcement of decisions in matters of matrimonial property regimes). If the scope had also included other issues related to marital relations, the structure of the book would have been too complicated. However, it would be welcome if the author publishes his opinion on these issues in the future.

The research questions are well formulated: a) are the existing restrictions on the choice of the applicable law desirable (with other words: should the (future) spouses have a broader possibility to determine the applicable law, which also would make it possible to choose one single law applicable to all aspects of their marital relationship)?; and b) which law should be applicable in absence of a choice of law agreement? Tovar Galván has chosen to answer these questions from an economic perspective. This is a very innovative approach. This approach made it necessary to pay extensive attention to the discipline of law and economics (economic analysis of the law). For that reason, the book first explains the method of economic analysis of law in general and then focuses on the rules on marital relationships and finally on private international law rules relating to aspects of marital relationships.

The Preface comprehensively sets out the focus of the different chapters and the motivation for them. Interim findings at the end of each chapter facilitate the reader in following the development of the author's argumentation. The chapters are consciously linked with each other by making some "bridging" remarks. The Introduction describes the three relevant international and European instruments with special attention for the choice of law possibilities for the spouses and the default rule if a choice of law is lacking. Weaknesses are pointed out in a concise, but convincing manner. Paradoxes are well criticized. The first four chapters explain the main approach to the economic analysis of legal rules. Good examples demonstrate the relevance for marriage law, with special attention for the differences between mandatory and default rules in this branch of the law. Chapter Four also gives a very good resumé of the argumentation developed so far and includes an excellent "bridge" to the discussion on how to deal with legal pluralism, which is discussed in Chapter Five. In Chapter Five a very important point is made: *dépeçage* increases the so-called transaction costs for the spouses. This is really a strong argument in favour of allowing the parties a wide choice of law for the whole of their legal relationship. Furthermore, avoiding high transaction costs is also of paramount importance, when trying to find an appropriate default connecting factor for cases where no choice of law is made. However, the transactions costs could also be used as an argument in favour of unification of laws (in this cases of marriage related rules). This issue is discussed in Chapter Seven, Section 4.4. where Tovar Galván argues that working on an optional code is welcome, but only to the extent that it does not stop initiatives to eliminate barriers to the freedom of choice of law. Chapter Seven also deals with the different arguments in favor of giving (future) spouses a wider possibility of making a choice of law. The arguments in favor of this are developed well. However, one must also ask whether (future) spouses in a purely domestic setting should have the right to opt out from the application of their national law. To do so could be appropriate for future spouses who are both residing in the same country of which they are nationals, but who will have their first marital residence abroad. And should nationals belonging to a religious minority be allowed to make a choice of law in favor of the law of the country of their ancestors? One even can raise the question, whether perhaps all (future) spouses should have the possibility to make a free choice of law? That would create a real free competition between legal systems.

This book will hopefully get the attention of the community of private international law because of its innovative approach and inspiring (sometimes even provocative) suggestions. It certainly deserves to be considered in all committees working on the development of instruments in the field of family law and related issues. I sincerely hope that Tovar Galván will continue to contribute to discussions on a better private international law which pays proper attention to the needs of people living in a cross-boundary relationship, in particular their need to have legal certainty without being frequently confronted with high bills from legal experts in private international law.

Prof. Dr. Gerard-René de Groot
Emeritus Professor of Comparative Law and Private International Law,
Maastricht University (The Netherlands) and Professor of Private Law,
University of Aruba (West Indies)

PREFACE

The variety of legislation at an international level represents a barrier for married couples planning to reside in another country. Each movement between jurisdictions can cause significant changes in the rights and obligations derived from a marriage, as courts can use different approaches to determine the legal system – or legal systems – governing relationships with international connotations. To address this issue, the European Union has decided to take matters into its own hands. With a view to assuring the proper functioning of the internal market, it has promoted the creation of three international instruments[1] dealing with the determination of the applicable law to legal issues arising from marriage: the Hague Protocol of 2007;[2] Regulation 1259/2010;[3] and Regulation 2016/1103.[4] The material scope of application of each of these instruments only focuses on one specific aspect of the marriage, namely maintenance obligations, divorce and property regime. As a result, not all legal effects arising from the marriage are covered by those instruments. Conflict of laws rules applicable to *inter alia* the names of the spouses, the validity of their marriage, or ownership of personal effects of the marital relationship have not been harmonized. Nevertheless, the efforts of the European Union must not be underestimated, not only because the newly regulated aspects of the marriage are of great importance in the daily life of spouses, but also due to the large number of states that have incorporated these rules into their national legal systems. Currently, they are

---

1 To these instruments should be added Regulation 2016/1104 that regulates property issues of registered partnerships. See: Council Regulation (EU) 2016/1104 of 24 June 2016 implementing enhanced cooperation in the area of jurisdiction, applicable law and the recognition and enforcement of decisions in matters of the property consequences of registered partnerships [2016] OJ L183/30.

2 Council Decision of 30 November 2009 on the conclusion by the European Community of the Hague Protocol of 23 November 2007 on the Law Applicable to Maintenance Obligations [2009] OJ L331/17 (hereafter Hague Protocol of 2007). For the competence of the EU in topics related to the harmonization of conflict of laws rules in the area of family law, as well as its role within The Hague Conference, see: Martiny (2008) 189–190.

3 Council Regulation (EU) No. 1259/2010 of 20 December 2010 implementing enhanced cooperation in the area of the law applicable to divorce and legal separation [2010] OJ L343/10 (hereafter Regulation 1259/2010).

4 Council Regulation (EU) 2016/1103 of 24 June 2016 implementing enhanced cooperation in the area of jurisdiction, applicable law and the recognition and enforcement of decisions in matters of matrimonial property regimes [2016] OJ L183/1 (hereafter Regulation 2016/1103).

used by domestic courts to resolve conflict of laws in marital matters in more than half of the Member States of the European Union.[5]

Notably, these instruments grant spouses the possibility to determine by themselves the law governing their relationship. They also contain specific conflict of laws rules for cases where spouses have not made use of party autonomy. However, although the creation and entering into force of these instruments represent a significant improvement over the previous situation, there is still room for improvements in their content. On one side, the restrictions imposed on the spouses' freedom of choice are significant compared to the broad discretion people have in the field of international contract law pursuant to the Rome I Regulation. Whereas contractual parties are permitted to choose the legal system they regard as the most appropriate when contracting with other individuals, the freedom of choice granted to spouses is much more restricted: Spouses are only able to designate a law which the law-maker considers closely connected to their relationship. In contracts involving consumers, passengers and employees, the party autonomy is also restricted. However, this limitation is based on the need to protect a vulnerable party from abuses by their counterpart. In the case of the marriage, there is apparently no need to impose protective restrictions on spouses, unless one believes that marriage is also a legal relationship typically characterized by the presence of a weaker and a stronger party. On the other side, it is also striking that the logic behind the determination of the applicable law in the absence of a choice of law agreement is very dissimilar from one instrument to the next. Marriage is not addressed as a legal relationship that requires a consistent and uniform treatment. Instead, the marriage has been divided into separate aspects – maintenance, divorce and property regime – in which divergent legal techniques are used to determine the applicable law in the absence of a choice of law agreement. As a consequence, a legal proceeding between spouses can be subject to several legal systems in the aftermath of the application of these legal instruments. Furthermore, under certain circumstances the default rule included to resolve the conflict of laws can undermine legal certainty, as the determination of a governing law might be based on facts occurring after the conclusion of the marriage that can be manipulated by one spouse unilaterally to assure the application of a law favorable to their own interests.

The aim of this book is to present a new approach in the understanding of marriage and marriage law that in turn serves as a cornerstone for the creation of a conflict of laws system that prioritizes predictability and congruency in

5 The Protocol 2008 has been also signed by non-Member States of the European Union such as Brazil, Cyprus, Kazakhstan, Republic of North Macedonia, Serbia and Ukraine. For information about contractual parties to the Protocol of 2007, see: <https://www.hcch.net/en/instruments/conventions/status-table/?cid=133>.

the determination of the applicable law. The objective is by no means to depict a detailed set of legal provisions settling any question about the resolution of conflict of laws. The goal is more modest, as it intends to answer a few specific but very important questions for any individual involved in a marriage with international connotations:

- Should spouses (and prospective spouses) be allowed to choose the law applicable to maintenance obligations, divorce and property regime? If so, to which extent should their party autonomy be restricted?
- Which connecting factor is the most appropriate for the determination of the applicable law in absence of a choice of law agreement for maintenance obligations, divorce and property regime?

Different methods might be used to respond to these main questions; here the economic perspective is the chosen path. Thus, before dealing with the specific inquiries, one devotes attention to a preliminary question:

- What is the economic rationale behind marriage and marriage law?

The book moves away from the methodology traditionally used by legal scholars to face challenges posed by legal relationships linked to two or more jurisdictions. It benefits from some ideas and concepts from economics to reframe questions related to the determination of the applicable law and to provide new answers to them. The use of economics in the analysis of the law is promising on two levels: First, it offers a theory to understand and predict the effects of a law on the behavior of people. Second, economics provides a normative standard – the concept of economic efficiency – for evaluating legislative reforms.

For the purpose of this book, the use of economic theory means concretely: first, marriage is regarded as a contract in an economic sense; that is, as an instrument that builds trust between individuals to make exchanges of complementary and reciprocal efforts. It is assumed that two persons agree to enter into marriage because it enables them to invest energy, time and other precious resources to obtain assets of monetary and non-monetary value for both of them. Second, private law is conceived as a system of incentives with a specific objective: to promote the emergence of these collaborative dynamics by removing obstacles to the conclusion of voluntary agreements aimed at obtaining benefits from cooperation. Third, the system of conflict of laws is not understood as a separate entity from the substantive regulation. Rather, it is seen as part of the private law which, although it focuses on a specific task – determining the law applicable to legal relationships – is subject to similar principles to those underlying the substantive law. Private international law is therefore understood as an integral part of the whole. Marriage law and international marriage law are regarded as two sides of the same coin, in the sense that they are part of a single system serving the same objective. Fourth, the determination of the applicable law is not primarily grounded on the search for the legal system that is most closely connected to the relationship. Rather, it is based on whether the connection of the legal relationship with a legal system fosters the rise of a cooperative dynamic between spouses.

The book's conclusions are the following: First, the options available to the spouses to choose the applicable law should be much broader than those currently offered by the aforementioned international instruments. From an economic point of view, it is desirable that spouses are allowed to choose freely the governing law of their marriage without major restrictions. Second, in the absence of a choice of law agreement, the employment of a single and common rule for the determination of the applicable law to issues related to maintenance obligations, divorce and property regime is recommended. It is concluded that the law of the country of the spouses' first common residence – or, subsidiarily, the law of the place of celebration of the marriage – is the most appropriate connecting factor for the resolution of a conflict of laws.

1. SCOPE OF THE BOOK

The book is only focused on conflict of laws issues related to the marital aspects covered by the Hague Protocol of 2007; Regulation 1259/2010; and Regulation 2016/1103, namely: maintenance obligations; divorce and legal separation; and property regime of the spouses. It presents two general conflict of laws provisions for the determination of the applicable law: one focused on the regulation of party autonomy, the other on the applicable law when spouses have not chosen a law governing their relationship. By way of example, the following topics are within the scope of conflict of laws rules and subjects of the analysis: conditions for being entitled to receive maintenance payments during the marriage and after its dissolution or annulment; the basis for the calculation of the amount to be paid; statute of limitation; conditions for obtaining a divorce or legal separation; waiting periods imposed for initiating a proceeding on divorce or legal separation; establishment and termination of a property regime; determination of assets included and excluded from that regime; daily management and liquidation of the matrimonial property; rules for the division and assignment of common assets; and rights and duties related the disposal of separate and common property.

The book does not deal with questions related to jurisdiction and recognition of decisions rendered abroad. The effects of the marriage *vis à vis* third parties – in particular obligations of spouses towards their children – also fall outside of the scope of the proposed conflict rules. The book does not cover questions about inheritance issues, personal effects of the marriage, names of the spouses, validity of the marriage, capacity for marriage, creation and extension of rights *in rem* and any other further topic excluded explicitly or implicitly from the scope of application of the aforementioned international instruments. The book also does not dwell on further matters that are not regulated by the general rule, but in separate provisions within domestic statutes or international instruments on conflict of laws. By way of example, the following topics are excluded from the scope of the analysis: definition and extension of concepts such as habitual residence, domicile or effective nationality; issues arising from the qualification; questions related to the adaptation of substantive or conflict of laws provisions to attain coherence in the application of the private international law system; formal validity of marital contracts and choice of law agreements; and determination of the applicable law in situations where the *lex causae* contravenes the *ordre public*. The scope of the book is strictly confined to presenting the economic rationale of marriage law; establishing the extension of the freedom of choice granted to the spouses; and drafting a general rule for the determination of the applicable law in the absence of a choice of law agreement.

Finally, the analysis does not cover conflict of laws issues arising from the engagement, concubinage or contractual forms of civil union between two adults for organizing their joint life such as for example the French civil solidarity pact.[6] The book makes, however, no distinction between heterosexual and homosexual marriages. Its conclusions apply to marital relationships regardless of the gender of the spouses.

2. STRUCTURE OF THE BOOK

The book is divided into four sections. The Introduction serves as a preamble for the whole book. There, a general overview of the issues caused by legal pluralism as well as the strategies used in the Hague Protocol of 2007, Regulation 1259/2010, and Regulation 2016/1103 to confront them will be given. Case law as well as the national law of five states – Germany, Italy, Malta, Netherlands and Switzerland – are used to illustrate the legal troubles that spouses involved in an international relationship may experience as a consequence of the enforcement of the rules included. It is not the intention to carry out an exhaustive analysis of the rules contained in those international instruments, or of the motives leading law-makers to regulate in a certain way. The objective of this preambular chapter

6 For the difference between registered partnership and marriage and their treatment in EU instruments see: Joined cases C-122/99 P and C-125/99 P D. and *Kingdom of Sweden v. Council of the European Union*, paras. 36 et seqq.

is showing, in a simple and summarized way, the practical problems arising from their application and drawing attention to the need to use a single and congruent approach for the resolution of conflict of laws.

Part I of the book is devoted to analyzing the objectives pursued by individuals entering into marriage; and the underlying rationale of a number of legal provisions in substantive marriage law. *Chapter 1* is focused on showing that marriage can be seen as a contract in an economic sense; that is, a tool that by building trust in spouses permits them to cooperate to obtain assets of monetary or non-monetary value. The next chapters go a step forward and demonstrate that legal provisions in modern legislations are in line with this view of the marriage. *Chapter 2* presents the economic reasons for the existence of limits on the promises between spouses that can be legally enforced. It also explores the economic logic behind some typical remedies – alimony and waiting periods to initiate a divorce proceeding – provided by marriage law once a marital crisis has started. *Chapter 3* deals with the cases that justify restrictions on party autonomy, as well as the rules applicable to the relationship of spouses in the absence of a bespoke agreement configured by them. *Chapter 4* summarizes the topics discussed in the previous chapters and leads back to the initial question of how to deal with the existence of different legal systems at an international level.

Part II of the book deals entirely with the conflict of laws dimension of the marriage. *Chapter 5* shows the costs generated by legal pluralism and the role of the private international law as the promoter of legal transactions of any kind in the international arena. *Chapter 6* envisions a positive dynamic that could emerge if spouses in international relationships were free to select the law they deem the most appropriate for their marriage. In order to carry out this analysis, an analogy with regular markets will be made. It will be argued that in a situation where there are no barriers for the determination of the applicable law, the behavior of individuals and states will resemble the behavior of consumers and suppliers. Based on theoretical and empirical arguments, the plausibility of the emergence of a law market – an authentic regulatory competition between jurisdictions – for marriage issues is discussed. *Chapter 7* is focused on presenting the most salient advantages of party autonomy in international marriage law in a more systematic way: legal certainty; greater chances to find suitable regulation; safeguarding the rights of minorities; greater coherence and flexibility of the legal system; innovation and experimentation in the law-making process; tendency for spontaneous harmonization; and incentives for the formalization of relationships. *Chapter 8* deals with the connecting factor stipulated by law when spouses have not designated a specific set of rules applicable to their relationship. The chapter concludes that the use of the first place of residence seems to be the most appropriate connecting factor, as it not only provides a high degree of legal certainty, but also reduces costs needed to get information about the content of the law. The place of conclusion of the marriage is put forward alternatively as a subsidiary connecting factor for those cases where spouses have never had a common place of residence.

The Conclusion displays the principal findings in a summarized way. The ideas put forward in the previous chapters are concretized by the presentation of specific subjective and objective connecting factors that prioritize predictability and congruency for the determination of the applicable law to matrimonial issues.

In sum, this book offers a holistic framework – including the substantive and conflictual dimensions of the legal relationship – to understand and regulate marriage from a *law and economics* perspective. It not only describes the nature of marriage as a contract in an economic sense, but also shows the economic rationale behind several legal provisions at substantive and conflict of laws levels.

Rorick Tovar Galván

ACKNOWLEDGMENTS

This book is based on a PhD dissertation defended in March 2020 to obtain the doctoral degree at the University of Bern. I must confess that writing the dissertation was much more difficult than I first thought, not only because of the effort and dedication required to do the research – there are some footnotes in the book that took a whole day to chase down – but also because of the emotional ups and downs involved in writing it: One day one can feel like superman for having a novel idea, and the next day one feels helpless or even dejected for being unable to find a solution to a particular problem, for not being able to express an idea clearly, or for realizing that the previous day's idea is actually not quite as brilliant as one thought. However, maybe writing a dissertation is – from an observer's position – like having a baby: no matter how much you scream and suffer during labor, when you see the result, it is only natural to instantly forget all about that. Likewise, it is very likely that after a short time due to this *selective amnesia*, you will even feel willing and ready for the next one. Be that as it may, what I will never forget are all those people who in one way or another have helped to carry out this personal project.

First, I would like to thank my *Doktorvater* Prof. Dr. Gerard-René de Groot for his always clear and precise recommendations, as well as for his patience and continuous personal support during the whole preparation time. Because of his legal knowledge, experience, and way of being, Prof. de Groot is the doctoral supervisor that everyone wishes for. I would also like to thank Prof. Dr. Florian Eichel for agreeing to be the second supervisor of the manuscript, for his accurate observations – exactly 618 on the final draft of the dissertation – and for all the support and encouragement he has given me during the last months to prepare the text for publication – *vielen Dank Florian, ich werde das nie vergessen!* I would also like to thank Prof. Dr. Gisela Rühl for having listened attentively to the main thesis of the book in its preparatory phase and for having made remarks, which I certainly took into consideration in the development of the book. In this regard, I must say that Prof. Dr. Rühl's work *Statut und Effizienz* not only served me as an inspiration for the development of the whole second part of this book, but also as *vade mecum* to solve any theoretical doubts and as a reference point to contrast the conclusions I was arriving at.

My infinite gratitude goes to Prof. Dr. Alberto Achermann for being the first to see in my thesis a possible topic for a dissertation and for giving me the opportunity to be part of the project *The Law and Economics of Migration Policy* at the University of Bern. If it was not for Prof. Achermann, I would have never even started this book – *¡muchísimas gracias por todo tu apoyo Alberto!* In the same vein, I would like to thank Prof. Dr. Gianni D'Amato and all the people at *NCCR on the move* for all their work in organizing activities and workshops aimed at expanding the horizons of doctoral students and making us see that migration and mobility should certainly be analyzed from more than a mere legal angle. I would also like to thank Intersentia for considering my text for a publication, for the valuable suggestions to improve the structure of the book and for the professional and thorough work in editing and proofreading the final text of the manuscript.

Many thanks also to all my direct supervisors and colleagues during my PhD-student period at the University of Bern – PD Dr. Marion Panizzon, Dr. Philip Hanke, Marek Wieruszewski, Dr. Stefan Schlegel, Dr. Barbara von Rütte, Dr. Martin Hemmi and Muriel Schiessl – for their constructive comments and specially for kindly listening to me thousands of times talking about the central thesis of the book. A special mention goes to my good friend Dr. David de Groot for the interesting and enjoyable discussions at the pub *Schanze*, which certainly helped me to develop many of the ideas presented in the book. More than thanks for their kindness and tolerance, I would also like to apologize to Stefanie Schaller and the staff of the *Juristische Forschungsbibliothek* at the University of Bern for the clutter of books and papers that characterized my desk at the library.

My thanks go of course also to my family – Tania, Sebastián, Mörli and Yulo – for their support and above all for putting up with me during the whole process of preparing the book. *Dir sit z Beschte, was mä säch cha wünsche. Merci, dass dr so sitt, wi dr sitt!*

Finally, there is one person whose comments, corrections, suggestions and above all, hard criticism were decisive in the development of the book: Francesco Zanetti. Thank you very much for all your patience and attention you paid to each of the drafts you read as well as for your accurate observations to improve the text. This book is entirely dedicated to you – dear friend Francesco.

CONTENTS

PART I. ECONOMICS AS A POINT OF DEPARTURE TO EXPLAIN THE SUBSTANTIVE RULES ON MATRIMONIAL ISSUES

LIST OF CASES

SUPRANATIONAL JURISPRUDENCE

COURT OF JUSTICE OF THE EUROPEAN UNION

NATIONAL JURISPRUDENCE

GERMANY

ITALY

MALTA

NETHERLANDS

SPAIN

SWITZERLAND

UNITED STATES

INTRODUCTION

Uncertainty and Inconsistency Surrounding the Determination of the Applicable Law in the EU Instruments on Matrimonial Issues

The objective of this section of the book is to highlight significant problems in terms of unpredictability and inconsistency caused by the current widespread method to resolve conflict of laws in marriage law. It serves as a concrete reference point to show the need for legal amendments and even for a shift in perspective to address the legal challenges posed by international marriages in the present-day context. Since an examination of the existing national conflict of laws systems would certainly go well beyond the objectives of the book, the analysis will only focus on the most recent and successful – according to the number of adhesions – international instruments on marriage law: the Hague Protocol of 2007; Regulation 1259/2010; and Regulation 2016/1103. In their preparatory work not only leading national case law and domestic statutes on conflict of laws from a variety of countries were considered, but also the existing conventions on international marriage law. Furthermore, the wide acceptance by states[7] and novelty of these international instruments make them a meaningful reference material for drafting future sets of conflict of laws rules on marriage law and for writing judicial opinions on this subject. Therefore, the concerns and legal flaws discussed in this section of the book might be already present – or will be present – in many jurisdictions, where these instruments are not in force.

It is not the aim to conduct a comprehensive analysis of the provisions included in each of them, or to refute the motives that led the international law-makers to regulate in one way or another. Rather, this Introduction invites the reader to reflect on the practical problems that the application of these instruments to concrete cases entails. In particular, it underscores the complexity of their legal provisions, the uncertainty created by their conflict rules, the unnecessary imposition of limits on the freedom of choice, and the

7 In this book, the style followed for the word "state" is lower case for countries, and capitalised for US States.

need of a stronger coordination between the legal provisions contained in these instruments.

Against this background consider the following situation:

> María Isabel – daughter of Spanish migrants living in Berne – had moved to Maastricht to continue her studies. Upon arriving, her plans took an unexpected turn when she met Giovanni – an Italian-Spanish national and former school sweetheart – with whom she quickly and hopelessly fell in love once more. After a while, they got married in a church in Palermo – the place of residence of the groom's grandmother – and eight months later moved to Aachen, a German city located only 40 km away from Maastricht, where Giovanni planned to open a bar.
>
> Step by step María Isabel noticed that her husband was not exactly prince charming. Not only did he often organize gambling activities in his bar and was suspiciously friendly with practically all the female clients; he also became his own best customer, leading to a lot of lost revenue as well as clients due to the many arguments he had after "testing" the quality of his products. One day she even discovered that he planned to use their savings to start a new business, but this time on a beautiful beach in Malta. When confronted, he told her not to worry, because he had already got a place to live. It was a bit small, so he wanted to move there alone first until he would be able to find something bigger for both of them later.
>
> In the eyes of María Isabel, this revelation was the straw that broke the camel's back. So, she went back to Switzerland to stay with her parents. Once there, her mother advised her to contact a divorce attorney. She also reminded her daughter that she should not to be concerned about the costs of starting a new life, as some years ago she had inherited a property in Spain from her late grandmother. In the end, they arrived at the conclusion that the first step should be to hire a lawyer to make a fresh start as soon as possible. The father – who had listened attentively – asked: "... but which lawyer, one specialized in Spanish, Dutch, German, Italian, Maltese or Swiss law?"

1. LEGAL PLURALISM AND ITS ADVERSE EFFECTS ON MARRIED COUPLES

The existence of multiple legal systems is a major issue for married couples with distinct nationalities, owning property abroad or having resided in at least two countries in the past. Any of these circumstances can cause significant changes in the rights and obligations derived from their marriage, since different legal rules could potentially be used by courts to resolve legal disputes between them. In a context where it is increasingly common to meet and initiate relationships with persons from around the world, or move from one jurisdiction to another, it can be very difficult for people to ascertain the outcome of proceedings on a marital union because a foreign – and in many cases unknown – law could ultimately be applied to their legal relationship. Duties of the spouses during the marriage, as well as the legal consequences of the dissolution of their marital bond – which could also be caused by the death of one spouse – might be confusing or even unexpected from the perspective of the spouses due to the application of an alien legal system to the case.

Think for example of the time needed to get divorced. In the introductory example,[8] the woman is determined to demand a divorce to move on from a difficult situation. But, what if the husband does not agree? Can she initiate the proceeding without the consent of her husband? The answer to this question depends indeed on the law applicable to the case. If Dutch[9] or Spanish[10] law applies, she would have no problem to start the divorce immediately, as the consent of one of the spouses is enough to bring the case before a court. However, the situation changes if another legal system applies. Italian law requires a waiting period of one year before initiating a divorce proceeding when one of the spouses objects.[11] Swiss law for its part requires two years,[12] whereas German law demands three years.[13] The situation in Malta is even more complicated, as the law requires that the couple live separately for a period of at least four years even when both of them desire to get divorced.[14] One could think that the law in Malta is a bit strict in these matters. However, when comparing the current

---

8 See this chapter *in initio*.

9 Art. 1:150 Dutch Civil Code. See also Vlaardingerbroek (2016) 72.

10 Provided that three months have at least elapsed since the date of celebration of the marriage (Art. 81 Spanish Civil Code). See Castilla (2011) 265. In the following, the term "Spanish law" refers only to the rules contained in the Spanish Civil Code (*Real Decreto de 24 de julio de 1889*).

11 Art. 3 of Law No. 898 of 1 December 1970. See also Cian et al. (2016) 191 et seqq. Until 2015 according to Italian law an application for divorce could be filed only if a legal separation of the spouses had previously been established or declared by a court and if at least three years had elapsed between the date of that separation and the date on which the application for divorce was filed with the court. In this regard the CJEU established in Case C-249/19, *JE v. KF* (para. 44) that "Article 10 of Regulation 1259/2010 must be interpreted as meaning that the expression 'where the law applicable by virtue of Article 5 or Article 8 makes no provision for divorce' applies only where the foreign law applicable makes no provision for divorce in any form". The *lex fori* should not be applied if the law designed by the regulation requires a legal separation of three years as a condition to fill the divorce. See para. 26.

12 Art. 114 Swiss Civil Code. See also Hausheer et al. (2010) 119; Tuor et al. (2015) 211–212.

13 Art. 1566 para. 2 German Civil Code. See also Weber (2017) 921. In Germany even when both spouses desire a divorce, it is necessary to be separated for one year to file for divorce. See for example Oberlandesgericht Hamm, 03.12.2012, II-7 WF 239/12 (application of German law and rejection of the divorce petition because the spouses – both with Turkish nationality – did not meet the requirement of living separately to get a divorce).

14 See Art. 66B para. *(a)* Maltese Civil Code. See also Mangion (2012) 112; Pietsch (2012) 427.

legislation with that in force until 2012, it seems rather progressive, as before then divorce was not permitted in that country.[15]

Regarding maintenance obligations,[16] there are also substantial differences across the legal systems. In the north of Europe – especially in the Nordic countries – the chances of obtaining alimony from the other spouse are very low.[17] A little further to the south such cases are not entirely uncommon.[18] Based on the principle of gender equality, a husband could certainly demand maintenance payments if the circumstances merit it.[19] Thus, depending on the law applicable to the case, an alimony right in favor of a person like Giovanni should not be ruled out, especially if he is unemployed at the moment of the divorce.[20] Furthermore, the method used to calculate the payments is very different from country to country. In Switzerland[21] and Germany,[22] the amount is determined by the concrete needs of the beneficiary. But in Italy, until 2017,[23] the determination depended primarily on the lifestyle of the spouses before the divorce.[24] Large sums of money

---

15 Pietsch (2012) 426. Currently, the Philippines and Vatican City are the only states where divorce is still not permitted.

16 In some countries, for example Spain, the payment received after the dissolution of the marriage is called *pension compensatoria*. This legal institution has a similar purpose to maintenance obligations. The Protocol of 2007 is for this reason applied by local courts for the determination of the law applicable to *pensiones compensatorias*. See for example: Audiencia Provincial León no. 38/2015, 27 February 2015 (application of Spanish law to a *pension compensatoria* based on Art. 3 of the Protocol of 2007); Audiencia Provincial de Islas Baleares no. 332/2017. 19 October 2017 (application of Spanish law based on the residence of the creditor. The application of the Protocol of 2007 is based on Case C-220/95 *Antonius van den Boogaard v. Paula Laumen*).

17 Regarding the possibility to obtain maintenance from a former spouse in Sweden, Finland or Norway see: Boele-Woelki et al. (2003) 54, 38, 26 respectively. See also: Henrich (2013) 60.

18 For a general view of the practice in European countries see: Boele-Woelki et al. (2003) 9–54.

19 See for example: Tribunale di Roma, 14 June 2019 (in this case the husband – resident in Italy – claimed maintenance from the wife, residing in Spain. He argued that he had left his job in order to allow his wife to continue with her career. Summary available at: <http://www2.ipr.uni-heidelberg.de/eufams/index.php?site=entscheidungsdatenbank&lang=en>, EUFAMS code ITF20190614a).

20 In countries like Switzerland for example, social assistance – *Sozialhilfe* – has a subsidiary character. It is granted only if the alimony received from the ex-spouse does not cover the basic needs of the person. Regarding the regulation of social assistance for spouses in Switzerland see: Freivogel (2007).

21 Hausheer et al. (2010) 131; Tuor et al. (2015) 235 et seqq. See also BGer 20.8.2008, 5A_95/2008.

22 Maurer (2017) 1035 et seqq.

23 Rinaldi (2017).

24 For the equalization function of maintenance obligations – *functione perequativa del asigno di divorcio* – see Wiedemann & Pertot (2021) 231. See also Boele-Woelki et al. (2003) 22–25.

far beyond the needs of the beneficiary were granted by Italian courts even in situations where they had a more than sufficient salary to cover their needs.[25] Recently, the Italian rules have been modified.[26] However, the Italian law continues to be attractive for potential maintenance creditors, as the amounts ordered by their courts are still above the average in the region, and because there is no expiration date to these payments. In contrast to countries like Netherlands, where according to the law alimony is granted – as a general rule – for a maximum period of five years,[27] in Italy such an obligation generally terminates only with the remarriage of the beneficiary.[28]

Finally, there are also significant differences in the default and mandatory rules applicable to the property regime of spouses. Some legal systems are based on the principle of separate property, while others are based on the principle of community of property. Under the separate property regime, the goods acquired or owned by a married person are considered the spouse's separate property and remain this way during and after a marriage. Although this system prevails in the jurisdictions of common law tradition, in some civil law countries and certain jurisdictions in Spain – such as the Balearic Islands[29] or Catalonia[30] – this system is applied as the default statutory regime.[31] In practice, the application of – for example – Catalonian rules to a marriage could lead to a situation where one of the spouses might end up empty-handed. That is the case because this legal system – unlike for example the German or the Swiss one – does not grant rights over gains accrued during the marriage to the other spouse.[32] Each spouse retains exclusive ownership of their property during and after the marriage. Actually, most jurisdictions – at least in continental Europe – are based on the community of property. This, however, does not guarantee that the outcome of the division of the common property will be equitable. In the Netherlands and Italy for example, the default regime is the community of property. However, whereas in Italy only assets acquired during the

---

25 The case of the former Italian Prime Minister Silvio Berlusconi is very illustrative of this principle. The first instance court ordered him to pay his second wife, Veronica Lario, a monthly allowance of 3 million euros. After he appealed the decision, the monthly payment was reduced to 1.4 million euros. See: Henrich (2013) 58.

26 Rinaldi (2017).

27 For the new law on maintenance obligations between spouses and exceptions to the general rule see Reinhartz & Vlaardingerbroek (2021) 904. Before 1 January 2020 the maximum period in Dutch law was 12 years according to Art. 1:157 para. 5 Dutch Civil Code.

28 Cian et al. (2016) 198. See also Wiedemann & Pertot (2021) 736–737.

29 Art. 3 para. 1 Compilation of Balearic Civil Law. See also Cuena (2011) 479 et seqq.

30 Art. 231-10 para. 2 Catalonian Civil Code. See also Cuena (2011) 113 et seqq.

31 Some Autonomous Communities in Spain are able to enact their own legislation in family law.

32 Molina et al. (2011) 254.

marriage are divided after the divorce, the Dutch legal system is rather more inclusive, at least for marriages celebrated before 2018:[33] not only those acquired during the relationship, but also those that spouses had before getting married – including donations, legacies and inheritances – become part of the community of property of both spouses.[34] The application of the Dutch legislation means that – with certain exceptions – the spouses have rights over all assets, regardless of the moment or circumstances in which they were acquired. Thus, the money obtained from the sale of a legacy – let's say from a plot of land left by a late grandmother – might then be divided between both spouses, even if it was acquired long before the wedding.

Although many people may ignore it, the specific legal system applicable to a case is of the utmost relevance as it determines not only the extent, but also the very existence of rights and obligations assumed with the celebration of marriage. The application of one or another law can cause significant costs as well as the loss of prerogatives with repercussions in the present and the future. Legal uncertainty and opportunistic behavior are probably the most conspicuous problems arising from legal pluralism at an international level. The first refers to the lack of awareness about significant changes in the rights and obligations of spouses as a consequence of the application of an unexpected law. The second speaks to the opportunity each spouse has to initiate a legal proceeding in a specific place or at a specific moment to gain advantages with the application of favorable legal rules to the case.[35] Added to this are expenses incurred to gather information about the contents of a foreign law; possible errors made by courts when foreign law applies to the case; and incongruences and further inconveniences that the application of different laws to the legal relationships of a single person entail. It should be pointed out that the initial example given above only refers to countries located in Europe. If one considers the different views on marriage and family and their legal regulation around the world, the situation could be even more disconcerting.

According to data published by the European Union in 2010, the total costs from legal pluralism were close to 1.1 billion euros per annum in Europe alone.[36] It was estimated that in 2007 of the approximately 122 million marriages in the EU, around 16.3 per cent had some kind of international element.

---

33 Reinhartz & Vlaardingerbroek (2021) 880. A new law on matrimonial property came into force in the Netherlands on 1 January 2018. From that date onwards, unless otherwise stipulated by prenuptial agreement, a limited community of property regime applies to all marriages contracted in the Netherlands (new Art. 1:94 Dutch Civil Code). See in detail Reinhartz & Vlaardingerbroek (2021) 880–882.

34 Vlaardingerbroek (2016) 69.

35 Parisi (2007) 2. For the definition, reasons and problems related to forum shopping see: Ferrari (2017) 792–796.

36 epec (2010) 9–10.

Circa 16 million were marriages of spouses with different nationalities, and 3.5 million couples – with the same nationalities – lived outside of their country of origin. In sum, according to the survey, about 40 million individuals – that is, a higher number than the population of a country such as Poland – were involved in a marriage that could be subject to at least two legal systems of countries located inside or outside of the continent. Based on the steady increase of people moving around in the region, this number is expected to be even higher at the time of reading this.

2. CONFLICT OF LAWS SYSTEM AS A MECHANISM TO TACKLE LEGAL PLURALISM

The specific strategies adopted by states to resolve issues arising from legal diversity are manifold. Notwithstanding, it is possible to identify two main approaches to resolving the conflict of laws. The first one is the application of the national law, regardless of the international elements a given case may have.[37] This approach facilitates the work of judges, as they will be able to use their own law to decide over a case. Not only fewer errors, but also greater speed in the resolution of disputes is expected as a consequence of the application of the law of the court to cases with international elements.[38] That way of resolving the problem, however, can also lead to the application of a law having little or even no link to the couple, or the proliferation of parallel proceedings where different rules are applied to the same matter, because multiple jurisdictions could consider themselves competent to resolve a single case.[39] This approach might thus entail not only the application of unknown law from the perspective of the couple as well as the use of legal provisions contrary to the sense of justice or fairness; it could also create perverse incentives for each partner to initiate a legal proceeding in a specific jurisdiction – so-called forum shopping – on the basis of advantages from the application of this court's law.[40]

The second approach allows the application of foreign legal provisions by national courts. For this purpose, the legal system provides rules – in following conflict of laws rules or "conflict rules" – aimed exclusively at determining the

---

37 For *lex fori* as *lex decisoria* see: Requejo (2017) 1106–1108. For the definition and historical development of unilateralism in private international law, see: Franq (2017) 1779–1783.

38 Parisi & O'Hara (1998) 390; Requejo (2017) 1105.

39 Updated information, as well as a global view of the legal rules for the determination of the competent jurisdiction for questions related to maintenance, divorce and property regime in EU Member States can be found in: Stone (2018) 599–618, 703–708, 723–728.

40 For a definition, reasons and problems related to forum shopping see: Ferrari (2017) 792–796. See also: Parisi & O'Hara (1998) 390.

specific legislation to be used by the local courts to resolve the case.[41] The term "connecting factor" describes the element of the conflict of laws rule used to link a factual situation with the law of a particular jurisdiction.[42] Although the chosen factor might serve specific objectives pursued by the legislator, in general connecting factors are designed to appoint the law most closely connected with the issue at stake.[43] In theory, as long as all national conflict of laws systems pursue this objective, they contribute to the international uniformity of decisions, as following the same principle guarantees the application of the same law regardless of the place where the case is ultimately settled.[44] According to this second approach, the application of foreign legal provisions is accepted as long as they do not disturb the normal functioning of the administration of justice. The immediate application of *lex fori* might be prescribed; however this measure is generally confined to procedural aspects or as a means of protecting the public policy.[45]

3. HARMONIZATION OF CONFLICT OF LAWS RULES TO OVERCOME PROBLEMS FROM COMPETING SYSTEMS

In the past, conflict of laws systems contained few conflict rules, each with wide scopes of application, guaranteeing not only predictable connections, but also uniformity in the application of the law.[46] In the case of marriage, the *lex fori* was commonly applied by courts to resolve disputes between spouses, since many countries assumed that the resolution of family matters concerned the public policy of the forum.[47] Some jurisdictions, however, used the nationality – of both or only one spouse – as the decisive element for the

41 For the divergence between unilateralism and multilateralism in the private international law, see: Franq (2007) 1786.

42 Mansel (2017) 441.

43 Mansel (2017) 442. Regarding the role of the law with the closest connection for the determination of the applicable law in Europe, see: Rühl (2017) 1387–1388.

44 The determination of the applicable law might be based on guaranteeing the interstate or international uniformity of decisions. According to the dominant thought in the USA – for example – choice of law principally serves to resolve conflicts between the interests of the various States of the federation. See: Rühl (2017) 1387–1388. Regarding the role of the interests of the States in the resolution of conflicts of laws and the so-called "American Conflict of Law Revolution" see: Silberman (2017a) 66 et seqq.

45 For the use of the *lex fori* as a protection of the forum's interests and as a reaction to the difficulties encountered in the application of foreign laws see: Requejo (2017) 1105.

46 Mansel (2017) 451.

47 A debate focused exclusively on the different criteria used to determine the applicable law to the marriage was held on the occasion of the drafting of the 1951 Convention relating to the status of refugees. See: UNHCR (1990) 65. Currently, however, the CJEU has imposed some limits to the margin of discretion Member States have at the moment of assessing the

determination of the applicable law to the case.[48] As a result, the outcomes of proceedings involving international marriages were to a certain point foreseeable, as the range of possible laws was reduced to these two options – nationality or forum. Since the the middle of the last century the situation has changed in a number of countries in Western Europe, as new connecting factors were introduced.[49] Gradually, the *lex fori* and the nationality lost their preponderance in favor of other connecting factors such as the place

recognition of marriages celebrated by EU citizens abroad. Member States, for example, could not rely on their own national legislation to refuse the recognition of same-sex marriages celebrated in another country. See Case C-673/16 *Coman and Others v. Romania*. See also Gray (2021) 77.

48 By the early 50s the following countries applied the law of the country of nationality to at least one aspect of the marriage, e.g. property regime, maintenance support, divorce or requirements for the conclusion of a marriage. The following list refers to private international law provisions in force before 1953: *Egypt* (Art. 11.1 Egyptian Civil Code); *Albania* (Art. 5 Introductory Act to the Albanian Civil Code); *Belgian Congo* (Art. 8 of the Law of 18 October on the government of the Belgian Congo); *Bulgaria* (Art. 24 Law of 5 August 1949 Act on Persons and the Family); *China* (Art. 10 of the Law of 5 August 1918 on the application of foreign law); *Denmark* (Art. 53 Law of 18 March Act on the Effects of Marriage); *Germany* (Arts. 13, 15, 16 Introduction to the German Civil Code); *Dominican Republic* (Art. 170 of the Dominican Civil Code), *Finland* (Art. 2 law of 5 December 1929 on Family Law with International Character); *French protectorate in Morocco* (Art. 8 of law of 12 August 1913 on the Civil Position of French and other Foreigners in the French protectorate in Morocco); *Greece* (Arts. 13, 14 Greek Civil Code); *Israel* (Art. 64.2 Palestine Order in Council 1922, as amended by Palestine Order in Council 1923); *Italy* (Arts. 17, 20 Italian Civil Code); *Japan* (Arts. 14, 15, 16 Law of 21 June 1898 on Application of the Law), *Yugoslavia* (Art. 82 Fundamental Law on Marriage of 3 April 1946), *Cuba* (Art. 91 Cuban Civil Code. The law of the country of nationality applied, but only for foreigners residing on the island for less than two years); *Austria* (Arts. 6, 7, 8 Statutory Order of 25 October 1941 on Harmonization of the International Family Law); *Poland* (Art. 12.1 Law of 2 August of 1926 on Private International Law); *Portugal* (Art. 1107 Civil Code); *Romania* (Art. 86 Law of 21 February 1928 on Personal State); *Sweden* (sections 1 and 2 of chapter 3 of the law of 8 July 1904 on Marriage, Guardianship and Adoption); *Switzerland* (Arts. 7c, 7e, 7h, 8 Federal Law of 25 June 1891 on the Civil Relationships of Domiciled Persons); *Syria* (Arts. 14, 16, 17 Syrian Civil Code); *Czechoslovakia* (Arts. 10, 13, 15 Law of 11 March 1948 on Private International Law and the Legal Situation of Foreigners in Civil Law), *Hungary* (Art. 16.1 Law IV/1952 on Matrimony, Family and Guardianship). With few other exceptions, the law of the forum was used to resolve questions related to the marriage in the rest of the countries – in particular in those of common law tradition. For a French and German translation of all cited laws see: Makarov (1953).

49 The Hague Convention of 24 October 1956 on the law applicable to maintenance obligations towards children was the first international instrument using the place of residence as main connecting factor for the determination of the applicable law in family matters. Subsequently, the Convention of 2 October 1973 on the Law Applicable to Maintenance Obligations included the habitual residence of the creditor as the connecting factor for cases involving maintenance between spouses. See Basedow (2015) 314 et seqq. Before the entry into force of this instrument, Switzerland was the only jurisdiction that used as main connecting factor for maintenance between spouses the law of the common domicile of the spouses. See: Schnitzer (1957) 426–427; Verwilghen (1975) 432 et seqq. Interestingly, the Hague Convention of 1902 relating to the settlement of guardianship of minors was the first international instrument to include the habitual residence as the criterion for the determination of the applicable law. See Art. 3 of the Hague Guardianship Convention of 1902.

of celebration of the marriage, the country of residence of the couple or even the law chosen by the spouses.[50] These connecting factors, however, were not used to determine the legal system governing the whole relationship, but only the applicable law to particular aspects of the relationship like validity of the marriage, the conditions for divorce, division of the property, etc. The institution of the marriage was thus split into separate sub-issues that could be subjected to different legal systems.[51] Furthermore, as time goes by, the specific connecting factors used by courts began to diverge significantly from one country to another. The objective of achieving international uniformity of decisions became less feasible due to the plethora of approaches to resolving conflicts of laws.[52] To have an idea about the dimension of the problem in Europe, one can cite a comment made by a scholar in the middle of the 1990s, for whom the system of private international law in the region seemed like a "jungle that can confuse even Europeans and that an outsider without guidance may easily become lost in".[53]

In this context, the European Union decided to take matters into their own hands.[54] With a view to assure the proper functioning of their internal market, it promoted the creation of common rules for the determination of the applicable law to marriage.[55] Although not all Member States have agreed to be part of the process of harmonization in the area of marriage law, the results achieved are without a doubt a major step forward in comparison to the previous situation in Europe. To the present day, these common rules are in force in more than a half of the Member States of the European Union, and so the law applied to a case should be the same if a legal proceeding is initiated in any of these countries.[56]

---

50 Martiny (2008) 191; Bogdan (2007) 303 et seqq. For the specific connecting factors used in European countries before the entry into force of the instruments see: Bonomi/Explanatory Report (2013); epec (2006); epec (2010) for maintenance, divorce and matrimonial property regime respectively.

51 This trend can also be observed in international instruments dealing with marital issues. The conflict of laws rules applicable to maintenance and property regime are regulated separately in different Hague Conventions. They also contain different connecting factors for those aspects. For details about the *ratio* behind the conflict rules in the 1978 Hague Matrimonial Property Regimes Convention and the 1973 Hague Maintenance Convention, see: Verwilghen (1975); Von Overbeck (1978).

52 Raupach (2014) 2.

53 This commentary appears in the book *Conflict of laws in Western Europe: A guide through the jungle*. See: Reimann (1995) XXI.

54 Martiny (2008) 187. Specific competence as regards private international law was conferred upon European legislators at the end of the 1990s. It was included in Art 61(c) in conjunction with Art 65(b) of the Treaty of Amsterdam (today: Art 81(1) and (2)(c) of the Treaty of Lisbon). See: Basedow (2000) 687 et seqq.

55 For the competence of the EU in topics related to the harmonization of conflict of laws rules in the area of family law as well as its role within The Hague Conference see: Martiny (2008) 189–190.

56 It was estimated that the harmonization of conflict of laws rules saves between 2,000 to 3,000 euros per case. See: European Commission MEMO/11/175 (2011) 3.

4. LEGAL UNCERTAINTY AND INCONSISTENCY IN THE EU INSTRUMENTS ON PRIVATE INTERNATIONAL LAW

The establishment of a unified system of choice of law might offer a number of advantages over the situation in which every state has its own system. It could lead to an increase of legal certainty, more international uniformity of decisions and greater protection of the legitimate expectations of people.[57] Seen from the point of view of the European Union, it might lead to the reduction of barriers to the free movement of people, as well as to developing an enhanced area of freedom, security and justice.[58] In general, there are few doubts about the potential benefits of building a common system of private international law. However, carrying out a harmonization of conflict of laws rules is no easy feat in practice. It ultimately means the imposition of limits on the sovereignty of the states. In the case of marriage law, the situation is indeed very complicated, as one of the central features of this area of law is the existence of restrictions and imposition of duties on the spouses, justified in the name of morality or preservation of public values. It is then no surprise that even though the process of harmonization was finally carried out between only a reduced number of countries, it took a long time and was made in a piecemeal fashion. The creation of these common conflict rules lasted more than 20 years. Furthermore, marriage had to be dismembered into different facets and subjected to separate negotiations to be able to achieve an agreement. As noted above, there is not just one, but three different international instruments dealing with the determination of the applicable law to the same legal institution – the Hague Protocol of 2007; Regulation 1259/2010; and Regulation 2016/1103 – to allow countries to choose the specific aspects of marriage they want to harmonize.[59] The results of having opted for a sectorial approach – in addition to the general difficulties to reach a consensus – had a negative impact on the final outcomes of the harmonization.[60] Next, the rules in the absence of a choice of law will be discussed. Later on, attention will be paid to issues related to the regulation of party autonomy.

---

57 Basedow (2000) 703.

58 See extensively in: Bogdan (2007) 78–88.

59 Netherlands and Sweden – among other Member States – did not participate in the enhanced cooperation on Regulation 2016/1103. In those countries, however, the Protocol of 2007 as well as Regulation 2016/1103 do apply.

60 Bonomi (2020) 36–40.

4.1. DRAWBACKS OF THE LEGAL PROVISIONS ON CONFLICTS IN ABSENCE OF A CHOICE OF LAW AGREEMENT

Having a variety of instruments on international marriage law is not in itself negative, but the lack of an integrated and consistent approach to resolving conflict of laws and the absence of coordination between these instruments, is.[61] It is striking, for example, that each of them uses different connecting factors for the determination of the applicable law. Although they refer to a single legal relationship, the instruments prescribe dissimilar techniques to resolve conflicts of laws and include exceptions to the application of foreign law that apparently are not related to one another. Furthermore, they leave a great deal to be desired in terms of legal certainty. All of them put forward the predictability of the litigation's outcomes and the protection of the legitimate expectations of the parties as the principal reason to justify the harmonization.[62] However, in many cases their provisions do not allow the parties to determine with certainty the specific legal system applicable to a case. Sometimes, the determination of the applicable law is based on circumstances whose occurrence could only be noticed shortly before the beginning of the legal processing.[63] In other instances, they grant a significant margin of discretion to the court resolving the conflict of laws, leading to great incertitude.[64]

4.1.1. The Conflict Rule for Maintenance Obligations

The Hague Protocol of 2007 governs the determination of the law applicable to maintenance obligations.[65] This international instrument applies regardless of whether the payments are demanded as an accessory claim in the framework of a proceeding dealing with a divorce, division of common property or any

61 Rühl (2014a) 336.

62 Bonomi/Explanatory Report (2013) 41; recital 9 Regulation 1259/2010; recital 15 Regulation 2016/1103. See also: EPEC (2006) 7, 9, 13, 16, 21, 32, 48, 53, 56, 57, 58, 59, 67, 69, 70, 72–77, 81, 86, 87; EPEC (2010) 33, 34, 40, 47 51, 90, 91, 98, 99, 106, 143, 149.

63 See Art. 3 Hague Protocol of 2007; Art. 8 Regulation 1259/2010. See in detail in this chapter Sections 4.1.1. and 4.1.2.

64 See Art. 5 Hague Protocol of 2007; Art. 26 Regulation 2016/1103. See in detail in this chapter Sections 4.1.1. and 4.1.3.

65 In some countries, for example Spain, the payment received after the dissolution of the marriage is called *pension compensatoria*. The Protocol of 2007 however also applies for the determination of the law applicable to the *pension compensatoria*. See: Audiencia Provincial León no. 38/2015, 27 February 2015 (application of Spanish law to a *pension compensatoria* based on Art. 3 of the Protocol of 2007); Audiencia Provincial de Islas Baleares no. 332/2017, 19 October 2017 (application of Spanish law based on the residence of the creditor. They based their decision on Case C-220/95 *Antonius van den Boogaard v. Paula Laumen*).

other main claim.[66] As long as there is a requirement to resolve a dispute revolving around maintenance issues, the Hague Protocol of 2007 applies to determine the law governing this particular aspect of the case.[67] Article 3 of the protocol establishes as the general connecting factor the habitual residence of the creditor:[68]

> Article 3 [Hague Protocol of 2007]: General rule on applicable law
>
> (1) Maintenance obligations shall be governed by the law of the State of the habitual residence of the creditor, save where this Protocol provides otherwise.
> (2) In the case of a change in the habitual residence of the creditor, the law of the State of the new habitual residence shall apply as from the moment when the change occurs.[69]

---

66 The CJEU has established some criteria to differentiate between maintenance and matrimonial property regime. See Case C-220/95 *Antonius van den Boogaard v. Paula Laumen* para. 22 et seqq. See also Case 143/78 *Jacques de Cavel v. Louise de Cavel.*

67 Bonomi/Explanatory Report (2013). See also: Andrae (2014) 569–557. The Hague Protocol allows contracting states to establish the existence of a relationship from which the claim is derived. See Bonomi/Explanatory Report (2013) 25, 27. For the personal scope of the Hague Protocol see: Gray (2021) 89–92.

68 An overview of the existing jurisprudence of the ECJ shows that the determination of the habitual residence is primarily based on the length of the duration of the residence (but, in Case C-90/97 *Robin Swaddling v. Adjudication Officer* para. 30 it was mentioned that "the length of residence in the Member State cannot be regarded as an intrinsic element of the concept of residence"); the intention to remain (Case T-90/92 *Pedro Magdalena Fernández v. Commission of the European Communities* para. 22); and other factors as whether the abode was purchased or leased, the existence of employment or business ties and family links in the country (Case C-372/02 *Roberto Adanez-Vega v. Bundesanstalt für Arbeit* para. 32). See Gray (2021) 135–137; Viarengo (2014) 556–557. For German case law on the determination of the residence see: Oberlandesgericht Koblenz, 18.03.2015, 13 UF 825/14 (discussing the determination of the residence of a child – apparently – living in Luxembourg but attending the school in Germany). In Switzerland the concept of habitual residence is defined in Art. 20 of Federal Act on Private International Law: natural persons have habitual residence "in the state where they live for a certain period of time, even if this period is of limited duration from the outset". For the concept of habitual residence in Switzerland see BGer, 26.9.2002, 5C_139/2002 consideration 2.2.

69 For case law on Art. 3 of the Hague Protocol of 2007, see for *Germany*: Oberlandesgericht Hamm, 22 April 2016 – II-3 UF 262/15 (ruling that The Hague Protocol of 2007 does not apply to the Islamic "morning gift" – a copy of the *Quran* and an English gold sovereign – as it was regarded as an engagement present, but it does apply to the "evening gift" – fifteen thousand dollars – because such a gift had – according to the court's view – the character of maintenance); Oberlandesgericht Hamm, 6 May 2016–9 UF 196/14 (discussing the possibility to apply the conflict rules of the Protocol of 2007 to a preliminary question – paternity – in a case involving maintenance for a child). For *Italy*: Tribunale di Padova, 4 August 2015 (application of the law of the place of residence of the debtor. The case involved a bigamist debtor. Summary available at: <http://www2.ipr.uni-heidelberg.de/eufams/index.php?site=entscheidungsdatenbank&lang=en>, EUFAMS code ITF20150804); Tribunale di Padova, sezione prima civile, 13 January 2017 (Application of the law of the country of residence of the creditor. Summary available at: <http://www2.ipr.uni-heidelberg.de/eufams/index.php?site=entscheidungsdatenbank& lang=en>, EUFAMS

The existence and amount of the obligation, the conditions to receive the payments, the criteria for its termination, enforceability of maintenance agreements and other questions related directly to maintenance during the marriage or after its dissolution will be resolved according to the law of the place where the beneficiary lives when the proceeding is started.[70] The drafters of the protocol were aware that the use of this connecting factor would lead to a change of the applicable law if the creditor moves to another country, and subsequently initiates a proceeding.[71] For this reason, they included in Article 5 an exception to the general rule by applying the law most closely connected with the marriage.[72] At the request of one of the parties, the law of the place of residence of the creditor will not apply if the law of another jurisdiction is more closely linked.[73] The article goes on to say that the place of their last common residence should merit special consideration at the moment of determining this close connection of the relationship with a jurisdiction:

> Article 5 [Hague Protocol of 2007]: Special rule with respect to spouses and ex-spouses.
>
> In the case of a maintenance obligation between spouses, ex-spouses or parties to a marriage which has been annulled, Article 3 shall not apply if one of the parties

---

code ITF20170113); Tribunale di Roma, 6 June 2018 (application of the *lex fori* to a divorce. The spouses have different nationalities and never lived in the same country. Summary available at: <http://www2.ipr.uni-heidelberg.de/eufams/index.php?site=entscheidungsdatenbank&lang=en>, EUFAMS code ITF20180606a); Tribunale di Parma, sezione prima, 6 May 2019 (application of Italian law to the maintenance claim of the wife and French law to the maintenance claim of the daughter of the creditor since they lived in different countries. Summary available at <http://www2.ipr.uni-heidelberg.de/eufams/index.php?site=entscheidungsdatenbank&lang=en>, EUFAMS code ITF20190506). For *Malta* see: Civil Court (Family Section), 9 December 2020. ECLI:MT:FMLJ:2020:124443 (Application of Maltese Law to a case in which the creditor of the obligation resided in Malta. The court, however, did not mention the conflict rules of the Protocol of 2007 for the determination of the applicable law, although the debtor claimed in the defense that he was no longer living in Malta). For *Netherlands* see: Rechtbank Amsterdam 10 October 2018, ECLI:NL:RBAMS:2018:7107 (determining the applicable law based on the residence of the creditor). For *Spain*: Audiencia Provincial Barcelona no. 496/2013, 27 June 2013 (application of Municipal law – Catalonian law – based on Arts. 3 and 16 of the Protocol of 2007); Juzgado de Violencia sobre la Mujer Cornellà de Llobregat no. 32/2015, 15 July 2015 (application of Municipal law – Catalonian law – based on Art. 3 of the Protocol of 2007 but without taking into consideration the rule contained in Art. 16 of the Protocol of 2007); Tribunal Superior de Justicia Aragón no. 27/2015, 6 October 2015 (application of Municipal law – Aragonese law – based on Arts. 3 and 16 of the Protocol of 2007); Audiencia Provincial de Islas Baleares no. 332/2017, 19 October 2017 (application of Spanish law based on the residence of the creditor. According to the *lex causae* – *in casu* Spanish law – the payment is granted only for a specific period).

70 Andrae (2016) 569–570, 57. For the material scope of application of the protocol see: Hausmann (2018) 442–444; Mankowski (2016) 41–50.

71 Bonomi/Explanatory Report (2013) 41.

72 For the exceptional character of this provision see: Mankowski (2016) 125.

73 Bonomi/Explanatory Report (2013) 43; Mankowski (2016) 117.

> objects and the law of another State, in particular the State of their last common habitual residence, has a closer connection with the marriage. In such a case the law of that other State shall apply.[74]

At first glance this provision seems appropriate, as it avoids unexpected alterations in the conditions for receiving and paying maintenance caused by an eventual change of residence of the beneficiary of these payments.[75] However, rather than reinforcing the predictability, the special rule undermines it, because no clear basis is provided for the determination of this close connection.[76] As it simply assumes a mere preference for the last common residence, courts remain obliged to analyze any possible fact surrounding the relationship in order to determine the linkage.[77] When commenting on this article, the explanatory report of the protocol suggested that the authority "shall have regard to all the connections of the marriage with the various countries concerned" to resolve the conflict of laws.[78] It further advises that different circumstances, such as for example the place of celebration of the marriage; past places of residence of the couple (including the one prior to the marriage); the country where the children are living; and the location of the divorce or separation should be considered along with the place of the last common residence in order to determine the law most closely connected.[79] Thus, if – as is not unusual in international marriages – the couple has been in touch with multiple countries, predicting the law governing their relationship in advance can become very complex due to the high number of circumstances that could

---

74 For case law on Art. 5 of the Hague Protocol of 2007 see for *Germany*: Bundesgerichtshof, Urteil vom 26 Juni 2013 – XII ZR 133/11 (establishing the closer connection of the marriage with German law based on the nationality of the common children and the last common residence of the spouses). For *Spain*: Audiencia Provincial Barcelona no. 308/2015, 12 May 2015 (non-application of the law of creditor's habitual residence because another State – *in casu* Germany – has a closer connection to the case); Audiencia Provincial de Barcelona no. 580/2018, 12 September 2018 (non-application of the law of the creditor's habitual residence because another State – *in casu* Uruguay – has a closer connection to the case); Audiencia Provincial Barcelona no. 334/2019, 7 May 2019 (non-application of Art. 5 of the Protocol of 2007. In this case the couple had previously lived in several countries – in Germany between 1996–2004, in China between 2004–2011, in Singapore between 2011–2014 and finally in Belgium between 2014–2016. The proceeding was initiated in 2016; the habitual residence of the spouses was Belgium. In accordance with Art. 3 of the Protocol of 2007, the court finally applied Belgian law).

75 Bartl (2012) 97.

76 Mankowski (2016) 118.

77 The closest connection with the last common residence mentioned in Art. 5 of the Protocol is no legal presumption, but a mere indication. See: Andrae (2014) 583; Hausmann (2018) 457; Mankowski (2016) 125.

78 Bonomi/Explanatory Report (2013) 45.

79 Bonomi/Explanatory Report (2013) 45, 47. See also: Andrae (2014) 583–584; Mankowski (2016) 124–127; Staudinger (2018) 1297.

be considered relevant or decisive when establishing the applicable law.[80] Planning their life prudently – e.g. deciding to stay at home to take care of the children – gets complicated further due the practical unfeasibility of knowing either: whether in the future this marriage will be in some way connected with a certain law; or the influence that seemingly mundane situations – as moving to another jurisdiction or acquiring a nationality – will have on the decision of the authority assessing a close connection.

4.1.2. The Conflict Rule for Divorce and Legal Separation

The rules for the determination of the governing law of the divorce – and legal separation – are prescribed in Regulation 1259/2010. The conflict rules contained herein establish the legal system applicable to resolve questions about specific requirements for demanding legal separation or dissolution of the marital bond; the need to be separated for a period of time before initiating a divorce proceeding; consequences derived from a temporary reconciliation of the spouses, assuming that separation is needed; whether an inquiry may be carried out to determine if either of the spouses has contributed to the breakdown of their marriage; and rules determining the burden of proof and raising presumptions of law.[81] In short, the law designated by this instrument controls the conditions and promptness for obtaining a dissolution or loosening of the marital ties.[82] Just like the Hague Protocol, Regulation 1259/2010 also bases the resolution of the conflict of laws on the application of the legal system most closely connected with the relationship.[83] The difference between both instruments lies in the introduction of specific provisions to determine the linkage of the marriage with a certain jurisdiction. The Regulation leaves a significantly smaller margin of discretion to the courts,

80 Andrae (2014) 585; Mankowski (2016) 126–127.

81 For the limits, see recital 10 of Regulation 1259/2010. This instrument, however, does not cover private religious divorces. See Case C-372/16 *Soha Sahyouni v. Raja Mamisch* paras. 39, 48. See also Oberlandesgericht München, 2 June 2015, 34 Wx 146/14. In Germany the application of Regulation 1259/2010 to private divorces by means of analogy is controversial. For the non-application see Oberlandesgericht München, 14 March 2018 – 34 Wx 146/14. For the application of the Regulation by means of analogy to private divorces see: Oberlandesgericht Düsseldorf, 15 February 2018 – I-13 VA 6/16.

82 For the scope of application of Regulation 1259/2010 see in deteil: Andrae (2014) 282–283, 302, 312–313; Franzina (2011) 101–105; Hausmann (2018) 70–81. See also Oberlandesgericht Hamm, 22 April 2016 – II-3 UF 262/15 and Oberlandesgericht Düsseldorf, 16 June 2016 – II-5 UF 81/16 (ruling that Regulation 1259/2010 does not cover issues related to pension rights adjustments between spouses).

83 See: recital 21 of Regulation 1259/2010. See also: Franzina (2011) 116. For another view see Andrae (2014) 290.

as it includes a cascade of connecting factors[84] for the determination of the applicable law:

> Article 8 [1259/2010]: Applicable law in the absence of a choice by the parties.
>
> In the absence of a choice pursuant to Article 5, divorce and legal separation shall be subject to the law of the State:
>
> (a) where the spouses are habitually resident at the time the court is seized; or, failing that
> (b) where the spouses were last habitually resident, provided that the period of residence did not end more than 1 year before the court was seized, in so far as one of the spouses still resides in that State at the time the court is seized; or, failing that
> (c) of which both spouses are nationals at the time the court is seized; or, failing that
> (d) where the court is seized.[85]

---

84 Commonly called Kegel's ladder. See Franzina (2020) 94–95.

85 For case law on Art. 8 of the Regulation 1259/2010 see for *Germany*: Oberlandesgericht Stuttgart, 17 January 2013, 17 WF 251/12 (non-application of Art. 3 of Regulation 1259/2010 and application of the law applied by the court to grant legal separation – Italian law – to a conversion of legal separation into divorce in accordance with Art. 9 of Regulation 1259/2010); Amtsgericht Berlin-Schöneberg, 20.08.2013, 22 F 171/12 (denying the petition for divorce, since abandoning the marital bedroom – in contrast to abandoning the marital home – is no ground for divorce according to Thai law); Oberlandesgericht Nürnberg, 31 October 2013–10 UF 1073/13 (non-application of Art. 3 of Regulation 1259/2010 and application of the law applied by the court to grant legal separation – Turkish law – to a conversion of legal separation into divorce in accordance with Art. 9 of Regulation 1259/2010); Oberlandesgericht Hamm, 22 April 2016 – II-3 UF 262/15 (application of German law based on the residence of the spouses); Thüringer Oberlandesgericht, 4 January 2018–1 WF 713/17 (application of German law based on the residence of the spouses). For *Italy*: Tribunale di Parma, sezione prima, 6 May 2019 (application of Italian law to legal separation based on the residence of the spouses); Tribunale di Modena 26 January 2016 (non-application of Art. 8 and application of the *lex fori* since the petition requested legal separation – a legal institution that is not regulated by the law designated by Art. 8 – *in casu* Moroccan law. The court based its decision on Art. 10 of Regulation 1259/2010. For the analysis of this case see: Falconi (2018) 576–578). For *Malta* see: Court of Magistrates (Gozo) Superior Jurisdiction Family Section, 15 January 2021. ECLI:MT:GFML:2021:124921 (application of Maltese Law to the conversion of a legal separation into divorce. Although the spouses had resided in different countries for one year at the time the proceeding was initiated, the court did not base the application of Maltese law on Regulation 1259/2010. This instrument was not even mentioned in the judgment). For *Spain*: Audiencia Provincial Barcelona no. 756/2014, 4 December 2014 (application of Municipal law – Catalonian law – based on Art. 8(a) of Regulation 1259/2010 but without mentioning Art. 15); Audiencia Provincial León no. 38/2015, 27 February 2015 (application of Spanish law based on the common residence of the spouses); Juzgado de Violencia sobre la Mujer Cornellà de Llobregat no. 32/2015, 15 July 2015 (application of Municipal law – Catalonian law – based on Art. 8(a) of Regulation 1259/2010 but without taking into consideration the rule contained in Art. 15 of Regulation 1259/2010); Tribunal Superior de Justicia Aragón no. 27/2015, 6 October 2015 (application of Municipal law – Aragonese law – based on Art. 8(a) and 15 of Regulation 1259/2010); Audiencia Provincial Barcelona no. 334/2019, 7 May 2019 (application of the last common residence of the spouses to the case).

Additionally, according to Article 9, if a legal separation is converted into a divorce, the law applicable to the divorce should be that used by the court to grant the legal separation previously:

Article 9 [Regulation 1259/2010]: Conversion of legal separation into divorce

1. Where legal separation is converted into divorce, the law applicable to divorce shall be the law applied to the legal separation, unless the parties have agreed otherwise in accordance with Article 5.
2. However, if the law applied to the legal separation does not provide for the conversion of legal separation into divorce, Article 8 shall apply, unless the parties have agreed otherwise in accordance with Article 5.[86]

Clear rules for the resolution of conflicts of laws seem to be a step forward in terms of predictability and certainty.[87] However, the intricacies of the provisions make the determination of the concrete law applicable to a case difficult in practice, as up to five connecting factors have to be taken into consideration: common place of residence; last habitual residence of the couple; state of nationality of both spouses; *lex fori*; and the law used to grant the legal separation.[88] The problems of Regulation 1259/2010 are, however, not only limited to the unnecessary degree of complexity imposed for the determination of the governing law. The connecting factors still allow subsequent change of the governing law, as the habitual residence at the time the court is seized is included as the prime connecting factor: thus, moving from one country to another – even if only one spouse does it unilaterally – can lead to the application of a different legal system to resolve the case. All things considered, Article 8 makes the applicable law dependent on the actions of the spouses during the course of their marriage, even when a factual marital crisis has already erupted.[89]

At first glance, one could think that moving from one country to another to avoid the application of some rules could only be done by wealthy people or only in extreme cases, but that might not necessarily be true. The freedom of movement guaranteed in Europe, together with technological advances – e.g. teleworking – make it much easier for ordinary people to change their

86 For German case law see: Oberlandesgericht Stuttgart, 17 January 2013, 17 WF 251/12 (non-application of Art. 3 of Regulation 1259/2010 and application of the law applied by the court to grant legal separation – Italian law – to a conversion of legal separation into divorce in accordance with Art. 9 of Regulation 1259/2010); Oberlandesgericht Nürnberg, 31 October 2013–10 UF 1073/13 (non-application of Art. 3 of Regulation 1259/2010 and application of the law applied by the court to grant legal separation – Turkish law – to a conversion of legal separation into divorce in accordance with Art. 9 of Regulation 1259/2010).

87 Andrae (2014) 290.

88 Franzina (2011) 115.

89 Andrae (2014) 291; Raupach (2014) 194–195. See also Franzina (2020) 104–105.

residence from one country to another. Indeed, the COVID-19 pandemic has shown the capability of employers and employees in several labor sectors to adapt themselves quickly and without major difficulties to remote working models.[90] Besides that, many metropolises are located near the borders of their countries – think for example of the cases of Geneva and Lyon; Salzburg and Bratislava; or Tallinn and Helsinki – so that changing residence to a neighboring country does not require an insurmountable effort. To that should be added that many cities located at the border tend to expand into the other country to form a single conglomeration with foreign suburban areas. For some individuals, changing their residence to another country simply means moving to another neighborhood.[91]

4.1.3. The Conflict Rule for Matrimonial Property

The conflict rules for matters of the matrimonial property regime are set down in Regulation 2016/1103. Just as in the other two cases, this international instrument applies regardless of whether the claim has an accessory character or not. As long as a part of the demands refer to the proprietary and related financial consequences of the marriage – in particular the existence, determination, daily management, division and protection of common assets – the rules contained in this instrument apply to determine the law governing this issue.[92] Article 26 of Regulation 2016/1103 also contains a hierarchical set of connecting factors for the determination of the applicable law. However – in contrast to Regulation 1259/2010 – it provides a solution enhancing the stability and predictability of the resolution of the conflict of laws:

> Article 26 [Regulation 2016/1103]: Applicable law in the absence of a choice by the parties:
>
> 1. In the absence of a choice-of-law agreement pursuant to Article 22, the law applicable to the matrimonial property regime shall be the law of the State:
>   (a) of the spouses' first common habitual residence after the conclusion of the marriage; or, failing that

90 Fana et al. (2020) 8 et seqq.

91 The territory of the European Union is to a large extent – about 40 percent – made up of border regions. Indeed around 30 percent of the total population resides there. See: Schneider et al. (2021) 5.

92 See recital 18 of Regulation 2016/1103. The Regulation encompasses decisions of the daily management of the common property as well as those arising upon separation and divorce, see Art. 3 of Regulation 2016/1103. According to the CJEU (Case C-558/16 *Doris Margret Lisette Mahnkopf* paras. 31 et seqq.) the equalization of accrued gains in the case of death – in accordance with Art. 1371 of the German Civil Code – falls, however, outside the scope of application of Regulation 2016/1103. See also Bonomi (2020) 33.

(b) of the spouses' common nationality at the time of the conclusion of the marriage; or, failing that
(c) with which the spouses jointly have the closest connection at the time of the conclusion of the marriage, taking into account all the circumstances.
2. If the spouses have more than one common nationality at the time of the conclusion of the marriage, only points (a) and (c) of paragraph 1 shall apply.
3. [...][93]

The primary connecting factor put forward by the Regulation is the law of the state of the spouses' first common residence after their marriage.[94] Thus – *prima facie* – the law governing the property regime of the spouses will not change by actions performed unilaterally by one spouse after its celebration. The other connecting factors included in the instrument are for cases where spouses have never lived together, which is an exceptional situation.[95] This change of approach in the determination of the applicable law is welcome. The use of the first common residence usually provides legal certainty to the spouses, and enables them to know in advance – even before the celebration of their marriage – the specific legal system governing the financial aspects of their relationship. However, the regulation also includes, in Article 26 paragraph 3, an exception to the use of the first common residence that again inserts uncertainty into the determination of the governing law:

Article 26 [Regulation 2016/1103]: Applicable law in the absence of a choice by the parties:

1. [...]
2. [...]
3. By way of exception and upon application by either spouse, the judicial authority having jurisdiction to rule on matters of the matrimonial property regime may decide that the law of a State other than the State whose law is applicable pursuant to point (a) of paragraph 1 shall govern the matrimonial property regime if the applicant demonstrates that:
(a) the spouses had their last common habitual residence in that other State for a significantly longer period of time than in the State designated pursuant to point (a) of paragraph 1; and

93 Art. 26 para. 3 is discussed below.
94 As recital 49 of Regulation 2016/1103 states that "[t]he first common habitual residence of the spouses *shortly after* marriage should constitute the first criterion" (emphasis added), some authors affirm that spouses should establish their common residence within a period of up to six or eight months in a specific jurisdiction to regard it as their first common residence. See: Coester-Waltjen (2018) 203; Hausmann (2018) 234; Looschelders (2018) 843.
95 In those special cases, the law applicable will be that of the spouses' common nationality at the time of the conclusion of the marriage. If they do not have the same nationality, the law which is most closely connected with the couple at the time of the conclusion of the marriage will be applied. See in detail: Coester-Waltjen (2018) 201–206.

(b) both spouses had relied on the law of that other State in arranging or planning their property relations. [...][96]

In order to avoid situations in which the law applicable to the matrimonial property regime is not connected to the circumstances, the judicial authority might apply the law of the last common habitual residence of the couple. This substitution occurs for example when the spouses have lived there for a longer period and both have relied on the law of this country in planning and handling their property.[97] The aim pursued by this provision is understandable. The problem is the technique employed to reach this objective. As the Regulation does not specify how to determine if the spouses have relied on the use of this law for arranging their affairs, it becomes difficult to predict in which cases the change of law will finally occur.[98] All in all, although the Regulation was thought to remove obstacles to the free movement of people, it might end up complicating the situation of those who have changed their residence during the course of their marriage.[99] The approach employed compromises the determination of the applicable law, as in some cases the spouses will have difficulties in knowing whether their last or first place of residence will ultimately be used by the court to resolve their case.[100] In a context where it is not uncommon to move from one country to another, this legal provision might end up creating more problems than solutions for the spouses.

Finally, it is also important to note that Article 26 paragraph 1 refers to the common nationality at the time of the marriage, while under Article 8 of the Regulation 1259/2010 the common nationality at the time the court is seized is critical. Furthermore, as noted by Andrea Bonomi those regulations do not even consistently address the issues resulting from a plurality of nationalities: "while the Matrimonial Property Regulation [Article 26 paragraph 2] excludes

---

96 The excluded paragraphs read as follows: "The law of that other State shall apply as from the conclusion of the marriage, unless one spouse disagrees. In the latter case, the law of that other State shall have effect as from the establishment of the last common habitual residence in that other State.
The application of the law of the other State shall not adversely affect the rights of third parties deriving from the law applicable pursuant to point (a) of paragraph 1. This paragraph shall not apply when the spouses have concluded a matrimonial property agreement before the establishment of their last common habitual residence in that other State."

97 Hausmann (2018) 235; Looschelders (2018) 844.

98 See Martiny (2020) 257. Furthermore, as the conflict rule grants the possibility to demand the application of the law of the last common residence only with *ex nunc* effects, the Regulation opens up the possibility that the marital regime will be governed by two different sets of legislation.

99 Coester-Waltjen (2018) 207, 209–210.

100 Coester-Waltjen (2018) 210–211; Hausmann (2018) 236; Looschelders (2018) 844.

nationality when the spouses share more than one common nationality, a similar rule is lacking in the Rome III Regulation".[101]

4.1.4. Practical Problems Arising from the Application of the Legal Provisions to a Single Case

Analyzed one by one, the instruments dealing with the determination of the applicable law do not seem promising for individuals immersed in a marriage with international connotations. In terms of predictability and simplicity, all of them still leave much to be desired. However, when they are applied jointly, the situation is even more problematic. This shall be illustrated by continuing our introductory example:[102] If Giovanni finally decides to move to Malta and demands the payment of maintenance, the law applicable would be that in force in Malta, as this country is the habitual residence of the creditor at the moment of initiating the proceeding. However, if one of them decides to refute the application of the law of the habitual residence, the law most closely connected with their marriage takes its place. As the Hague Protocol of 2007 states, that last common place of residence should be given special consideration when determining the linkage, so the law of Germany would apply, as this was the country where they lived together for the last time. It is, however, important to note that there is no guarantee that the court will ultimately opt for German law, as the couple had contacts with many jurisdictions.[103] According to the protocol, the law that has a close connection with the relationship should apply. Thus, other considerations, such as the fact of having a common nationality or having lived in another country for a long time, might be taken into account at the moment of determining the governing law.[104] Regarding the divorce, Regulation 1259/2010 designates the law of the last country of residence as the governing law if spouses do not live in the same jurisdiction at the time the court is seized. This legal system, however, applies only if the period of residence did not end more than one year before the court is seized, provided that one of the spouses still lives in that country. As neither Giovanni nor María Isabel still live in Germany, the next connecting factor should be used: the common nationality – that is, Spanish law.[105] Finally, the applicable law to the property

---

101 Bonomi (2020) 38.

102 See this chapter *in initio*.

103 Andrae (2014) 583.

104 Andrae (2014) 583; Hausmann (2018) 457; Mankowski (2016) 125.

105 For the sake of simplicity, the Italian nationality of the husband is not considered. However, the determination of the applicable law when the person has multiple nationalities is controversial as Regulation 1259/2010 does not provide a clear answer to resolve this issue. In some countries the domestic conflict of laws system contains rules that resolve such cases which could be used by national courts to fill gaps left by the Regulation. According to the Swiss private

regime will – arguably – be Dutch law, as the Netherlands was their first common place of residence after the conclusion of their marriage.[106]

In sum, three legal systems would likely apply to the case in absence of a choice of law agreement: Maltese law – or German law if one of the spouses refutes its application – for maintenance issues; Spanish law for questions related to the divorce; and Dutch law to disputes regarding the matrimonial property regime of the couple.

4.2. DRAWBACKS OF THE LEGAL PROVISIONS ON CHOICE OF LAW AGREEMENTS

One of the most notable and useful prerogatives included in the Hague Protocol of 2007, Regulation 1259/2010 and Regulation 2016/1103 is the possibility to individually determine the applicable law. Spouses are not only allowed to indicate at any time – before and after the conclusion of their marriage – the exact legal system governing their relationship, but also to subsequently change a law previously agreed upon. The freedom of choice in marital issues is by no means an innovation introduced by any of these instruments; the validity of choice of law agreements can be traced back to an expert opinion delivered by the French jurist Charles Dumoulin in 1527.[107] Notwithstanding this, its express

international law, for example, if a person is national of several states, the nationality of the state with which the person is most closely connected applies for purposes of the applicable law (See Art. 23 Swiss Federal Act on Private International Law). There are, however, jurisdictions where courts give priority to the law of the court (*lex fori*) if the nationality of the person corresponds to the place where the case is discussed. According to Art 5 of the Introduction to the German Civil Code, for example: "If reference is made to the law of a country of which a person is a national and where this person is a bi- or multinational, the law applicable shall be that of the country with which the person has the closest connection, especially through his or her habitual residence or through the course of his or her life. *If such person is also a German national, that legal status shall prevail*" (emphasis added). The application of German law may, however, depend on whether the nationality corresponds to a Member State of the European Union. For the application of Regulation 1259/2010 by German courts in cases involving individuals with multiple nationality, see in detail: Andrae (2014) 291–293.

106 As long as it is proven that they lived in Germany for a longer time than in the Netherlands, and that both relied on the German law when arranging or planning their property, the application of Dutch law will be rejected. See: recital 50 of the Regulation 2016/110. If German law applies, will ultimately depend on whether both relied on the German law when arranging or planning their property. The regulation however does not specify the scope of this assertion or any way to demonstrate it.

107 The opinion referred to the law applicable to the property regime of spouses. See: Ancel & Lequette (2001) 134; Corneloup (2013) 15; Gamillscheg (1955) 110 et seqq. However, an even earlier example – in the second half of the 11th century – of an express choice of law clause can be found in the marriage settlement concluded by the Princess of Leon Jimena and "El Cid Campeador" Rodrigo Díaz de Vivar. See: Juenger (1982) 297.

inclusion is a significant milestone, not only because in several jurisdictions spouses were previously not allowed to designate the law applicable by themselves at all,[108] but also, if they were permitted, party autonomy was often restricted to specific aspects of the relationship and subject to varying requirements for its substantive validity.

The inclusion of the freedom of choice in family matters is usually seen as a result of the widespread acceptance of party autonomy as a guiding principle in the area of international contract law.[109] In countries where the choice of law for marital issues was not possible before the implementation of the instruments, individuals were already allowed to specify the law applicable to their contracts dealing with the sale of goods and immovable property, provision of services, rental of assets, tenancy, franchise and many other private arrangements.[110] However, despite the parallels in the regulation of party autonomy in contract and marriage law, there are also significant differences between them. In contract law, parties can choose freely the governing law.[111] Restrictions on the freedom of choice exist only in protection of those individuals regarded as vulnerable by the law, in particular consumers and employees.[112] Besides that, people are permitted to select any legal system. Furthermore, their choice of law is not subject to any formal requirement, it may be expressed or even just implied from the circumstances or the terms used by the parties at the moment of drafting a contract. There are certainly limits to the freedom of choice. But they lie in the defense of the interests of third parties, the safeguards of international public policy and the protection of certain individuals that are unable to negotiate the terms of their contracts according to the substantive law.[113]

Marriage law does not follow this model, as the choice of law is significantly restricted and subject to a number of conditions for its validity. Agreements on

---

108 Before the entry into force of the 2007 Protocol, only Sweden and the Netherlands allowed spouses to choose the applicable law for disputes on maintenance obligations. See: Permanent Bureau Prel. Doc. No. 2 on Maintenance (2003). For the Dutch decision that allowed the choice of law for maintenance issues (decision issued on 21.02.1997 by the Hoge Raad in the Nederlands, RvdW 1997, 56 = NIPR 1997 Nr. 70) see: Boele-Woelki (1998).

109 Bartl (2012) 104–105; Bonomi/Explanatory Report (2013) 51; Corneloup (2013) 17.

110 Party autonomy in contract law is regulated in Article 3 of the Rome I Regulation (Regulation (EC) No 593/2008). This Regulation applies to all EU Member States except Denmark. Denmark is, however, part of the 1980 Rome Convention, which also allows the free choice of the applicable law to contracts.

111 It is, however, disputed if the parties may only choose rules of law that are generally regarded on an international, supranational or regional level as neutral. See: Mankowski (2017) 103 et seqq. See also Girsberger et al. (2021) 43 et seqq.

112 Mankowski (2017) 106, 167. Regarding the limits imposed on party autonomy for contracts involving consumers and employees, see: Palao (2017) 581 et seqq.; Wilderspin (2017) 455 et seqq.

113 See: Magnus (2017) 50–51.

choice of law might also be subject to scrutiny well beyond the protection of the *ordre public* or the interests of third parties. Furthermore, spouses are generally only able to designate a legal system with which they are closely connected.[114] Finally, there is no common approach among the instruments when establishing limits on the freedom of choice.

4.2.1. Mismatch and Lack of Congruency

There are significant disparities in how party autonomy is regulated across the three instruments. Not only the options at the disposal of the individuals but also the conditions for their enforceability differ from one instrument to the next.

4.2.1.1. Agreements on the Law Governing Maintenance Obligations

The Hague Protocol of 2007 provides expressly for the possibility to choose the applicable law in Articles 7 and 8.[115] It is quite remarkable that despite being the oldest of the analyzed instruments, this protocol offers the widest range of options. Along with the *lex fori*, the law of the nationality and the habitual residence of either spouse can be chosen. Couples are also allowed to make the law governing their maintenance obligations depend on the legal system applicable to the property regime, or the dissolution of their marriage.[116] Notwithstanding that, the Hague Protocol of 2007 is also the instrument that regulates the limits of party autonomy less precisely, as well as the one that provides greater leeway to the courts to decide on the enforceability of choice of law agreements.

---

114 Corneloup (2013) 19; Kroll-Ludwigs (2013) 475–476.

115 The 1973 Hague Maintenance Convention does not expressly provide the possibility to choose the applicable law. Swiss courts have assumed that this instrument does not allow the parties to choose their law. See BGE 119 II 167, 171. See also Kren Kostkiewicz & Eichenberger (2015) 28. Dutch courts, however, interpreted this convention the other way around, that it does not prevent a choice of the applicable law to maintenance obligations. See Hoge Raad 21 February 1997, ECLI:NL:HR:1997:ZC2288.

116 For case law on choice of law agreements see for *Germany*: Oberlandesgericht Hamm, 22 April 2016 – II-3 UF 262/15 (establishing that there is no choice of law agreement even though a foreign legal institution – the *mahr* – was mentioned in a marital agreement concluded by the spouses); Kammergericht Berlin, 3 February 2017–16 UF 77/16 (discussing the validity of a contract by which the husband agreed to pay 135,000 € – 500 gold coins as *mahr* – in case of divorce). For *Italy*: Tribunale di Padova, prima sezione civile, 8 September 2017 (choice of the national law of the spouses – *in casu* Moroccan law – to apply to the payment of a lump sum of 2,000 €. Summary available at <http://www2.ipr.uni-heidelberg.de/eufams/index.php?site=entscheidungsdatenbank&lang=en>, EUFAMS code ITF20170908); Tribunale di Pordenone, 30 June 2015 (choice of law of the nationality of the wife – Brazilian law. Summary available at <http://www2.ipr.uni-heidelberg.de/eufams/index.php?site=entscheidungsdatenbank&lang=en>, EUFAMS code ITF20150630).

The freedom of choice is provided in two different variations:[117] one for the purpose of a particular proceeding, the other for all future disputes. The first variant in Article 7 is restricted to one option – the *lex fori* – and to a single dispute. Once the proceeding is over, a new agreement on choice of law is necessary to avoid the application of the default conflict rule, even if the dispute is subsequently discussed in the same country and before the same authority:[118]

> Article 7 [Hague Protocol of 2007]: Designation of the law applicable for the purpose of a particular proceeding:
>
> (1) Notwithstanding Articles 3 to 6, the maintenance creditor and debtor for the purpose only of a particular proceeding in a given State may expressly designate the law of that State as applicable to a maintenance obligation.
>
> (2) [...][119]

Regarding this first variant, one should note that in contrast to some other aspects of marriage law, the *res iudicata* in cases involving maintenance support has a relative character. Any party can request an adjustment of a decision if he or she believes that a change of circumstances merits a review of the judgment.[120] Thus, the practical usefulness of this option is very questionable, due to the relative ease with which agreements on choice of law can be set aside by either of the spouses: if one of them – debtor or creditor – considers the effects of the judicial decision detrimental to their interests, all he or she has to do is simply initiate another proceeding in order to escape the effects of the law previously jointly agreed upon. Just by demanding an adjustment of the payments, the affected party can leave behind the one-off agreement and achieve the application of another legal system – the one designated by the default conflict of laws rule – to the case.[121]

The second variant is in Article 8. This provision allows individuals that are over the age of 18 and do not suffer from an impairment of their personal

---

117 Bonomi/Explanatory Report (2013) 23.

118 Andrae (2016) 707; Bartl (2012) 104; Staudinger (2018) 1302.

119 The excluded paragraph reads as follows: "A designation made before the institution of such proceedings shall be in an agreement, signed by both parties, in writing or recorded in any medium, the information contained in which is accessible so as to be usable for subsequent reference."

120 For a general description of the substantive regulation of maintenance obligations in several countries around the world see: Permanent Bureau Prel. Doc. No. 2 on Maintenance (2003); Permanent Bureau Prel. Doc. No 3 on Maintenance (1999). For German case law: Oberlandesgericht Hamm, 22 April 2016 – II-3 UF 262/15 (establishing that there is no choice of law agreement even though a foreign legal institution – *mahr* – was mentioned in a marital agreement concluded by the spouses).

121 Andrae (2014) 590.

faculties to choose among a wide range of possibilities.[122] This option dictates that the designated law will apply to any future legal proceeding between the spouses.[123] However, unlike in the previous case, the choice of law in this variant is subject to further restrictions.

Article 8 [Hague Protocol of 2007]: Designation of the applicable law:

(1) Notwithstanding Articles 3 to 6, the maintenance creditor and debtor may at any time designate one of the following laws as applicable to a maintenance obligation –
   (a) the law of any State of which either party is a national at the time of the designation;
   (b) the law of the State of the habitual residence of either party at the time of the designation;
   (c) the law designated by the parties as applicable, or the law in fact applied, to their property regime;
   (d) the law designated by the parties as applicable, or the law in fact applied, to their divorce or legal separation.

(2) Such agreement shall be in writing or recorded in any medium, the information contained in which is accessible so as to be usable for subsequent reference, and shall be signed by both parties.

(3) Paragraph 1 shall not apply to maintenance obligations in respect of a person under the age of 18 years or of an adult who, by reason of an impairment or insufficiency of his or her personal faculties, is not in a position to protect his or her interest.

(4) Notwithstanding the law designated by the parties in accordance with paragraph 1, the question of whether the creditor can renounce his or her right to maintenance shall be determined by the law of the State of the habitual residence of the creditor at the time of the designation.

(5) Unless at the time of the designation the parties were fully informed and aware of the consequences of their designation, the law designated by the parties shall not apply where the application of that law would lead to manifestly unfair or unreasonable consequences for any of the parties.

First, the law designated does not govern either the validity or extent of a waiver of the right to maintenance, or the conditions for renouncing the right to receive support, according to Article 8 paragraph 4. Regardless of the designated law,

---

122 See for a detailed account: Mankowski (2016) 158. Regarding the possibility to choose the law of the nationality of one of the spouses see for *Germany*: Oberlandesgericht Hamm, 22 April 2016 – II-3 UF 262/15.

123 For a description of the options at the disposal of the spouses, see in detail: Andrae (2016) 711–714; Mankowski (2016) 152–158.

a waiver of maintenance is governed by the law of the place of residence of the creditor at the moment of concluding the choice of law.[124] Therefore, it can then happen that much later a distant law – one with which they now have only a tenuous or very recent connection – ultimately applies in a future proceeding when determining the validity of a renunciation.[125] Furthermore, it is surprising that the drafters of the protocol did not specify whether this provision only refers to cases in which the creditor renounces their right, or rather, if it also covers situations in which the choice of a particular legal system leads to the loss of the right to be the beneficiary of support.[126] It is not clear, either, whether the law agreed upon by the parties will finally apply, for example in cases in which the maintenance statute does not allow for retro-active payments, or to situations where the loss of maintenance is the result of being declared culpable for the dissolution of the marital union, celebrating a new marriage or expiring periods of prescription.[127]

Second, Article 8 paragraph 5 states that authorities have the power to set aside the law chosen if they think it leads to an unreasonable result or a manifestly unfair position. As this provision is separate from the public policy clause, it can be interpreted that the non-application of the designated law is not restricted to severe cases.[128] The protocol does not specify *when* the choice of law might lead to a manifestly unfair position.[129] Scholars suggest that the assessment should be done in comparison with the law that would apply according to the default connecting factor,[130] so that the bigger the difference in the amount to pay, the more likely it is regarded as inappropriate.[131] Being so, the desired legal certainty is heavily impaired, as the actual enforceability of the choice of law would ultimately depend on the

---

124 Bartl (2012) 108; Staudinger (2018) 1307. The idea behind Art. 8 para. 4 might be protecting the creditor from suffering the negative consequences of agreeing to a particularly unprotective law. See Gray (2021) 88. For German case law see: Oberlandesgericht Hamm, 22 April 2016 – II-3 UF 262/15 (mentioning that the Hague Protocol explicitly states that the question of whether the creditor can renounce his or her right to maintenance, should be determined by the law of the state of the habitual residence of the creditor at the time of the designation).

125 Bartl (2012) 109–110.

126 According to some reputed scholars, the designation of a law granting no maintenance is considered a renunciation of maintenance. See: Mankowski (2016) 163; Staudinger (2018) 1308.

127 The awarding of a lump sum should, however, not be regarded as a renunciation of a maintenance right according to the explanatory report. See Bonomi/Explanatory Report (2013) 59.

128 Staudinger (2018) 1308.

129 Staudinger (2018) 1308.

130 Staudinger (2018) 1308; Mankowski (2016) 164.

131 Andrae (2016) 718.

law applicable in the absence of a choice of law. Thus, in order to determine if the chosen law could be set aside by the authorities, it is necessary to know the future place of residence of the creditor or the legal system closest to the spouses' relationship, as one of those two laws would apply in absence of a choice of law. As neither of them can really be known in advance – for example at the moment of the conclusion of the marriage – spouses would end up having no certainty about whether their choice of law agreement will ultimately be enforced.

It seems that the drafters were aware of this problem. The protocol states that in case the law designated leads to an unreasonable result or a manifestly unfair position, the law chosen will notwithstanding be applied if: "at the time of the designation, the parties were fully informed and aware of the consequences of their designation".[132] The intention is good; however, it does not solve the problem. On the one hand, both conditions – to be fully informed and aware of the consequences – are very difficult to prove in a legal proceeding. They require that the person knew the advantages and disadvantages of the legal system that would apply in absence of a choice of law agreement, which – as explained above – is very difficult to determine in advance. Furthermore, a number of scholars reckon that being counseled by an expert adviser that knows and explains the contents of both legal systems – the one that would apply normally and the one chosen – might not be enough. It should also be necessary to prove that the information was processed properly and understood by both spouses.[133] These authors, however, do not mention any specific means to prove this in the context of a legal proceeding.

On the other hand, even if it can be proven that both spouses were fully informed and aware, it would be very odd that the choice of law would ultimately be allowed, as it is about permitting the enforcement of an agreement that leads to "manifestly unfair or unreasonable consequences for any of the parties". By definition, any judicial decision is supposed to be coherent and just. Thus, it is very difficult to imagine that a court that considers the effects of a choice of law "unreasonable" or "manifestly unfair" would still accept that situation merely because both parties were aware of its effects.

---

132 Article 8 (Hague Protocol of 2007), paragraph 5: (emphasis added) "(5) *Unless at the time of the designation the parties were fully informed and aware of the consequences of their designation*, the law designated by the parties shall not apply where the application of that law would lead to manifestly unfair or unreasonable consequences for any of the parties."

133 See for a detailed account: Andrae (2014) 593; Mankowski (2016) 165–166. For a different view, see: Henrich (2013) 60–61.

4.2.1.2. Agreements on the Law Governing the Divorce or Legal Separation

As in the case of the protocol, the party autonomy of the spouses has a prominent role in Regulation 1259/2010:

> Article 5 [Regulation 1259/2010]: Choice of applicable law by the parties
>
> 1. The spouses may agree to designate the law applicable to divorce and legal separation provided that it is one of the following laws:
>   (a) the law of the State where the spouses are habitually resident at the time the agreement is concluded; or
>   (b) the law of the State where the spouses were last habitually resident, in so far as one of them still resides there at the time the agreement is concluded; or
>   (c) the law of the State of nationality of either spouse at the time the agreement is concluded; or
>   (d) the law of the forum.

It is remarkable that spouses are allowed to choose the *lex fori* not only for one, but for all future disputes between them.[134] Thanks to this new option,

[134] See: González Beilfuss (2020a) 76; Gruber (2013) 43. See also: Andrae (2014) 284; Hausmann (2018) 91. For case law on Art. 5 Regulation 1259/2010, see for *Germany*: Oberlandesgericht Nürnberg, January 31, 2013, 7 WF 1710/12 (validity of a choice of law agreement – Kazakh law – concluded during the course of a divorce proceeding); Oberlandesgericht Hamm, 07.05.2013, 3 UF 267/12 (discussing the validity of a tacit choice of law agreement in favor of Iranian law); Oberlandesgericht Hamm, April 2016 – II-3 UF 262/15 (asserting that there is no choice of law agreement according to Art. 5 of Regulation 1259/2010 since the marital agreement only refers to the Islamic "morning gift" and other issues related to the celebration of the marriage); Kammergericht Berlin, 3 February 2017–16 UF 77/16 (choice of German law by a woman of Iranian nationality and a man of both Iranian and German nationality). For *Italy*: Tribunale di Padova, 24 November 2015 (choice of the common nationality of the spouses – Colombian law. Summary available at <http://www2.ipr.uni-heidelberg.de/eufams/index.php?site=entscheidungsdatenbank&lang=en>, EUFAMS code ITF20151124); Tribunale di Belluno, 27 October 2016 (choice of the common nationality of the spouses – *in casu* Albanian law – in order to get divorced without fulfilling the requirements of Italian law. For the analysis of this case see: Falconi (2018) 571–572); Tribunale di Treviso 20 September 2016 (tacit choice of law agreement – the woman bases the divorce petition on legal provisions of the Moldovan Civil Code, the husband bases his defense also on Moldovan law. For the analysis of this case, see: Falconi (2018) 573–575); Tribunale di Padova, prima sezione civile, 8 September 2017 (choice of the law of the common nationality of the spouses. Summary available at: <http://www2.ipr.uni-heidelberg.de/eufams/index.php?site=entscheidungsdatenbank&lang=en>, EUFAMS code ITF20170908); Tribunale di Alessandria, sezione civile, 11 December 2017 (validity of a choice of law agreement by the wife alleging the use of foreign law – Romanian law – and the husband did not contest its application. Summary available at: <http://www2.ipr.uni-heidelberg.de/eufams/index.php?site=entscheidungsdatenbank&lang=en>, EUFAMS code ITF20171211); Tribunale di Torino, 1 June 2018 (rejection of a choice of law agreement because the foreign law – Argentinian law – would allow the immediate dissolution of the marriage.

spouses are able to accomplish a synchronization between *lex causae* and *lex fori* by concluding a choice of court agreement that also designates the law of the forum as the applicable law. That means not only a lower likelihood of errors in the application of the law and greater speed in the resolution of the case;[135] such a combination also costs less for the spouses, as neither translations nor the services of legal experts in foreign law will be necessary to achieve the dissolution of their marital bond.[136] However, in contrast to the protocol, for questions related to their divorce, spouses are not allowed to choose the law of residence of either of them as governing law. If they want to designate the law of the country where only one of them is habitually resident, they must both have lived there together before the conclusion of the choice of law agreement.[137] The assumption was probably that the parties are informed about the content of their chosen law.[138] However, if that was the aim, it is not clear why they can designate the law of the nationality of either of them, even if this law has no link with the other spouse.[139] Instead of limiting the range of options, forcing them to consult a legal expert – requiring the notarization of the choice of law agreement – would have been

According to the court the application of the foreign law would be contrary to the best interest of the child: "*non risponde all'interesse dei figli*"); Tibunale di Roma, 2 March 2018 (application of the national law of the spouses – Albanian law. The divorce was granted without a period of legal separation which is required according to Italian law). Summary available at <http://www2.ipr.uni-heidelberg.de/eufams/index.php?site=entscheidungsdatenbank&lang=en>, EUFAMS code ITF20180219); Tribunale di Firenze, sezione prima, 16 May 2019 (choice of the national law of the wife – in *casu* Moroccan law. The agreement allowed the spouses to circumvent the application of Italian law which required a three-year period of legal separation as a condition to file for divorce). Summary available at <http://www2.ipr.uni-heidelberg.de/eufams/index.php?site=entscheidungsdatenbank&lang=en>, EUFAMS code ITF20190516); Tribunale di Novara, 16 May 2019 (choice of the national law of the spouses – Albanian law. The agreement allowed the spouses to circumvent the application of Italian law which required a three-year period of legal separation as a condition to file for the divorce). Summary available at <http://www2.ipr.uni-heidelberg.de/eufams/index.php?site=entscheidungsdatenbank&lang=en>, EUFAMS code ITF20190516a). For *Spain*: Audiencia Provincial Castellón no. 43/2015, 27 April 2015 (accepting the validity of a tacit choice of law agreement made by the spouses. Although the spouses concluded no explicit choice of law agreement, the court applied Romanian law since both based their allegations on this law); Audiencia Provincial Barcelona no. 334/2019, 7 May 2019 (rejection of the validity of a tacit choice of law agreement in a case where the court of first instance incorrectly applied the law of common nationality of the spouses – Spanish law – without opposition from the spouses. Both spouses lived in Belgium when the divorce proceeding was initiated).

135 González Beilfuss (2020a) 75; Wennersbusch (2018) 99.

136 See: Hausmann (2018) 91. For the advantages of choosing the *lex fori* once the proceeding was already initiated see: Raupach (2014) 166–167.

137 Otherwise the choice of law will be invalid. See González Beilfuss (2020a) 73.

138 See: recital 18 of Regulation 1259/2010. See also: Raupach (2014) 164–165.

139 Wennersbusch (2018) 99–100.

a better way to guarantee informed decisions. No international instrument, however, mentions such a requirement for the conclusion of choice of law agreements.[140]

In terms of legal certainty, Regulation 1259/2010 seems to be a step forward in comparison with the protocol, as it states expressly that issues regarding the material validity of the choice of law agreement will be determined by the law designated by the parties:

Article 6 [Regulation 1259/2010]: Consent and material validity

1. The existence and validity of an agreement on choice of law or of any term thereof, shall be determined by the law which would govern it under this Regulation if the agreement or term were valid.
2. Nevertheless, a spouse, in order to establish that he did not consent, may rely upon the law of the country in which he has his habitual residence at the time the court is seized if it appears from the circumstances that it would not be reasonable to determine the effect of his conduct in accordance with the law specified in paragraph 1.

Article 6 paragraph 2 introduces a degree of uncertainty as it establishes that the habitual residence at the time the court is seized would apply for determining the existence of the choice of law agreement.[141] Courts must make a concrete comparison between the two legal systems to assert whether it would be unreasonable for a person to select the chosen law.[142] However, the margin of discretion of the court is restricted, as this provision stipulates the particular circumstances – determination of the existence and validity of an agreement – in which courts are allowed to apply this connecting factor.[143] Thus, it is expected that the law designated will in most cases apply on any issue related to the divorce.[144]

4.2.1.3. Agreements on the Law Governing the Matrimonial Property Regime

The approach used to regulate party autonomy for questions about the property regime is similar to the one used for the divorce. There are, however,

140 See: Art 7, Art. 8 Hague Protocol; Art. 7 Regulation 1259/2010; recital 47, Art. 23 Regulation 2016/1103. The Regulation 1259/2010 and Regulation 2016/1103 stipulate the application of additional rules on form according to the law of the spouses' common residence at the time the agreement on choice of law is concluded. For a critique on those provisions see González Beilfuss (2020b) 85–87.

141 It was affirmed that a mistake due to a misunderstanding of a foreign language could fall within the scope of Art. 6 para. 2. See Joubert (2020) 84.

142 It was even affirmed that it is only required to show that the reference to the applicable law appears to be unreasonable. See Joubert (2020) 86.

143 Hausmann (2018) 95.

144 Franzina (2011) 122.

differences – again – in the range of possibilities that can be chosen by the spouses:

Article 22 [Regulation 2016/1103]: Choice of the applicable law

1. The spouses or future spouses may agree to designate, or to change, the law applicable to their matrimonial property regime, provided that that law is one of the following:
   (a) the law of the State where the spouses or future spouses, or one of them, is habitually resident at the time the agreement is concluded; or
   (b) the law of a State of nationality of either spouse or future spouse at the time the agreement is concluded.
2. Unless the spouses agree otherwise, a change of the law applicable to the matrimonial property regime made during the marriage shall have prospective effect only.
3. Any retroactive change of the applicable law under paragraph 2 shall not adversely affect the rights of third parties deriving from that law.

According to Article 22 of the Regulation 2016/1103, along with law of the country of nationality of either spouse, they can also choose the law of the state where one of them is a habitual resident at the moment of the conclusion of the choice of law agreement. Spouses can so designate the law of the country where only one of them lives, regardless of whether this place was their last common habitual residence. However – and in contrast to the other instruments – the Regulation on matrimonial property does not include the option of the *lex fori*.[145] It is interesting to note that Regulation 2016/1103 allows for the designation of the court located in the country where the marriage was concluded to resolve disputes related to the matrimonial property of the spouses. But if this option is taken, they will then not be able to compel this court to use its own law to resolve the case as this option is not provided by the Regulation.

4.2.1.4. Practical Problems Arising from the Application of the Legal Provisions to a Single Case

Let us return to the introductory example[146] to analyze two possible scenarios: one where spouses conclude a choice of law agreement at the time of the celebration of their marriage; and another where this idea arises right before a legal proceeding is initiated.

---

145 Hausmann (2018) 228; Looschelders (2018) 841.

146 See this chapter *in initio*.

In the first case, Giovanni and Maria Isabel have three options for issues related to maintenance obligations: Spanish, Italian and Dutch law. If they settle for the law of the country of the nationality of one of them, Dutch law will still govern questions about the renunciation of maintenance rights, as the Netherlands was the place of residence of the future creditor at the moment of concluding the choice of law agreement.[147] That happens even though they have only lived there for a brief period of time, neither spouse has Dutch nationality, and at the time of initiating a proceeding neither of them will be significantly connected to this country. Furthermore, regardless of whether Spanish, Italian or Dutch law is chosen, the determination of whether the chosen law leads to an unreasonable result or a manifestly unfair position should be made on the basis of the law of the future place of residence of the creditor (Maltese law) or the law most closely connected with the case (presumably German law).

For questions related to the divorce and property regime, the range of options is the same. However, in order to determine whether the spouses have given their consent validly, either of them can require the court to apply the law of the place of their residence at the time it is seized of a future proceeding.[148] Maltese or Swiss Law might then end up playing a role in the dispute, when deciding on the material validity of the agreement. It is interesting to note that although both of them have lived the largest part of their lives in Switzerland and consequently – most likely – are familiar with the content of this legal system, they are not allowed to choose the Swiss law.[149] Unfortunately, the drafters of the international instruments did not consider that currently the effective linkage that individuals have with the country of their nationality or residence has in many cases lost much of its former importance. The fact that children of migrants do not automatically acquire the citizenship of the country where they have spent their whole life might lead to situations where they feel total familiarity with the traditions and social customs, as well as with the law in force in a country that is not the country of their nationality. It is clear that the drafters were aware of the ever-increasing movement of people and the issues that it could cause for spouses. They however seemed to ignore the effects that the migration of parents ends up having on their children. And in the same vein, the possibilities that people currently have to move from one jurisdiction to another implies a weakening of the connection with the country where a person is currently – in a maybe short-lived moment – staying.

If Giovanni and Maria Isabel desire to agree on the applicable law once they are not living together anymore, the range of possibilities would be different.

[147] See: Art. 8 para. 4 *in fine* Hague Protocol of 2007.

[148] It was argued that the imposition of formalities to the determination of the applicable law makes Art. 6.2 of the Regulation 1257/2010 unnecessary. See Joubert (2020) 84.

[149] Swiss law is no option even if the Swiss conflict of laws rules apply to the case See: Art. 49, 52, 61 (Swiss Federal Act on Private International Law).

The Spanish and Italian legal systems remain as options as those of their nationalities. Maltese and Swiss law appear as available alternatives, but only for questions related to maintenance obligations and property regime, but not for the divorce according to Regulation 1259/2010, as their last common residence was not located in either of these countries.[150] It is also noteworthy that German law is not an option at the disposal of these spouses, although this legal system would likely be regarded by a court as the one most closely connected with their marriage. Regardless of the time they have spent in this country during the relationship, and how well informed they actually might be about the law's content, the choice of this legal system is not an option. The same restriction exists for the law of their first place of residence, independently of the preference they might have for the Dutch law or the degree of information they have about its content after having lived there. The possibility to choose Dutch law has expired as they do not live there anymore at the time the proceeding is initiated. Paradoxically, both legal systems would, however, apply to the relationship – German law for questions related to maintenance,[151] Dutch law for issues arising from the property regime[152] – in absence of a choice of law.

4.2.2. Limited Range of Eligible Options

As noted above, in contract law the freedom of choice is limited to certain types of contracts. Consumers and employees – for example – are not allowed to freely determine their applicable law. The reason for this limitation is the possibility that professionals in a business activity and employers can take an undue advantage of the vulnerability of their counterpart and manipulate them to choose a legal system with legal provisions that benefit exclusively them.[153] That consumers and employees are in need of special protection by the legal system seems to be largely undisputed in Europe.[154] National laws agree that there are factual imbalances and clear inequalities between employee and employer, as well as consumers and suppliers of consumer goods, that justify the introduction of limitations in the substantive law for the sake of the weaker party. The introduction of constraints on choice of law agreements on these types of contracts follows the same logic: limitations are needed to address

---

[150] If the divorce proceeding is issued before a Swiss court, Swiss law would always apply to the case. According to the Swiss conflict of laws system, spouses are not allowed to choose the law applicable to their divorce. See: Art. 61 of the Swiss Federal Act on Private International Law.

[151] Art. 5 Hague Protocol of 2007.

[152] Art. 26 Regulation 2016/1103.

[153] Other contracts – e.g. transport and insurance contracts – are also subject to certain limitations based on similar reasons. See: Magnus (2017) 50.

[154] For a view of the protection granted by European substantive legislation to consumers and employees, see: Potz & Runggaldier (2012) 521–523; Rösler (2012) 369–370.

differences in the factual negotiating positions of the involved parties that impede them from assessing and weighing the consequences of their own actions correctly.[155]

Modern marriage law, however, is based on the opposite principle. Spouses are regarded as equals. Neither of them is seen as weaker or stronger in the relationship; quite the contrary, equality between spouses is by and large recognized at a constitutional level in basic principles like sexual or gender equality.[156] In fact, the substantive law in the vast majority of legislative regimes allows spouses to alter the effects of their marriage in accordance with their particular preferences.[157] Key issues like the system of property ownership as well as the extension of maintenance obligations could be the subject of a legal contract in many countries.[158] There is, then, a tacit consensus in modern legal systems that recognizes that all spouses – regardless of their gender, social position or education level – have the same capability to determine their own destiny.

If the legal situation of spouses is not tantamount to that of employees or consumers, it is not clear why spouses are not allowed to choose the law governing their marriage with the same freedom as they can do for other contracts. Limiting their freedom of choice based on the presumption of a weaker party in the relationship seems contradictory in light of the ample margin of discretion afforded to spouses to regulate individual marital issues in national legislation.[159] Furthermore, even if the existence of a vulnerable party in a marriage is conceded – that is, accepting that one of the spouses as a general rule has the capacity to manipulate the other to the point of choosing a law contrary to their own interests – it is highly questionable whether the restrictions imposed on the freedom of choice will effectively prevent abuses. While in the case of consumer or employment contracts the protection consists in assuring that certain mandatory legal provisions of the country with which the weaker party is more related cannot be derogated from by a choice of law,[160] in the case of the marriage this does not occur. Quite the contrary, the allegedly stronger party can impose their personal law preference on the other, since spouses, according to the three instruments, can agree on the application of

---

155 Wilderspin (2017) 455.

156 For Europe see: Coester-Waltjen (2012) 1157.

157 Franzina (2011) 108. For a view of legal issues related to marital agreements in a number of European countries, see: Scherpe (2012a) 1135. The actual content of marital agreements can, however, be reviewed by the courts in most jurisdictions. See: Scherpe (2012a) 1136.

158 For the increasing importance of party autonomy in substantive family law in France, Italy, England, Japan, Germany and Islamic countries see: Gebauer & Huber (2017). For a European perspective regarding the regulation of marital agreements, see: Scherpe (2012a) 1137–1138; Scherpe (2012b).

159 Wennersbusch (2018) 100.

160 Wilderspin (2017) 483.

the law of the state of the nationality of either of them, regardless of whether their partner is informed about its contents or whether they are in some way connected with this law. Furthermore, the Hague Protocol of 2007 as well as Regulation 2016/1103 even permit the designation of the law of the place of residence of each of the spouses at the time of the conclusion of the choice of law agreement.

Be that as it may, the need to protect individuals from their own decisions is based on factual imbalances that characterize certain relationships, caused mainly by three sources: mental or intellectual disadvantage, economic dependence, or information asymmetry.[161] The first one does not need to be explained any further; it refers to prohibitions affecting minors or adults in a situation of incapacity. Restrictions on party autonomy based on these circumstances are unquestionably necessary. The second type particularly affects employees as they – in general – depend on their work to meet their basic needs. Given that for most people their salary is the sole or at least the most important source of income, there is a risk that employees feel compelled to accept the application of a law to their contracts which is not in their best interests. The imposition of limits on the freedom of choice in contracts involving employers and employees seems logical, due to the disequilibrium present in most relationships of this type. The third source of imbalance – information asymmetry – refers to situations where one of the parties typically has more or better information than the other. That occurs in consumer and employee contracts, as the costs of acquiring knowledge about the contents of the chosen legislation is typically disproportionate to the expected benefit obtained from such information for consumers and employees. Thus, they are routinely poorly informed – or even completely uninformed – about the contents and quality of the applicable law. Their contractual counterparty, by contrast, might be constantly engaged in cross-border activities and have an incentive to be informed about the benefits of other laws. Consequently, they have an informational advantage with which they can exploit consumers and employees by resorting to choice of law clauses.

Limiting the freedom of choice in marriage law suggests that any of these sources of vulnerability would be typical in a relationship of two spouses: that there would be a maturity inequality; that one of them would be financially dependent on the other; or that one spouse would be poorly informed about the contents of one law in comparison to the other. Whereas in the case of contracts concluded by children, employees or consumers – respectively – the probabilities that this will occur are high, in the case of a marriage it does not

---

161 For the application of these concepts as reasons to impose restriction on party autonomy in private international law, see: Rühl (2014a) 343 et seqq. For marriage: Kroll-Ludwigs (2013) 471.

seem entirely clear.[162] Assuming the presence of any of these vulnerabilities in a marriage hints at a stereotypical understanding of men and women. In any case, it seems contradictory that in those countries where the aforementioned international instruments are in force, individuals – including spouses – are free to choose the law applicable to any other contract regardless of its economic impact. As is well known, the Rome I Regulation does not impose restrictions on the party autonomy of contractual parties. Thus, as paradoxical as it may seem, a spouse cannot choose freely the applicable law for the determination of assets included in or excluded from their marital regime, but the same person is free to choose the law applicable to the sale or donation of assets included in their patrimony – as for example a car, shares, a house or a whole company – if the counterpart is a third party or even the other spouse.[163]

It is important to note that the protection granted by contract law to certain groups of people is not founded solely on possible damage to these parties. Someone taking an undue advantage of economic dependence or information asymmetry could occur in every contract. The crucial issue is whether this occurs consistently and regularly.[164] Thus, in contracts where the imbalance becomes a feature of the relationship – most notably in contracts involving minors, employees or consumers – the freedom of choice is restricted. But if both contractual partners have as a general rule the same capabilities, the principle should remain the same, so that they can freely choose the law applicable even if that might sometimes lead to disadvantages.[165] People can make mistakes or even be fooled at the moment of choosing the applicable law. However, private law and private international law is based on the idea that notwithstanding the risks, the benefits brought on by party autonomy outweigh the potential negative effects that this freedom could cause. That does not mean that people have lost the protection of the law completely, as there are other mechanisms – e.g. the doctrine of error or lesion – that can be used by courts to avoid the enforcement of detrimental choice of law agreements. Furthermore, the *ordre public* clause[166] as well as the *loi d'application immédiate* will in no

---

162 Kroll-Ludwigs (2013) 471–473, 483.

163 Magnus (2017) 431. See also Case C-249/19 *JE v. KF* para. 29 (ruling that in disputes about assets only proprietary legal relationships between spouses resulting directly from the matrimonial relationship or its dissolution should be regarded as part of the scope of the marital statute. Contracts concluded between them with no connection to their marriage are therefore not covered by the marital instruments, but by conflict rules of other instruments – i.e. the Rome I Regulation.

164 For the reasons behind the protection of the weaker party in European private international law see: Rühl (2014a).

165 Kroll-Ludwigs (2013) 487. See also: Wennersbusch (2018) 100.

166 Regarding the application of the public policy clause contained in the Protocol of 2007 and Regulation 1259/2010, see for *Germany*: Oberlandesgericht Hamm, 22 April 2016 – II-3 UF 262/15; Kammergericht Berlin, 3 February 2017–16 UF 77/16 (discussing the validity

case be derogated from by a choice of law.[167] Thus, courts have means to avoid negative effects arising from party autonomy.[168]

5. CONCLUDING REMARKS

In general, the results achieved by the harmonization of the conflict of laws rules in Europe should be regarded as an improvement in comparison to the previous situation. Individuals can now be sure that the outcome of a proceeding will – mostly – be similar if a court located in any of these countries is seized to settle their case. However, in view of the above, there are still shortcomings negatively affecting the predictability and congruency of the conflict of laws system. First, it is puzzling that each instrument contains different rules for the determination of the applicable law in absence of a choice of law agreement – different default connecting factors. The lack of consistency across instruments, however, not only concerns the default rules; it also affects the regulation of private autonomy as choice of law agreements are subject to dissimilar limits and conditions for their enforceability. Furthermore, the number of options at the court's disposal is also different from one instrument to the next without a sound justification. Second, determining the law governing a relationship in advance can be very difficult – sometimes even impossible – if a choice of law agreement is not concluded. The determination of the applicable law is in many instances based on facts whose occurrence could only have happened shortly before the beginning of the legal processing. Third, a paternalistic view of a couple infuses the establishment of limits on party autonomy. Spouses are only

of an agreement by which the husband has to pay 135,000 € to his wife in case of divorce. The spouses concluded a contract in which they designated German law as applicable law); Oberlandesgericht Hamm, 22 April 2016 – II-3 UF 262/15 (establishing that a marital agreement subject to Lebanese law is contrary to German public policy because the woman – under this legal system – would not be entitled to maintenance payments if she files for divorce); Oberlandesgericht Hamm, 07.05.2013, 3 UF 267/12 (discussing the effects of a repudiation – *talaq* – made by a woman in accordance with Iranian law). For *Italy*: Tribunale di Torino, 1 June 2018 (rejection of a choice of law agreement because the foreign law – Argentinian law – would allow the immediate dissolution of the marriage. According to the court the application of the foreign law would be contrary to the best interest of the couple's child: "*non risponde all'interesse dei figli*").

167 Regarding the role of the *loi d'application immédiate* in the analysis of the enforceability of choice of law agreements on family issues, see: De Groot (2001) 625–626. Currently, however, the CJEU has imposed some limits on the margin of discretion of Member States recognizing marriages celebrated by EU citizens abroad. Member States, for example, cannot rely on their own national legislation to refuse the recognition of same-sex marriages celebrated in another country. See Case C-673/16 *Coman and Others v. Romania*. See also Gray (2021) 77.

168 For a different view see: Wennersbusch (2018) 101–103; 164.

allowed to choose a legal system with which they are closely connected. This would not be controversial, if it were not for the fact that in all countries where the instruments are in force, individuals are permitted to choose any law they deem appropriate for their other contractual relationships.

After having carried out this analysis of the international instruments, four different – but also concurring – objectives pursued by their legal rules can be identified: achieving legal certainty; the application of a law linked to the relationship; prevention of abuses; and – to the extent possible – the application of a law in accordance with the preferences of the spouses. All of them are undoubtedly desirable. The problem is that there is no systematic approach that assigns an order of precedence to these goals. This has ultimately resulted in a legal regulation devoid of consistency, discordant and even with some contradictions. The following chapters will now provide a structure that orders these priorities in the creation of conflict of laws rules. It has the particularity that it moves away from the traditional methodology used to confront the challenges posed by legal pluralism in the area of marriage law. The model presented borrows some ideas and concepts from economics to reframe the problems and provide answers from a different perspective. The introduction of economics into the analysis of the legal regulations of the family might sound unconventional. However, this underlying logic can be uncovered in the *ratio* of several legal provisions of substantive law. The objective of Part I of the book is explaining what the marriage is – from an economic perspective – and showing how this view can be used to explain the contents of a number of legal provisions in modern states' legislation on marriage law. Later on – in Part II – the book will apply these ideas in the analysis of the conflict of laws rules.

PART I

ECONOMICS AS A POINT OF DEPARTURE TO EXPLAIN THE SUBSTANTIVE RULES ON MATRIMONIAL ISSUES

The aim of this part of the book is twofold: setting forth the contractual nature of marriage as well as the economic rationale behind this legal institution, and showing that an economic rationale indeed underlies many provisions of marriage law in modern legislation. Accordingly, this part is divided into four chapters: In the first one – Chapter 1 – the reasons to consider marriage as a contract and its function as an economic means will be discussed. A hypothesis about the reasons that motivate individuals to get married will be presented. This chapter suggests that marriage can be understood as a device that encourages spouses to make investments in the household, just as it imposes legal consequences in case the relationship ends prematurely or when certain promises made by the spouses are not delivered as agreed. Next, the book focuses on outlining the main tasks of marriage law and describes the economic logic of a number of substantive legal provisions governing the marriage. In Chapter 2, criteria will be discussed to delimit the promises that should be enforced by the courts. This chapter also shows the efficiency of some characteristic remedies provided by the law in the event of a marital crisis. Chapter 3 is focused on providing a conceptual framework that explains the economic rationale of the limitations to party autonomy, as well as the logic behind rules that can be overridden by the spouses. The last section – Chapter 4 – is devoted to summarizing the topics discussed and serves as a prelude to the next part of the book, which is entirely focused on solutions for the issues arising from the potential application of different legislation to marriages with international connotations.

CHAPTER 1

MARRIAGE AS A CONTRACT AND ITS ECONOMIC FUNCTION FOR THE SPOUSES

When people are asked why they got married, the most common answer is love.[169] I have no doubt that this feeling is the motor that drives most people to take the great leap. However, this sentiment alone does not seem to be a sufficient reason for people to get married. There are many couples that despite being in love are not legally bound to their partners. Indeed, most individuals experience such a feeling with great insensitivity at the beginning of a relationship, but they usually wait for a time – months or even years later – before deciding to marry.[170] Love is crucial to stop the search for a potential partner to found a family with,[171] but there must be something more explaining the decision to get involved in a legal relationship with another person. Being more pragmatic, one can assume that – aside from love – the reason lies with the age of the people, or even the pressure from the rest of the

169 A study made about college students from India, Pakistan, Thailand, Mexico, Brazil, Japan, Hong Kong, the Philippines, Australia, England and the United States confirms that people regard love as an important factor for getting married. There are, however, differences among the cultures. Love tended to be most important in Western and Westernized nations in comparison to Eastern nations. To the question "If a man (woman) had all the other qualities you desire, would you marry this person if you were not in love with him (her)?" the responses varied across cultures: The percentage of people answering "yes" was greatest in India and Pakistan – 49.0% and 50.4% respectively – in comparison to other countries: Thailand (18.8%); the Philippines (11.4%); Mexico (10.2%); England (7.3%); Hong Kong (5.8%); Australia (4.8%); Brazil (4.3%); United States (3.5%); Japan (2.3%). This study, however, confirmed that men and women within the same culture value the importance of love equally for getting married. See: Levine et al. (1995) 554, 561.

170 For some data about the duration of courtship before marriage in North America with special emphasis on individuals who were already married, see: O'Flaherty & Workman Eells (1988) 501–504.

171 This is valid for all Western and Westernized nations. See: Levine et al. (1995) 561. In fact, arranged marriages occur in 85% of tribal cultures, however, the capacity for amorousness – falling in love – is universal. See: Weisfeld & Weisfeld (2018) 7–8.

society. It is no coincidence that people living in a certain territory decide to get married at a similar age.[172] Marriage is a very contagious phenomenon. Once one receives the first wedding invitation of a peer, they continue to crop up and sooner or later attending wedding receptions as a bachelor starts being the exception. Reaching a certain age prompts individuals to formalize their relationship; even more so when other individuals of the same age do the same. However, this factor cannot sufficiently explain the reasons to get legally involved with another person. One cannot deny that the so-called biological clock urges people to have children and start a family. However, maturity does not seem to impel them to rush to the civil registry office or city hall to get married, but simply to seek a greater stability in their relationship and to settle down. After all, having children and cohabiting with another person are possible without any formal agreement in practically all modern societies.[173]

Love, customs, age and many other factors undoubtedly play a major role when thinking about marriage. Still, none of them can explain by itself why people not only carry out ceremonies in the presence of family and friends, but are also willing to formalize their desire to stay united before an authority – in most cases a state-run one – and to commit themselves to fulfill a number of duties, thereby sacrificing other interests and future life choices.[174] Assuredly, analyzing why people marry is complicated, because of the great number of factors that could influence their decision. Notwithstanding, this is by no means a characteristic unique to marriage. Many decisions – even the most common ones – are also influenced by a number of variables. Many of them can go unnoticed by a casual observer, although they might be of pivotal importance for them. Think for example of the place that you frequent at the weekend to have a drink. The specific reasons why you visit this place could be diverse: the cost of the beverages, the quality of the offered fare, the courtesy of the waiters, the location of the restaurant or the funny jokes of the owner. If the price were to suddenly double, a rude waiter were hired, it moved to another city, the supplier of the products changed or the owner started making racist jokes, your preference for that restaurant would most likely change. Depending on their virulence, any one of these changes may lead you to look for another place to have your weekend drink. However, not only changes in the specific reasons you would mention

172 For uniformities over time and across countries in the age patterns of first marriages, see: Coale (1971) 193–199.

173 Ukraine, Lithuania and Russia show the lowest incidence of cohabitation among partnered individuals aged 15–44: less than 20% were cohabiting in 2010. On the other hand, cohabitation is more frequent in Sweden and Estonia, where more than half of partnered people under 44 cohabited. See: Sánchez Gassen & Perelli-Harris (2015) 431.

174 Cohen (2002) 10.

as causes to go to this place influence your decision. Nobody would say that the reason for choosing a certain restaurant is that it serves drinks in glasses. Despite that, it is very probable that if your favorite restaurant changed that – although small – detail, and began to serve the coffee, wine or beer in plastic cups, you would never come back.

Something similar could be said about the law and marriage. Although people can answer that love, age or certain attributes of their partner[175] are the most important factors that influence their decision, other issues – such as the legal regulation – can also be very important. In fact, a number of studies[176] have shown that a recently modified marriage law has measurable repercussions not only for the average marriageable age or the duration of the premarital relationship. They can also alter the intensity of the effort put forth in a relationship, and even the willingness to celebrate a marriage at all. Jurisdictions that have introduced a no-fault divorce system have, for example, experienced changes in the average capital investment of spouses in a relationship,[177] as well as an increase in the duration of the premarital courtship and the average age to get married.[178] It is unclear how highly people rank the significance of the legal regulations at the moment of the decision to marry. However, there are good reasons to believe that the content of the legal rules does play a role in the deliberations of those thinking of making or accepting a wedding proposal.

The following lines are concentrated solely on the legal regulation of marriage. They do not analyze all possible considerations that could influence the decision to get married. The analysis only focuses on a single factor, one that often goes unnoticed by the people: the legal configuration of marriage. The point of departure of the analysis assumes that people decide to get married

175 According to a study conducted in five different cultures, the most determinant factors for mate selection are: compatibility, physical attractiveness and resources. The perception of spousal attractiveness was significantly correlated with marital satisfaction in each culture. Silveri & Samayoa (2018) 218.

176 Allen (2002) 191 et seqq.; Brinig & Crafton (1994) 869, 885 et seqq.; Landes (1978) 35–36, 58 et seqq.; Matouschek & Rasul (2008); Mechoulan (2006) 143–174; Rasul (2005) 30–69; Smith (2012) 212 et seqq; Stevenson (2007) 75, 81 et seqq.; Yurko (2014).

177 It was found that the introduction of unilateral divorce reduces investments in all types of marriage-specific capital considered except home ownership. Investments in the acquisition of home ownership, however, seem to depend on the law governing the division of property between spouses. It was also found that newlywed couples in states that allow unilateral divorce are about 10% less likely to be supporting a spouse through school. They are 8% more likely to have both spouses employed in the labor force full time and are 5% more likely to have a wife in the labor force. See: Stevenson (2007) 75, 77.

178 According to a study, the average age of marriage increased by nine months in jurisdictions that have introduced no-fault divorces in comparison to those that have not. Allen (2002) 191, 206.

because they expect to be better off within the framework provided by the law. Marriage will be presented as a means to achieve easier and safer personal objectives – such as for example having children, raising a family or acquiring property – as it allows one to reinforce one's trust in the partner and so assures mutual cooperation. With this in mind, the overall objective of this chapter is to emphasize the contractual nature of marriage, as well as its significance in enabling the spouses to obtain assets of high value for both of them. It begins with a general explanation of the function of the private and the contractual law from an economic perspective. Afterwards, the chapter focuses on the economic nature of marriage and the reasons driving people to formalize their relationship.

1. THE ECONOMIC FUNCTION OF CONTRACTS

In general, when people hear the word "economics", they tend to think about money. However, economics comprises much more than that. It is rather about how individuals weigh options of almost every conceivable sort, regardless of whether they have a monetary value or not. Scholars on economics define their field as "a science which studies human behavior as a relationship between ends and scarce means which have alternative uses".[179] Accordingly, economics studies how individuals choose among alternatives available to them, in a context where the subject of their decisions – the resources – are not infinite. The word "resources" should here be interpreted in the broadest sense, as it does not refer exclusively to traded goods in regular markets, but includes any – material or non-material – assets, with or even without a monetary value in regular markets, such as for example time, information, education, etc.[180] The decision whether you or your partner should do the dishes tonight, make a charitable donation, change career or accept a job offer can all be analyzed economically. Decisions taken by governments are often discussed in economic terms, due to their direct impact on the pockets of the people. However, most of the daily or life choices

179 Robbins (1932) 15. For the importance of the definition given by Robbins and its reception in economic writing see: Backhouse & Medema (2009a) 225; Backhouse & Medema (2009b) 805.

180 Becker (1990) 5–6. As a positive science, economics aims to develop theories and hypotheses that yield valid and meaningful predictions about phenomena in the real world. In contrast to a positive analysis, a normative one asks in which direction the behavior of people should be guided to achieve a particular goal. For the difference between positive and normative economics in the analysis of legal institutions, see: Parisi (2004). See also: Carrascosa (2011) 28; Mankiw (2012) 30–31; Miceli (2004) 1; Trebilcock (1997) 3–8.

made by spouses, governments or any other individual or collective entities can also be explained economically, regardless of whether their outcomes would be expressed in monetary terms.

1.1. PRIVATE LAW FROM AN ECONOMIC PERSPECTIVE

A central problem of economics is how a society makes use of its scarce resources to achieve the highest possible satisfaction of the wants of all the people that it comprises of. From an economic standpoint, any measure taken by a government – including enacting laws – ought to pursue this objective.[181] The economic analysis of law – also known as *law and economics* – is an application of this perspective to legal rules.[182] When evaluating the desirability of legal rules, it is important to discern whether they contribute to the maximum satisfaction of the wants of the people and avoid wasting resources.

To better appreciate how scholars of law and economics understand the private law, the basic idea behind contractarianism is helpful.[183] According to this view, legal rules are the result of an agreement between the members of a society, with the aim of protecting each of them from the actions of the others and so achieving their maximum prosperity, in compliance with the *status quo* that existed when the contract among the members of the society was concluded.[184] The *status quo* – also known as original allocation of resources – refers to the property rights over the resources as they stand at the moment of the conclusion of the social contract. Scholars on law and economics are well aware that this *status quo* is not the most desirable situation, since resources are wasted, as they may be in the hands of persons who do not necessarily value them the most. To resolve this issue, those scholars rely on the capacity of millions of firms and households to make exchanges.[185] The idea is that individuals carry out the allocation of the resources in a society through voluntary transactions, and so achieve an improved situation where the resources end up in the hands of those that value them the most.[186]

181 Schäfer & Ott (2004) 3–4.

182 For a general explanation of economic reasoning to the analysis of legal institutions as well as some basic concepts used by scholars on law and economics see: Cooter & Ulen (2016) 3 et seqq.; Posner R. (2014) 3 et seqq.

183 Wittman (2000) 1073. For an application of contractarianism as a tool for lawyers and economists see: Kraus (1998) 229 et seqq.

184 Cooter & Ulen (2016) 178.

185 Schäfer & Ott (2005a) 72.

186 Garcimartín (2002) 129; Mankiw (2012) 10–11; Ogus (1989) 399; Streit (1995) 64–65.

They – the persons – are primarily responsible for addressing the waste created by the acceptance of the *status quo*. No centrally-planning administrator[187] should – as a matter of principle – decide on the allocation of resources existing in the society, as this task corresponds primarily to the individuals that compose it.[188] The place where individuals turn their evaluations into actions is the market; the framework within which this happens is the private law. Therefore, private law is not understood as a neutral entity, but as an institution with a specific purpose: enabling, facilitating and promoting a decentralized system of decision-making. Its main roles are protecting the rights acquired by individuals over the existing resources, enforcing the promises related to the transmission of those rights, and avoiding that individuals generate any harm to the rest when they try to obtain resources of any kind. The economic rationality of property, contract and tort law can be explained in those terms, as they are focused predominantly on one of these purposes: protection of property rights; enforcing of promises related to exchanges; and avoidance of – or compensation for – damages caused.[189] In principle, private law should not, by itself, distribute rights or legal positions.[190] Its task is rather recognizing the original allocation prior to the social contract by protecting the private property of individuals over resources, and enabling the free transfer of these resources between individuals as long as their actions do not harm others.

Modern economics uses the concept of efficiency to evaluate the suitability of policies or decisions taken by a government or private individuals.[191] This concept refers to a state where the resources of a society are in the hands of the individuals who value them most, so that the resources cannot be reallocated

187 Garcimartín (2002) 129; Hayek (1969) 254; Sacks (1988) 866. For a discussion about the relative efficiencies of planned economies see: Moroney & Lovell (1997) 1086 et seqq. From a critical point of view see Caraballo-Arias et al (2018).

188 For the use of concepts such as externalities, asymmetric information or constraints affecting decision-making as reasons for limitations to party autonomy see Chapter 3. However, the system is based on the idea that, as a matter of principle, every person knows better than anybody else – including the state – which goods fit them and their interests. See: Hayek (1948d) 15. See also: Ogus (1994) 16. For a discussion about the different justification of the freedom of choice offered by classical liberals or libertarians see: Trebilcock (1997) 8–9.

189 Ogus (1994) 16–17; 19–20; Trebilcock (1997) 9–18. From this perspective family law is understood as a branch of law having a twofold function: a contractual one regarding the situation of the spouses and a protective one in respect to the situation of the children. See: Posner R. (2014) 165.

190 There are, however, exceptions to this statement. Private law norms – for example – may legitimately be used to redistribute wealth if alternative methods of doing so in public law are more costly or intrusive. See: Kronman (1983) 770.

191 For different uses of the term efficiency see: Cooter & Ulen (2016) 13–14. See also: Carrascosa (2011) 25.

anymore to make one individual better off without making at least one individual worse off.[192] This objective will be achieved through voluntary transactions. Thus, measures taken by governments – including the enactment or repeal of laws – that facilitate the realization of exchanges between people are regarded as efficient.[193]

The injustices derived from the acceptance of the *status quo* – in particular, the arbitrary concentration of certain goods in the hands of the few when the social contract was concluded – are of the utmost importance not only for economics but also, of course, for the law. However, from an economic point of view, addressing the resulting social and economic inequalities in the society does not primarily concern the private law, but other areas of the law like tax law, health law and other branches of the public law.[194] It is there where the state can perform a planning and allocative function and where principles of social and redistributive justice find their place. From an economic perspective, private law is focused on ensuring that the resources – through free and voluntary exchanges – get passed from one hand to another, and so ultimately end up in the hands of individuals that value them the most.[195] This, however, does not mean keeping the private law from intervening in the market. A system based on the free exchange of goods and services can certainly fail. If that is the case, the imposition of limits on party autonomy might be unavoidable to assure an efficient allocation of resources. Later on,[196] it will be shown how certain categories of market failures – externalities, asymmetry of information, constraints affecting decision-making and a monopolistic position – can describe situations that merit a restriction of party autonomy in contracts as well as in marriage law.

1.2. CONTRACTS AND CONTRACT LAW FROM AN ECONOMIC PERSPECTIVE

When analyzing a contract, economists start from the premise that the values given to goods, services or any other promised asset are personal and unique.

---

192 For the concept of economic efficiency see: Rühl (2016) 47–49. Trebilcock & Keshvani (1991) 534; Wittman (2000) 1073. For the implementation of the concept of efficiency in the analysis of conflict of laws rules see: Rühl (2016) 53–57.

193 Posner R. (2005) 1583. Limits to this assumption will be discussed below. However, as a matter of principle, legal rules that remove obstacles for the conclusion of voluntary agreements between people will be seen as economically desirable. For a distinction between the different criteria of economic efficiency see: Coleman et al. (1989) 642 et seqq.; Rühl (2016) 47–49.

194 Garcimartín (2002) 129; Ogus (1994) 26. See also: Cooter & Ulen (2016) 7.

195 Cooter & Ulen (2016) 92.

196 See Chapter 3 in this book.

The assessment of rights and obligations involved in an economic transaction ultimately depends on the subjective preference of every single person. The individual motives that cause people to desire certain assets are mostly not taken into consideration when carrying out an economic analysis. More important is the fact that people have their own desires, and these desires – and their intensity – vary from one individual to another. Contracts will likely be made between individuals that own diverse – tangible or intangible – assets and value them differently. When two persons meet, and each of them considers that the value of what they have and potentially would give, is less than the value of what the other has and potentially would receive, an exchange between them will probably take place.[197] Reaching an agreement to exchange these goods would thus generate benefits for both parties. From an economic perspective, a contract is viewed as a means that permits individuals to be engaged in a cooperative dynamic and to benefit from their joint effort. It is a tool that allows persons to achieve a state in which one person's gain does not depend on another's loss; both parties come out as winners after the execution of the contract, as they both profit from the surplus generated by the cooperation.[198] Let us look at an example to make this idea clearer:

Consider the case of somebody who is thinking of selling his car, after determining that the pleasure of owning and driving it is worth at least 8,000 euros (8,000 €). Someone else is looking at buying a car. Both meet, and after inspecting the vehicle, the potential buyer calculates a maximum price he is willing to pay for the car. Let us assume this person – the potential buyer – decides that the pleasure of owning and driving the car is worth up to 10,000 €. Assume also, that neither of them knows exactly the value assigned by the other person.

An agreement between them means that a good valued by one person at 8,000 € would pass to another who values it at 10,000 €. These distinct subjective preferences create a surplus of 2,000 €, which will be split between the two. The outcome of the transaction hinges ultimately on the price they agree on. As per the value assigned by each of them, the seller will not accept less than 8,000 €, and the buyer will not pay more than 10,000 €, so the price must be somewhere in between. Note that the price will not necessarily be 9,000 €. It rather depends on the negotiating skills of both actors. If, after bargaining, the price is set at 9,500 €, the surplus value will be divided unequally. The seller would profit by 1,500 €, whereas the buyer, only 500 €. If the price is 8,100 €, the seller would get just 100 € profit whereas the buyer would benefit by 1,900 € in contrast. However – and that is the point I wish to make here – whatever the price may be

197 Ogus (1994) 27.

198 Ogus (1994) 15. See also: Kirchner (2006) 44; Schäfer & Lantermann (2006) 92.

that they finally agree on, both will benefit from the transaction, since seller and buyer will receive a good of a higher value to themselves – the money or the car respectively – than what each of them must deliver to the other party.

When exchanges are voluntary and parties are informed enough about the content and consequences of the transaction, an agreement leads to a win-win solution for all the people involved. The movement of a resource from the party who values it less to another who values it more means gains for both of them in comparison to their situation before the exchange.[199] This idea can be used to analyze all kinds of agreements: in a labor contract, employees submit to the commands of an employer because of the belief that the salary compensates the efforts put into the service for their new patron. And *vice versa*, an employer hires a worker because he values the work done more than the salary he will pay. The same applies to housing rental contracts: a tenant rents a house because he thinks that the cost of the rent is lower than all the benefits of living in the chosen neighborhood. The landlord, for his part, accepts the contract, because to him receiving monthly payments is worth more than living in this house himself. Even contracts that do not include an exchange of money can be explained in these terms. Individuals that set up a business – two youngsters that want to build a computer prototype in their garage or two enterprises that plan to launch an innovative technological gadget – do that with the intention of using the capabilities of their partner for their own benefit. The central point of these arrangements is providing and exchanging complementary and reciprocal services between them to achieve a common goal. It is a kind of swap, in the sense that each partner puts his own skills and abilities at the disposal of the other to obtain assets that are difficult or even impossible to get alone.[200]

In all these examples, the agreement between individuals in pursuit of an exchange leads to a positive change in their situation. As long as the contract is performed in the terms agreed upon, both are better off, since they obtain – each from their own perspective – something of a higher value in exchange for another thing of lesser worth. A contract – in the widest sense of the word – is an instrument that permits both partners to improve their initial situation. As long as these voluntary transactions leave the participants better off without making any other person – somebody within or outside of the contract – come off worse, they should be encouraged, since their realization not only means

199 Cooter & Ulen (2016) 75; Leib (2009) 684.

200 The same can be said about agreements that do not involve assets with a monetary value. Think for example of the case of two friends that arrange to go out together. They do that, because being accompanied not only is more fun that being alone, but also allows them to accomplish other objectives such as, for example, getting to know other people. See: Leib (2009) 684–687.

the betterment of the situation of two people;[201] from a global perspective, voluntary transactions also increase the welfare of the whole society by the surplus created by the execution of the contract. Afterwards, there is more of a resource and that can in turn be exchanged further in order to improve the situation of somebody else.[202]

From the above, economists conclude the following: while the objective of a contract is to procure gains for both contractual parties - a win-win outcome - the basic purpose of contract law is, and should be, to provide a framework within which individuals can more easily and freely enter into agreements between them to obtain mutual gains.[203] Contract law - from an economic perspective - has as its goal the removal of obstacles that prevent or discourage individuals from making voluntary transactions, as their realization contributes to the improvement of the situation of the participants and of the society at large.[204] Legal rules that are in line with this goal - facilitating the conclusion of contracts - are regarded as efficient.

2. THE ECONOMIC FUNCTION OF MARRIAGE

The previous thoughts apply to transactions involving market goods. However, can this logic also be used to analyze an agreement as unique as a marriage? Can marriage be understood as a simple means to be involved in an exchange with another individual? Is marriage a mere instrument to improve one's situation? In the opinion of some scholars the answer to these questions is yes.[205] They argue that people do not act randomly when they decide to get married. Individuals decide to be engaged in a long-term relationship with the expectation of obtaining benefits from this agreement. Already at the beginning of the seventies, a seminal - theoretical - academic paper was published on this idea. It was the first to propose that marriage could be successfully analyzed

201 MACKAAY (2013) 421, et seqq.

202 For different views about the role of contract law from an economic perspective, see: MACKAAY (2013) 243 ff.

203 GUNST (1994) 144; MACKAAY (2013) 414.

204 CARRASCOSA (2011) 34; Posner R. (2005) 1583.

205 For literature about the characterization of marriage as an economic means, see the compilation of scholary works made by DNES & ROWTHORN (2002). There are, however, different approaches describing the economic nature of the marriage as a contract. Some literature for example emphasizes that the main function of marriage is to serve as a signaling device, a tool to convey credible information about themselves to others. For the difference between the marriage as a relational contract and marriage as a signal, see: SCOTT & SCOTT (1999); TREBILCOCK (1999).

within the framework of modern economics.[206] Since that moment, several publications – many of them of an empirical kind – have appeared where marriage, divorce and decisions concerning the household are analyzed in terms of bargaining and rational choice.[207] In the last few years, the earlier models have been complemented with psychological insights to improve them and to better reflect the real behavior of people.[208] The idea was – and continues to be – to provide a powerful framework and gain new insights into family organization.[209]

2.1. CHARACTERIZATION OF MARRIAGE AS A CONTRACT IN AN ECONOMIC SENSE

Different arguments can be put forward against treating marriage as a mere economic means. One can rebut its economic function based on the fact that not the parties themselves, but the state defines and specifies the central duties and privileges arising from their marriage.[210] In addition, the lack of clarity about the exact obligations assumed by each spouse could also undermine the idea of presenting marriage as an instrument to improve their situation.[211] Its long-term nature – sometimes perpetual, as intended in the marriage vows – as well as the presence of love – an irrational feeling, impossible to control – do not favor its comparison with other agreements in regular markets.[212] Finally, the difficulty to determine the subject matter of the marriage makes regarding it as a contract in the terms described above also problematic.[213] However, although most of these observations are accurate, they do not affect the contractual essence of the marriage. They rather highlight the singularities of matrimony in comparison to other types of contracts.[214] Actually, most of these peculiarities are present in other kinds of legally enforceable arrangements concluded in regular markets. Let us analyze each of these concerns with the exception of the last one – the subject matter of the marriage – which will be discussed separately later.

---

206 Becker (1973). According to this seminal paper the marriage takes place when there is a surplus to be gained for the two individuals in comparison to the situation of staying single. The gains derived from specialization – the division of labor between the spouses – will encourage individuals to form a marital union. See: Becker (1974); Mortensen (1988).

207 See for example the literature cited in this chapter.

208 Frey & Eichenberger (1996); Gigerenzer & Todd (1999); Todd & Miller (1999).

209 Estin (1994) 999.

210 Brinig & Crafton (1994) 870.

211 See: Teitelbaum (1988) 801, 805; Brining (1994) 870; Cohen (2002) 13.

212 Brinig & Crafton (1994) 870.

213 Teitelbaum (1988) 806–807; Regan (1993) 35–42.

214 Cohen (2002) 10.

First, there are several legal agreements regulated by imperative rules that significantly restrict the maneuverability of parties to negotiate the content and range of the obligations they assume. Not only public contracts – those where federal, state or local governments are the counterpart in the relationship – but also some purely private arrangements are strongly regulated by the law. Agreements on assisted reproduction – especially when a monetary exchange is involved – are an example of contracts where the freedom of the parties is heavily restricted.[215] As mentioned in the Introductory chapter, nowadays many legal systems permit spouses a considerable degree of flexibility to regulate the effects of their marital union. Acceptance of divorce settlement agreements, the possibility to conclude contracts on maintenance support, as well as the inclusion of different property regimes all demonstrate an increasing degree of freedom that spouses enjoy according to several law systems.[216]

Second, a lack of clauses that fully detail the contents of marital duties is not entirely accurate. Several legal systems stipulate with great care the range of duties and rights of spouses after the emergence of a marital crisis. In some jurisdictions, for example, the law allows spouses to determine by a simple calculation – or with the help of a computer program – the amount to be paid as alimony during or after a divorce.[217] The absence of a detailed specification of the obligations of both spouses *during* their relationship – that is, before a marital crisis – is, to some extent, accurate. To this author's knowledge, no legal system includes a catalogue of obligations and rights for married people in the same way as is prescribed, for example for tenancy agreements. However, their absence does not mean that those obligations do not exist. Quite the contrary; the complexity of marital duties and especially the major difficulty in determining with accuracy the specific tasks to be carried out in the future, make the establishment of an itemized list very difficult. The almost infinite set of duties each spouse must perform, as well as their changing nature over the course of time, make any attempt at naming them all in an agreement or

---

215 For differences in the regulation of surrogacy laws in the United States and other countries, as well as the commercial dimension of this contract, see: Guzman (2016) 628, 640. For an economic analysis of the legal regulation of these contracts see: Trebilcock & Keshvani (1991) 582 et seqq.

216 For a comparative analysis of the regulation of the marriage in jurisdictions in Europe and the role currently played by party autonomy in their law, see: Boele-Woelki et al. (2004); EPEC (2006); EPEC (2010); Permanent Bureaus Prel. Doc. No. 3 on Maintenance (1999); Permanent Bureau Prel. Doc. No. 2 on Maintenance (2003).

217 Australia, Denmark, Finland, New Zealand, Norway and Sweden are *inter alia* countries where the support is determined through an administrative process. In all of these jurisdictions guidelines specify the amounts to be paid by maintenance creditors. Countries such as Germany or Switzerland use tables to calculate the monthly amount. The methods employed in those jurisdictions enhance the predictability of judicial decisions. See: Permanent Bureau Prel. Doc. No. 2 on Maintenance (2003) 47, 48, 51, 59, 60, 63, 64.

the law meaningless.[218] Furthermore, while the spouses are still married, the costs of negotiations are generally low in comparison to other kinds of legal relationships. The immanent proximity of the contractual parties allows them to arrange the creation, modification or abolition of duties between them according to the current necessities easily and quickly.[219] In fact, marriage is not the only contract with such characteristics. Employment agreements are another example of a contractual relationship without a detailed list of the specific obligations assumed by the worker due to the diversity of the tasks they usually perform. The specific duties are rather left to common practices or the needs of the employer as they arise during the time of the employment. Although a work schedule and the salary are usually specified, the chores to be assumed by the worker as well as the intensity with which they should be performed are specified in an informal way. In any case, marriage is in no way a journey into the unknown. The duties as well as the intensity with which they should be performed can be inferred from customs, social usages and especially on the basis of the prenuptial relationship.[220] This period of time is of crucial importance to establish what each of them expects from the other after the marriage is officially celebrated.

Third, the long-term nature of the contract does not seem to be an obstacle for the consideration of the marriage as a contract either. Many legal agreements are concluded without specifying the moment at which they will be terminated. It is not uncommon for real estate rentals, for example, to be concluded without specifying the moment when the tenant must leave the house.

Fourth, the presence of love is not a unique feature of a marriage either. This feeling could be present at the conclusion of any contract. A sale agreement between father and son, for example, could not only involve strong filial love between the parties, but this sentiment could even be the very cause that motivated the transfer of property. In the same vein, donations *inter vivos* are regarded as contracts in most legal systems, regardless of the reasons that lead the donor to make the donation. Besides that, one cannot affirm that in none of these cases does the realization of the contract bring no benefits to the parties. The presence of altruism – the state in which the welfare of one person is a positive function of the welfare of another – can explain the economic logic behind such contracts perfectly.[221] Finally, although a marriage could be

218 Cohen (2002) 13; Scott & Scott (1998) 1249.

219 For an economic analysis of negotiations (coasian-bargains) between spouses, see: Skåtun (2017).

220 Cohen (2002) 11.

221 Estin (1994) 1013–1016; Kronman (1985) 20; Posner R. (2014) 161. Regarding the existence of interdependent utility in the context of the marriage see: Friedberg & Stern (2014) 1156.

the culmination of a strong romantic relationship, most individuals take this important step a long time after they have initiated the relationship. It is not unusual that the decision to get married is not only taken when the individuals know each other relatively well, but also after considerable time for reflection.[222] Although the marriage is certainly based on an emotional and physical attraction, in general the individuals analyze trade-offs and sacrifices – e.g. those related to their professional development – before they enter into matrimony.[223]

2.2. SUBJECT MATTER OF MARRIAGE FROM AN ECONOMIC PERSPECTIVE

The unique features of marriage seem to be no impediment to regarding it as a contract in the terms explained above. At least formally, it is not that different from other arrangements with contractual status according to the law. However, to be able to undertake a thorough economic analysis, it is necessary to know more about its nature, namely, about the reasons that cause individuals to take such a decision. Similarly to a tenant agreement that allows the use of a house in exchange for rent, marriage must also have a characteristic objective. There should be a specific reason why so many people conclude this contract.

Men and women, men and men, and women and women can obtain major benefits from each other if they decide to have a close relationship. Each of them has assets that can be exchanged: companionship for the present and the future, physical and economic protection, sex and – probably the most important – procreation and time to raise children are only a few examples.[224] However, they alone do not suffice as reasons that cause individuals to engage in a legal relationship such as marriage, considering the attendant restrictions to their freedom as well as the high costs in case of a failure. After all, in modern societies all these assets – companionship, procreation, protection, sharing the cost of board and lodging, etc. – could be achieved without any formal agreement, but by simple cohabitation. What is more, although it is true that the sole conclusion of a marriage could bring about other immediate benefits – social acceptance, the right to stay in a country, tax benefits or even exemption from military

---

[222] For data about the duration of courtship before marriage in North America with special emphasis on individuals who had already been married see: O'Flaherty & Workman Eells (1988) 501–504.

[223] Analysis of data compiled in different cultures suggests that economic factors affect the incidence of marriage and age of marriage. In hard economic times, the marriage rate declines, marriage age in turn drops during prosperous times. See: Weisfeld & Weisfeld (2018) 11. See also: Weisfeld et. al. (2018) 330.

[224] Child-rearing is also an issue to be considered when analyzing the situation of same-sex couples. Not only because technological advances allow same-sex partners to procreate. But also, because adoption by same-sex couples is currently legal in many countries.

service – it is in no way the general rule that people get married based solely on those advantages.[225]

So maybe the most important gain from matrimony is not related to a specific performance delivered by one or both parties. It rather refers to something much broader that comprises many potential benefits of being married: Trust. Being more specific, the essence of marriage is giving stability and confidence to each spouse so they can continue making meaningful expenditures – especially of time – to obtain a variety of tangible and intangible goods whose value could be distinctly diminished if the union came to a premature or unforeseen end.[226] The conjecture is that people formalize their relationship with the objective of solidifying a bond they already have and so obtain greater security for themselves. For the price of restricting their freedom and establishing specific consequences in case of termination, a marriage allows individuals to invest effort, time and other resources in the present and future to obtain assets of higher value that are otherwise impossible or very difficult to obtain on their own. The decision is thus based on the belief and hopes that individual self-fulfillment – one's aspirations, ambitions and desires – will benefit from a substantial investment in a knowing, stable, and long-term relationship.[227]

2.3. MARRIAGE AS AN ECONOMIC MEANS

Although there are differing views about the role of marriage,[228] it is here assumed that the principal reason why two individuals decide to initiate a marital relationship is capturing the "surplus" derived from this union in comparison to the situation of remaining single.[229] The utility does not directly depend on the goods or services acquired by them in the marketplace, but on the commodities produced together as a consequence of the division of labor and the assignment of specific tasks performed by each of them.[230] It is different from simple cohabitation, because it is much costlier for the parties to exit this relationship, which encourages both partners to be thoroughly engaged in their partnership. Thus, marriage becomes a mechanism that maximizes the benefits

---

225 Wedgwood (2016) 32. There are however some studies showing certain influence of tax law on the willingness of heterosexual and same-sex couples to get married. See: Zelder (2002) 160.

226 Cohen (2002) 12; Scott & Scott (1998) 1256–1259; Scott & Scott (1999) 214.

227 Scott (1990) 12. See also: Cooter & Ulen (2016) 305; Cohen (2002) 13; Scott & Scott (1999) 212–213.

228 Some literature emphasizes, that the main function of marriage is serving as a signaling device, a tool to convey credible information about themselves to others. See: Bishop (1984) 245–262; Trebilcock (1999) 249–253.

229 Becker (1973) 814; Landes (1978) 40; Matouschek (2008) 59.

230 Becker (1973) 816.

created by their joint work, as it provides more stability for the relationship to gain – material and immaterial – worthwhile assets for each spouse in the future.[231] Marriage is here understood as a device that fosters cooperation by inducing both parties to make sizable investments that they would not make if the partnership could easily be broken. Marriage imposes significant legal consequences if one of them abandons the other, or in situations in which the relationship is dissolved due to unexpected events such as the death of one of the parties. Thus, it inspires great confidence in the spouses to be more committed to their joint work.[232]

It is true that many advantages could play a pivotal role, when a specific person analyzes the pros and cons of getting married. Singular circumstances such as for example receiving an inheritance, obtaining a residence permit or fulfilling a religious duty can be decisive in the calculation of the benefits of a particular case. But regardless of such short-sighted effects, generally the focus of the interest – at least legally speaking – lies in what would happen if a marital crisis were to occur, or the marriage were dissolved for any other reason. The motives driving people to get married should then somehow be related to the effects of the termination of the relationship; that is, what one should give, receive or retain when that time comes. It is therefore no surprise that maintenance support, the criteria for getting divorced and the division of assets between partners come to the mind when hearing the words "marriage law".

This view is supported by empirical data. A number of studies have shown that changes in the legal regulation of marriage affects the behavior of people significantly.[233] Jurisdictions that have liberalized rules on divorce or limited compensations after the dissolution of the marital bond have experienced a diminution of marriage rates[234] and a delay in the age of first marriage.[235] Although it is disputed whether a liberalization of marriage is positive or negative,[236] there is, however, a consensus that a reduction or an increase in

231 Scott & Scott (1998) 1254–1255. The division of labor, specialization of training and clarity about the assignment of tasks between two persons as reason to get married is common across different cultures. Weisfeld et. al. (2018) 319.

232 Brinig & Crafton (1994) 872; Cohen (2002) 12; Scott & Scott (1998) 1259; Trebilcock (1999) 245.

233 Allen (2002) 191 et seqq.; Brinig & Crafton (1994) 869, 885 et seqq.; Landes (1978) 35–36, 58 et seqq.; Mechoulan (2006) 143–174; Rasul (2005) 30–69; Smith (2012) 212 et seqq; Stevenson (2007) 75, 81 et seqq.; Yurko (2014).

234 There is evidence that states which have restricted alimony in the event of a divorce have a significantly lower percentage of married women aged 25–34. See: Landes (1978) 36, 58.

235 According to a study, the age of first marriage increased by nine months in those states that have introduced the no-fault divorce in comparison to those that have not. Allen (2002) 191.

236 An empirical study, however, has shown that no-fault divorce laws reduced violence toward wives. The same study showed that the introduction of no-fault divorce reduced the suicide rates in adult women. See: Stevenson & Wolfers (2006).

the costs of terminating a marriage – or more precisely, the legal effects once a marital crisis occurs – has a direct impact on those that are thinking of formalizing their relationship. Following on from what the authors of one book on this topic said, "as far as one can tell from the econometric evidence, it [the law] matters quite a lot".[237]

2.4. INVESTMENTS MADE BY SPOUSES IN THE HOUSEHOLD

Another author has stressed the nature of the marriage as a pre-commitment strategy used as a tool of self-management – comparing entering into marriage with Ulysses ordering his crew to lash his body to the mast of his ship to resist the sirens.[238] But the reason behind marriage is not – at least in most cases – to prevent dying at the hands of a dangerous female creature. More than a way to control future impulses, marriage rather encourages the partners to make couple-specific investments.[239] Now the question arises: What are these special investments and assets in a marriage? Is it only about the money and other pecuniary goods?

Certainly not. The economic analysis of marriage is based on the idea that a household is the most basic production unit of a society.[240] However, not only the commodities that spouses acquire in markets, but also their skills and abilities are inputs that produce many tangible and intangible assets which do not necessarily have to be traded on a market. The outputs of a marriage have a value to the spouses; but this value need not necessarily be expressed in pecuniary terms. Children, for example, are regarded as one of the most important outputs of a marriage.[241] Evidently, the specific investments made in a relationship could consist of cash contributions, work or goods. However, the most salient investment – at least for young couples – is not a market commodity; it is the time and effort needed to raise the children. One can say, then, that marriage is a contract, but a special one – in comparison, for example, with a sale contract – as it also generates outputs which cannot be sold on regular markets, even though they have enormous worth for the spouses. A paradigmatic example of this is their children.

Furthermore, marriage also defines the baseline under which several different arrangements of little and great importance are agreed upon. These

237 Dnes & Rowthorn (2002) 3. For some literature outside the law and economics field about the influence of the law on the behavior of spouses in different cultures, consult: Weisfeld & Weisfeld (2018) 14 et seqq.
238 Scott (1990) 40.
239 Cohen (2002) 12; Scott & Scott (1998) 1254–1255.
240 Becker (1973) 815; Posner R. (2014) 159, 163.
241 Cohen (2002) 15.

arrangements are related to specific tasks to be performed during the whole relationship, and go from who should bring the child to their drums lesson or cook this weekend to the time span for which one of them has to stay at home to raise the offspring. As a marriage imposes costs on the party that attempts to end the relationship unilaterally, it encourages continued compliance with the specific tasks agreed upon by them to obtain and maintain assets with or without a monetary value but of great importance for them as a couple.

2.5. SOCIETY'S PARTIAL ASSUMPTION OF PROCEDURAL COSTS TO ACHIEVE PROPER ADMINISTRATION OF JUSTICE

As seen above, there are outcomes of a marriage that cannot be traded in markets for monetary benefits. Thus, it could happen that regardless of the effort invested in the relationship, one or both of the spouses are not in a position to pay the costs of the resolution of a dispute by a court. In this context, requiring parties to assume all legal fees – including legal representation – would discourage individuals from initiating proceedings due to the uncertainty surrounding any trial of the issues. Whereas in commercial disputes, parties can include legal costs in the price of their products, that is not possible in a marriage because of the non-monetary nature of many of its outcomes.[242] For this reason, it does not seem unreasonable that part of the costs of legal proceedings is partially borne by society in the form of lower court fees or making a public lawyer available.

Requiring the total internalization of all judicial costs by the spouses would stop people from initiating proceedings. Courts could make mistakes. Furthermore, sometimes it is not possible to foresee the outcome of a proceeding, due to the necessity of proving allegations or the lack of precision in some legal provisions. Subsidizing a part of the costs of a proceeding in family law is a suitable solution to allow people – in real world circumstances – to enforce their rights.[243] The costs of proceedings should therefore not be totally borne by the spouses, but a part of them must under certain circumstances – depending on the economic situation of the spouses – be transmitted to the rest of society in order to encourage the realization of contractual cooperative dynamics.[244] Thus, measures reducing the costs of the administration of justice in resolving marital disputes will be regarded as desirable, but only if they do not reduce the assistance granted to spouses lacking the necessary financial resources to fund their proceedings.

---

242 Scott & Scott (1998) 1242.

243 Cramton (1982) 553–554.

244 For a study measuring the effectiveness of legal aid on needy people involved in legal proceedings related to family law, see: Owen & Portillo (2003).

3. CONCLUDING REMARKS

Marriage has been presented as a contract in an economic sense, a tool whose primary purpose is creating incentives between the partners to cooperate in order to obtain benefits of great value for them. By establishing specific consequences in the case of premature termination and mutual obligations in the event of a rupture, marriage motivates spouses to invest considerable efforts in the relationship. Its main appeal lies precisely in maximizing the fruits of the join work.

It remains to be seen whether legal provisions in modern legislation are actually in line with this view of marriage. The next chapters are devoted to addressing this question.

CHAPTER 2

EXPLAINING ENFORCEMENT OF PROMISES IN SUBSTANTIVE MARRIAGE LAW FROM AN ECONOMIC PERSPECTIVE

The previous chapter concluded that the aim of contract law is facilitating the realization of agreements between individuals. This conclusion is based on the idea that voluntary exchanges not only improve the situation of the people involved, but they also assure a suitable allocation of the resources in a society. As long as these exchanges do not negatively affect individuals that have not chosen to incur these costs, they ought to be supported by the law. Party autonomy seems to be the corner-stone of the economic and legal system. In the case of marriage, however, spouses do not enjoy the same freedom that people in contract law have. There are significant restrictions on the specific obligations they can agree on in the framework of their marital relationship. Furthermore, the consequences of the termination of a marriage are unique when comparing them to transactions concluded in regular markets. If marriage is a contract, it is then necessary to explain why these differences exist. The first section of this chapter focuses on the reasons why not all promises between spouses must be legally enforced. The second explores the economic rationale behind the remedies commonly provided by marriage law

1. ECONOMIC RATIONALE BEHIND THE DETERMINATION OF ENFORCEABLE PROMISES

The law provides legal means with which individuals can enforce their promises to one another.[245] Promises come in all varieties, including promises to provide a good in exchange for money; promises of employment; promises to create

[245] BRINIG (2000) 2.

a business; and, of course, the promise of being together in sickness and in health, until death do us part. One can also think of promises like staying faithful, quitting smoking, respecting the partner or keeping them company. The key question is: Which promises should be legally enforceable – or to be more specific – which arrangements deserve the protection of the legal system?[246]

1.1. SPECIALIZATION IN THE ADMINISTRATION OF JUSTICE AS A COST FACTOR

In 1776 Adams Smith explained the gains of productivity through the division of work.[247] Using a pin factory as an example, he argued that producing pins in a system where the entire process is divided up among the workers would generate very large increases in productivity. According to him, the key factor affecting the productivity is the amount of time that workers spend switching from one task to another. A division of work allows them to focus on a narrow range of tasks and so gain much more experience and ability to perform their activity efficiently. He concluded that the assignation of a single task to each worker will enhance the level of production of any factory.[248] The division of the law into different branches – public and private law or tort and contract law – can also be seen as a mechanism that enhances the productivity of the legislators, courts and legal practitioners in their job:[249] a natural response of society to the increasing number of situations regulated by law, as well as the growing volume of disputes resolved by courts. Delimitating the subjects covered by a specific area of law enables a more complete exploitation of the division of labor, and so an improvement of the productivity of law-makers and courts.[250] Accordingly, marriage law is understood as a result of this specialization, so that it only focuses on a special kind of contract regulating the realization of investments in a specific production unit: the household. Thanks to this limitation, not only fewer errors and greater speed and precision in the analysis of the cases will be achieved; it also allows law-makers to design rules that respond better to the specific preferences and needs of prospective spouses. Rather than a burden, the restriction of the subject matters covered by the marriage law acts in favor of the interests of the law's addressees.

---

246 Miceli (2004) 109.
247 Smith ([1776] 1976) 7.
248 Smith ([1776] 1976) 7, 13.
249 Wittman (2000) 1088.
250 With a similar view in other contexts see: Posner R. (2014) 731.

This delimitation of marriage's scope does not contravene the function of the private law of promoting agreements that reallocate resources in a society. Spouses are not prevented from concluding transactions. They simply have to use a different body of rules or resort to a different court when enforcing promises beyond the limits of what is regarded as a strictly matrimonial issue. Spouses continue being free to make exchanges of any type to improve their situation. Contracts about the realization of tasks – within or outside the house – in exchange for money, between spouses, are still possible. Their enforceability will simply depend on whether they fulfill the requirements and conditions prescribed by other branches of law, such as for example employment law. The same applies to contracts with which spouses buy or sell property or those that determine what happens with their assets after their death. They remain outside of the scope of marriage law, so that the conditions for their enforceability and interpretation – default and mandatory rules – will be subject to other areas of law.

Although different reasons can be put forward, the availability of only a limited number of matrimonial property regimes, as well as the restrictions on modifying their content, can also be seen as an expression of the economic principle of specialization. Instead of alleging protection of third parties or paternalism, the limitation on party autonomy might rather promote the development of more accurate rules and jurisprudence and assure informed decisions by the spouses.[251] It expedites the resolution of disputes and reduces errors in the implementation of the law, as the application of a fixed set of rules allows legal practitioners to become more skilled in their use. The limitations also permit people to be more aware of the exact contents of the rights and obligations arising from their marriage. Not only a reduction of procedural costs, but also better predictability of the proceedings' outcomes are achieved thanks to the existence of a *numerus clausus* and a reduction of the margin of discretion to modify the provisions of a matrimonial regime.[252] According to this view, the freedom to introduce changes in the regulation of the law is not *per se* positive or negative, but it depends on whether the benefits are higher than the costs it triggers. Part II of this book argues that allowing alteration of the legal regulation applicable to the property regime – and other aspects of the relationship – *via* choice of law agreements is a promising way to reduce such costs.

---

251 The limitation reduces administrative and information costs. For a similar view, see: Trebilcock (1999) 253. This idea can be used to analyze restrictions on the creation of new property rights – *numerus clausus* – in property law. See: Merrill (2000) 38–42. For a different view, see: Rudden (1987).

252 Scott & Scott (1999) 216.

1.2. AMBIGUITY OF SPECIFIC TERMS AS A COST FACTOR

Marriage is a contract in the sense that it generates valuable assets through the imposition of obligations on the parties. However, it has distinctive features that differentiate it from other legally-binding agreements concluded in regular markets. One of them is its long-term nature. Being so, drafting rigid rules in a marital agreement might be counterproductive, due to the difficulty to foresee the prospective needs and preferences of the spouses or their future personal situation. If one cannot predict the number of children, time available, future salaries or even the couple's place of residence in the medium term, it would be insensate to specify at length the obligations – e.g. hours per week devoted to raising children – to be performed by each party during the whole duration of the relationship. Meticulousness could become a straitjacket that might prevent individuals from achieving their personal goals, as it would oblige them to fulfill their promises regardless of their personal situation in the future.[253] Thus, it would be a mistake to assume that arrangements between spouses with a wide margin of discretion are simply products of negligence. Quite the opposite, they might respond to the desire to minimize the costs of adjusting their behavior to varying circumstances and the occurrence of events that are impossible to predict.[254] The longer a relationship, the more advisable is evading rigid rules.[255] Flexible, adaptable or even ambiguous terms should not be attributed to incompetence. They are necessary or even unavoidable in complex relationships of long duration.[256]

However, this does not mean that courts are obliged to resolve every problem arising from a lack of clarity in the drafting of a contract. Determining the real intentions of the parties when duties are not precisely defined could be excessively costly, not only in terms of time but especially due to the high probability of making mistakes. Thus, courts must be allowed to refuse to enforce promises when their meaning is difficult to interpret.[257] The significant costs

---

253 Scott (1987) 2020. See also: Scott & Scott (1999) 218–220.

254 It was also suggested that a lack of specification in the obligations assumed by the spouses would give bad signals about their intentions and expectations of the relationship. *Fiancées* will be reluctant to propose the conclusion of a contract regulating the division of property in the event of a divorce, because to do so would lead the other to believe that the chance of success of their marriage might be lower or the probability of divorce greater. See: Spier (1992) 433.

255 Epstein (2014) 301, 317–318.

256 Scott & Scott (1998) 1249, 1253.

257 Posner R. (2005) 1587, 1593, et seqq.; Posner R. (2014) 99. The idea is to prevent an overuse of common resources. See: Cooter & Ulen (2016) 147.

of setting the legal system in motion justify the rejection of the enforcement of promises whose degree of imprecision prevents courts from ascertaining – with reasonable accuracy and affordability – the true intentions of the parties. An equitable distribution of household chores, moderation, support, respect and faithfulness are not only important obligations on which most marital relationships are based; they can also be used as a key reference point to calibrate the degree of cooperation and effort invested into the marital relationship. However, the difficulty to determine the exact meaning of these terms according to the expectations of each spouse – not to mention issues linked to the presentation of adequate evidence in the context of a legal proceeding – makes it necessary to reject agreements that attempt to link specific consequences to breaches of these obligations.[258] This does not mean that the law should avoid any regulation of the marital life that includes a certain margin of discretion in its interpretation. On the contrary, as was said before, flexibility is necessary in relationships of a long duration. But some arrangements between spouses must be rejected based on the difficulties of determining the meaning of the expressions used by the parties.

The significant problems in terms of unpredictability – for spouses – and unnecessary increase of workload – for judges – linked to the use of imprecise terms can be seen in jurisdictions in which the culpability of one spouse for a marriage's breakdown plays a role in the resolution of matrimonial disputes. A Maltese case illustrates how time-consuming and absurd it could be discussing evidence on this matter in the course of a legal proceeding.[259] In this case, the plaintiff and defendant consumed rivers of ink trying to prove the guilt of their ex-partner. Bizarre arguments such as "[I] caught him, the defendant, masturbating [...] together with his fetish for watching pornographic material" or "[she] was unfaithful because she started showing a keen interest in Facebook" were used to prove the blameworthiness of the counterpart. In this case, the owner of a local bar was even called as a witness to determine the times each spouse was in the bar alone or with other friends. If one takes into consideration that costs of legal proceedings on matrimonial issues are partially assumed by the state, it is no surprise that most modern legislation has eliminated the need of proving the guilt of one spouse for irretrievable breakdown as a cause for divorce.

In sum, the enforceability of promises and appropriateness of legal provisions are subordinated to the costs that their interpretation causes. Thus, not all commitments between spouses will necessarily be enforced by the

---

258 The rationale is similar to the one behind penalty default rules. See: Ayres (1998) 587. In detail: Ayres & Gertner (1989) 95, et seqq. See also: Posner R. (2005) 1587–1588.

259 Civil Court (Family Section), 9 December 2020. ECLI:MT:FMLJ:2020:124443.

competent jurisdiction. Enforceability requires that the content of an obligation encompasses an adequate degree of objectivity that enables an interpretation at a reasonable cost.[260] This condition explains why a number of promises – despite their importance for the relationship, such as for example those mentioned above – are most likely not going to be legally enforced.[261]

1.3. EXTRALEGAL MECHANISMS AT THE SPOUSES' DISPOSAL AS A COST FACTOR

Further restrictions on party autonomy are justified because other means can encourage cooperation at much lower costs, and consequently make the intervention of a court unnecessary. In fact, nobody gets married with the expectation that all vows exchanged will be enforced by a court in case of non-fulfillment. People want their partners to keep their promises. They also regard marriage as a suitable mechanism to assure the fulfillment of the underlying obligations. However, people also know that a marriage is much more than a body of legal rules, as there are also non-legal mechanisms that can be used to achieve their objectives.[262]

1.3.1. Endogenous Extralegal Mechanisms

A marriage is a long-term relationship composed of a large number of mutual obligations whose performance are often mutually dependent. The relationship between spouses could thus be seen as a repeated game, in which each of them has the opportunity to reward – or if necessary, to punish – the other for the performance of their duties during each round.[263] Regardless of whether their arrangements could be legally enforced, the marital dynamic provides spouses with the necessary tools to encourage their partner to fulfill a number of promises. Each of them has the opportunity to give their best when it is their turn to perform a duty. The incentive to cooperate lies in knowing that if one of them delivers their promise in the terms agreed upon – or fails to do so – the other has the opportunity to do the same in the future.[264]

It is inevitable that either of the spouses will be tempted to act selfishly, if they think that the benefits of a certain activity – working late, having some

---

260 Posner R. (2005) 1593.

261 This does not preclude spouses from using private mediators – arbitrators, marriage counselors, etc. – to resolve disputes related to vague or ambiguous duties assumed by them.

262 Scott & Scott (1998) 1249; 1284.

263 Cooter & Ulen (2016) 209.

264 Scott (1987) 2024–2025.

drinks with friends or buying expensive shoes – are greater than the expected returns of another task their partner must carry out next.[265] However, because they are in a long-lasting relationship, a cooperative pattern will emerge. As each spouse is aware that their partner could decide not to comply with their tasks, they will take their current choices into consideration, not only for the present, but also for future situations.[266] The fact that nobody obliges them to deliver on certain promises paradoxically pushes them to cooperate with each other. The non-enforcement of such promises does not seem counterproductive; it drives them to resolve their matters on their own. Game-theory specialists have studied in detail the strategies used by individuals in situations where they have the opportunity to cheat each other. They have discovered that in repeated games the strategy called *tit for tat* – first cooperate and then replicate the partner's previous action – not only provides the best outcomes, but also tends to emerge spontaneously in virtually every situation.[267] Despite its name, which emphasizes an adversarial root, its nature is largely cooperative when analyzing its outcomes due to the resulting equilibrium.[268] In the marital dynamic, *tit for tat* not only encourages the fulfillment of promises, but also serves as a feedback mechanism that allows spouses to adjust their behavior constantly to the demands of the other. It yields good results in changing environments, even if the expected behavior is not precisely defined. It is a suitable device to signal both bad and good practices, even without the need to spell out what one exactly expects from the other. The success of this dynamic is not based on the creation of a hostile environment, where each wrong action will be punished by the other, but on knowing that the present collaboration – from cleaning up after a dinner with friends, up to raising the children during their first years – will be rewarded by performances of equal value in the future.[269]

The fact that courts can refuse to analyze some claims about a specific division of tasks in the household does not mean that people cannot assure the fulfillment of these promises. Obligations that concern fundamental issues, such as respect and equity in a marriage, can be enforced successfully by endogenous extralegal mechanisms developed by the spouses on their own.

---

265 Scott & Scott (1999) 228–229.

266 This prediction does not require that spouses be wholly rational decision-makers. It only assumes self-interested behavior played out in a variety of contexts. Each spouse adapts through trial and error to the strategy that – from their perspective – appears to be the optimal one. See: Scott (1987) 2026; Scott & Scott (1998) 1286; Scott & Scott (1999) 229.

267 Axelrod (1984) 14–15, 19–20, 27 et seqq. For "lock in effect" in relational contracts see: Scott (1987) 2026 et seqq.; Scott & Scott (1999) 229.

268 Cooter & Ulen (2016) 299.

269 For some evidence about domestic labor as an incentive for the other spouse to increase waged labor in developing countries see: Walther (2017) 357, 378–379.

Something similar occurs with rules designed by the spouses to decrease the likelihood of certain undesirable events happening. *Tit for tat* becomes useless when one of them has already had an affair. It can, however, help enforce rules of behavior – e.g. limiting the number of pub nights – and so prevent the probability that marital infidelity occurs in the first place.[270]

1.3.2. Exogenous Extralegal Mechanisms

Tit for tat may be insufficient to prevent non-cooperation in certain situations, due to the significant costs of monitoring some duties.[271] A marriage is composed of many *facere* and *non-facere* obligations performed within and outside of the household. In some cases, the success of endogenous strategies might require a high degree of supervision of the activities in progress to ensure that they are on-course and on-schedule to meet the desired objectives. For this reason, in marriages as well as in any other long-term relationships, social norms play an important role in the dynamic of cooperation.[272]

Unlike a simple cohabitation, marriage is subject to many social conventions that impose duties on the spouses in order to reinforce mutual cooperation and discourage a breach of core promises. Once people get married, the behavior of society toward them changes. Everybody expects the spouses to respect social rules that – although unwritten – are of paramount importance for the whole group. It is not only about the question of "when does the baby arrive?", but also "did you remember your wedding anniversary?", "are you really coming alone tonight?" or "is he married?"[273] Many social customs and traditions serve as precautionary measures to make a breach of marital duties more difficult, enforce commitments or expedite investments.[274] Individuals know the importance of such mechanisms: the announcement of the engagement, the conclusion of the marriage in a public space, as well as the organization of a wedding reception, apprise the whole community of the conclusion of a serious commitment and a change of status. The celebration of wedding anniversaries, the habit of using a specific title – Mrs. – the change of the surname

270 *Tit for tat* could, however, also create a very negative spiral in a relationship, and so trigger a dangerous dynamic of retaliatory actions between the spouses. Scott & Scott (1999) 229.

271 Leib (2009) 678; Scott (1987) 2040.

272 Scott (1987) 2041; Scott (1990) 52; Trebilcock (1999) 245; Weisfeld & Weisfeld (2018) 10.

273 Scott & Scott (1998) 1289–1291; Wedgwood (2016) 33, 37.

274 An anthropological study shows that in many cultures couples are discouraged from divorcing or separating by social pressure – in particular from parents and friends. See: Weisfeld & Weisfeld (2018) 10.

and the custom of wearing a wedding ring serve as constant reminders for the partner and all members of the society of the existence of this marriage.[275]

The logic behind all these traditions is not only to warn conspecifics of the existence of a kind of property right over the partner, and making it clear that in case of a transgression "you will have to deal with me". Much more than a kind of scent mark, the objective is to announce to the whole group – males and females – that they are empowered to demand a certain behavior or even enforce social punishments if one spouse attempts to infringe on commonly expected marital obligations when the other partner is not present. Exogenous extralegal mechanisms do not reduce the risks to zero. Indeed, that would be counterproductive, since social rules need not necessarily reflect the preferences of the spouses. However, they increase the costs of breaching certain promises and contribute to the cooperation between spouses. Acts of infidelity, for example, are costly not only because of the need to keep it a secret from the partner, but also because they must be kept hidden from friends and family. Regardless of how good the relation with a close relative or a friend is, they generally do not tolerate that their own son, sister, father or best friend has an affair.[276] Moreover, since such an act is repudiated by most members of society, it might even be necessary to hide the existence of the marriage from the mistress or lover, which makes things even more difficult.

1.4. LEGAL ENFORCEMENT OF PROMISES BETWEEN SPOUSES

Although extralegal mechanisms can be of great help, they may be insufficient to ensure a cooperative equilibrium between spouses. The efficiency[277] of exogenous mechanisms rests on the extent to which these social rules are internalized by the parties and the severity of the penalties imposed on transgressors.[278] Since the expected behavior is defined from the outside,

275 Scott & Scott (1999) 230.

276 Scott & Scott (1998) 1290; Scott & Scott (1999) 230; Weisfeld & Weisfeld (2018) 10. For the importance of traditions, see also: Hayek (1948d) 23.

277 Throughout this book the term "efficient rules" refers to legal provisions – or any other legal measure taken by governments – that facilitate the emergence of cooperative dynamics between people. Legal provisions that eliminate barriers to the conclusion of contracts – or any other kind of voluntary agreement – are regarded as efficient, as contracts are the typical means used to depict the terms in which such dynamics will be carried out. This is based on the idea that continuous conclusion of voluntary agreements between people transfer existing resources into the hands of those that value them the most. See: Chapter 1 Section 1.1 and Section 1.2. *in fine*. For situations meriting the imposition of restrictions on the freedom to conclude voluntary agreements – externalities, asymmetry of information, constraints affecting decision-making and monopolistic positions – see: Chapter 3 Section 1.

278 Scott & Scott (1998) 1268; Scott & Scott (1999) 231.

they may be contrary to the needs of the spouses or simply insufficient to encourage cooperation. They could be too loose or too restrictive for the needs and preferences of a specific couple. Endogenous mechanisms are also by no means faultless. Even long relationships finish eventually, which makes *tit for tat* insufficient to encourage further cooperation. The end does not necessarily refer to the couple's divorce – that is just the formalization of the end. It rather alludes to the moment at which the opportunity costs of fulfilling a promise are higher than the benefits that the continuation of the cooperative game generates. In broad terms, the end refers to the moment when a marital crisis has begun, and consequently retaliation or rewards do not have an impact on the behavior of the other anymore.[279]

In such a context, legal enforcement is needed to buttress trust and assure an optimal investment level.[280] It is necessary to build confidence between the parties, so that the quality and quantity of the resources exchanged approximate as closely as possible to the investments that they would make if they could fully rely on each other. However, one has to consider the significant costs of setting in motion the judicial administration, as well be aware of the existence and effectiveness of extralegal enforcement mechanisms. To reach an optimal degree of cooperation, most legal systems use the following strategy: legal enforcement of long-term contracts is not primarily focused on the time during which the relationship works. The surplus generated by the cooperation is enough to foster the emergence of non-legal mechanisms that assure the desired performance. To reduce costs, legal mechanisms are only made available at the moment at which the relationship deteriorates; that is, at the time at which continuing with the cooperative game generates only modest profits in comparison to the benefits that a termination of the relationship would grant. Thus, agreements about maintenance payments, division of the property and – more recently[281] – causes to apply for a divorce are subjects of analysis by courts.[282]

---

279 Axelrod (1984) 10, 174. The key to the success of repeated games lies with the possibility each player has to punish the other in a subsequent round. If the game has an end, the one who made the first move can have no possibility to retaliate in the last round. Knowing this, they could refuse to invest in the penultimate round, which in turn creates a spiral of mutual distrust in the third-but-last round and so on: if both know that in the future, there is a point in the game where there is no possibility for retaliation, they will reject long- or even medium-term risks. Knowing that there is an end to the cooperation game could lead to an under-investment in the relationship. Such a dynamic may have an impact on the relationship of spouses. See: Scott (1987) 2033.

280 Scott (1987) 2042, et seqq.; Scott & Scott (1998) 1294; Scott & Scott (1999) 235. For issues related the "end game problem" in relational contracts see: Cooter & Ulen (2016) 301.

281 Some jurisdictions in the United States have recently introduced an optional regime – known as covenant marriage – that places stricter limits on exiting the marital union. For information about the covenant marriage and its effects in the State of Louisiana see: Sanchez et al. (2001).

282 Scott & Scott (1998) 1304.

Full legal enforcement of intramarital pledges concerning – for example – division of the household chores, time dedicated to childcare, cohabitation, determination of the parties' domicile or other matters of a similar nature does not generally need to take place if a dispute between the partners occurs before the marital crisis. Extralegal mechanisms are better at assuring the fulfillment of these promises due to their lower cost and capability to reveal the subjective expectations of each spouse.[283] During the time when the spouses are convinced that this is an indefinitely repeating game, there is no great need to intervene, since they are capable of creating internal mechanisms to incentivize cooperation. However, the success of these mechanisms is heavily subordinated to the enforcement of clear rules that structure the end of the game. Since neither exogenous nor endogenous mechanisms provide an adequate solution after a marital crisis, the coercive power of the state is a good alternative to fill this gap. Legal enforcement of promises related to the termination of a marriage becomes the corner-stone on which the robustness and strength of extralegal mechanisms rely. The potential use and success of these mechanisms depend directly on the belief that in case they are not enough to discipline the behavior of the partners, there is at least one other way to recover a part of the investment or mitigate the damage caused by a breach.[284] This is not to say, however, that the law must never enforce any agreement that aims to regulate certain obligations during a marriage, or more precisely, before a marital crisis. It does not mean, either, that any agreement about the termination of a relationship must be enforced by the courts. Marriage law must find an equilibrium in the use of its enforcing power, so that it entices the blooming of private mechanisms that incentivize cooperation but at the same time discourage parties from behaving opportunistically.

Which of these mechanisms could determine both – the promises that should be enforced before and after a marital crisis and the legal consequences of breaking them – will be revealed later.[285] In fact, that is the question around which a great deal of Part II of this book revolves. For now, it is important to stress that cooperation does not need the legal enforcement of all pledges made by the spouses. Focusing on only a part of them – especially those referring to their obligations when a marital crisis has begun – seems to be enough to encourage cooperation. The existence of extralegal mechanisms allows legislators and courts to choose only a group of obligations to be subject of the coercive power of the state, without reducing the willingness of the spouses to cooperate.

---

283 Scott & Scott (1999) 237.

284 Cooter & Ulen (2016) 301.

285 See Chapter 6 in this book.

2. ECONOMIC RATIONALE BEHIND REMEDIES IN MARRIAGE LAW

Now it is time to analyze if there is also an economic rationale behind the remedies commonly used by the law in the event that one or both spouses decide to terminate the relationship prematurely. Marriage law presents two particularities when compared to contract law. On the one hand, although a unilateral termination of a marriage is allowed in practically all legal systems, most of them do not grant it automatically. It is necessary – except in specific circumstances as for example domestic violence – to wait for a time to get divorced if one of spouses does not agree with the dissolution.[286] On the other hand, marriage law contemplates the possibility to demand payments in the form of maintenance obligations. Qualifying conditions, the duration and calculation of such payments differ strongly from one country to another. However, the institution of maintenance exists in virtually all legal systems.[287] Next, the book focuses on exploring the economic rationale behind these particularities. It will be shown, that although such practices have a historic background, their survival in modern marriage law can be explained due to their suitability to encourage a cooperative dynamic between spouses. They should not be regarded as an anachronism, but rather as an interesting incentive promoting investments in the relationship.

2.1. WAITING PERIODS IN CONTESTED DIVORCES

Specific or literal performance is a remedy used by courts consisting of ordering the parties to perform their obligations in the strict terms in which they were assumed. As marriage is a legal institution thought to last the whole life of the parties – until death do them part – the application of the doctrine of literal enforcement would not permit a divorce when one of the spouses still desires

---

286 For some references consult Introduction Section 1 of this book. For differences in the regulation of waiting periods in European countries see: EPEC (2006) 6, 38 et seqq.

287 According to the preliminary documents of the drafting process of Protocol 2007, the Family Law regimes of all the State members of the Hague Conference contain a duty of support between individuals bound by marriage. Furthermore, with the only exception of Israel, such a duty exists even after the dissolution of the marital bond. See: PERMANENT BUREAUS PREL. DOC. NO 3 ON MAINTENANCE (1999); PERMANENT BUREAU PREL. DOC. NO 2 ON MAINTENANCE (2003). In general, the payment of alimony terminates on the occurrence of certain facts such as the remarriage of the creditor. See for example: Art. 763 Czech Civil Code; Art. 1444 para. 2 Greek Civil Code; Art. 145 para. 3 Bulgarian Family Code; Art. 301 para.10 Belgian Civil Code; art 763 Czech Civil Code; s. 79 and s. 82 Latvian Civil Code; Art. 130 para. 2 Swiss Civil Code – or cohabitation with another partner – see for example: Art. 1586 German Civil Code; Art. 1:160 Dutch Civil Code.

to be married. Currently, there is a clear trend in comparative law not only to allow the dissolution of a marriage, but also to grant a divorce even without the need of proving wrongdoing by either party.[288] However, most legal systems still include a degree of a specific performance, requiring a waiting period before granting a divorce if only one of the spouses requests the termination of the relationship. A number of laws inside and outside of Europe require the continuation of the marriage for a certain period of time – one, two, three or even four years – regardless of whether one of the spouses has expressly announced their desire to get divorced immediately.[289]

At a first glance one might think that the requirement of a waiting period is useless as a measure to encourage cooperation. Since courts do not have the instruments to enforce standards of fulfillment of marital duties, it would be futile to oblige the couple to stay together when one of them is not willing anymore. However, from an economic perspective, literal enforcement has two advantages. First, marriage includes benefits that do not depend on the fulfillment of specific obligations by the counterpart. Society not only imposes duties on the spouses, but it also grants them a number of prerogatives and privileges that could be lost if the marriage is terminated. These refer not so much to the social position of the spouses in front of other people; nowadays, they also concern the legal *status* of the spouses in a country and specific benefits derived from being married to a national of that state. The termination of a marriage could *inter alia* mean the non-renewal of a residence permit and consequently the impossibility of continuing working, or even being removed from the country. Furthermore, it could lead to a loss of revenue and so to the necessity of one or other spouse being cast precipitately into the labor market. A sudden termination of a relationship could generate losses that are not only difficult to measure, but also to replace by means of monetary compensation. Thus, requiring the specific performance of the marriage contract for a period of time seems a suitable remedy to prevent injuries whose value could be hard to assess for a court[290] or the calculation of which would even be unaffordable for the other spouse. Waiting periods can be an efficient mechanism that dispenses with the need for complex calculations to determine the exact damage suffered

---

288 A number of jurisdictions – some of them located in Europe – still require an "irretrievable breakdown", however proving it is not complicated, as in general it is only necessary to demonstrate a factual separation for a certain period of time. See Boele-Woelki (2005) 53, et seqq. In the United States, however, despite the clear liberalization of the rules of divorce in the whole country, some jurisdictions have more recently introduced an optional regime – known as covenant marriage – that places stricter limits on entering and exiting the marital union. For information about covenant marriage and its effects in the State of Louisiana see: Sanchez et al. (2001).

289 Boele-Woelki et al. (2004) 18; Moore (2016).

290 Kronman (1985) 26; Scott (1990) 76. For costs related to the calculation of damages see: Posner R. (2014) 167.

by one spouse as a consequence of an abrupt termination of the relationship. Second, the fact alone of being married after the marital crisis could generate costs for the one that wants to leave immediately. Not only social punishment, but also the legal impossibility to celebrate a new marriage – at least for a period of time – could push this party to the negotiating table. The obligation to remain married could put the side that refuses the dissolution in a better position to demand a more favorable divorce-agreement and so cover the investments made by them throughout the relationship.[291]

Thus, this specific performance can be attractive for prospective spouses and consequently efficient in the sense that it increases trust in the institution of marriage. The imposition of a waiting period to obtain a divorce could motivate further investments in the marriage, since it mitigates the negative impact of a possible non-cooperation in the future. It has particular importance in marriages, as here parties often assume costs asymmetrically over time.[292] However, a system based solely on specific performance is not enough to encourage an optimal level of cooperation between spouses.[293] Since its effectiveness depends on every individual's costs of remaining married, it does not necessarily assure efficient results. For some people, the social or legal prerogatives granted by society or the state for the simple fact of being married – social acceptance, right to stay in a country, etc. – could be irrelevant, too insignificant or even worthless. Furthermore, the benefits for one spouse of getting divorced could not always cause equal losses in the other, so that the imposition of a waiting period would have no effect on the negotiation outcome of the separation agreement. For these reasons, the use of literal performance as a means to generate cooperation is generally restricted to a limited period of time.[294]

2.2. MAINTENANCE OBLIGATIONS AFTER THE DISSOLUTION OF MARRIAGE

To make it clear from the outset, non-compliance with promises is not necessarily undesirable from an economic perspective. As long as the benefits of a breach are higher than the losses caused for the counterpart, non-compliance should be allowed as long as the aggrieved party is compensated.[295]

---

291 Scott & Scott (1998) 1281; Posner R. (2014) 167–168.

292 Scott & Scott (1998) 1262; 1275.

293 Against this position see: Cohen (2002) 31–33.

294 Boele-Woelki et al. (2004) 18; Moore (2016). Even a covenant marriage permits a divorce after a period of time. See: Sanchez et al. (2001).

295 According to Campbell "[f]ar from it being the function of the law of contract to (so far as possible) prevent breach, the function of that law is to make breach possible, although on terms which the law regulates". See: Campbell (2005) 456.

As was explained before, the aim of a contract is facilitating the conclusion of agreements, as their realization increases the welfare of society due to the surplus created by the execution of that contract.[296] If the termination of a given marriage creates benefits that exceed the damage it causes for the other spouse, so that they could be indemnified in some way for their loss, that breach should not only be allowed but encouraged.[297] Being so, marriage law – from an economic perspective – should not seek to discourage the termination of any relationship. A divorce could lead to the emergence of another relationship, which could mean benefits for the one desiring the break-up, the other spouse and even for other members of society. Most legal systems in the world seem to follow this logic, as they allow spouses to get divorced even when one of them does not agree with that decision at first. However, at first glance, it might not be clear why marriage law – unlike contract law – is not designed to compensate one party for the injuries caused by the premature termination of the relationship. In general, the law does not seek to redress the harm caused to the "victim", but only stipulates an eventual payment based on the needs of the spouse. According to some legal systems,[298] the prior conduct of one spouse can influence the payments required after the divorce. However, maintenance obligations – if they are finally granted – are generally calculated not on the basis of the damage suffered, but rather on the specific needs of the creditor.[299]

This special feature of marriage could be explained by taking into consideration that in regular (non-marital) contracts the payment of the contractual indemnity – actual damages, lost profit, consequential damages, etc. – assumes the existence of a guilty party.[300] Thus, in general the solution for a contractual default is not cumbersome: the party who breaches the contract will be held responsible for the costs arising from the non-compliance with the promise. In the case of the marriage, however, the situation is a bit more complicated. It can be that the one who intends to terminate the marriage or breaks a marital promise may not necessarily be the "cheater", but the victim. Furthermore, more often than not, the desire to

---

296 See Chapter 1 Section 1.2.

297 For the concept of efficient breach of contract see: Goetz & Scott (1977). See also: Cooter & Ulen (2016) 307 et seqq.; Craswell (1992) 809; Friedman (2000) 163; Macaulay (2007); Posner R. (2014) 129 et seqq.

298 See for example Arts. 27, 60 Polish Family and Guardianship Code (Act of 25 February 1964).

299 The Protocol 2007 even obliges contracting States to take into consideration the needs of the creditor as well as the resources of the debtor when determining the amount of maintenance. See Art. 14 of the Protocol of 23 November 2007 on the Law Applicable to Maintenance Obligations.

300 From an economic perspective, "guilty" is the cheapest-cost-avoider. For the application of this concept in marriage law, see the next chapter.

get divorced or a breach of a conjugal duty might be caused by the actions of both spouses.[301] In this context, a system that assigns blame based on the desire to terminate the relationship or the breach of a specific promise will not necessarily deliver efficient outcomes – that is, adequate incentives to cooperate in the framework of the household – as it does not allow the whole picture to be seen in order to distribute the responsibility.[302] Furthermore, as noted before, it is not possible to enforce all obligations that surround a marriage. The high costs of enforcing each promise make it necessary to impose limits on these claims. Fundamental issues like fidelity, respect, equality and many others – despite their importance – are outside of the oversight of the authorities. They are rather subject to the aforementioned extralegal mechanisms. Thus, it might happen that one or even both partners are not – even from the very beginning – satisfied with the outcome of their marriage, because they were unable to reach a suitable degree of cooperation. The quantity and quality of the performance of agreed upon obligations may not match the expectations of the spouses over the whole duration of the marriage. The decision to terminate the marriage could then respond to their behavior of not adequately fulfilling their obligations due to the lack of an adequate – legal or extralegal – mechanism to enforce them.

For this reason, most examples of legislation rely on a system that promotes cooperation by imposing consequences without denouncing a culpable party. Both spouses are – up to a certain point – seen as responsible for the damages caused by the break-up, as both had and have the capacity to influence the occurrence of the causes triggering the termination and the scale of the injuries.[303] To encourage cooperation and generate trust, the law uses an approach inspired by the concept of strict liability: responsibility irrespective of the degree of culpability of the creditor.[304] The law makes a spouse responsible for the damage or loss suffered by the other regardless of their own fault, negligence or intention, so that the claimant only has to prove the occurrence of an event – i.e. lack of adequate financial means – to receive compensation. The idea is to encourage both of them to avoid situations that could lead to the lack of adequate means of other in the future. Many jurisdictions use this approach to determine payments in favor of one spouse in the context of

301 Scott & Scott (1999) 226.

302 Scott & Scott (1998) 1297.

303 Both spouses end up sharing the risks of the rupture. Scott & Scott (1998) 1268, 1310; Scott & Scott (1999) 222.

304 Alimony is then described as a (self-)insurance. See: Scott & Scott (1998) 1273; Trebilcock & Keshvani (1991) 557.

a divorce.[305] They make one of the spouses responsible for a certain harm – e.g. the fact that the partner does not have financial means to cover essential needs after the marital crisis[306] – regardless of whether or not the debtor has provoked the harm with their own actions. As said before, legal systems limit the amount of payments and determine the conditions to receive maintenance differently. Although some of them use the lifestyle of the spouses during their marriage to ascertain the amount to be paid, currently there is a trend toward establishing ceilings for these payments.[307] The economic rationale is to avoid situations where the potential creditor takes more risks, because they know that another person will bear the costs of these risks. By using the needs of the creditor as a yardstick for the maintenance obligation, the law discourages the potential creditor from remaining at home and not seeking an income.[308] Since only their minimal needs will be covered, they would be better off if they worked – at least partially – outside of the house. This strategy is also used by insurance companies when determining the amount paid to a policy-holder: to avoid a *moral hazard*,[309] the compensation does not cover the full amount of the damage, but only a part of it, so that it encourages the injured party to themselves take protective measures and so reduce the loss. The existence of a maintenance obligation also becomes an incentive for the potential debtor to motivate and even support the other to find gainful employment during their marriage, because if not, this person would be liable for higher payments in the future.[310]

However, it is important to stress that the efficiency of such a mechanism in a concrete case relies on the actual preferences of the individuals. Sometimes such limits to the maintenance payments might not reinforce cooperation. The problem is that when the law imposes ceilings to the compensation, it also indirectly puts limits on the investments of the spouses: they will not be willing to invest more than what they can receive in the case of a divorce. If one spouse is ready to give up their career and focuses entirely on the household, and the other agrees with this decision, a system that imposes limits on compensation

305 For detailed information about the substantive regulation of maintenance obligations in several member States of the Hague Conference see Permanent Bureaus Prel. Doc. No. 3 on Maintenance (1999); Permanent Bureau Prel. Doc. No. 2 on Maintenance (2003). See also Boele-Woelki et al. (2004).

306 The term "after the marital crisis" is used as maintenance obligations might be ordered by the judge when spouses are married regardless of whether either of them have the intention to initiate a divorce or legal separation proceeding.

307 Boele-Woelki et al. (2004) 77–78.

308 Scott & Scott (1998) 1313–1314.

309 Moral hazard is an economic term that refers to the lack of incentive to guard against risk where one is protected from its consequences. See: Cooter & Ulen (2016) 48.

310 Scott & Scott (1998) 1313–1314.

would prevent this division of labor. The law could become a problem for all those that want to make high non-monetary contributions to the household, as the damage from a potential termination of the marriage would outweigh the potential compensation by far.[311]

The solution to this problem is not – as some authors claim – establishing a system to compensate "perfectly" for the losses suffered as a consequence of a premature termination of a marriage.[312] Practical reasons make determining the lost-opportunity costs of a marriage – the benefits someone could have gained instead of being married – impossible; not to mention the calculation of the moral damage or any other disadvantage suffered as a consequence of the breakdown. The solution to this problem lies – in this author's opinion – in giving the spouses a margin of discretion to alter the general rules used by the law to determine maintenance obligations. Later on – in Part II of the book – the conclusion of choice of law agreements as a suitable solution will be highlighted.

3. CONCLUDING REMARKS

The reduction of costs of operating the legal system and avoidance of errors in the administration of justice were presented as the main reasons to regard only one group of arrangements as legally enforceable. Through these limitations the productivity of the courts increases; rules that better respond to the needs of spouses are developed; and mistakes in the interpretation of the spouses' obligations are reduced. Extralegal mechanisms that encourage cooperation between the spouses release the courts from enforcing all the promises, and allow them to focus on only one set of arrangements, in particular those referring to the time after the outbreak of a marital crisis.

Waiting periods and maintenance obligations respond to a similar logic. As it is very difficult – and costly – to identify and calculate the damages from a breakdown case-by-case, the law assigns strict obligations to compensate the parties for the negative effects from a premature termination of a relationship. Waiting periods are thought of as a mechanism to compensate for prerogatives that spouses enjoy for the sole reason of being married to a person – as for example a residence permit. By requiring the continuation of the relationship during a period of time, courts are discharged from the necessity to precisely determine the damages from the loss of such prerogatives and to calculate an appropriate compensation for them. The obligation to pay maintenance was in turn described as an ingenious mechanism to cover financial losses without

311 Scott & Scott (1998) 1241.

312 Posner R. (2014) 171; Trebilcock & Keshvani (1991) 556; Williams (1995).

needing to establish a guilty party. As the desire to terminate the marriage or the non-fulfillment of a marital duty may stem from the behavior of the other spouse or even both of them, the law relies on a system that establishes a supportive obligation based on an objective fact: the lack of financial means of the partner and the capacity of the other to support them. The trend to include ceilings on the amount paid in modern legal systems, as well as to limit the obligation to cover basic needs of the creditor, are mechanisms to avoid a *moral hazard*.

CHAPTER 3

EXPLAINING MANDATORY AND DEFAULT RULES IN SUBSTANTIVE MARRIAGE LAW FROM AN ECONOMIC PERSPECTIVE

The previous chapter has described the economic rationale underlying some peculiarities of marriage law. It explained that the non-enforcement of some marital promises and basic legal remedies lower the costs of the administration of justice. However, the legal regulation of marriage goes beyond those features, as the law contains other – optional and imperative – rules for the spouses. If we assume that marriage is a contract – a tool to encourage the realization of investments in order to generate mutual benefits – it is necessary to demonstrate that the legal provisions in marriage law actually respond to this logic. The following pages are focused on providing a conceptual framework that explores in a comprehensive manner the economic rationale behind mandatory and default rules. Although it is undeniable that culture, belief, religion and other local features influence law-making, marriage law – as it has developed in a number of modern national laws – can be understood as a coherent system of incentives that induce cooperation between spouses in the same way as contract law does with contractual parties. The chapter is divided into two sections. In the first one, the cases that justify the imposition of restrictions on the freedom of choice are discussed. The second deals with the nature of default rules and their importance in the context of marriage.

1. RULES OF OBLIGATORY COMPLIANCE FOR THE SPOUSES

From an economic point of view, allowing individuals to decide freely with whom to contract and permitting them to define the conditions that govern these relationships is very welcome. This freedom would contribute to maximizing the benefits from their transactions, and accelerate the allocation of resources to those that value them at most.[313] However, not all transactions

[313] See Chapter 1 Section 2 in this book. See also: Kronman (1977) 370; Riley (2000) 370.

lead to an improvement, as some arrangements can generate damage, injuries or other costs to contractual or external parties. A system based on the free exchange of goods and services can certainly fail. If that is the case, the imposition of limits on party autonomy is unavoidable to assure an efficient allocation of resources. It is here where provisions of obligatory compliance come into play.[314] The economic theory of contract regulation borrows from the economic theory of market regulation when evaluating the cases in which mandatory rules are necessary. Categories of market failures – externalities, asymmetry of information, constraints affecting decision-making and monopolistic position – are used to describe situations that merit the imposition of limits on party autonomy in contract law.[315] Based on those categories, this section explores the reasons why some rules have lost their mandatory nature over time, as well as the economic logic underlying several provisions of obligatory compliance still in force in a number of modern legal systems. Restrictions on the possibility to waive maintenance support; formalities for the conclusion of contracts between spouses; a minimum age of marriage; and the prohibition of agreements precluding the possibility of divorce will, *inter alia*, be explained with the aid of these economic concepts.

1.1. EXTERNALITIES AS LIMITS ON THE SPOUSES' FREEDOM OF CHOICE

In general, the term externality refers to positive or negative effects experienced by third parties as a consequence of an activity. Contract law is prevalently interested in negative externalities, caused by agreements concluded by others than those that suffer the adverse effects. Their emergence can lead to the intervention of the law – *via* limitations to party autonomy – to avoid such damage.[316] In the following, I refer to this negative type when using the term externality succinctly. Virtually all transactions can produce some degree of harm, loss, damage or any other cost to third parties. Buying a car, for example,

314 Cserne (2011) 64. These rules are known as imperative, immutable or mandatory rules, and can be classified in two groups. The first group restricts the contractual freedom of parties by means of forbidding the conclusion of some agreements. The second group requires certain actions before – or during – the exchange of the promises, such as for example the presence of a notary, for the conclusion of a contract. The rules of the second type do not seek to ban agreements but assure that individuals are aware of possible negative effects of their actions and lessen potential harm generated by a contract. See: Ayres (1998) 585–586.

315 Cooter & Ulen (2016) 294–295; Trebilcock & Keshvani (1991) 550.

316 According to the Coase-Theorem, this depends on the presence of high transaction costs. The implications of this theorem in the analysis of the legal institutions will be discussed in Chapter 8 Section 4.2.2.

could harm all those that were interested in the same vehicle. The decision of two persons to sit on a bench in a park to have a conversation could disturb others who prefer peace and quiet. Even an agreement of two individuals to wear certain clothing could offend the sense of decency of some people. It is clear that if all these spillovers would count as reasons to ban the realization of arrangements, freedom of contract would be at an early end.[317]

By establishing cases which justify the inclusion of rules that limit the freedom of people, contract law is not interested in every loss or cost that may arise from the conclusion of an agreement. More important is whether the contract leads to a reduction or deprivation of the enjoyment of legally recognized rights over certain assets. Establishing whether a limitation of contractual freedom is necessary does not depend on the physical or psychological state of third parties as a consequence of the conclusion of an arrangement between two persons. It rather hinges on whether the realization of this contract impedes other individuals from exercising a power over a resource,[318] assuming that the law – in particular the rules of constitutional, property or inheritance law – considers the affected person entitled to exercise such a power. If that is not the case, there is no need to limit contractual freedom to protect them, regardless of how adversely affected the individuals themselves feel.[319] To summarize, restrictions based on externalities simply recognize the old adage "freedom ends where another person's [legal] right begins".[320] Think, for example, of the restrictions imposed on parents on the use and destination of assets belonging to their children – e.g. Art. 1643 German Civil Code, Art. 167 Spanish Civil Code, or Art. 324 Swiss Civil Code. Although they are generally allowed to administrate these goods, legal systems tend to include limits to their actions. Arrangements of the parents about the disposition of these goods might have

317 Langbein & Yost (2009) 294; Trebilcock (1997) 58.

318 The word resource should here be interpreted in a broad sense, as it does not refer exclusively to traded goods in regular markets, but also to any – material or non-material – asset that can be used to obtain material or non-material benefits, for instance, time or education.

319 For the concept of externality and situations that merit an intervention to avoid negative spillovers on third persons see: Cooter & Ulen (2016) 296; Hermalin et al. (2007), 3, 30–34; Mankiw (2012) 196; Rühl (2011) 216–217; Schäfer & Ott (2004) 108–110; Shavell (2004) 77–78; Veljanovski (2007) 38–40.

320 The classic formulation of the so-called harm principle can be traced back to John Stuart Mill's essay *On Liberty*: "The object of this Essay is to assert one very simple principle, as entitled to govern absolutely the dealings of society with the individual in the way of compulsion and control, whether the means used be physical force in the form of legal penalties, or the moral coercion of public opinion. That principle is, that the sole end for which mankind are warranted, individually or collectively in interfering with the liberty of action of any of their number, is self-protection. That the only purpose for which power can be rightfully exercised over any member of a civilized community, against his will, is to prevent harm to others". See: Mill (1859/1999) 5.

to fulfill certain requirements – e.g. a permission of the court – or be subject to a control *a posteriori* to avoid damage or loss – that is, externalities – to the children.[321]

Limitations on party autonomy based on the contravention of the *ordre public* follow a similar logic. They respond to the desire of protecting certain rights granted to all the members of a society.[322] The prohibition of polyandry, polygyny or same-sex marriages might be economically grounded on the idea that a legal recognition of these relationships would negatively impact the rights of other members of the society.[323] Whether such unions actually generate externalities will depend on how adversely affected by those kind of unions the majority of people living in a certain jurisdiction feel.[324] The invalidity of marriages celebrated with the sole objective of obtaining a residence permit in exchange for a payment follows a similar logic, as this measure seeks to avoid the effect of externalities from those private arrangements on other members of a society.[325] This prohibition, however, is not aimed at avoiding moral damage, but it prevents individuals from benefiting, without compensating the whole group in the form of creating a family: that is, a basic production unit in the society. The invalidity of such marriages seeks to avoid what economists call the "free-rider problem".[326]

---

321 Trebilcock (1999) 253.

322 Calabresi & Douglas (1972) 1112; Schäfer & Ott (2012) 607.

323 The externality argument against polygamy or same-sex marriage goes like this: "A part of a voluntary but 'immoral' activity spills over onto 'moral' people, who are annoyed by the way of life of 'immoral' people [...] Then, the way of life or the acts of some people can be said to offend the majority. Their acts or transactions have negative external effects of such a magnitude that they can harm the social order itself". See: Hatzis (2006) 58. However, almost a decade ago – at a time when same-sex marriage was still not recognized in the United States – an empirical study was conducted to evaluate whether legally recognizing (or prohibiting) same-sex marriage had any adverse impact on societal out-comes of "traditional family values". The conclusions were that the argument that same-sex marriage poses a negative externality on society is untenable. See: Langbein & Yost (2009). Whether polygamy actually generates externalities on the rest of the society is by no means sure. Be that as it may, the prohibition of polygamy is based on the belief that such marriages generate spillover on the rest of the society. See: Hatzis (2006) 56.

324 In general, whether same-sex marriages – or interracial marriages – are allowed need not depend on economic considerations, but on values of justice related to the protection of fundamental rights of the people. The use of economics in the analysis of legal institutions does not seek to replace the idea of justice, but simply to complement it. In Chapter 7, it will be shown that the elimination of barriers to the choice of law might help accelerate the introduction of reforms in conservative legal systems, as it lets people see with their own eyes whether a different regulation – or legalization – of the marital union actually generates externalities in their society.

325 The movement of individuals from one country to another can also be analyzed in those terms. The question of whether migration gives rise to externalities depends on who – the migrant or the individuals living in the host country – has the right over migration as a kind of "property right". See: Schlegel (2017) 47–48.

326 For the free-rider problem with public goods see: Mankiw (2012) 220.

Negative spillovers are more likely in situations where multiple individuals are entitled to an asset at the same time. If two or more individuals are allowed to simultaneously profit from a single resource, the actions of one could easily impede – or at least undermine – the exercise of the right of the other.[327] Mandatory rules are often imposed to delimit the exploitation of this resource – the use of the common asset – and so avoid that the unilateral enjoyment interferes with the rights of another person. This idea was previously used to explain the existence of limits on the enforceability of promises. In order to avoid externalities from an excessive use of the judicial system – e.g. slowness in the resolution of disputes due to a back-log of cases – the law might expressly or tacitly impose limits on promises made by the spouses that can be settled before a court. In this vein, the imposition of formalities for the conclusion of agreements between the spouses – e.g. requiring a written form – can also be seen as a way to reduce the costs of the administration of justice.[328] They can serve as proof of the existence of a contract, and so facilitate the conduct of the judiciary process. The same applies to requirements like the presence of a notary in civil law countries: the mediation of a legal expert not only guarantees more informed decisions, but also makes the work of courts easier, as notaries bear the burden of translating the wishes of the couple into proper – legal – terminology. Their contribution in the procedural economy consists in avoiding the use of ambiguous or inaccurate terms that might complicate the resolution of disputes.[329]

1.1.1. Role of Other Mechanisms to Mitigate Externalities

The fact that an activity performed in the context of a marriage generates externalities does not automatically justify a ban in marriage law, as there might be other options to resolve this issue at a lower cost. The question of whether a legal ban is needed, depends on whether the costs of monitoring the behavior of people, and setting in motion the judicial system, are less than the harm generated by this action. Some externalities can successfully be discouraged by extralegal mechanisms without statutory prohibitions, as the mere existence of social rules might deter individuals from performing these acts.[330] In other

---

327 This situation is known as the tragedy of the commons in economic literature. See: Trebilcock (1997) 13–15; Cooter & Ulen (2016) 139. See also: Trebilcock & Keshvani (1991) 551.

328 See: Ayres (1998) 587. In detail: Ayres & Gertner (1989) 95, et seqq.

329 Arruñada (1996) 8.

330 For the effectiveness of social rules in the context of marriage, see Chapter 2 Section 1.3. See also: Weisfeld & Weisfeld (2018) 10; Scott (1987) 2041; Scott (1990) 52; Trebilcock (1999) 245.

cases, legal prohibitions are unquestionably necessary to avoid harm to third parties or even the spouses themselves. However, it is important to not only consider the incidence of a given action. The benefits from the division of labor and – consequently – the possibility that other areas of the law might be better suited to resolve an issue should also be taken into consideration.[331] The elimination of the *saevitia mariti* and *saevitia patres* – the prohibition of using cruelty to *discipline* members of the family – from practically all modern legislation on marriage can be explained this way.[332] Although combating domestic violence is a priority of most legal systems, modern ones do not contain express provisions in marriage law against this scourge anymore. The inclusion of violence against a spouse or child as a specific statutory offense or aggravating factor in criminal law is nowadays the most commonly used option to combat violence in the context of a marriage.

1.1.2. Risk as Justification for Mandatory Rules

Some mandatory rules are not based on the imminent occurrence of harm, but on an increase of the probability that this harm might occur. By imposing limitations on party autonomy, the law might also seek to reduce risky activities that can later – potentially – lead to damage. In the case of marriage, the ban of the renunciation of maintenance support – irrespective of paternalistic reasons – can be justified by the increased probability of the generation of negative spillovers not only on the renouncer, but also on third parties, like the state or the common children of the couple. Contractual arrangements aimed at extinguishing the right to claim maintenance – or any other compensatory allowance after the divorce – might generate externalities to the state because it must provide financial aid to any person in need living in its territory. If spouses were free to agree on the renunciation of any compensation, one of them could benefit from the work of the other in the household without bearing the future costs of this decision, as the state would assume them though social assistance programs. The unenforceability of such contracts can then be seen as a measure to prevent a spouse from transferring the costs of the investments made by their partner to the rest of the society.[333] The generation

331 Scott & Scott (1999) 233–234.

332 Some countries, however, still include the *saevitia mariti* – excessive harshness towards the spouse – as grounds for divorce (See for example Art. 48 Costa Rican Civil Code). In practice, those legal systems indirectly support mistreatment, as it is necessary to be treated "cruelly" to obtain the divorce, accepting mistreatments as long as they are not "cruel". For the regulation of the *saevitia mariti* in Costa Rica see: CIJUL (2006).

333 Regarding the externalities of divorce and their impact on the welfare-state, in particular the fact that a part of the costs of the divorce are – or should be – borne by the state, see: Bourreau-Dubois & Doriat-Duban (2016).

of externalities for the state can also explain why some jurisdictions regard agreements between spouses that prevent the compensation of contributions into a pension fund as invalid.[334] The idea is the same: avoiding the opportunity for spouses to extricate themselves through a private contract from the costs of their partner's decision to stay at home.[335]

However, not only the state, but also the children could suffer from certain agreements concluded by spouses as for example those aimed at eliminating maintenance in favor of any of them after the dissolution of a marriage.[336] In situations in which individuals have no right to compensation for a premature termination of a marriage, one spouse may use common children as a means to push for a better position in the negotiations, to get the payment of "voluntary" compensation or even to assure the continuation of the marriage. The non-enforcement of agreements by which a spouse waives the possibility to receive maintenance payments in the future – or a compensatory allowance after the divorce – can be seen as a way to avoid cases in which, as a matter of necessity, the person who has expended more time in the household uses the children as bargaining chip to assure the coverage of personal needs. Such a limitation on the party autonomy of spouses could be seen as a means to avoid situations that jeopardize the well-being of the children, or in economic terms, the potential generation of negative externalities in third parties.

1.2. ASYMMETRIC INFORMATION AS A LIMIT ON SPOUSES' FREEDOM OF CHOICE

The law might also prevent the enforcement of contracts when a lack of information affects the interests of the parties negatively. That occurs particularly when one party knows much more than the other and this person tries to exploit this imbalance in the negotiations. Mandatory rules can impose a positive duty to disclose specific information or perform certain actions to guarantee informed decisions about the features of the exchanged assets and the risks of the contract.[337] Rules requiring a medical certificate before the celebration

334 See for example Art. 122 para. 1 Swiss Civil Code: "Where one of the spouses or both spouses belong to a professional pension scheme for old age, survivors and disabled persons, and if neither of the spouses has become a recipient of contributions from such a professional pension scheme, each spouse has a claim to one half of the assets of the other spouse, calculated for the duration of their marriage, according to the provisions of the Federal Statute on Free Movement of 17 December 1993. Where the spouses have mutual claims, only the difference is to be divided."

335 *Ibid.*

336 Kronman (1985) 21; Cohen (2002) 27.

337 Cooter & Ulen (2016) 297.

of a marriage[338] or the presence of a notary for the conclusion of marital agreements are examples of imperative rules assuring legally informed decisions.[339] Notwithstanding, although it is desirable that people are informed about the consequences of their actions, not every rule should be made imperative just because it encourages them to make more informed decisions. Restrictions on party autonomy always entail costs for the people concerned. Visiting a notary – for example – will surely make people more aware of the legal effects of a contract. However, notaries do not work for free. Mandating their presence for any agreement between spouses could be counterproductive, as that could prevent spouses – in real life – from organizing their relationship according to what they deem appropriate.

1.2.1. Failures Caused by Asymmetric Information

The problems from a lack of information were well illustrated by the parable of the market for lemons in a seminal paper written by the economist George Akerlof,[340] published in the early seventies.[341] In this essay, he explained that in regular markets consumers acquire information about goods and services before purchasing them. In many transactions, the quality of the goods or services could be known by simple observations. In other cases, however, the quality of the goods – referred to as "experience goods" – will only become evident with their ordinary and repeated usage. By purchasing "experience goods", people can gain knowledge of the characteristics of their product, but only after they have paid for and then used it.[342] In situations in which there is no mechanism that transmits information about the quality of a product, buyers will tend to value good or bad products equally, since they cannot discriminate between them. As a consequence, sellers will refrain from offering high-quality products due to the low price they would receive for these goods. According to Akerlof, this dynamic – which it is provoked by the lack of information – may produce a race to the bottom, since the existence of bad products may make the sale of good ones difficult. In the worst case, low-quality products may ultimately drive out high-quality ones from the market.[343] Although it is not explicitly mentioned in Akerlof's paper, it follows that there is a potential role for the state to correct

---

338 See for example Art. 98.IV Mexican Federal Civil Code.

339 Arruñada (1996) 9. For a historical overview of the role played by notaries in France to resolve problems of asymmetric information see: Hoffman et al. (1998).

340 A lemon is a term used in colloquial speech to describe an unreliable used car, prone to break down soon after being purchased; often having been superficially repaired to hide structural flaws. The opposite, an actually good used car, is called a peach.

341 Akerlof (1970).

342 Mackaay (2013) 417–418.

343 Magat (1998) 308.

such a failure by means of imposing legal rules that oblige one or both of the parties to disclose information.[344]

1.2.2. Asymmetric Information in Marriage

In the specific case of marriage, problems caused by a lack of information certainly exist. Grooms resemble "experience goods", in the sense that it is not possible to determine either their future level of engagement in the relationship or the extent of their investments into the marriage. By getting married, people run two big risks: adverse selection and moral hazard.[345] The first refers to a lack of information about the real intentions and plans of their partner at the moment of celebrating the wedding. A marriage proposal could be driven by the need of a residence permit or only by the youthful – and ephemeral – beauty of the partner, rather than by their sincere desire for building a family and create a lifelong project.[346] The second risk – moral hazard – concerns the difficulty to predict whether the behavior of the partner after the conclusion of the marriage will match the challenge of having a family.[347] It may occur, for example, that once the marriage is celebrated, one of the spouses loses interest in undertaking an economic activity, since they know that they will be supported economically by the other. In the same vein, it could also happen that after children arrive, one still behaves as if they had no responsibilities, since he or she knows that the other will do all the child-rearing.

In the case of marriage, however, problems related to the lack of information are significantly reduced due to the fact that people – in particular in Western countries – usually experience long periods of courtship and engagement before deciding to get married.[348] This custom lets prospective spouses discover the real intentions and capabilities of the other party. The period of time during which individuals are dating or cohabitating could be understood as a bargaining phase, where both of them acquire mutual knowledge of personal characteristics of each other. In this time, they have to actually decide if it is worth forming a joint venture[349] with the

344 For an economic justification of rules protecting consumers based on the problem demonstrated by Akerlof's "lemons" see: Stuart (1981).

345 Zelder (2002) 158–160. For a more accurate definition of concepts like experience goods, adverse selection and moral hazard see: Spence (1973); Magat (1998); Cooter & Ulen (2016) 48–49.

346 Zelder (2002) 158.

347 Walther (2017) 358.

348 For data about the duration of courtship before marriage in North America, with special emphasis on individuals who had already been married, see: O'Flaherty & Workman Eells (1988) 501–504.

349 In legal jargon the term *joint venture* refers to a business entity created by two or more parties, generally characterized by shared ownership, shared returns and risks, and shared governance. Here this term is used in a more broad sense.

other person.[350] During this phase, they not only get to know the personal preferences and needs of their potential partner; more importantly, they have the opportunity to see the capacity of the other to accommodate their behavior to changing environments, as well as to have a better awareness of personal attributes and skills of their potential partner. The function of courtship or engagement time, from an economic perspective, resembles a trial period or a free sample offered by a business in regular markets. It serves as a test of important qualities like companionship, fidelity, professional ambitions, sexual performance[351] etc. Thanks to this mechanism, people can get a better idea of the actual suitability of their partners to support a long-term relationship.[352]

In general, modern practices such as living together or long periods of courtship are better suited to avoid problems of adverse selection or moral hazard. However, in some jurisdictions vestiges of legal rules that are a reminder of a time when appropriate practices to combat asymmetry of information were not available can still be found. Some jurisdictions still require the taking of a blood test as a condition of celebrating marriage, in order to avoid the transmission of venereal diseases after the conclusion of a marriage.[353] There is no doubt that in the past such a rule made sense from an economic perspective, since it obliged the spouses to disclose information that was difficult to gather before the wedding night. Currently such a requirement might not be of great help to resolve damage arising from the asymmetry of information, as in general couples have intercourse or even cohabit together before their marriage.[354]

---

350 According to a study, 85% of Americans report having experienced at least one non-marital breakup after a serious relationship with another person before getting married. See: DeLecce (2018) 265.

351 This idea applies not only to modern Western societies. In fact, about two-thirds of tribal societies do not restrict premarital sex. Weisfeld & Weisfeld (2018) 11.

352 Some measures taken by governments might lead individuals to reduce their period of courtship and so increase the probability of a failed marriage. Most countries, for example, require the celebration of marriage to allow certain foreigners to move to the country of origin of their partner. The law so indirectly pushes individuals to bypass the period of courtship. It is then no surprise that the rates of divorce tend to be higher between partners of different nationalities as they might have less time to get to know each other. A temporary residence permit before a marriage would resolve these problems.

353 The Mexican Federal Civil Code goes even much further: a certificate signed by a qualified physician who assures that they do not suffer from syphilis, tuberculosis, or any other chronic and incurable disease that might be contagious or hereditary must be sent to the judge responsible for the civil registry. See Art. 98.IV Mexican Federal Civil Code.

354 Concerning Art. 98.IV Mexican Federal Civil Code: a study conducted in 2006 in Mexico showed, that the median age for women of their first sexual intercourse is 19.3 years, and the median age of their first marriage is 22.3 years. In this context the medical certificate requirement would not help to prevent disease transmission; it would however inform them of the fact that they already have a disease. See: Juárez et al. (2010) 11.

In some countries, where cohabitation is not an option and people marry at an early age, the law requires the presence of a legal guardian,[355] whose expertise helps prospective spouses to make an informed decision about the characteristics of their partner and the contents of the obligations in their marital contract. Rules that encourage endogamy and push young people to marry individuals of the same religion or ethnicity assure that they know the family of the prospective spouse, and have an idea of the principles, traditions and beliefs under which their future partner was raised. All those measures can be understood as a means to combat problems from asymmetric information in the context of a marriage.[356] In Islamic marriage law, the *wali* – the legal representative of the spouses[357] – has an equivalent economic function in the marriage dynamic. He has a very similar role to that of a stockbroker in stock markets: the *wali* must care for the interests of his client, by assessing accurately the risks of an investment under uncertainty. His function is to combat problems of asymmetric information in the context of a marriage.[358] In an environment where it is not even possible to have moderate periods of courtship, relying on the services of an adviser can be of great help for the spouses. Indeed, the presence of a *wali* – at least for women – is mandatory in many Arabic countries.[359] Societies where cohabitation is socially accepted, or the marriage is preceded by a long-term romantic relationship, rarely rely on mandatory rules to combat asymmetry of information about personal attributes of the partners. If they exist, these rules are rather there to assure that people gain knowledge about the contents of laws and are aware of the legal effects of their actions. Not only the presence of a notary to alert the parties to relevant changes in the system of matrimonial property, but also the requirement of celebrating the marriage before an authority – whose task is precisely reading out the rights and duties arising from a marriage – are measures to guarantee informed decisions.

In sum, the appropriateness of imperative rules combatting asymmetric information depends on the reality and time where they are applied. The practices and traditions in a society determine the suitability of mandatory legal provisions aimed at disclosing information. Local factors will finally

355 Arshad (2010) 49–50.

356 For the use of intermediaries as a strategy to overcome asymmetry of information between contractual partners in France in the 18th century, see: Hoffman et al. (1998) 499, 526.

357 For the different kinds of guardianship existing for Muslim marriages, see: Arshad (2010) 49–50.

358 This relationship is here analyzed in terms of principal-agent literature. See: Zelder (2002) 160.

359 Arshad (2010) 50.

determine their efficiency – that is, if they actually encourage cooperation between spouses.[360]

1.3. DECISION-MAKING CONSTRAINTS AS A REASON FOR LIMITS ON SPOUSES' FREEDOM OF CHOICE

The defense of the freedom of choice is based on the idea that it – in most cases – generates benefits for those who use it. But if this freedom in particular circumstances leads to an inappropriate allocation of resources and causes damage to the involved individuals, it should be restricted. Supporting blindly a *laissez faire, laissez passer* stance would discourage people from performing exchanges and encourage some to take advantage of other people's errors to obtain gains, which in turn would diminish the general willingness to make exchanges.[361] In those cases, limits on the freedom of choice are not only advisable, but necessary to avoid a race to the bottom; that is, a negative spiral that sooner or later ends up affecting the correct functioning of the whole system.[362]

1.3.1. Age and Disorders Affecting a Person's Judgement

The realization of transactions only leads to the betterment of the situation if parties are capable of acting rationally when deciding to assume an obligation.[363] They should be capable of ranking the expected outcomes from the least preferred to the most preferred, and then choosing the best one.[364] They must also take into consideration the present and future costs of their decisions.[365] Lacking these minimal skills will hamper an allocation of resources in the terms explained above. Constraints imposed on people based on their age or serious mental

---

360 Throughout this book the term efficient rules refers to legal provisions – or any other legal measure taken by governments – that facilitate the emergence of cooperative dynamics between people. Legal provisions that eliminate barriers to the conclusion of contracts – or any other kind of voluntary agreement – are regarded as efficient as they – contracts – are the typical means used to depict the terms in which such dynamics will be carried out. This is based on the idea that the constant conclusions of voluntary agreements between people – i.e. the engagement in cooperative dynamics – allows the existing resources to end up in the hands of those that value them the most. See: Chapter 1 Section 1.1 and Section 1.2. *in fine*.

361 See: Stucke (2013) 173. See also: Demsetz (1969) 1 et seqq.; Schäfer & Ott (2005a) 82.

362 See: Stucke (2013) 173.

363 Posner R. (2014) 3.

364 Individuals must have transitive preferences and seek to maximize their utility: "If some good or bundle of goods denoted A is preferred to another good or bundle of goods denoted B and B is preferred to a third good or bundle of goods denoted C, then it must be the case that A is preferred to C". See: Ulen (2000) 792. See also: Craswell (1992) 807.

365 Schäfer & Ott (2005a) 59–60.

disability are aimed at avoiding situations where there is a clear risk that these minimal skills are not present.[366] These people are prevented from marrying as it is assumed that they are not able to take decisions rationally. In general, their preferences are not stable enough, and they are not able to weigh the – present and future – costs of being in a long-term relationship appropriately, so the law restricts their freedom of choice.[367]

The adequacy of this measure is not based on the fact that no minor – or person affected by a severe mental illness – is actually able to take decisions on their own. There are cases of teenagers with a high degree maturity that are perfectly capable of weighing the risks and benefits of their choices. However, in general, most of them are not able to ponder accurately the consequences of important decisions like getting married when they are 14 or 15 years old. Imposing a minimal marriageable age assumes that the benefits of this restriction – in terms of what it would mean for the administration of justice to conduct a case-by-case analysis – outweigh the costs to all those that are in fact mature enough to understand the consequences of their actions. The costs imposed are not too high: mature teenagers that want to marry are only compelled to the wait for a time – in general the time needed to reach the full age – to see their wishes fulfilled.

1.3.2. Dire Circumstances Provoked by One of the Parties

Think for example of the case of two individuals: Maria Elżbieta and João. Both of them got married, believing that matrimony is the best way to improve their situation. If, shortly after the wedding, Maria Elżbieta desires to dissolve the union and the law imposes a waiting period of three years to initiate a contested divorce proceeding, she must wait that long if João does not agree with an immediate dissolution of the relationship. But, what if the motive that drove Maria Elżbieta to accept the proposal in the first place was the promise by João not to harm her family? Should she be obligated – from an economic point of view – to bear the consequences of a premature termination of their relationship? Should a marriage be valid if it was motivated by blackmail or threats?[368]

The answer is obviously no. Regardless of the moral perspective, there are economic reasons to disregard marriages – and in general any contract – concluded under these circumstances.[369] First, those agreements do not

366 Ulen (2000) 798.

367 Cooter & Ulen (2016) 295; Kronman (1983) 786; Trebilcock (1997) 150.

368 In fact, establishing a clear difference between threats and offers is by no means easy. Threats reduce the possibilities open to the recipient of a proposal, whereas offers expand them. Threats are then coercive, while offers are not. For a discussion about the difference between both concepts and its implications in the economic analysis of the law see in detail: Trebilcock (1997) 79–84; Cserne (2011) 65, et seqq.

369 Cooter & Ulen (2016) 295, 347–349; Scott & Scott (1999) 214.

create wealth from the point of view of the society as a whole, but a mere redistribution of assets between two persons. The freedom of choice is guaranteed because the realization of voluntary exchanges creates a surplus for both parties.[370] In the case of blackmail or threats, there are no mutual gains, but one side simply benefits at the expense of the other. The initial situation of the counterpart does not improve; it just avoids a harm that will not be compensated if the offer is rejected. Enforcing promises in these situations would endorse threats – that is, a kind of negative externality – as a strategy to make profit.[371] Second, although contracts made under dire constraints can sometimes accidentally generate a benefit for both parties, enforcing such contracts could create perverse incentives. Some individuals could invest resources to become professionals in extortion or specialize in seeking out others that suffer from some sort of impaired judgement. Such a specialization would lead to a reduction of any benefit obtained randomly, and in the long run create a dynamic of zero-sum games without any improvement in welfare from an aggregate perspective. Allowing these acts would lead to a downward spiral that lowers the social product by channeling resources into making threats, searching for incompetent people and developing protective measures against them. This situation would represent a waste from a utilitarian standpoint, while at the same time undermining the functioning of the allocation system, as fewer people would be motivated to use the market – the conclusion of voluntary agreements – as a mechanism to satisfy their needs.[372]

Marriages celebrated under dire circumstances should be unenforceable, even if the exploited party does not agree with the invalidity of their marriage. The contrary would encourage aggressors to perform undue acts, as their actions would be validated by the law. By making the victim entirely financially and emotionally dependent, it would not be difficult to obtain consent in the future. The restriction imposed on the freedom of choice of the victim – no validation *a posteriori* even with their consent – is founded on the downwards spiral that tolerating such situations would cause for the whole group. That, however, must not affect the rights of the victims to demand compensation from the aggressor. Together with the corresponding penal sanctions, the application of the legal concept of putative marriage can help mitigate harms caused.

---

370 See Chapter 1 Section 1.2.

371 Stucke (2013) 174. See also Cserne (2011) 65–66; Mackaay (2013) 461. For a discussion about the difference between coercion and offers from a law and economics perspective, see: Cserne (2011); Kronman (1980).

372 Doing so would only give an incentive to spend more on fraud protection – a deadweight loss from society's point of view. Kronman (1983) 767; Posner R. (2014) 119, 123; Friedman (2000) 152. In detail see: Cserne (2011).

1.4. MONOPOLISTIC POSITION AS A LIMIT ON SPOUSES' FREEDOM OF CHOICE

Whereas in a competitive situation prices are "controlled" by the market, as potential buyers are able to find substitutive products when a good is overpriced, in a monopolistic one the consumers do not have this option due to barriers barring the entry of competitors. The lack of alternatives forces people to consume products regardless of whether the price exceeds by far the good's costs of production. This ultimately leads to a deadweight loss, that is, a level of production below the one the society needs.[373] Furthermore, in this context, suppliers have no incentive to innovate and offer better quality goods as they know that whatever happens, their products will always be sold – monopolistic markets let suppliers *rest on their laurels*.[374] One type of restriction on the party autonomy of spouses can be explained as a mechanism to deal with these kind of failures in the system. The non-enforcement of marriages celebrated under extreme conditions and the invalidity of spousal agreements aimed at eliminating the possibility to get divorced avoid a monopolistic position in the "market for spouses".

1.4.1. Dire Constraints not Provoked by One of the Parties

Imagine the case of a woman – Myriam Elisheva – who in a cold winter night runs out of gas in a lonely place next to a miners' camp after dining with some friends in a nearby restaurant far away from her home. The temperature outside is −10 °C and she is in the company of her 11-year-old son. Someone knocks on the car window, and offers her 5 liters of gas for 50,000 €. In the face of certain death, she accepts the terms of the transaction; however, the next day she goes to the court to invalidate this contract.

Civil legal systems apply the doctrine of *laesio* – lesion[375] – to allow parties to rescind, resolve or request the invalidity[376] of contracts concluded under

---

373 Depoorter (2010) 501; Mankiw (2012) 310–313; Posner (2014) 336.

374 See: Cooter & Ulen (2016) 363; Mackaay (2013) 142–143; Posner R. (2014) 342.

375 See for example Art. 1406 of the Civil Code of Quebec which contains a definition of lesion.

376 The specific remedy depends on the domestic law applicable to the case. For example, according to Art. 1407 of the Civil Code of Quebec: "A person whose consent is vitiated has the right to apply for annulment of the contract; in the case of error occasioned by fraud, of fear or of lesion, he may, in addition to annulment, also claim damages or, where he prefers that the contract be maintained, apply for a reduction of his obligation equivalent to the damages he would be justified in claiming". French law does not provide for the invalidity, but for the rescission of the contract. According to Art. 1681 of the French Civil Code purchasers can even opt to pay the balance of the fair price in order to avoid the rescission of the contract: "In the case where the action for rescission is entertained, the purchaser has the choice, either to return the thing while taking back the price which he paid for it, or to keep the tenement while paying the balance of the fair price, after deducting one-tenth of the total price. A third party in possession has the same right, save his warranty against his seller".

such circumstances.[377] This doctrine is not only a moral imperative, but has also an economic *rationale*, as it avoids price-fixing that exceeds the costs of production massively due to a lack of competitors offering substitutive products. This way the law avoids that people are discouraged from performing economic activities – in this case traveling, dining in a restaurant, spending time with friends, etc. – due to risks – an engine failure, multiple flat tires, etc. – that are difficult to predict. The unenforceability of contracts concluded in such contexts also discourages individuals from searching for situations where they can ask for exorbitant prices, not because of the quality of their products, but simply as a consequence of the lack of competitors – i.e. their monopolistic position.[378] In those situation courts should – from an economic perspective – intervene by modifying the price.[379]

Arrangements between spouses celebrated under dire circumstances could also be rejected by courts based on the same arguments. If it is demonstrated that the consent was given in a state of despair – e.g. religious persecution, a natural catastrophe – as no other options were available to avoid an evil with incommensurable consequences, a marital agreement – or even marriage – must not be enforceable.

1.4.2. Non-Enforceability of Agreements Preventing a Spouse from Requesting a Divorce

Freedom of choice is the corner-stone on which private law – and by extension marriage law – is built from an economic view. Based on this, one could conclude that, if two individuals agree on banning the possibility to get divorced in the future, this contract should be necessarily enforced. However, this reasoning is flawed because such an agreement might create a dominant position in the market of spouses, inasmuch as it gives a spouse a veto power affecting not only their counterpart, but also other individuals.[380] Let us look at an example to make this idea clearer.

> After hearing the advice of their priest Marie Isabelle and Jean – a young couple – agree on the indissolubility of their marriage unless both of them consent. Over time,

---

377 An equivalent – but not equal – doctrine is applied in common law countries under the name unconscionability. For similarities and differences between them, as well as an explanation in English about the regulation of this legal concept in civil and common law countries: Browne & Biksacky (2013) 240 et seqq.

378 Cserne (2011) 64; Cooter & Ulen (2016) 298, 347–349; Mackaay (2013) 462–463.

379 Prohibiting any price increase in situations of shortage – e.g. gasoline after a hurricane – is, however, counterproductive, as this would discourage sellers from making an effort to supply products under difficult circumstances. See: Posner R. (2014) 128.

380 Paternalism can also be used as ground for the non-enforcement of contracts that stop one spouse from initiating a divorce; the spouses are thus protected by law from contracting away to great a part of their personal liberty. It was also affirmed that the economic reason for the

Jean feels, despite every effort, that there is something missing in his wife. One day he meets Roberto Ricardo who – after the best two weeks of Jean's whole life – asks to marry him.

As the conclusion of a second marriage depends entirely on the willingness of Marie Isabelle to divorce, she has the opportunity to make demands that exceed the costs of the termination of the relationship. The enforceability of the contract would permit her to exploit the willingness of Jean to pay her compensation to the maximum – in terms of time, money or any other resource – which will also affect Roberto Ricardo, as it will diminish the capacity of Jean to invest in the new relationship. The conclusion of a contract banning the possibility to unilaterally request a divorce creates a monopoly from the perspective of Roberto Ricardo, as it allows a third person – Marie Isabelle – to fix the price of his preferred option at her whim.

Against this reasoning one could argue that the contract must be enforced anyway because Roberto Ricardo has – in same way as consumers in regular markets – the freedom to find someone else if he thinks the costs are too high. However, the situation of prospective spouses differs from consumers in regular markets, due to the difficulties of actually finding the fitting partner. At first glance one could assume that – at least in Western countries – the "market for spouses" is highly developed, due to the ease with which people interact with each other. However, finding a spouse is by no means easy, because it is a "barter market": people not only face the daunting task of finding a person to whom they are willing to promise a lifelong conjugal relationship, but this person must also make the reciprocal promise to them.[381] Whereas in regular markets exchanges are easy, due to the medium of money, in the case of marriage, each candidate is obliged to find a trading partner who fits their expectations and in turn is interested in them. Economists call this situation double coincidence of wants,[382] a requirement – a transaction cost – individuals face in barter markets when carrying out an exchange.[383] In real life the situation of prospective spouses is therefore more complicated than that of consumers. Although there are many single individuals in the marriage market, most of them are not close substitutes for one another. The double coincidence of wants significantly reduces the number of options at their disposal. Individuals cannot simply look for another person once they have found their soulmate, because most likely no substitute exists that meets

invalidity of such contracts is the same as that behind the non-enforcement of contracts by which one party agrees to be the slave of another in return for food, shelter or education See: Kronman (1983) 764, 775, 777–778.

381 Cohen (2002) 18.

382 Jevons (1893) 3.

383 For issues arising from double coincidence of wants in markets lacking a medium of exchange like money, see: Ostroy & Starr (1990) 26.

their preferences, and who at the same time is ready to be with them. In such a context, it is counterproductive to allow individuals to eliminate unilateral divorce, because it reduces the supply and creates a dominant position due to the lack of substitutive "products" in the market.[384]

Finally, it should be noted that the non-enforceability of agreements preventing the divorce not only avoids a shortage in the "market of spouses";[385] it also prevents individuals from *resting on their laurels* once they have found their partner, as the possibility of divorce introduces a competitive element to the relationship. The threat of a unilateral divorce fosters further investments in the relationship even after the conclusion of the marriage. By leaving the door open to a one-sided termination, partners are encouraged to innovate and give their best to keep the "flame burning" in their marriage.

2. RULES GOVERNING THE RELATIONSHIP IN ABSENCE OF AGREEMENT BETWEEN SPOUSES

The economic analysis of the law assumes that the objective of individuals concluding a contract is not only determining what the tasks assumed by each of them are, and specifying the payments or benefits received in exchange for the performance of these tasks; it also surmises that people expect that further disputes will be resolved, even if they have not set out a specific solution for them. Default rules fulfill this objective. They allocate potential risks surrounding the realization of a transaction, and so clarify which party should bear or avoid the consequences of the occurrence – or non-occurrence – of events affecting the normal unfolding of the relationship.[386] The task of default rules – from

384 It should be noted that economic theory does not entirely reject monopolies. In intellectual property law, for example, inventors are rewarded with the exclusive right to exploit their inventions during a period of time. The idea is to encourage them to take risks by assuring them exclusivity during a time span. The existence of waiting periods in the context of unilateral divorces can be compared with the time-limited monopoly given to inventors, as this obligation also assures exclusivity – a temporary veto right – that can be used to obtain benefits. In fact, marriage can be seen as tool to create a temporary monopoly between two individuals. See: Friedman (2000) 172.

385 Contrary to the position defended here, others argue that the power to make an enforceable promise of this sort – waiving the right to ask for a divorce – might facilitate the communication of information regarding the promisor's sincerity and future intentions. It was even suggested that a ban on such agreements makes this communication more difficult and may even exclude some candidates from the marriage market altogether. These authors conclude that paternalism is the reason for banning contracts that prohibit the initiation of a divorce proceeding unilaterally. See: Kronman (1983) 776, et seqq.

386 Dnes (2018) 102–103. See also: Cooter & Ulen (2016) 292–293; Craswell (2000) 1; Haro (2004) 185; Posner R. & Rosenfield (1977) 88.

an economic perspective – is to offer "backup" solutions for unforeseeable contingencies during the relationship.[387]

2.1. DEFAULT RULES IN CONTRACT LAW

Think, for example, of a contract concluded between a farmer and a firm, where the former delivers potatoes at the end of the season. In order to assure the benefits generated by the relationship, it is not enough to only agree on the quantity and the price. It is also necessary to provide answers to questions about: the place of delivery; who must pay the shipping costs; if there is interest to pay in case of payment default; what the standard of care is; and many other issues related directly and indirectly to the transaction. It would be ideal if the parties arrived at a bespoke solution by themselves right at the beginning, and so resolve any questions or problems that might arise before, during and after the performance of the contract. However, one cannot expect that people actually do that, due the practical difficulties of envisaging a specific answer for every possible circumstance of the future. Default rules offer remedies for all those situations where individuals were not able, were not willing, or simply forgot to provide a remedy for a contingency.[388] These provisions are of the utmost importance, as they avoid spending time and resources on imagining all sorts of obstacles, that in some far-fetched way might affect the performance of the contract negatively, and on coming up with a specific solution for those scenarios.[389] Both figuring out and negotiating are not only costly and cumbersome, but also unattainable due to the infinite number of contingencies that could affect the performance of a contract. By providing rules that resolve controversies in a specific and predictable way, the legal system provides security and instills confidence in the parties, so that they know that whatever happens, there is always a solution for potential disputes even if they have not expressly planned for those cases.

---

387 According to Craswell "The law could simply refuse to enforce any contract that does not provide all the answers about how it should be performed. However, such a solution would itself be a 'default rule': it would be a legal rule defining the obligations (or lack of obligations) that must be used when a contract does not itself specify what rules should govern. As long as actual contracts fall short of full completeness, default rules are not so much a choice but a logical necessity". See Craswell (2000) 2.

388 Ayres & Gertner (1989) 93; Cooter & Ulen (2016) 293; Coleman et al. (1989) 640, 673; Schäfer & Ott (2012) 433; Whincop & Keynes (2001) 34.

389 Craswell (2000) 4; Whincop & Keynes (2001) 34–35.

2.2. DEFAULT RULES IN MARRIAGE LAW

Marriage law does not seek to put pressure on people to formalize their romantic relationships; it simply facilitates the legal union for all those that freely and voluntarily desire a closer and stronger bond with their partner. In order to achieve this goal, marriage law – in the same way as contract law – should fill lacunas left by the spouses about the exact way in which their duties – those agreed on by them and those imposed by mandatory rules[390] – have to be carried out practically. By providing solutions for contingencies happening throughout their relationship, the law makes spouses feel confident to invest more in the relationship and so obtain greater gains from the joint work with their partner.[391]

2.2.1. Majoritarian will of the Parties as the Default Rule

In economics, there are different opinions about how law-makers should fill gaps in contracts.[392] The most widely accepted one is to use the rule that most individuals would choose if they could contract in a costless way.[393] Legal provisions following this logic are known as majoritarian default rules. According to this approach, gap-filling rules should mirror what the majority of individuals would agree on if they had negotiated over that specific issue. They reflect the hypothetical will of the parties; that is, the solution at which they would have arrived if they had expressly bargained over that issue at the moment of the contract's conclusion.[394] As these provisions reflect the

390 The payment of a periodic maintenance obligation to a partner in need could be regulated by a mandatory rule. However, whether such an obligation has to be paid monthly, weekly or annually might be subject to a default rule, such as for example: "in absence of an agreement the payments should be delivered at the end of the month". The performance of mandatory rules could – to some extent – then be subject to default rules, providing that spouses have a certain margin of discretion in the way they must be executed.

391 Scott & Scott (1998) 1306.

392 For a brief summary see: Craswell (2000) 2 et seqq. See also: Posner R. (2005) 1596 et seqq.

393 Ayres (1998) 586. See also: Cohen G. (2000) 82; Coleman et al. (1989) 641; Posner E. (2005) 585; Posner R. (2005) 1585; Posner R. & Rosenfield (1977) 88; Scott & Scott (1998) 1306; Schäfer & Ott (2012) 455–457; Veljanovski (2007) 123. For some caveats to this assertion see: Craswell (1992) 808, 815 et seqq. Some default rules might, however, be designed to create incentives in the parties to negotiate a specific solution for a given contingency. For the concept of penalty rules, see: Ayres & Gertner (1989) 90, 97. The actual existence of penalty default rules in modern legal systems is, however, controversial. See: Posner E. (2005); Whincop & Keynes (2001) 36.

394 A similar view can be found in a text written by Jeremy Bentham more than 150 years ago: "[O]bligations may be distinguished into original and adjective. I call those original, of which express mention is made in the contract itself: I call those adjective, which the law thinks proper to add to the first. The first turn upon events which the contracting parties have foreseen; the others upon events which they could not foresee. [...] It is thus that in

preferences of most members of a society, majoritarian default rules will also minimize the costs of negotiations in the whole society, as individuals would spend less time and other resources on thinking of designing solutions for any event that could prevent achieving their goals.[395] In general, efficient legal systems are those with default rules that are rarely overridden by the parties, as this means they are fulfilling their task of minimizing costs of transactions from an aggregate perspective.[396] Contrarily, if individuals constantly contractually override the default rules, it must be interpreted as a signal that it is time to make adjustments in the law.[397]

2.2.2. Silence as a Default Rule

One should not think that efficient legal systems must contain an exact solution for any issue that could arise between spouses. As the preferences of spouses might dramatically change over time, sometimes it is advisable to abstain from intervening, to encourage spouses to find a rule that fits their preferences and needs at the precise moment when a certain contingency appears. As noted before, marriage is much more than a body of legal rules. Spouses have not only legal mechanisms, but also extralegal ones at their disposal to assign responsibilities between them and so reach a cooperative equilibrium without the need of judicial intervention. Thus, when the law refuses to provide a default solution for a specific dispute between spouses – e.g. which partner has the last word if they are not able to decide on the marital domicile – we must not automatically infer that the legal system is deficient. The rationale behind this gap could rather be the assumption that the majority would prefer to resolve this issue by themselves instead of resorting to a court.[398]

---

every country the law has supplied the short-sightedness of individuals, by doing for them what they would have done for themselves, if their imagination had anticipated the march of nature." See: Bentham (1843) 191–192.

395 Ayres (1998) 586; Kronman (1983) 766 *in fine*; Posner R. & Rosenfield (1977) 89; Posner R. (2005) 1583; Scott R. (1990) 607; Scott & Scott (1998) 1300.

396 Empirical evidence has, however, shown that individuals tend to value certain rights more simply because they already have them. This tendency might then lead individuals to prefer the application of a default rule not necessarily because it corresponds to their preferences, but just because their familiar legal system would apply this rule in the absence of an agreement. This phenomenon is called the endowment effect or *status quo* bias. For its implications and relevance in legal analysis, see: Korobkin (2002). For the endowment effect and other cognitive biases to be considered when drafting mandatory and default rules, see: Sunstein (2000).

397 Posner R. (2014) 99; Scott & Scott (1998) 1251.

398 This solution seems "appropriate when it is cheaper for the parties to negotiate a term ex ante than for the courts to estimate ex post what the parties would have wanted". See: Ayres & Gertner (1989) 93.

2.3. THE CHEAPEST-COST-AVOIDER PRINCIPLE

As was explained before, agreements of any kind generate a surplus that will be divided between the partners.[399] The higher this surplus is, the better for the parties, as it means an increase of the gains for each side.[400] Based on that, one can assume that the preferred default rules are those that – at the moment of the conclusion of the contract – would have increased the surplus of the contract the most.[401] As individuals seek to maximize the benefits from their contracts, these rules would naturally avoid that parties have to negotiate a bespoke solution for the exchange.[402]

Law and economics scholars have developed a criterion that addresses this objective. It is known as the "cheapest-cost-avoider" and applies to situations where it is necessary to assign responsibilities for events affecting the expectations of individuals involved in a legal relationship negatively.[403] This criterion stipulates that the party which could have averted or mitigated the occurrence of an undesirable contingency at the lowest cost should be the one to prevent it.[404] The idea is to encourage the individual who can control a risk more easily – e.g. because this person is better informed about the probability of a risk – to take the necessary precautions and avoid the undesirable situation.[405] This contractual party will only be liable as long as the potential damage is reasonably avoidable: for liability to occur the costs of preventing or mitigating the undesirable event should thus be lower than the benefits obtained from its avoidance.[406]

2.3.1. Efficiency of Default Rules Following the Cheapest-Cost-Avoider

The suitability of rules following the cheapest-cost-avoider can be appreciated from two perspectives: From the point of view of society as a whole, these rules

---

399 The surplus is the sum of the gains obtained by each party as a consequence of the realization of a contract. See Chapter 1 in this book.

400 See Chapter 1 Section 1.2.

401 See: Scott R. (1990) 602.

402 Cohen G. (2000) 83; Posner R. (2005) 1588; Posner R. & Rosenfield (1977) 89.

403 This criterion is also called the "cheapest-cost-bearer", "cheapest-risk-bearer" or "least-cost-avoider". Following the terminology used by Guido Calabresi in the analysis of the rules of tort law – Calabresi (1970) – the term "cheapest-cost-avoider" will be used hereinafter. Although this concept is usually employed as a point of departure for allocating responsibilities in contract law, it was first conceived as a method to determine liability in tort law. For an in-depth analysis of the economic implications of the cheapest-cost-avoider, see in detail: Gilles (1992).

404 Provided that – as it occurs in most real-world situations – transaction costs prevent a Coasian bargaining. See: Demsetz (1972) 25–26. The meaning of Coasian bargaining and its implication in the design of default rules will later be discussed in Chapter 8.

405 De Geest et al. (2002) 167; Garcimartín (2002) 134–135; Demsetz (1972) 27; Posner R. & Rosenfield (1977) 91.

406 Schmidtchen et al. (2007) 76. See also: Friedman (2000) 162; Garcimartín (2002) 136.

require fewer resources to resolve conflicts between its members. If avoiding an undesirable event would cost 20 € for one party and 50 € for the other, allocating accountability according to the cheapest-cost-avoider means saving 30 €. These savings could then be used to make further investments in other transactions with the same or other partners. Economic resources will not be wasted, but rather used for the satisfaction of further needs. From the perspective of the parties, the cheapest-cost-avoider is also advantageous, as the relationship will create more profits not only for one, but for both parties so that each of them will be willing to offer more to the other in order to reach an agreement. Let us look at an example to better understand this idea:

Suppose a photographer values one of his pictures at 100 €, while another – a potential buyer – values it at 200 €. If they meet and have the opportunity to talk about the picture, it is very probable that a transaction between them will come about. As explained before,[407] the final price of the object will depend on their negotiating skills. In order to facilitate the calculations,[408] let's say that both are equally skilled negotiators and consequently – *ceteris paribus* – they agree on 150 € as the purchase price (= [200 + 100] / 2). Assume now, that the prevention of a certain risk will cost 20 € for the seller and 50 € for the buyer. Now, who should assume these costs?

Allocating the prevention costs to the buyer would reduce the gains from the contract in comparison with the alternative solution. As explained in Chapter 1, the gains are the difference between the price agreed on by the parties and the subjective appraisal of the exchanged asset according to the personal needs and preferences of each of them.[409] Thus, if the buyer values the picture at 200 € and pays 150 € in the end, he would gain 50 €, but if he has to invest 50 € to avoid the risk – because he is regarded as liable for the occurrence of this event – the subjective value of the picture is not 200 € anymore, but rather 150 € (200 – 50). He must deduct from his original value the cost he has to pay for the prevention of the contingency. After the negotiation, the final price would be 125 € (= [150 + 100] / 2). The equal gains for each party would be down to 25 € (= [150 – 100] / 2). Contrarily, if the risk is allocated to the seller – the cheapest-cost-avoider – the gains for both would be higher. The picture's subjective value for the seller is higher, as he has to add 20 € to his original subjective value to avoid the risk. However, the new equilibrium is preferable to the previous one, since the gains for each of them will be greater. On the basis that the seller's subjective value is now 120 € (100 + 20), the gains for each of them will be 40 € (= [200 – 120] / 2). Thus, even though the resulting price will be

407 See Chapter 1 Section 1.2 (illustrated by the car purchase scenario).

408 The application of the cheapest-cost-avoider would increase the surplus of the contract even if the parties are not equally good at negotiating, and the transaction were more beneficial for only one of them. See Chapter 1 Section 1.2.

409 See Chapter 1 Section 1.2.

a bit higher – 160 € (= [200 + 120] / 2) – allocating the risk to the cheaper-cost-avoider yields 15 € extra gain for each party compared with the other solution.

Filling gaps in a contract according to the cheapest-cost-avoider maximizes the parties' benefits from their transaction.[410] For this reason, it is assumed that this corresponds to the hypothetical will of the parties – the solution at which they would arrive if they had negotiated the allocation of that risk between them. It is efficient, because it increases the gains of the transaction and leads to greater incentives to conclude even more transactions, as people can rely on the law to provide optimal risk allocations.

2.3.2. Cheapest-Cost-Avoider in Disputes between Contractual Parties

The idea of taking into consideration the cost of the prevention of an undesirable event at the moment of determining the default responsibility has its roots in the Learned-Hand-Formula. In 1947, the US judge Billings Learned Hand introduced this solution to deal with the standard of care for the tort of negligence.[411] His formula states that the behavior of an individual should be regarded as negligent when that person refuses to invest in the prevention of a risk, if these investments are less than the "expected value of the risk". This last term is understood as a mathematical ratio – a multiplication – between two variables: the probability that an event will occur, and the magnitude of the resulting harm. In the field of contract law, the formula can be used to allocate responsibilities in a variety of cases.[412] Think for example of the case of a businessman that has missed his flight because the taxi that took him to the airport had a tire puncture. The taxi company and the affected person have not negotiated a specific solution for this mishap. That being so, it is necessary to determine who must assume responsibility for the consequences of this event; here, who must cover the cost of buying a second airplane ticket.

If the delay occurred because the driver had no spare tire, the taxi company should be liable, as the cost of having an additional pneumatic (B) is low, especially considering that all new cars are delivered with a spare tire. And the risk of a puncture is fairly high (P) in a vehicle that is frequently used as a work tool to carry people from one place to another. Furthermore, it is to be expected that clients transported to the airport could miss their flights (L), if they do not arrive on time as a consequence of the car breaking down. Thus, one can summarize that if no spare tire is in the vehicle, the taxi company should be regarded as negligent. The situation, however, changes, if not just one but rather all four tires burst. In this scenario, the company should not be liable for the

---

410 Schäfer & Ott (2012) 435–436.

411 *United States v. Carroll Towing Co.* 159 F.2d 169 (2d Cir. 1947) 243.

412 With a similar example see: Haro (2004) 186–187.

missing three spare tires. The cost of having four spare tires (B) would simply be too high. Such an investment would not be rationally justified, due to the low probability (P) of such an incident, in conjunction with the high cost of preventing it. Here the passenger should bear the cost of missing the plane. As a summary of the Learned-Hand-Formula, negligence is proven if the effort to prevent a risk (B) is less than the value of the damage (L) times the probability of its occurrence (P):

$$(B) < (L) \times (P) = \text{negligence}$$

Let us say that the damage of missing a flight is 400 €. Now we assume for the first case, that the burden of maintaining an additional pneumatic in the car is 10 € for every 10 years, and the probability of having a puncture is 10 incidences per 10 years, or one each year. For the second case, we assume that the cost of having four spares is 3,000 €,[413] and the probability of having all tires burst is one every 10 years. The results of applying the Learned-Hand-Formula are the following:

First case:	10 < [400 x 10/10 (= 400)]	Negligence.
Second case:	3,000 > [400 x 1/10 (= 40)]	No negligence.

The Learned-Hand-Formula and the cheapest-cost-avoider have in common that they do not care which person has actually *caused* the undesirable event. The cause of the delay is probably the same in both cases: a stranger broke a bottle in the street. The relevant question is rather whether the occurrence of the damage – missing the flight – could be reasonably prevented by taking into consideration not only the magnitude of the damage and costs of prevention, but also the probability that it might actually occur.[414] Based on this reasoning, the cheapest-cost-avoider suggests that if both contractual parties could avoid the occurrence of an event – that is, taking into consideration damage, costs of prevention and probability of the occurrence – the law should allocate the responsibility to the one who could more easily – at lower costs – avoid the undesirable contingency.

2.3.3. *Cheapest-Cost-Avoider in Disputes between Spouses*

The following example shows the application of the criterion of the cheapest-cost-avoider in a case involving spouses.

> After several years of marriage, Maria Elisabet announced to her husband, Ivan, her wish to get divorced. Upon the wife's insistence to a divorce, Ivan suggested

413 100 € for each extra spare plus 2,700 € to alter the car's trunk to have space for four spare tires without less space for passenger baggage.

414 De Geest et al. (2002) 167–168.

> living separately for a while, before talking about this issue again but also accepted an agreement specifying the division of the common property in case of a divorce. In the common property were two identical pictures, taken and developed by both of them together. They decided that each of them would receive one of the pictures in the event of divorce and that all the common property – including both photographs which were hanging in the living room – should stay there during the period of separation. They further agreed that Maria Elisabet would live in the family house in order to take care of Pablito – their 11-year-old son. After one year, Maria Elisabet communicated to her husband in a notarized letter her desire to initiate the divorce proceeding immediately. In the same letter, she expressed regret that he would not receive his picture in the same condition as he remembered it, because Pablito had used it as a dartboard with some friends when she was away for a business meeting. She also wrote that such an incident would not have happened if he had installed a safely system that alerted him when the child played around the prized object. She thought keeping the surviving picture in exchange for adequate compensation would be fair. The husband immediately claimed the remaining picture for himself because in his opinion she should have hired a sitter to avoid these situations.

Neither spouse is interested in money. Each of them wants to keep the picture. The agreement about the distribution of common assets, however, does not specify a solution for such a contingency. It is then necessary to fill this gap by a default rule.

According to the cheapest-cost-avoider, it is not relevant which party was the real originator of an event: that could be subjective and susceptible to vastly differing interpretations. In our case, both could be seen as accountable, as they together conceived Pablito, the real cause of the damage. More important are two matters: First, whether the potential damage was reasonably avoidable, taking into consideration its dimensions, the cost of prevention and the probability of occurrence. Second, which of the spouses – according to the events and the arguments provided by the parties – was in a better position to avoid the undesirable situation? That is, which of them is the person who would have to invest less resources to prevent an 11-year-old child from destroying the picture: Ivan – by installing an alarm system – or Maria Elisabet – by having a sitter that keeps an eye on her son when she has to leave him at home alone? On the basis that the value of the damage and probability of its occurrence are the same here, the cost of prevention is the only variable to consider when determining the responsibility. After eliminating the equal variables, we have:

(Babysitter's costs) in comparison with (Alarm's costs)

Because hiring a sitter is most likely the more economical solution in terms of effectiveness and money, the responsibility for the avoidance of the undesirable event should be allocated to the wife. This decision is not only based on the fact that the sitter would have avoided the damage caused to the picture, but it would also reduce the probability that further damage had happened to other objects or even the child himself.[415] Thus, although buying an alarm system only costs once in comparison to the other alternative, hiring the services of a person to look after the boy costs less, as it prevents further harm to the interests of the couple. Hence, Ivan will receive the picture.

2.4. THE PARSIMONY PRINCIPLE

Sometimes it is very difficult – or even impossible – to determine an allocation of responsibilities between contractual parties that assures an increase of the surplus created by the legal relationship. The complexity of certain risks, and the number of factors that could influence the outcome of a rule – or set of rules – might make another approach to defining the hypothetical will of the parties necessary.[416] Another aspect to be considered when designing default rules is their implementation by courts. Rules that are easy to deploy are more suitable, as they allow for a rapid settlement of disputes and a lower incidence of errors.[417] If the cheapest-cost-avoider test does not indicate a clear solution, it will be assumed that rules that are easily applied by the administration of justice would be those that the parties would have agreed on.

Philosophers use the term "Principle of Parsimony" or "Ockham's razor" to describe the problem-solving principle establishing that the simplest answer – the alternative with the least assumptions – should generally be preferred.[418] The application of this principle calls for pragmatism in the law-making process. Not only disregarding obscure legal lucubrations to resolve conflicts, but also favoring established solutions – past law and local customs – as blueprints to fill gaps in a contract: if it is not possible to determine the default rule that increases the surplus, the rules hitherto used in a jurisdiction should continue being applied by the courts. Analogies and other legal techniques used by traditional legal scholars to interpret the existing positive law will provide solutions when the law does not contain a clear answer to gaps left by the parties.

---

415 At the moment of determining the individual who is in a better position to bear the cost arising from the occurrence of adverse events, not only the immediate expenditures needed to avoid them, but also further gains for each party derived from the investment should be taken into account by the judge or legislator at the moment of establishing the default rule. See in detail Chapter 8 Section 4.2.2.

416 Garcimartín (2002) 135.

417 Craswell (2000) 9.

418 These terms refer to medieval philosopher William of Ockham's dictum "*pluralitas non est ponenda sine necessitate*" – plurality should not be assumed without necessity – which is commonly interpreted in the sense that complicated explanations of observed phenomena should not be accepted without proof of their necessity. See: Helmholz (2006) 111.

Think of the default rules applicable to the property regime of spouses. Which set of rules is the most efficient for the division of assets after the dissolution of a marriage is difficult to calculate abstractly? There are a number of factors that influence the specific regime that would best encourage individuals to engage in a cooperative dynamic. Some legal systems are based on the principle of separate property of the spouses, while others are based on the principle of community of property. There is also an intermediate type of regime, in which there is no transfer of property between the spouses, but the spouse who has accumulated higher values during the marriage is obliged to compensate the other. Furthermore, a number of laws do not even mention the concept of matrimonial property, but they treat personal and patrimonial obligations as if they were the same. Within this variety, knowing which regime is the one that increases the surplus created by a marriage the most is not possible through identifying the cheapest-cost-avoider, as it is not clear what the probabilities, costs of prevention or damages involved are. The inadequacy of the cheapest-cost-avoider as a tool is even more obvious when answering a single question of a specific regime. According to the community of property, all or parts of the movable and immovable property held or acquired by one party are transformed into common patrimony of both spouses. It is not clear how the cheapest-cost-avoider method could decide whether the community of property should include assets acquired before the marriage, or whether donations or inheritances should be regarded as part of the joint property.

If a group of law-makers are charged with providing a new default property regime for spouses, a wise solution would be to continue with the rules that have been used by the courts in the past. The suitability of this solution does not rely on an efficient allocation of risks between spouses. It is rather based on the fact that the judges know how to interpret this regulation, so that a greater celerity and fewer errors in the resolution of disputes will be achieved.[419] To provide responses to disputes at lower costs – in terms of time, effort and errors – law-makers can choose to simply keep the current legal state of affairs, as that has positive effects for the people.

It is important to emphasize that the use of this approach should be accompanied by a monitoring system that allows law-makers to detect whether these rules still fit the expectations of the spouses. Default rules should – from an economic perspective – reflect what spouses would agree on if they had negotiated over the specific issue. They should be changed if they do not match the current needs and preferences of the people.[420] In Part II of this book, it will be shown that having an efficient conflict of laws system – one that allows

419 Craswell (2000) 10.

420 See in this chapter Section 2.2.1.

individuals to choose the applicable law to their legal relationships – is crucial for the introduction of reforms and the evolution of the law in accordance with the will of the people.

3. INTERIM FINDINGS

By taking into consideration that marriage can be seen as a contract in an economic sense – an instrument aimed at improving the situation of the parties – this chapter explained not only the function of several legal provisions in modern marriage law, but also some legislative changes that have occurred in the last years in this area of the law. The model presented above does not explain every mandatory or default rule included in any given national marriage law. Some of the provisions contained in them – regardless of how modern the legal system at stake is – depart significantly from the goal of achieving efficiency and are based on other objectives. The chapter does, however, paint a general picture without investigating the specific substantive regulation in force in each jurisdiction in the world.

To what extent this helps create an efficient system of conflict of laws – a regulation above the regulations – will be discussed in the next part of the book. Before that, the next chapter will summarize the most salient findings discussed up to now in this and the previous chapters.

CHAPTER 4

SUBSTANTIVE MARRIAGE LAW FROM A LAW AND ECONOMICS PERSPECTIVE

The right to marry is recognized in a number of domestic laws and international conventions as being of pivotal importance for the proper and harmonious development of a person. The US Supreme Court has attested to the constitutional status of the marital bond on several occasions.[421] The Council of Europe regards the right to marry as a basic human right, when it states in Article 12 of the European Convention on Human Rights: "men and women of marriageable age have the right to marry and to found a family, according to the national laws governing the exercise of this right". The right to marry and right to found a family is also included in Article 9 of the Charter of Fundamental Rights of the European Union. A similar provision is contained in many international documents, like the International Convention on Civil and Political Rights (Article 23 paragraph 2), the American Convention on Human Rights (Article 17 paragraph 2) and the Universal Declaration of Human Rights (Article 16 paragraph 1).[422]

The recognition of the right to marry as one of the basic freedoms has helped abolish discriminative restrictions and expanded this right to groups of people who were not formerly permitted to celebrate it. Although the legislation of a number of national jurisdictions still constrains this right, there is a clear trend to protect and safeguard it regardless of the religion, race or gender of the prospective spouses. The invalidity of laws prohibiting interracial unions, as well as the extension of marriage rights to same-sex couples[423] are a consequence of the recognition of its fundamental status. However, such recognition in

---

421 For references to the constitutional status of marriage in the United States of America see: *Loving v. Virginia*, 388 U.S. 1 (1967); *Obergefell v. Hodges*, 135 S. Ct. 2584, 2628 (2015). In the first decision – *Loving v. Virginia*, 388 U.S. 1 (1967) – the U.S. Supreme Court declared illegal laws banning interracial marriage as violations of the Equal Protection and Due Process Clauses of the Fourteenth Amendment to the U.S. Constitution. In the second one – *Obergefell v. Hodges*, 135 S. Ct. 2584, 2628 (2015) – the U.S. Supreme Court ruled that the fundamental right to marry is guaranteed to same-sex couples by both the Due Process Clause and the Equal Protection Clause of the Fourteenth Amendment.

422 For case law on the legal recognition of same-sex marriages in Europe see De Groot D.A.J.G. (2021) 240 et seqq.

423 For an outstanding historical analysis of the legal recognition of same-sex marriages in Europe see De Groot D.A.J.G. (2021) 233 et seqq.

domestic legislation and international conventions does not help to explain why people get married or what the logic underlying marriage law is. The regulation of marriage in international conventions as well as the development of this right by supreme or international courts establishes limits to the discretion of law-makers when regulating marriage. But such insights – despite their importance – are not enough to deduce the central features of this institution in modern legislation.

The previous chapters shed some light on the content of marriage laws. Instead of starting with the letter of the law, basic economic principles were used to deduce a model that outlines the current regulation of marriage, independently of the place where a concrete law is enacted. Two assumptions were made: Individuals perceive marriage as a contract in an economic sense; and law-makers support the conclusion of these contracts as long as they respect constraints that are similar to those existing in regular markets. Based on those assumptions, it was possible to develop a kind of map that explains the main features of marriage in modern legal systems. A number of questions remain open. The model presented above only allows for a general view of the logic behind the provisions of marriage law. These ideas will, however, be of the utmost importance in the next chapters, to develop a system of conflict of laws rules that determines the law applicable to marriages with international connotations efficiently.[424] Before addressing the international regulation of marriage, let us look in a summarized form at the principal findings of the previous chapters.

1. ECONOMICS OF MARRIAGE LAW

Economics understands the private law as a promoter and facilitator of exchanges between members of a society. The role of the law is enabling the functioning of a decentralized system of decision-making that allocates resources according to the principles of a market economy. Contract has a central role in this system of laws, as it makes the realization of more transactions between members of the society possible. Since it triggers certain consequences if one of the parties is not

424 Throughout this book the term "efficient rules" refers to legal provisions – or any other legal measure taken by governments – that facilitate the emergence of cooperative dynamics between people. Legal provisions that eliminate barriers to the conclusion of contracts – or any other kind of voluntary agreement – are regarded as efficient as contracts are the typical means used to depict the terms in which such dynamics will be carried out. This is based on the idea that the constant conclusion of voluntary agreements between people – i.e. the engagement in cooperative dynamics – allows that the existing resources end up in the hands of those that value them the most. See: Chapter 1 Section 1.1 and Section 1.2. *in fine*. For situations meriting the imposition of restrictions on the freedom to conclude voluntary agreements – externalities, asymmetry of information, constraints affecting decision-making and monopolistic positions – see Chapter 3 Section 1.

willing to fulfill their promise, people feel confident to run the risk of relying on another individual when making an exchange. Marriage has been described as having the same objective as the contract. It was depicted as an instrument that builds trust between two individuals to make exchanges of complementary and reciprocal efforts within the framework of the household. An intimate cooperative dynamic with another person is possible – at least in modern societies – without the need of being married. Couples can have babies, raise a family or acquire joint property without a marriage certificate. However, a legal bond creates a stronger commitment due to the emergence of legal repercussions in the event of an unexpected termination of the relationship. Marriage builds trust in prospective spouses to make bigger investments, especially at different stages of the relationship. The rules of marriage law in modern legal systems seem to reflect this logic. Although marriage is not expressly regarded as a mere instrument aimed at improving the initial situation of spouses, the legislation in force in a number of legal provisions induces people to obtain the benefits from joint cooperation in the household. In general, the law provides regulation that encourages spouses to make significant investments and so increase their well-being from the surplus generated by a more intensive cooperation. To promote such cooperation, marriage law – likewise contract law – fulfills three main tasks: enforcement of promises, enactment of imperative rules and provision of default rules.

The enforcement of promises does not mean that any discord between spouses must be resolved by a court. Since a part of the costs of legal proceedings are assumed by society, it is necessary to use a filter to avoid an overcrowding of the judicial system. Thus, not all but only a sub-set of promises will be legally enforced by courts. However, this restriction does not necessarily lead to a reduction of the willingness to cooperate between parties, as endogenous and exogenous mechanisms can assure a cooperative equilibrium in a relationship. The success of extralegal mechanisms is, however, heavily subordinated to the legal enforcement of clear rules when the relationship does not work anymore. Their adequacy to promote cooperation depends directly on the belief that if they are not enough to create an equilibrium, there is at least one more way to recover a part of the investment or mitigate the damage of a marital crisis. Legal enforcement in long-term contracts like the marriage exists, but it is not primarily focused on the time during which the relationship is strong. The benefits of joint work give rise to non-legal mechanisms that assure the desired performance of promises. To reduce costs, legal mechanisms are rather triggered at the moment in which the relationship has deteriorated; that is, at the time when the cooperative game only generates modest profits in comparison to the benefits of exiting the relationship. Legal enforcement is thus mainly focused on questions related to the effects of the termination of the relationship. The second task – enactment of imperative rules – refers to the imposition of restrictions on the party autonomy of spouses. From an economic point of view, promoting the realization of transactions, allowing individuals to decide freely with whom to contract, as well as permitting them to define the conditions that govern their relationships, are positives. However, not all exchanges of promises necessarily lead to an improvement in aggregate terms, as the realization of some agreements could impose costs on other individuals that have not chosen to incur them, or even cause harm to one of the parties. The economic theory of contract regulation resembles the economic theory of market regulation when establishing the cases in which mandatory rules are necessary. Categories of market failures are used to describe situations that merit the imposition of imperative rules. The generation of externalities justifies the imposition of limits on promises enforced by courts. Restrictions based on public policy or the protection of the interests of third parties – such as for example the children – can be economically explained drawing upon the concept of negative externality. Asymmetric information was described as the economic reason for the existence of formalities, like the presence of a notary, public deed or other formal requirements to grant validity to agreements concluded by spouses. A lack of stability in the preferences of some individuals justifies the requirement of a minimum age to celebrate a marriage. Those who are impaired by a severe mental illness or learning disability are similarly barred from entering into a marital relationship. Finally, the problems generated by a monopoly position justify the imposition of limits on those who desire to conclude an agreement aimed at eliminating or imposing greater barriers to the possibility of a unilateral divorce. The last task of marriage law is the provision of dispositive rules to fill lacunas in the regulation of the relationship. It would be ideal if the parties arrived at a bespoke solution for any problem arising over the course of their partnership by themselves. However, this cannot realistically be expected due to the difficulty of imagining all sorts of problems in the future and providing individual solutions for each of them. In order to solve this matter, the law provides default rules. These rules reflect the hypothetical will of the parties; that is, the solution at which they would arrive if they had expressly bargained over that term of their contract. It is assumed that the preferred rules will be those that increase the total gains generated by the cooperation the most. However, it is sometimes difficult to determine which rules meet this goal. Preferring the current state of affairs – maintaining the legal *status quo* – will be the strategy used to fill gaps in contracts, as it reduces the costs of the implementation of the law by dipping into tradition and past legal precedents. It is assumed that the hypothetical will of the spouses corresponds to rules that avoid the incidence of errors and allow for rapid dispute settlement by the courts.

In sum, marriage does not eliminate the risk that a planned investment loses its value by a unilateral decision or by a fortuitous event. It does, however, provide more security in comparison than cohabitation, since it imposes legal obligations and rights in case something unexpected occurs. Neither marriage, nor any other contract can prevent abandonment, marital crises or the death of a partner. However, it employs mechanisms that make that situation much more bearable, which ultimately works as a lure to make further investments in the household.

2. LEGAL PLURALISM AND MARRIAGE IN AN INTERNATIONAL CONTEXT

Economics provides a language to describe the logic behind a number of provisions in marriage law. However, that is not enough to make specific recommendations. An efficient marriage law should provide a legal framework that encourages the blooming of cooperative dynamics between spouses. But applying this idea to real situations could lead to widely different outcomes, due to the wide margin of discretion left by this postulate.[425] For example, waiting periods for unilateral divorce are desirable from an economic perspective. But this statement does not answer the question of how much time spouses should wait to obtain their divorce. Should the waiting period be set to one, two, four, six or even 10 years? Furthermore, the suitability of norms always depends on the time and place where they are used. What may be efficient in one country could be irrelevant or even have a negative impact in another. As mentioned before, the presence of an adviser before the conclusion of a marriage could help in environments where spouses have no opportunity get to know each other before the wedding. But this adviser would make no sense in societies where individuals are used to long periods of courtship or even cohabitation before entering into a marriage.

Economics is not the panacea. It presents a model to see the contours of marriage law, but – honestly – the insights presented so far are not enough to draft a comprehensive set of rules covering the complexity of a marital relationship. Economic analysis of the law provides fresh and new ideas to better understand the behavior of individuals, but it still leaves unanswered a number of questions for the creation of a complete marriage law.[426] Notwithstanding, we can still discover interesting things about this topic. Although the insights presented above do not allow us to draft specific substantive rules on marriage law, they can be used to make a step forward and so create a legal framework that – by covering the interactions of multiple legal systems in the international arena – accelerates the emergence of concrete substantive rules that maximize

425 Kerber (2000) 74.

426 Grossbard-Shechtman & Lemennicier (1999). Some authors say that the evolution of the law to efficiency generates multiple equilibria, so that each legal system is potentially efficient and "there are multiple efficient doctrines depending on local determinants". See: Garoupa & Gomez (2011) 229.

the cooperation between spouses. On the following pages, the scope of the analysis will be extended. The effects of internationality – the costs, benefits and incentives that the plurality of legal systems creates – will be examined. However, the analysis will not be focused on describing the current trends in private international law. It will rather present a normative model for conflict of laws rules. This model is not only congruent with the ideas explained above, but also fleshes them out as it garners the maximum profit from the existence of different legal systems at an international level by providing answers that the model presented above was not able to respond to.

Let us finally uncover the linkage between legal pluralism and efficiency in marriage law.

PART II

ECONOMICS AS A POINT OF DEPARTURE TO BUILD A SYSTEM OF CONFLICT OF LAWS FOR MATRIMONIAL ISSUES

The next chapters are entirely focused on the conflict of laws dimension of marriage. Using the economic rationale outlined before, the way in which the conflict of laws system ought to be drafted is discussed. The goals – from an economic perspective – pursued by the substantive law are used as a point of departure for the analysis. Based on them, it is concluded that the application of the legal system chosen freely by the couple or – in absence of a choice of law agreement – the law of the country of their first common residence – or, subsidiarily, the place of conclusion of the marriage – are the most appropriate solutions for the resolution of a conflict of laws.

This part is divided into four chapters. Chapter 5 deals with the general objectives of private international law from a *law and economics* perspective. It establishes attributes of the conflict rule that encourage more legal transactions in the international arena. Chapter 6 explores the emerging dynamic once spouses are allowed to determine themselves the law they deem most suitable to govern their relationship. Chapter 7 presents the most salient advantages of party autonomy in international marriage law. Chapter 8 focuses exclusively on the applicable law when spouses have not made use of their freedom of choice.

CHAPTER 5

LEGAL PLURALISM AND ITS COSTS FOR MARRIED COUPLES

A marriage – or any other contract – linked to two or more legal systems entails significant risks and uncertainties for those bound by it. How this conflict of laws is resolved might generate unexpected benefits, but also serious disadvantages, as the application of an unexpected law can radically change the rights and obligations assumed by the parties. The situation of business partners is illustrative here, as it is possible to measure the dimension of the problem of legal pluralism. There are a number of empirical studies focused on international trade, underscoring its negative effects on the volume of exchanged goods.[427] These surveys confirm that borders clearly have an adverse impact on the willingness of people to make exchanges across them. It is interesting to note that, despite the efforts of governments to eliminate tariff barriers and other surcharges on imported and exported goods, the number of international transactions continues to be lower than of domestic ones. People have the tendency to invest more in domestic markets, despite the benefits of diversifying into foreign economies.[428] One study, for example, suggests that the mere existence of a border between two cities can decrease the trade volume five-fold.[429] Other surveys estimate that it could be between 12[430] and 20[431] times. Whatever the exact figure, all of them confirm the same basic fact: borders do matter, because they diminish the number of transactions that are realized between individuals located on different sides significantly.

---

427 See for example: Anderson & van Wincoop (2003); Brenton & Vancauteren (2001); Chen (2004); Engel & Rogers (1996); Helliwell (1997); Helliwell (1998); McCallum (1995); Obstfeld & Rogoff (2000); Rodrik (2004); Turrini & Van Ypersele (2006); Yi (2005).

428 Turrini & Van Ypersele (2006) 2.

429 Yi (2005) 26.

430 Helliwell (1997) 165.

431 Anderson & van Wincoop (2003); McCallum (1995) 615.

The reasons that explain this phenomenon – known as *border effect* in academic literature –[432] could be varied: distance between countries; linguistic and cultural barriers; transportation fees; practical difficulties to find an appropriate partner from afar; or economic inequalities.[433] However, it is remarkable that there are still big differences in the trade volume between neighboring countries which are very similar in terms of culture, language and economic welfare, compared to domestic trade.[434] Such disparities can even be found between those that – in addition to these similarities – have implemented policies to liberalize and deregulate their mutual trade, such as for example the United States and Canada.[435] The *border effect* suggests the existence of additional disincentives and barriers – *costs* – for the realization of international contracts in comparison to domestic ones.[436] Eliminating or reducing these costs is desirable from an economic perspective, as that would lead to more exchanges and consequently an increase in welfare in aggregate terms. In this regard, scholars in economics have started to pay much more attention to the law under which transnational activity is regulated.[437] International transactions of any kind have as their central characteristic the fact that they are concluded or performed in the shadow of at least two different legal systems.[438] Since private international law is the area of law dealing with conflicting legal systems, it seemed meaningful to focus on these rules to find out what their influence on the *border effect* is.

The *border effect* was first described in the context of market transactions. There is no study suggesting that the willingness of people to get married declines if an international element is present – or could do so in the short or long run. However, that does not mean that the disincentives, complications or awkwardness besetting business partners are not also affecting spouses. Quite the contrary, as it will be explained below, there are good reasons to believe that spouses and tradesmen – or tradeswomen – share the same quandary.

---

432 See in general: Brenton & Vancauteren (2001); Chen (2004); Evans (2003); Head & Mayer (2000); Helliwell (1997); Helliwell (1998); McCallum (1995); Obstfeld & Rogoff (2000); Rodrik (2000); Turrini & Van Ypersele (2006); Wei (1996).

433 Chen (2004) 93; Brenton & Vancauteren (2001) 1–2.

434 Carbonara & Parisi (2008) 340; McCallum (1995) 615.

435 According to surveys, the province of Ontario exported more than 12 times as much to British Columbia – another Canadian province – than to the state of Washington in the United States. This, even though the distances are virtually the same, and the population of Washington is bigger than that of British Columbia. The exact extent of the border effect in international trade is still disputed. However, it is uncontested among scholars that borders have a negative effect on trade; the mere existence of lines separating one country from another decreases the number of exchanges significantly. For the application of the gravity model to this case see: Head (2000) 9; Engel & Rogers (1996).

436 Carbonara & Parisi (2007) 369.

437 Schmidtchen (1995) 65.

438 Garcimartín (2002) 91, 127; Schmidtchen (1995) 66.

Building on these ideas, the aim of this chapter is to show the costs generated by legal pluralism for individuals involved in a marriage connected to at least two jurisdictions. It also explores the function of private international law from an economic perspective, to establish – from a normative point of view – concrete attributes of the conflict rule that encourage the conclusion of voluntary agreements between people. The chapter begins by explaining some basic concepts used by scholars in law and economics to analyze the problems of individuals involved in a relationship with international connotations. Next, it focuses on the role played by the accuracy, uniformity, consistency and simplicity of conflict rules for the emergence of cooperative dynamics. After that, the practical relevance of legal certainty is discussed. The last section summarizes the most salient findings of the chapter.

1. ECONOMIC ANALYSIS OF LEGAL PLURALISM

In the early nineties two economists – Dieter Schmidtchen and Hans-Jörg Schmidt-Trenz – began to extensively publish about the effects of legal pluralism on international exchanges and its link to the border effect.[439] Some of their conclusions are: First, the presence of varying legislation across the international arena does adversely affect the willingness of people to conclude international transactions. Second, this leads to an increase of the costs to carry out exchanges, which in turn triggers a reduction of the volume of international trade. And third, the cause of this phenomenon is what they called *constitutional uncertainty*.[440] According to these authors, the differences in trade volume are a direct consequence of the legal uncertainty – their constitutional uncertainty – arising from the looming application of either legal system to the relationship. This leads to a situation where individuals are reluctant to cooperate even if it is in their best interest to do so. In a clear reference to the prisoner's dilemma, the authors use the term transaction dilemma to illustrate the implications of this uncertainty for exchanges subjected to different laws.[441]

Their work was aimed at explaining the difficulties that business partners experience when making international transactions. However, their findings could be generalized to any contract with international connotations, as the root of the problem is not related to the nature of the obligations assumed by the parties.

439 See for example: Schmidt-Trenz (1990); Schmidtchen (1995); Schmidtchen (2002); Schmidtchen (2007); Schmidt-Trenz & Schmidtchen (1991); Schmidtchen & Schmidt-Trenz (2006).

440 See in detail: Schmidtchen & Schmidt-Trenz (2006) 331–339.

441 See section 1.2. below. Schmidtchen & Schmidt-Trenz (2006) 331 et seqq. See also Rühl (2011) 38; Garcimartín (2002) 95.

It rather lies with the conditions under which these contracts have to be performed. Their ideas could then also be used to understand and explain the negative effects of legal pluralism and the central role played by the system of conflict of laws rules in marriage.

1.1. CONSTITUTIONAL UNCERTAINTY

What are the consequences of the fact that the power of each state is limited to its own territory? Which problems do contractual partners encounter that do not exist in domestic transactions? Schmidt-Trenz and Schmidtchen see the answer to both questions in a special uncertainty. This uncertainty is described as "constitutional", because it arises after and despite the formation and organization – i.e. the constitution – of states.[442] Let us look more closely at what both authors mean when they use this term.

1.1.1. Law as an Incentive for Cooperation

Every transaction comprises a degree of uncertainty, as its success depends on whether the partner ultimately honors their promise. In some cases, the risk is small. Think for example of the situation of two farmers – let's call them Hans and Robert Ryszard – who consider a swap of potatoes and onions. Since the quality of the goods at stake can easily be observed prior to the transaction, and the exchange is carried out simultaneously, there is no need to reflect too much on the risks.[443] In such a situation, it is to be expected that both individuals will simply weigh the pure benefits of the exchange. As long as the value of what is received is higher than the value of what is delivered, an agreement between them will likely be reached.[444] However, in many other cases – as for example in a marriage – the promises are not simple barters. They rather entail specific investments and the performance of many successive obligations. Here the circumstances may push one of the parties to do their part before the partner reciprocates, so that a high degree of trust is necessary to reap the rewards of the transaction. The position of parties in non-simultaneous exchanges is often risky, as it is difficult to verify the reliability of the partner and consequently to feel confident that they will actually do their part.[445] It is ultimately ineluctable to rely on the goodwill of the other to uphold their promise, but at the same time keep in mind that there is always a risk of not being paid back.

---

442 Rühl (2011) 33. The term "constitutional uncertainty" has no legal connotation in the sense of constitutional law.

443 Kronman (1985) 9.

444 See Chapter 1 Section 1.2.

445 Kronman (1985) 10.

In non-simultaneous exchanges, focusing on the subjective value of the exchanged goods is not enough;[446] it is also necessary to consider the costs and probabilities of non-compliance carefully. The greater such a likelihood is, the less attractive a partnership with another person may seem. Each side will then presumably demand more from the other – a higher or lower price; more or less investments – to factor in the risks. As a result, the surplus of the contract will be reduced, and consequently fewer transactions will be concluded. It is here that the law becomes indispensable for economic actors, as it reduces the probability that things turns out different than expected. The threat of sanctions provided by a legal system discourages opportunistic behavior, as parties are entitled to resort to the courts in case the other reneges on their promise.[447] The law also offers a number of solutions – default provisions – to resolve any contingency emerging before, during or after the benefits of the contract are received. For individuals involved in a non-simultaneous transaction the law is of paramount importance. It becomes an essential condition to enable cooperative dynamics under these challenging circumstances.

1.1.2. Costs Arising from Overlapping Legal Systems at an International Level

The law allows people to plan their lives within the framework of the associated legal regulation. Thanks to it, they are able to evaluate whether it is worth initiating a partnership with another individual, determine the extent of effort to be invested in the relationship, and shape a preferred course of action to be followed during their lifetime. Decisions like having or not having children; refusing or accepting a job offer; staying in their home country or moving abroad; and raising a mortgage or selling a valuable asset to purchase real estate might – rightly – be influenced by the law applicable to marriage. Legal provisions about the calculation of maintenance obligations, time to initiate the divorce proceeding, or the regime of the property of the spouses could play a crucial role in the lives of spouses. Many people rely on the assumption that there is a mechanism – the law – that will ultimately back them up in case their relationship does not turn out as expected.

However, at an international level, the trust placed in the legal system is undermined because not only one, but a variety of laws compete with each other.[448] In contrast to a single jurisdiction, there is not one body of rules, but rather a number of distinct ones that could potentially be applied to the relationship. What is guaranteed and protected in one place will then not necessarily be so in another jurisdiction. Furthermore, it is possible that certain

446 For the concept of subjective value see Chapter 3 Section 2.3.1.

447 Garcimartín (2002) 98–99.

448 Schmidt-Trenz (1990) 168–169; Schmidtchen (1995) 69–70; Schmidtchen & Schmidt-Trenz (2006) 329. See also: Basedow (2006a) 58; Basedow (2006b) 230.

rights granted by legislation in one state are not even recognized by that of another. Entering into an international legal relationship could become a serious issue, as legal pluralism prevents the parties from knowing with precision if the expectations placed on a marriage – or any other contract concluded – will be respected.[449] The territoriality of the law – the fact that the power of states to enact and enforce laws is limited to their own jurisdiction – generates additional costs for contractual partners.[450] The potential application of unexpected laws to a contract compels people to learn more about the contents of the foreign law, and maybe even accommodate their behavior to strange – alien – provisions because these rules could ultimately govern their relationship. Unlike in domestic transactions, there are extra costs surrounding international contracts that are a disincentive for their conclusion.[451] These additional costs – *cost of internationality* – refer to the time, money and any other effort needed to know about the exact rights and obligations derived from the conclusion of a contract, and to the need for parties to adapt their goals and demeanor to those potential rules.[452] In sum, the fragmentation of the world into sovereign states leads to a situation where the obligations promised by parties will not necessarily be performed the way they should. This notion of "the way they should" depends completely on the particular law chosen by the authority of the jurisdiction where the legal relationship will eventually be discussed. Not only the enforceability of the obligations and the intensity with which they have to be performed, but also the validity of the whole relationship might be concerned. This fragmentation also creates the risk that gaps in the contract will be interpreted differently from how the parties may have surmised. Lacunas can ultimately be filled by extraneous or even bizarre default solutions, regardless of whether such loopholes were intentionally left open because both partners thought they would be filled with their envisaged default rules.[453]

Schmidt-Trenz and Schmidtchen coined the term constitutional uncertainty to describe the state of insecurity experienced by people bound by obligations connected to different legislative regimes,[454] which is caused by the very basic principle underlying the dominant Westphalian model of state foundation: sovereignty.[455] On a practical level, this expression – constitutional uncertainty – highlights the disincentive to cooperate arising from the lack

449 Rühl (2011) 35.
450 Schmidtchen & Schmidt-Trenz (2006) 344; Streit & Mangels (1996) 75.
451 Schmidtchen (1995) 63.
452 Garcimartín (2002) 131.
453 Schmidtchen (1995) 63; Schmidtchen (1995).
454 Schmidtchen (2007) 11; Schmidt-Trenz (1990) 232 et seqq. See also: Basedow (2006a) 58; Basedow (2006b) 230.
455 For further implications of the Westphalian doctrine of sovereignty in private international law see: Kramer (1991) 2140; Muir Watt (2011).

of a common mechanism clearly indicating the rules governing a contract.[456] The authors conclude that the creation of a system dealing with this issue is economically desirable, as without such a system people would be less willing to cooperate with others across borders.[457]

1.2. TRANSACTION DILEMMA

To illustrate the negative effects of the legal fragmentation, the authors draw upon the prisoner's dilemma.[458] Through the use of game theory, they demonstrate that two rational actors might not engage in a legal relationship with international connotations even though its realization is in their best interest. Their model was intended for the international trade of goods in regular markets. However, it could just as well be used to evince the problems of individuals involved in any marital relationship with international components. Their findings will now be expanded to show the importance – not only for contractual parties, but also for society as a whole – of having a reliable mechanism dealing with the problems of conflicting legal systems.

1.2.1. Zero-Sum Games

Imagine a world where there is no substantive legal system.[459] A place without a mechanism assigning property rights over resources, protecting the use of owned goods or guaranteeing the fulfillment of promises to exchange these resources.[460] Where there are people, there are also needs which could be satisfied either by their own efforts or through the work of others. Using the work of others could in turn be achieved in two different ways.[461] First: robbing others of their

---

456 Schmidtchen (1995) 70–72.

457 Interestingly, both authors do not look favorably upon the existing conflict of laws rules, but they prefer a private ordering system – a system created and operated predominantly by private actors. See: Schmidtchen (1995) 93–105; Schmidtchen & Schmidt-Trenz (1989) 31–35; Schmidt-Trenz (1990) 282; Schmidt-Trenz & Schmidtchen (1991) 332–336. See also: Basedow (2006a) 58–59; Basedow (2006b) 230–231; Rühl (2011) 39 et seqq.

458 Schmidtchen (1995) 90–93; Schmidtchen (2007) 13–20.

459 The objective of this example is only to illustrate the importance of the law for the realization of transactions of any type. The idea is to make an analogy with what some authors call the "state of nature". They use this term to explain the natural emergence of a legitimate political organization and laws without a ruler and without violating anyone's rights. See: Nozick (1974) 3–25.

460 This reality must not entirely be regarded as a fiction. Consider for example the situation of Goldminers in California in the 1850s, or most people in Western Europe in the early Middle Ages, after the collapse of Roman rule. See: Kronman (1985) 9.

461 In a state of nature, there are other ways to take advantage of the work of others; for example by the provision of voluntary hostages to the other party to generate trust. For the sake of simplicity, I will concentrate on only one means. For other methods to improve one's situation in the state of nature, see: Kronman (1985) 11–24.

resources to satisfy one's own needs. With appropriate methods and strategies, that option might seem appealing, as it offers immediate satisfaction. Thus, if Hans – the farmer in the previous example – lacks charcoal for heating, all he has to do is to go to the house of Robert Ryszard and take it to meet his needs. In the same vein, if Hans wishes to expand his crop field, he can simply occupy the plot of his neighbor to extend his arable land. In economic terms, these situations are known as zero-sum games. They describe an interaction between two actors, in which the gains or losses of utility of one of them are exactly balanced out by the losses or gains of the other; or to put it more simply: one side gains exactly as much as the other loses.[462] Therefore, like in a boxing match where the stronger fighter generally triumphs; or in football where the team with the most expensive players usually wins; in a world where the realization of such exchanges is the normal way of obtaining benefits from the work of others, the stronger and richer will have an advantage. They will be the ones who enjoy the existing resources, as long as they have the power to defend them from an assault of others.

Second: fortunately, zero-sum games are not the only way to capitalize on the work of others, it is also possible to come to terms with another individual and achieve a fruitful cooperation. Each side gets the resources they need through voluntary exchanges, so that the joint cooperation becomes the key to improve upon their starting position. A situation where individuals reach an agreement to cooperate for something of greater value is known as a non-zero-sum game in economics. It is characterized by the fact that the gains of one side *do not* balance out the losses of the other.[463] Quite the contrary, both come off better since they receive something of greater value than what they had invested. Contrary to the aforementioned examples where there is a vanquisher – an offender – and a loser – a victim – here we have two winners, as the initial situation of both is improved. The expression "non-zero-sum games" is nothing other than the terminology used by game theorists to designate situations where individuals conclude contracts.[464]

Now assume that Hans wants to retire and requires enough coal to stay warm during the winter, whereas Robert Ryszard is much younger and interested in having more land to grow more wheat. The first one owns cultivable land, but his age prevents him from using it. The second in turn has the strength to endure the winter without needing his whole coal and firewood stockpile. In a non-zero-sum game Hans and Robert Ryszard reach a voluntary agreement by which the young farmer hands over a portion of his stockpile right now in exchange

---

462 Baird et al. (1994) 317.

463 Baird et al. (1994) 50 et seqq.

464 Kirchner (2006) 44. For the economic rationale behind the conclusion of contracts see in this book Chapter 1 Section 1.2.

for the right to cultivate the soil of the elder man next summer. Although such a transaction would be beneficial for both farmers, in a world without a legal system it is very unlikely that they could reach an agreement. Because of the time-delayed performance, one side has to make the first move and is consequently in a disadvantageous position.[465] If there are no rules that protect the expectations created by the contract, nothing assures that – for example, in this case – the older one will actually honor his promise and allow the use of his land next year. The fear that the potential partner may not keep his promise pushes both of them to choose an option – retaining land and coal/firewood respectively – that, although not being the most beneficial solution, at least avoids losses.[466]

Individuals planning transactions with an international component experience the same feelings of insecurity.[467] Since their potential partners are typically far away, they cannot realize simultaneous exchanges. Lack of simultaneity is also an issue when an agreement – for example a marriage – is composed of a great number of successive obligations to be performed over time. Who makes the first step bears the risk of a non-performance by the other party, which makes the exchange less desirable.[468] The existence of a mechanism – clear rules – assuring the fulfillment of promises related to several legal systems is a requirement for the flourishing of non-zero-sum games at the international level.

1.2.2. *Requirements to Create a Favorable Climate for Cooperative Exchanges*

In general, the prevalence of non-zero-sum games in a society depends on two conditions. The first is the ability of people – especially of those in power – to realize the negative effects of zero-sum games, and to appreciate the advantages of cooperation. Society must be able to recognize that all kinds of encroachments – such as for example assaults and invasions – only result in short-term satisfaction, whereas in a system based on voluntary exchanges both groups – stronger and weaker ones – benefit. Individuals must then understand that a situation where resources are no longer invested in finding the most lucrative robberies or the best alarm systems, but channeled toward the production of assets that are appealing to the rest, is beneficial for all of them. They have to realize that gains from exchanges lead to a division of labor, which generates more productivity and thus a greater quantity and variety of resources at the disposal of the whole group.[469]

---

465 Carrascosa (2011) 36; Garcimartín (2002) 97–98; Hayek (1969) 257.
466 Kronman (1985) 10.
467 For a more complex modeling of the transaction dilemma see: Schmidtchen (1995) 90–93.
468 Carrascosa (2011) 88–89; Garcimartín (2002) 127–128; Rühl (2011) 36–37.
469 Garcimartín (2002) 96–97.

The second condition is the establishment of rules that define who is entitled to the existing resources, and protects expectations generated by promises about exchanging them.[470] The blossoming of cooperative dynamics requires, then, a legal system that defines property rights and assures the execution of contracts about the transmission of these resources in the terms agreed. In both cases this system must impose consequences for the non-observance of such rules. These requisites will in the following passages be called possessive security and transactional security.[471] These guarantees are the corner-stones for the functioning of a system based on voluntary exchanges, as they enable people to be involved in non-zero-sum dynamics.[472]

1.2.3. Supranational Rules on Private Law to Discourage Zero-Sum Games

The advantages of encouraging non-zero-sum games have been known for a long time. Even in ancient societies rules providing possessive and transactional security existed. Although the standard of protection granted by these laws was not the same among all societies, and they tended to change as time went by, all civilizations sooner or later formulated a set of rules that demarcated the rights and entitlements of people – or the community – over resources, and the conditions under which others could make use of those resources.[473] But, although societies were able to develop a system that encouraged the realization of non-zero-sum games with those living in their immediate surroundings, they were for the longest time unable to do the same for individuals located far away from them. When reviewing human history, border-crossing armed conflicts – which are nothing but a zero-sum game[474] – with the aim of robbing neighboring countries are a constant. Sometimes people forget that only 75 years ago in the very heart of Europe some governments regarded plundering the coal-mines of the neighboring country as well as claiming their fertile lands as legitimate. Zero-sum games in the international arena – like the one described between Hans and Robert Ryszard – were a valid option for the stronger European states to improve their situation at the expense of adjacent countries.[475]

To break with such a historical pattern, it is no surprise that governments have begun to develop a system setting out clear rules granting possessive

470 Carrascosa (2011) 45–46; Garcimartín (2002) 99.
471 Kronman (1985) 6–7. See also: Streit (1995) 62–63.
472 Schmidtchen & Schmidt-Trenz (2006) 344; Schmidtchen (2007) 9–10; Schmidtchen (1995) 69.
473 For the conditions for the emergence of property rights over resources in a society see: Demsetz (1974) 166–170.
474 Axelrod (1984) 76.
475 The provenance of the farmers' names used in the example was chosen deliberately to remember that this practice – plundering and invading – was actually employed by totalitarian regimes in Europe until well into the twentieth century.

and transactional security for transactions made at an international level. The development of mechanisms coordinating the legislation of different states in the last years could be explained as a consequence of – finally – understanding that the realization of zero-sum games must neither be tolerated domestically nor at an international level. Having a mechanism like private international law granting possessive and transactional security to individuals involved in an international transaction not only favors them; it also benefits the whole society, since it makes the cooperation more profitable and so prevents individuals and governments from resorting to undesirable strategies, that sooner or later would cause wide-ranging damage – negative externalities – to the rest of the people.[476] From an economic perspective, private international law has then as its overarching goal the encouragement of cooperative dynamics – and *vice versa* the discouragement of zero-sum games – in the international arena by upholding the rules defining property rights over resources and protecting expectations generated by promises aimed at exchanging them.[477] It maintains the effectiveness of the law in a context in which rights and obligations could be subject to several possible legal systems as a consequence of the connection of the relationship with multiple jurisdictions.[478]

2. FORMAL FEATURES OF THE CONFLICT OF LAWS SYSTEM ENCOURAGING SPOUSES' COOPERATION

Cross-border transactions would not disappear in the absence of a state-backed mechanism granting possessive and transactional security. As has happened since time immemorial, exchanges would still occur, but foreseeably at a lower volume due to the risks. In the case of marriage, it is also improbable that without a mechanism granting possessive and transactional security at an international level, zero-sum strategies would prevail, maybe as described by the myth of "The Rape of the Sabine Women". Notwithstanding, it would probably reduce the attractiveness of marriages as an instrument to improve the situation of people. Without private international law, fewer people would dare to change their residence, marry a foreign national or acquire property abroad, unless any of these actions generated a very large payoff that compensates for the loss

476 Garcimartín (2002) 128.

477 In other words, guaranteeing possessive and transactional security for international transactions. See: Basedow (2006a) 63; Basedow (2006b) 237; Garcimartín (2002) 103, 127–128. See also: Carrascosa (2011) 46.

478 The encouragement of cooperative dynamics not only requires reduction of transaction costs, but also interventions in case of market failures. See in detail: Rühl (2011) 208, 213. These issues as well as the role played by private international law in the regulatory competition will be discussed in more detail in Chapter 6.

caused by costs of internationality. As with business transactions, international marriages would not disappear, but be less common – and certainly less desirable – were it not possible to know at least a little about the legal consequences of their conclusion.

However, private international law does not solve all problems. Having a system of conflict of laws is essential to increase the number of cross-border exchanges. But, accomplishing that individuals are not discouraged from making transactions with international components depends on whether the system actually facilitates the realization of exchanges. The more the conflict rules strengthen the possessive and transactional security through the reduction of the cost of internationality, the more transactions will be made and consequently the more efficient the conflict of laws system will be.[479] The following features are essential to reduce the barriers to the realization of transactions: accuracy, uniformity, consistency and simplicity. Let us delve a bit more into their practical relevance for spouses involved in a relationship with international connotations.

2.1. ACCURACY

The more the law leaves the door open for the application of different legal systems to a contract, the less the willingness of the people to conclude one is. The lack of accuracy in the determination of the governing law triggers the need to invest more resources in ascertaining and ensuring the advantages achieved by the contract, which in turn decreases the benefits of the cooperation and – therefore – the preceding willingness to enter into cooperation with another person.[480] The potential application of multiple legal systems to a marriage – even if one knows exactly which laws might likely be applied by a court – forces diligent couples to modify their behavior to accommodate the mandatory rules in all of them. As these provisions are not subject to contrary agreements,

---

479 Throughout this book the term "efficient rules" refers to legal provisions – or any other legal measure taken by governments – that facilitate the emergence of cooperative dynamics between people. Legal provisions that eliminate barriers to the conclusion of contracts – or any other kind of voluntary agreement – are regarded as efficient as contracts are the typical means used to depict the terms in which such dynamics will be carried out. This is based on the idea that the constant conclusion of voluntary agreements between people – i.e. the engagement in cooperative dynamics – allows that the existing resources end up in the hands of those that value them the most. See: Chapter 1 Section 1.1 and Section 1.2. *in fine*. For situations meriting the imposition of restrictions on the freedom to conclude voluntary agreements – externalities, asymmetry of information, constraints affecting decision-making and monopolistic positions – see Chapter 3 Section 1. See also: Basedow (2006a) 63; Basedow (2006b) 237.

480 O'Hara & Ribstein (2000) 1152; Schäfer & Lantermann (2006) 91. See also: Gunst (1994) 136.

spouses must adjust their life plans to the imperative provisions of all possible laws to avoid eventual invalidity of their actions, rise of liabilities or any other undesirable effect imposed by these mandatory rules.[481] The lack of certainty will ultimately force them to comply with all of them at the moment of taking decisions in some way linked to their marriage. Furthermore, the lack of precision regarding the specific law governing the relationship also forces prudent parties to gather information about the non-mandatory provisions – all those in force in the legal systems at stake – and decide if those meet their preferences. That not only costs time and money for legal counsel; it also means understanding and processing all this information before assessing whether it is better to conclude a bespoke contract – a marital agreement – to repeal unsavory default rules.[482] Conflict rules that do not clearly indicate the applicable law become a major obstacle for those desiring to plan their life circumspectly.

In the light of this, it is striking that – as explained in the Introduction[483] – the last common residence of the spouses or the most closely connected legal system to the relationship are still used as connecting factors.[484] In a context where spouses could easily and effortlessly change their place of residence, find a job abroad or buy property in another country, the law that will finally be applied could be very difficult to predict not only ahead of time, but also right before the start of the proceeding. From the perspective of the court, determining the law governing the relationship based on facts occurring after the conclusion of the agreement might seem appropriate, as it assures the application of a law actually related to the case at stake. From the perspective of the spouses however, that could be perceived as a game of chance due to practical difficulties in predicting the circumstances that will surround them in the future – like their place of residence, acquisition of a nationality, place of residence of children, etc. – or the degree of importance that these events will have in the eyes of the court when determining the most closely connected legal system to the case.

A system focused on promoting the realization of the largest number of cooperative dynamics should avoid – as far as possible – the use of conflict rules that leave the door open to the application of a variety of legal systems.[485] The more precise and predictable the applicable law is, the better for the spouses, as this reduces costs and so maximizes the benefits from their cooperation.

---

481 The cooperation will then be discouraged as a consequence of an overregulation of their behavior. See: Guzman (2001) 906; Ribstein & O'Hara (2009) 25.

482 Rühl (2011) 209. See also Chapter 3 Section 2.2.1. *in fine*.

483 See Section 4.1. for the default conflict rule and Section 4.2.2. for ambiguities arising in the context of choice of law agreements.

484 Rühl (2006) 808.

485 Schack (2002) 190.

2.2. UNIFORMITY

The territoriality of the law – the fact that each state has the power to enact its own laws and reject the use of foreign provisions – leads to a situation where not only a variety of substantive rules exist, but also a wide range of private international law systems. When concluding cross-border transactions, people must always consider the possibility that a different approach, such as different conflict rules, will be used by a court if – as is usual in international cases – more than one jurisdiction is competent to resolve a dispute.[486] The Westphalian concept of sovereignty makes it necessary to consult foreign laws as a preliminary step before assessing the value of a transaction.[487] It might be a significant barrier for the realization of international exchanges, as major efforts are required to achieve possessive and transactional security.[488]

However, sovereignty is not an insurmountable hurdle, it can be overcome, and it even creates benefits from an economic point of view. On the one hand, sovereignty does not prevent states from transplanting successful conflict rules from another jurisdiction to their own, or reaching agreements with other states to apply common rules to cases with international connotations.[489] On the other hand, the prerogative of states to govern themselves can create novel and original conflict rules that might be more adequate than the standard solutions used by the rest of the countries. Indeed, modern conflict of laws rules – including those in supranational instruments – are the result of a process of trial and error, a synthesis of different approaches implemented over many years.[490] The legal diversity in conflict rules can be seen as a boost for the improvement of legal systems as it enables one to see favorable and unfortunate outcomes in similar and dissimilar realities caused by the use of distinct ways to confront the challenges posed by legal pluralism. This variety could bring forth the most appropriate solution for a conflict of laws, as it allows experimenting and so finding the suitable connecting factor.[491]

Still, a harmonization of private international law rules is also beneficial, as the use of a common approach to resolve conflict of laws reduces transaction costs for people as well. The system of conflict of laws should have what I would

486 Carbonara & Parisi (2008) 341.

487 For a discussion about the implications of the Westphalian doctrine of sovereignty in private international law, see: Muir Watt (2011).

488 Streit & Mangels (1996) 78–79.

489 The term "legal transplantation" refers to the "introduction, in national legal systems, of statutes and principles belonging to other systems, be they legal rules of other countries or customs whose acceptance is widespread". See: Carbonara & Parisi (2007) 368.

490 Smits (2002) 84.

491 Garcimartín (2002) 197 et seqq.; Vihanto (1992) 416. See in detail Chapter 7 Section 4.

like to call a *standardizing vocation*,[492] that is, states should try to achieve a harmonization, but not on a whim,[493] but based on the practical suitability of conflict rules to facilitate the realization of transactions. The idea is to promote initiatives aimed at coordinating the existing legal fragmentation, and to disseminate the positive results from the use of common conflict rules, but only among those countries actually willing to standardize their private international law. Such an approach – bottom-to-the-top – requires time and causes uncertainties, but it also makes the introduction of changes and innovations possible, as states remain free to experiment with different connecting factors.[494] This approach encourages the creation of international instruments on conflict of laws open to any state that would like to participate, but without denying them the possibility to withdraw, should they consider other conflict rules more appropriate. Thanks to this freedom, any state has the opportunity to assess the pertinence and adequacy of the harmonization by analyzing what happens in the unattached states.[495] The desire to attract more participants to an international agreement on conflict of laws, and the possibility for participants to withdraw, should motivate the harmonizers to develop efficient conflict rules and introduce timely corrections to their concept. So, as mentioned before in the case of divorce,[496] the right to dissent would prevent international law-makers from *resting on their laurels*.[497]

In any case, it is important to stress that it is neither desirable nor possible – at least in the current situation – to create a universal set of legal provisions to resolve the conflict of laws. States – as well as individuals – have dissimilar needs and incur different costs when implementing a particular law. As noted above, the application of the *lex fori*[498] is inadequate due to the uncertainties it creates. The use of a legal system that can be known beforehand is more adequate, as it avoids uncertainties for the spouses. This solution, however, presupposes that

---

492 The term *standardizing vocation* refers to initiatives aimed at the creation of international instruments open to the participation of states which are interested in harmonizing conflict rules in a specific area, but that also allow them to terminate their participation through a unilateral act.

493 Such as, for example, the creation of federal legislation for the case of the United States. See: O'Hara & Ribstein (2000) 1224; Kramer (1991).

494 See, for example, the Convention of 14 March 1978 on the Law Applicable to Matrimonial Property Regimes. Art. 30 of this convention permits its denunciation upon the fulfillment of minimal requirements by State parties of the convention.

495 For issues arising from the regulatory competition among choice of law systems see: Ota (2006) 7–8. For the advantages of the regulatory competition in general see: Vihanto (1992) 417–418.

496 See Chapter 3 Section 1.4.2.

497 Problems arising from agency costs – inefficiencies in the law caused by conflicts of interest between electors and political representatives – should also be taken into consideration at the moment of evaluating the economic desirability of a harmonization of conflict rules. See also: O'Hara (2000) 1577, 1580 et seqq.; O'Hara & Ribstein (2000) 1227. For agency costs in law-making, see in detail Chapter 7 Section 4.5.

498 See Introduction Section 2.

the administration of justice is capable of handling the costs of the application of foreign laws. Experience in other areas of the law – most notably in contract law – shows that countries like Germany, Switzerland or the Netherlands have enough resources to carry out this task.[499] Whether the judicial systems of countries like Mali, Myanmar or Haiti are able to bear these costs – such as for example translating foreign documents or accessing basic information about foreign law – is, however, questionable.[500] Issues like the degree of slowness of domestic judicial proceedings, incompetence of local authorities, and – above all – corruption in a given jurisdiction should always be considered when studying the effects of permitting the application of a foreign law.[501] The concept of *standardizing vocation* of conflict of laws rules thus accepts that the process of unification should be multi-speed. It does not rule out the promotion of initiatives aimed at harmonizing conflict rules. It does, however, remind us that not all states have the same resources to implement a new regulation and that a harmonization of conflict of laws – even among countries located in the same region – is sometimes neither possible nor desirable.

In sum, a harmonization of conflict rules enhances possessive and transactional security. Initiatives creating common rules on private international law should – from an economic point of view – be supported. However, tolerating a certain degree of diversity is also positive, as the quality of the harmonized rules can thereby be tested. Furthermore, the pluralism at this level is also the most appropriate way to overcome the very real problem that some countries have bearing the costs of implementation of the private international law system.[502] Uniformity is then a desirable attribute of the conflict of laws rule, but it – as everything in life, including getting married – has trade-offs.

2.3. CONSISTENCY

When answering all the questions arising from a legal dispute, the current conflict of laws system could use not just one, but a variety of connecting

499 It is not claimed here that the application of foreign law by domestic courts in these jurisdictions is without friction, but simply that despite the problems, the benefits seem higher than the costs. That is confirmed by the fact, that the number of states – at least in Europe – allowing the application of foreign law to cases involving family matters has consistently increased over the last years.

500 For costs created by the application of foreign law and ways to reduce them, see: Rühl (2007).

501 Schäfer (2001) 6; Schäfer & Lantermann (2006) 91–92.

502 As said before, the use of the *lex fori* creates uncertainties which might lead to a decrease in the number of exchanges. However, a deliberate or unintentional misapplication of foreign law could create even more uncertainties. In any case, countries that are not able to incorporate modern trends in private international law and participate in the current process of harmonization could find other ways to face legal pluralism – e.g. a harmonization of the substantive law or the creation of an optional marriage law – that respond well enough to the needs of the people within and beyond their borders.

factors to determine the law applicable to each of the claims.[503] The relationship could abstractly be divided into separate aspects, and each of them assigned a fitting connecting factor. The court has to first identify the nature of the action brought by the defendant, and then select the correct conflict rule. As a result, a single relationship might end up being subject to various different laws, depending on the number and nature of the claims raised in the legal proceeding.

But, in terms of costs, the application of a variety of legal systems to the same case is problematic even when the scope of the connecting factor is perfectly delimited, and the applicable law can be known before the conclusion of the contract.[504] The reason is that individuals normally can foresee neither the specific issue that will be a matter of dispute, nor the time when that will happen. At the moment of concluding a contract, individuals cannot predict whether – for example – questions related to the non-fulfillment of a formality, the responsibility for a poor or delayed performance, or the consequences of a premature termination of the relationship will be challenged in a proceeding taking place years later.[505] If multiple legal systems could be used by a court, diligent parties are again obliged to learn about the contents of all the possible applicable legislation to adequately assess the risks of their partnership.[506] The more connecting factors the relationship is subjected to, the greater the disincentives to concretize a contract as this will entail consulting a greater number of legal systems – or legal experts – to determine its real convenience. The use of a single conflict rule for the whole case is more efficient, as it makes possessive and transactional security easier to obtain.[507]

This should, however, not be overstated to the point of thinking that the drafting of a single conflict rule is enough to promote a great increase in the incidence of cooperative dynamics between people.[508] The use of a single legal system decreases transaction costs. But, there are circumstances where the application of a law other than the one governing the principal obligations is more convenient.[509] Not only questions of eminently procedural nature – e.g. rules regarding judicial notification or limitation periods to present documents to the court – but also certain particularities related to the performance of an obligation can be satisfactorily regulated by a different legal system. That is especially the case when the intervention of a third party is somehow required

503 Schmidtchen (1995) 80–81.
504 Carrascosa (2011) 65–66.
505 Kramer (1991) 2137.
506 O'Hara & Ribstein (2000) 1194, 1201.
507 O'Hara & Ribstein (2000) 1191, 1193–1194.
508 Jürgen Basedow commented that scholars of law and economics usually refer to "transactions" and their legal framework, although such a reference often includes, beyond contract law, all kinds of rules that might affect the performance and enforcement of the transaction significantly. See Basedow (2006a) 59–60.
509 Carrascosa (2011) 139; O'Hara & Ribstein (2000) 1194.

to perform them.[510] In contract law, for example, the application of the law of the place where an act is performed seems suitable for certain issues – e.g. inspections of merchandise, adherence to a holiday schedule or weighing and measuring goods – independently of the legal system applicable to the rest of the contract. In the case of a marriage, it would be perfectly understandable to use different conflict rules for questions about, for example, the time limit for contesting a claim; requirements for the conclusion of the marriage by domestic authorities; recording evidence of the needs and resources of creditors and debtors of maintenance obligations; or the nature of rights *in rem* relating to the common property of spouses. For practical reasons, the law of the country where the court is located, the marriage is concluded, the current place of residence of the spouses, and the place where their property is registered – respectively – shall apply to resolve these questions.

However, regardless of these exceptions, the principle still stands: the relationship should preferably be governed by a single legal system.[511] The inclusion of such *Teilfragen* (collateral questions) in the conflict of laws system is certainly possible, but it should be limited to exceptional cases where it is clear that the inclusion of a different connecting factor reduces the transaction costs for the parties significantly.[512] Unfortunately, the case of marriage can be seen as a paradigmatic example of how the current conflict of laws system can increase the costs for spouses involved in an international relationship unnecessarily. As showed before,[513] the legal framework for international marriages *dépeçages* it into different aspects – maintenance, divorce and property regime issues – and assigns separate approaches for each of them. Spouses are thus obliged to consult a variety of laws if the relationship is – or potentially could be – connected with different jurisdictions. From an economic point of view, there is no reason to treat substantive issues related to maintenance obligations, divorce or the property regime of the spouses differently, as none of them has an ancillary character, their concrete performance does not require the intervention of a third party, and all of them respond to the same logic: creating trust to invest more in the relationship.[514]

2.4. SIMPLICITY

One should never lose sight of the fact that the first addressees of conflict of laws rules of marriage law are not judges, or lawyers or legal advisors, but rather

510 The same applies to other questions related to validity of contracts – e.g. law applicable to the legal capacity of persons. See: Basedow (2006a) 59–60; Rühl (2011) 406–407.

511 Schack (2002) 184; Rühl (2011) 542.

512 See in detail: Rühl (2011) 376 et seqq., 402–407.

513 See Introduction Section 4.

514 For the economic function of the marriage see Introduction Section 2.

ordinary people: individuals that have neither the time nor the knowledge to understand the legalese which experts on law speak and write.[515] Thus, the realization of transactions will be facilitated if conflict rules are as simple as possible, with a clear and precise terminology and in plain language.[516] Legal provisions that can be easily comprehended by laypeople make less necessary an expert consultation, not only to determine the convenience of initiating the relationship, but also the consequences of the termination of the marriage.[517] Simplicity, however, not only means avoiding any unnecessary legal lucubration in the wording of the provisions, but also reducing the number of statements of facts – within the *Tatbestand* – and legal consequences – within the *Rechtsfolge* – in the structure of the conflict rule. Law-makers should create provisions that address the most common type of case.[518] They should avoid subsidiary connecting factors, as they might complicate the determination of the applicable law not only for the spouses, but also for judges.[519] The connecting factor used should span the widest range of cases and people. As mentioned before: slowness, incompetence and, above all, corruption in the administration of justice should always be considered when evaluating the efficiency of conflict rules – especially if they are designed to be in force in different jurisdictions. Although the inclusion of alternative cascading connecting factors might sometimes be unavoidable, the goal should be to include as few factors as possible in the conflict rule to improve its understandability and to simplify its application to a concrete case.[520]

The idea of simplicity encompasses not only the structure of the conflict of laws system, but also its content. The selection of a law to govern a relationship can generate high costs for one or both parties, as access to information is often difficult. The connecting factor should assure – to the extent possible – less expenditure when determining the specific rights and obligations assumed

---

515 Clarity should not be ignored in the economic analysis of the law, as unnecessary legal complexity can drive a misallocation of human capital and resources toward comprehending and complying with legal rules, and away from other productive ends. See: Katz & Bommarito (2014) 338.

516 Schack (2002) 196–197. For a discussion about the optimal complexity of legal rules from an economic perspective see: Kaplow (1995). For a framework measuring complexity of legal rules see: Katz & Bommarito (2014).

517 According to Louis Kaplow: "Actors seeking to comply with more complex rules may need to expend resources to learn how the rules apply to their contemplated acts. Moreover, because acquiring information is costly, some will choose not to learn the rules, so their behavior will not be guided by the rules' more precise commands. Finally, when rules are more complex, an enforcement authority typically will have to expend additional resources to determine whether a violation occurred or the severity of the violation". See Kaplow (1995) 151.

518 For issues arising from the complexity of conflict rules, see: Schack (2002) 183; Rühl (2011) 42

519 Questions about the correct interpretation of a conflict rule might lead to disputes at several stages of the appeals process. See: Schack (2002) 190.

520 Schack (2002) 197.

with the marriage.[521] Thus, the application of a legal system with some objective linkage to the spouses is preferred, as this would make use of pre-existing knowledge. However, the concrete determination of the governing law among all those connected in some way to the parties should not be justified by arguments other than economic rationality. It must represent an actual reduction of the costs for both parties. Thus, having a certain nationality or living in a certain jurisdiction should not by itself justify the application of a law. More crucial is to what extent the use of a connecting factor facilitates the parties being informed about the rights and obligations arising from the relationship.[522] The unique situation of each married couple makes the formulation of a conflict of laws rule that diminishes the costs of information in all cases impossible. For this reason, the efficiency of a rule will rather be measured by how much the information costs are reduced in the majority of cases. Further on, in the next chapters, objective criteria to achieve this goal will be discussed more in depth.

3. THE ROLE OF LEGAL CERTAINTY IN THE MARITAL RELATIONSHIP

Private international law is of key importance for the flowering of trade in the international arena. The performance of this set of rules to boost the number of transactions depends on certain attributes – accuracy, uniformity, consistency and simplicity – as they increase the possessive and transactional security required for the realization of exchanges. Omitting these attributes impacts negatively on the willingness of people to trade and decreases the surplus from transactions. However, whether in the context of the marriage a strengthening of possessive and transactional security will actually have significant repercussions in the life of spouses might be questionable. In commercial activities, the costs of information to gain certainty and predictability play a role in the decisions of trading partners. In the case of a marriage however, it is unclear if spouses actually pay much attention to the legal regulation of their relationship. Most do not consult specialists in marriage law to be made fully aware of the legal effects of the relationship. It seems that being only partially informed about the legal consequences of their acts is enough for most people.[523] If that is the case, one can conclude that an increase of the possessive and transactional security would only have a minimal impact on the decisions taken by them, and consequently any effort to enhance them would be trivial.

---

521 Rühl (2011) 209.

522 In Chapter 8, the importance of the cheapest-cost-avoider for the design of the conflict of laws rules will be discussed in detail.

523 For issues arising from bounded rationality see in detail Chapter 7 Section 2.

Notwithstanding this, the fact that individuals ignore a great deal of the rights and obligations arising from their relationship does not mean that certainty and predictability would not generate benefits for spouses. Possessive and transactional security are always important, even if people are not able – or willing – to be fully aware of the legal consequences of their marriage when making or accepting a marriage proposal.[524] First, it is not necessary to be completely informed about all the legal consequences of a marriage – or any other contract – to develop and deploy successful strategies. At the moment of taking decisions, individuals might only pay attention to one or a couple of legal effects to plan the course of action to be followed during their relationship. The exact time needed to initiate a divorce proceeding, the technical rules used by a court to allocate the common property or the simple right to receive maintenance covering basic needs could be – separately and on their own merit – reason enough for one spouse to reduce their worktime for raising the children.[525] Even without knowledge of the specific method of calculation, being aware of the existence of such a right might be enough to dare to take the leap. Similarly, moving abroad can be based just on the trust generated by the minimum amount of waiting time required to initiate a divorce proceeding. Knowing that a divorce cannot be demanded out of the blue means not being at the mercy of the partner, if a residence permit is linked with this marriage. In the same vein, knowing that only assets acquired after the conclusion of the marriage are subject to a division of property in case of a divorce, can motivate the parties to enter into this legal relationship. Being fully informed is not necessary to take appropriate decisions. More important is having one piece of knowledge that matters according to one's own particular situation. Sometimes a specific aspect of the regulation of maintenance payments is crucial; in other cases it may be the conditions for terminating the relationship or the distribution of assets after the marital crisis. Since it is impossible for law-makers to know which rules are important for every single person, all effects of the marriage must be – to the extent possible – predictable in order to avoid dashing their legitimate expectations. Low possessive and transactional security would punish those that want to plan their life prudently. It would become a disincentive for those willing to initiate or continue a long-term partnership with another person.[526]

Second, predictable rules give spouses the opportunity to figure out the legal consequences if not before, at least after the conclusion of their marriage. More often than not relationships do not end overnight, but they deteriorate as time goes by. Regardless of whether the couple was actually informed about the

---

524 O'Hara & Ribstein (2000) 1208. See also: Rühl (2016) 52–53.

525 For the suitability of one-reason decision-making see Gigerenzer & Goldstein (1999) 83 et seqq.

526 Bix (2002) 264–265.

regulation of their marriage before entering into it, predictability in the law is of the utmost importance, as it lets the spouses adjust their investments after the conclusion of the marriage to ameliorate *ex post* the costs to them of its termination. Without the need to discuss it with their counterpart, they can reduce future losses by changing their behavior in accordance with the allocation of rights and obligations stipulated in the applicable law. Thus, even assuming that spouses were not at all informed from the very beginning about the legal consequences of their marriage, unpredictable changes of the law would cause significant problems, as it prevents them from adjusting their own course of action to accommodate the applicable law when, over time, they envisage the rupture of the relationship and consequently a legal proceeding in the future. The uncertainty could indeed lead the spouses to assume the worst, and react by reducing their investment in the relationship immediately, which in turn might cause the same reaction in their partner. The lack of possessive and transactional security would thus trigger a downwards spiral with negative consequences for both of them. Again: since it is impossible for law-makers to know when things between any couple might start to go wrong, the effects of the marriage must be predictable at the earliest point in order to avoid dashing their legitimate expectations.

4. CONCLUDING REMARKS

Private international law does not necessarily assure by itself the willingness of people to conclude arrangements with international connotations. Having a system of conflict of laws is essential to increase the number of cross-border transactions. But, its capacity to encourage more cooperative dynamics depends on further attributes of the system: accuracy, uniformity, consistency, and simplicity. Accuracy means that conflict rules should strive to be precise – in particular – avoiding connecting factors that link the governing law to events whose occurrence could be envisaged only shortly before the beginning of the judicial proceeding. Uniformity refers to the benefits from the use of the same conflict of laws rules no matter where a legal proceeding is initiated. Consistency entails preferring the use of conflict rules that lead to the application of a single legal system to the whole relationship, as this reduces the costs of information for the parties. Finally, simplicity comprises two aspects of the conflict of laws rules: structure and content. The first wants to avoid obscure lucubrations in the wording of the rule, and achieve the preference of connecting factors that reflect the majority of cases. The use of cascading connecting factors within the conflict rule might be unavoidable, but it should be circumvented and relegated to exceptional cases for the sake of plainness. The second aspect calls for the application of a law whose content is easy to access for the parties. The legal system governing the relationship should be connected to the parties, as that requires fewer resources to get information about the rights and obligations assumed by them.

These attributes – accuracy, uniformity, consistency and simplicity – improve the system of conflict of laws, and spouses benefit even if they are only dimly aware of the regulation of their marriage. Possessive and transactional security allow them to find *ex ante* a promising course of action on the basis of easily understandable information, or to change *ex post* their old strategy if they notice that the relationship does not work out as expected. The next chapters will focus on applying these findings to international marriage law in order to provide concrete connecting factors to resolve conflict of rules. Following our familiar rationale, they depict the legal provisions that eliminate barriers for all those willing to formalize their relationship with the conclusion of a marriage.

CHAPTER 6

REGULATORY COMPETITION AND THE LAW MARKET FOR MATRIMONIAL ISSUES

One of the most notable novelties introduced by international instruments and national conflict of laws systems drawn up in recent years is the possibility to determine the law governing a relationship via a choice of law agreement. Since the late twentieth century, there has been a clear trend towards allowing individuals to select their specific set of legal rules themselves, not only in contractual disputes,[527] but also in those involving family matters.[528] There are,

---

[527] Party autonomy in international contract law is almost universally recognized. Prominent exceptions are *Brazil* (Art. 9.2. Introductory Act to the Norms of Brazilian Law. See: LIMA ET AL. (2017) 1935, although some authors do not enterely reject the possibility to choose the applicable law in Brasilian conflict of laws – see GAMA ET AL. (2021) 985–986); *Iran* (Art. 968 Iranian Civil Code, It is however allowed if both parties are foreoigners – see GIRSBERGER ET AL. (2021); YASSARI (2017) 2179); and *Saudi Arabia* (KRÜGER (2017) 2463). In *Bolivia, Chile* and *Colombia* the party autonomy is admitted but with a very limited scope of application (see GIRSBERGER ET AL. (2021) 39). *Uruguay* was part of this group, however the new legislation – Art. 45 of the Uruguayan General Act on Private International Law – allows contractual parties to choose freely the law governing their contract – see FRESNEDO DE AGUIERRE (2021) 1125; for the situation in Uruguay before the reform see IRIARTE (2017) 2632. For a comparative report on the regulation of the freedon of choice in international contracts in more than 70 jusrisdictions see GIRSBERGER et al. (2021) 33–42. See also: MANKOWSKI (2017) 104.

[528] By way of example, the following countries admit the determination of the law applicable to at least one aspect of the marriage: *Albania*: Art. 24 Private International Law Act; *Argentina*: Art. 2630 Civil and Commercial Code; *China*: Art. 24 Law of the PRC on the Application of Laws to Civil Relationships; *Dominican Republic*: Art. 44 Private International Law Act; Korea: Art. 38 Private International Law Act; *Lichtenstein*: Art. 20 Statute on Private International Law; *Norway*: CORDERO-MOSS (2017) 2396; *Russia*: Art. 161(2) Russian Family Code; Serbia: Arts. 74, 79 Draft of Private International Law Act; *Switzerland*: Art. 52 Private International Law Act; *Thailand*: Art. 25 Private International Law Act; *Turkey*: Art. 15 Private International Law Code. To this list one has to add those countries that are part of the 2007 Hague Protocol on the Law Applicable to Maintenance Obligations: *Austria, Belgium, Brazil, Bulgaria, Croatia, Cyprus, Czech Republic, Estonia, Finland, France, Germany, Greece, Hungary, Ireland, Italy, Kazakhstan, Latvia, Lithuania, Luxembourg, Malta, Netherlands, Poland, Portugal, Romania, Serbia, Slovakia, Slovenia, Spain, Sweden, Ukraine.* See also: CORNELOUP (2013) 15; BROSCH (2019) 1. For the regulation of party autonomy in the international instruments dealing with marital issues, see in detail: BROSCH (2019) 15 et seqq.

however, significant differences in the limits imposed on party autonomy in contract and marriage law. Whereas in regular contracts people have a wide menu to choose from – albeit limited in cases involving a weaker party – the freedom of choice granted to spouses is much more restricted. Contractual parties are permitted to choose the legal system they regard as the most appropriate according to their own interests.[529] In contrast, spouses are only allowed to designate a law which the law-maker considers closely connected to their relationship. They can choose between the law of their country of residence, the law of their nationality and – under certain conditions – the law of the forum.[530]

The introduction of party autonomy into international marriage law is a step forward in terms of efficiency.[531] Not only does it reinforce the predictability of the outcomes of legal proceedings, but it also clarifies the exact rights and obligations arising from a marriage.[532] Furthermore, the freedom of choice allows the designation of a single governing law to the most important aspects of a relationship that – given the options put at their disposal by the law – best responds to the preferences of these spouses. If the objective of private international law is the elimination of barriers hindering the emergence of cooperative dynamics, there is little doubt about the benefits of freedom of choice for achieving this purpose. Since the possibility to conclude choice of law agreements seems so advantageous from an economic point of view, it is worth asking why not further extend the number of the spouses' options? Why not allow them to choose with the same freedom they enjoy when concluding – for example – purchase contracts? The aim of this chapter is to theorize about the dynamic that could emerge if individuals were free to determine the law they deem most appropriate to disputes related to their marriage. In order to carry out this analysis, an analogy with regular markets will be made: the law will be

---

529 The Rome I Regulation grants contractual parties the possibility to choose from the worldwide menu of legal systems. According to Peter Mankowski, "Even if the contract at stake does present connections only with the States A, B or C, the parties are permitted to choose the law of D". See Mankowski (2017) 105.

530 See Introduction Section 4. In detail: Brosch (2019) 15 et seqq.; Gray (2021) 165 et seqq.

531 Throughout this book the term "efficient rules" refers to legal provisions – or any other legal measure taken by governments – that facilitate the emergence of cooperative dynamics between people. Legal provisions that eliminate barriers to the conclusion of contracts – or any other kind of voluntary agreement – are regarded as efficient as contracts are the typical means used to depict the terms in which such dynamics will be carried out. This is based on the idea that the constant conclusion of voluntary agreements between people – i.e. the engagement in cooperative dynamics – allows that the existing resources end up in the hands of those that value them the most. See: Chapter 1 Section 1.1 and Section 1.2. *in fine*. For situations meriting the imposition of restrictions on the freedom to conclude voluntary agreements – externalities, asymmetry of information, constraints affecting decision-making and monopolistic positions – see Chapter 3 Section 1.

532 Brosch (2019) 10–11; Corneloup (2013) 18–20.

treated like a product;[533] that is, an economic asset demanded and supplied by individuals and states. It is sought here to show that there are good reasons to assume that in a situation without barriers to the choice of law, the behavior of both agents – individuals and states – will be comparable to the behavior of consumers and suppliers. The place where the interaction between them would happen will be called the "law market".[534] The expression "law market" is used to depict a situation where individuals have the opportunity to select the law they consider the most suitable; and states compete with each other to offer legal rules that best meet the preferences of the people. This term is an explanatory resource used to better appreciate the potential behavior of states and individuals if legal systems did actually allow people to freely choose the law governing their relationships. With this market analogy, the behavior of the actors involved can be explained in simple terms, while also providing new insights into the advantages and hazards of a comprehensive freedom of choice in marriage law.[535]

This chapter begins with a description of the idea of the law market. Next, it delves into the theoretical framework of regulatory competition[536] and the incentives for spouses and states to be engaged in it. After that, some empirical data underpins the plausibility of the emergence of a market of law in marriage law. Later on, the discussion focuses on the desirability of such a dynamic, as well as the conditions needed to achieve efficient outcomes if the barriers to freedom of choice in marriage law were actually removed.

1. THEORETICAL FRAMEWORK OF THE LAW MARKET

Imagining law as a mere product, and individuals and states as its consumers and providers can be traced back to a seminal paper published in 1956 by the economist and geographer Charles Tiebout.[537] In this article, he argues that

533 Corneloup (2013) 20. See also: Bratton & McCahery (1997) 209; Eidenmüller (2009) 641; Garcimartín (2008) 255; Kerber (2000) 71; Kirchner (2004) 610; Romano (1985).

534 Ribstein & O'Hara (2009) 27, 66 et seqq.

535 In the last years, an increasing number of publications have spoken about the idea of a law market and regulatory competition in many areas of private international law. Its application in the analysis of the conflict rules of marriage law is, however, still sparse. See for example: Ribstein & O'Hara (2009) 161 et seqq; Lemke (2016). See also: Basedow (2015) 230 et seqq.; Brosch (2019) 9; Corneloup (2013) 20; Fulli-Lemaire (2017) 439–442.

536 The term "regulatory competition" describes "the activity of private or public lawmakers who intend to produce novel or alter current legislation in response to competitive pressure from other private or public lawmakers". See: Gödker & Hornuf (2019) 1787.

537 Tiebout (1956). See also: Gröteke (2007) 158; Gabor (2013) 2; Ribstein & O'Hara (2009) 27.

concepts such as shopping and competition could be applied to the public sphere and could explain decisions of local governments to provide public goods and the intent of people to reside in a specific place.[538] His model formulates that municipalities offer a basket of goods – roads, parks, schools, nurseries, etc. – in exchange for a price, which is paid by the residents in the form of taxes.[539] The decision of people to live in a certain community is influenced by a cost–benefit analysis between the set menu of public services, and the taxes required from this community.[540] Accordingly, similarly to how in regular markets competition leads to an efficient equilibrium between supply and demand, the Tiebout-model predicts that the decision of individuals where to live would also lead to an even balance between the provision of public goods and the preferences of the people.[541] Municipalities will not only try to offer good products at a low price to attract residents, but their basket of goods will also be affected by bids made by the surrounding localities.[542] Local governments will tend to copy offers made by successful municipalities and discard failed ones to obtain the greatest benefit from the movement of potential taxpayers to their own area. Before Charles Tiebout, it was assumed that there is no market-type solution to predict the level of expenditure on public goods. It was thought that individuals are only able to influence their services through the right to vote.[543] Pioneering in Tiebout's article was the idea that the decisions of governments could also be affected by the mobility of individuals. Mobility is seen as the central mechanism to reveal the preferences of the people about the correct amount of public goods,[544] as they not only express their opinions at the ballot box, but they also *vote with their feet*.[545]

1.1. REGULATORY COMPETITION AND CONFLICT OF LAW RULES

Although the work of Charles Tiebout only refers to public services offered by municipalities, there are no theoretical reasons to restrict the use of his

538 Tiebout (1956) 422 *in fine*. For a discussion about some assumptions underlying the Tiebout-model see: Trachtman (2000) 337 et seqq.

539 Oates (2006) 23, 27–28.

540 Tiebout (1956) 418. See also: Fischel (2000) 7; Oates (2006) 22.

541 Tiebout (1956) 422. See also: Bratton & McCahery (1997) 209.

542 Gröteke (2007) 159–160; Oates (2006) 22; Vihanto (1992) 412.

543 Musgrave (1939); Samuelson (1954); Samuelson (1955); Tiebout (1956) 416–418. See also: Fischel (2000) 7; Gröteke (2007) 158; Gerken (1995) 12.

544 Tiebout (1956) 418. See also: Oates (2006) 22; Gröteke (2007) 159; Garcimartín (2008) 254–255; Gatsios & Holmes (1998) 271.

545 Tiebout (1956) 420. See also: Bratton & McCahery (1997) 207–209; Fischel (2000) 7; Oates (2006) 22; Kirchner (2004) 612.

model to small communities. It is possible to expand its scope and analyze the functioning of bigger entities and more complex public goods such as nation states and legal systems. Under the keyword "international regulatory competition", the Tiebout-model is currently being applied to a broad range of legal fields at regional, national and international levels in a number of academic publications.[546] There, the effects of the liberalization of the choice of law have been analyzed in a number of areas such as tax law, competition law, contract law, corporate law and – to a very small extent – family law.[547]

Most of these publications understand the conflict of laws as the legal tool that makes the emergence of a law market possible in the first place. As this area of law is responsible for regulating the possibility, conditions and limits of opting out of the domestic law, scholars – especially those interested in the New Institutional Economics – have started to pay much more attention to the structure of conflict of laws rules and their influence on the enactment of local substantive laws.[548] From an economic perspective, conflict of laws is seen as a kind of referee in a game played at an international level. It aims – at this level – to bring order into the interactions of suppliers of laws by providing legal regulations where market failures cause inefficient outcomes. According to this view, conflict of laws has, then, the task of protecting competitiveness by safeguarding a legal framework that regulates the practices of the states – or any other provider of laws – in order to prevent party autonomy from generating undue costs – externalities – to other individuals or states.[549]

1.2. EXPECTED DYNAMIC IN THE LAW MARKET

The idea of a market of law must not be taken literally. Some caveats must be mentioned. On the side of demand, the decision of individuals to choose one or another legal system does not depend on an amount of money paid to states in exchange for its use. Their selection rather hinges on the content of

546 See: Gödker & Hornuf (2019) 1788. For an updated list of the most important publications about this topic see: Rühl (2017) 1515. See also: Bratton & McCahery (1997) 209–210; Gatsios & Holmes (1998).

547 For analysis regarding same-sex marriage see: Ribstein & O'Hara (2009) 161 et seqq. For the application of the Tiebout model to explain the evolution of US marriage law in the 19th and 20th centuries see: Lemke (2016).

548 Since the 1990s, German economists have paid particular attention to the link between conflict of laws and economics: Schmidt-Trenz (1990); Schmidt-Trenz (1991); Schmidtchen & Schmidt-Trenz (1989); Streit (1995); Streit (1996); Streit & Mangels (1996); Streit & Mussler (1995); Vanberg (1996).

549 Conflict of laws rules are seen as the guarantor of the proper functioning of competition between jurisdictions, just as competition law guarantees proper competition in markets for goods and services. Garcimartín Alferéz (2002) 118; Rühl (2011) 222–224; Rühl (2017) 1521; Streit (1996) 12–13.

the substantive legal provisions in force in that country. It is influenced by the solutions provided to resolve disputes between spouses, and the restrictions the chosen law imposes.[550] Generally speaking, the less the law reflects the preferences of the parties, the lower their willingness to choose it. It is assumed that this reluctance is based on the costs of negotiating and concluding additional marriage settlements – prenuptial or postnuptial agreements – to adjust their marriage to their preferences. Likewise, if the law imposed major constraints on party autonomy, spouses would avoid it, as it would prevent the customization of the relationship according to their particular needs.[551] On the side of supply, states do not ask for monetary compensation for the use of their law. Rather, they are mainly interested in promoting their domestic law in their own jurisdiction, due to the costs incurred by the administration of justice if couples increasingly opt out of using their local law. Furthermore, the non-use of the domestic law could generate losses for professionals living in the jurisdiction. Local lawyers, for example, would be particularly affected if people constantly chose foreign law, as their expertise would lose value. The use of domestic law abroad, in turn, is positive for them, due to a greater demand for their services.[552]

The consequences of allowing individuals to select their applicable law are varied. As mentioned above, choice of law agreements increase legal certainty, as a single law applies regardless of the moment or place where a legal proceeding is initiated. Party autonomy also gives spouses the opportunity to regulate their marriage according to their own beliefs, traditions and culture. The existence of various and diverse legal systems then becomes an advantage, as a greater diversity increases the chances of finding a law that effectively fits the preferences of a couple.[553] However, the elimination of barriers to the freedom of choice has further consequences. The increasing demand for a legal system can be understood as a sign of the suitability of the legal rules of this place. The rest of the states will have the opportunity to analyze these provisions, and consider possible reforms in their own domestic law. Successful legal provision in the legislation of other states on marriage law can more easily be identified – thanks to the choices made by spouses – and transplanted to other jurisdictions.[554]

---

550 See: Eidenmüller (2009) 642.

551 That, however, also includes the desire to opt out from legal systems that prevent spouses from restricting the termination of the relationship. Since the late 1990s, the market of law in the United States has seen the advent of "covenant marriages" – that is, unions between two persons that can only be dissolved under very restricted conditions such as adultery, felony conviction or abuse. See: Buckley & Ribstein (2001); Felkey (2011); White (2009).

552 Cuniberti (2013) 488; Eidenmüller (2009) 643, 647; Kobayashi & Ribstein (2013) 540; Ogus (1999) 408; O'Hara & Ribstein (2000) 1229; Ribstein & O'Hara (2009) 28, 74–75. For evidence regarding the current participation of lawyers in law-drafting activities, see: Kobayashi & Ribstein (2013) 539.

553 Gatsios & Holmes (1998) 273; Kirchner (2004) 615–616.

554 Bratton & McCahery (1997) 204; Eidenmüller (2009) 648, 653; Ogus (1999) 409.

Furthermore, the potential gains from the export of domestic law could encourage some jurisdictions to introduce innovations in their laws to make them more appealing for potential "customers".[555] Economic benefits from the use of domestic law abroad could encourage certain groups – e.g. local lawyers – to push law-makers towards introducing reforms in order to remain competitive in the international law market. The rest of the states would also benefit from this situation, as they would have the opportunity to observe the results of such reforms without the need to assume the costs. Jurisdictions that compete with each other become innovative laboratories, where different alternatives are put to the test. Law-makers serve as a kind of law scientists, who by trying to improve their own environment generate positive externalities for the rest, as their discoveries can subsequently be tested and replicated in other societies.

1.3. CURRENT SITUATION

As mentioned in the Introduction,[556] spouses are currently not allowed to freely choose the law applicable to their marriage. States either ban the choice of foreign laws completely, or – at the very least – demand the fulfillment of conditions to be able to select a specific legal system. National or international legislation that allows the choice of law requires the spouses to have a geographical or legal connection with the desired legal system to make their choice of law agreements valid. In general, spouses are only allowed to choose the law of their country of origin or the law of their place of residence for future disputes between them.[557]

The idea of a law market is to reframe the current situation and give people the opportunity to select a law based on its quality. Granting the possibility to designate the governing law – even with these limitations – is positive, as it allows spouses to have certainty about their rights and obligations. However, the elimination of all barriers for the choice of law would maximize these benefits, as it would not only let couples choose from more options, but also introduce a greater dynamism in the introduction of reforms in marriage law. The overwhelming preference of certain laws would help states detect better legal provisions in other legal systems. Furthermore, if a group of legal systems are systematically chosen more often, costs of the administration of justice will be reduced, as courts will apply these laws in the majority of cases.

---

555 Eidenmüller (2009) 643; Macey & Miller (1986) 496; Ogus (1999) 408, 412; O'Hara & Ribstein (2000) 1229; Ribstein (2004) 327. For some empirical data confirming this hypothesis, see in this chapter 3.1.2.

556 See Introduction Section 4.

557 For limits on party autonomy on family issues, see in detail: Brosch (2019) 15 et seqq. See also Gray (2021) 165 et seqq.

2. CONDITIONS FOR THE FUNCTIONING OF THE LAW MARKET

The mere existence of the freedom of choice is not enough to stir up competition among legal systems. The market of law presupposes that the consumers actually make use of the possibility of choosing another law, and that their decisions are driven by the concrete advantages a legal system grants. It is also required that states are concerned about the application of their own law and willing to adjust it according to the preferences of its addressees. In the following, these conditions will be scrutinized. It will be examined to what extent individuals are in a position to draw on party autonomy, and the incentives states have to be engaged in the law market. Some theoretical arguments about the expected responsiveness of individuals and states to freedom of choice will be described. Later on, in the next section, some empirical evidence supporting the plausibility of a market of law for marriage issues will be presented.

2.1. RESPONSIVENESS ON THE DEMAND SIDE

Legal rules and – even more so – legal systems are very complex; the content of a law is composed of many premises and consequences that are often very difficult to understand for laypeople.[558] The wide variety of situations covered by a law, in conjunction with the high number of technicalities, require special skills to understand the scope, extent and effects of legal rules as well as to compare legislative regimes in order to find the most convenient one. The practical difficulties of gathering information about the precise contents of a law have led some authors to call the rise of a law market into question.[559] There is little doubt that some individuals are ready to conclude marital agreements[560] and – where possible – to determine by themselves the law governing their obligations.

---

558 For an analysis of the degree of complexity of legal rules and sets of legal rules see: KATZ & BOMMARITO (2014).

559 KIENINGER (2002a) 83; KIENINGER, (2002b) 103; TJIONG (2002) 83; VOGENAUER (2013) 19.

560 The question how often spouses conclude marital agreements is tricky to answer. In Finland and France, it is estimated that around 20% of spouses have concluded a marital agreement. In Spain and The Netherlands, the percentage is above 25%. In other countries such as for example Lithuania, the percentage is only 2%. Lithuanian experts however recognize an increasing tendency toward formal agreements. See: BOELE-WOELKI ET AL. (2009) 295–302. Regarding trends, as well as the specific limitations in a number of countries for the conclusion of marital agreements within Europe and beyond, see: SCHERPE (2012a); SWENNEN (2015). As it is easier to choose a given body of rules, rather than customize one yourself, spouses are expected – at least on paper – to make use of the law market to more conveniently find legislation that meets their particular needs.

It is, however, hotly debated whether this decision would properly indicate the suitability of the chosen legal systems. As people are hardly ever in a position to be fully informed about the precise contents and extent of all legal provisions, they would most likely make mistakes when trying to choose the most suitable law.

Then again, complexity is not a unique attribute of legal rules. There are many services and products whose precise manner of operating is difficult to understand for people without this involving restriction in their capacity to choose when they are offered as available options. Think for example of a medical treatment. Although most people are only superficially aware of the mechanism of action and differences between treatments such as surgery, chemotherapy or radiation therapy, it is quite undisputed that patients should be the ones who decide on the treatment to be performed, if all of them appear as valid medical options to fight against a cancer they are suffering from. The same applies to further services and products traded in regular markets: the fact that commoners do not know how investment funds, cars or smartphones exactly work, is no reason to limit their capacity to choose among all the options at their disposal in these markets. Being fully informed about all the characteristics of a product is not a necessary condition for the efficient functioning of a market. If that were required, only simple products such as potatoes or onions would be allowed to be traded without an intervention of the government. Indeed, studies conducted in the last years have shown that consumers constantly rely on a limited number of features to take decisions about the convenience of a product – that is, without being aware of its exact *modus operandi* and – most important – that these decisions do surprisingly well at making accurate inferences in real-world environments.[561] Whereas one intuitively thinks that the optimal approach to choose among different options requires going through all the available information, deducing all the possible consequences and then calculating, based on the pro and costs of each alternative, the best option, experiments have shown that using a strategy by which one disregards most of the information available in order to rely on only a couple of attributes – those regarded as the most important – leads indeed to very good outcomes in many real-world situations.[562] It was demonstrated that successful decisions of great importance such as buying a house, choosing a career or even getting married are in reality based on a few good reasons, rather than a complex analysis of all their attributes.[563]

561 See for example: Czerlinski & Gigerenzer (1999); Gigerenzer & Todd (1999); Lenton et al. (2012); Todd & Miller (1999).

562 See: Gigerenzer & Todd (1999) 3 et seqq.; Czerlinski & Gigerenzer (1999) 98 et seqq.

563 Regarding empirical experiments about the way how individuals take decisions in the real world see: Czerlinski & Gigerenzer (1999) 98 et seqq; Gigerenzer & Todd (1999) 3 et seqq. For decisions related the choice of a partner see: Lenton et al. (2012) 456–457; Todd & Miller (1999) 288.

With this in mind, one can assume that individuals will only focus on specific solutions for particular issues – those regarded as the most relevant for each person – when choosing an applicable law.[564] The selection of a given legal system will then be made based on a reduced number of reasons, such as for example whether there is a division of property or not after the dissolution of the marriage, the waiting time to initiate a divorce, or the obligation to provide maintenance payments. The fact that each individual bases their decision on a particular aspect of the regulation will in turn help discover the superiority of certain legal systems over the rest. The constant preference of a certain law by individuals with different priorities will become a signal of the capacity of this set of rules to meet the requirements of all spouses. The wisdom of the crowd will set individual couples free of the burden to investigate every single option. As occurs with any product offered in regular markets, in a situation where people constantly make use of the possibility to choose, the most suitable legal systems would be revealed little by little. Subsequent legal innovations in key aspects of marriage would drive spouses to continue to choose a certain law, or rather replace it with another. Legal systems capable of rapidly adapting their rules to the preferences of the people would be those that ultimately remain at the forefront of the law market.

The fact that people are not fully informed about the contents of all legal provisions of a chosen law makes the occurrence of errors unavoidable. From a global perspective, however, the situation is not entirely reprehensible. The aggregate of all spouses would reveal the best rules through a process of trial and error.[565] The results of bad decisions will be taken into consideration by others, but also the contrary: good decisions made by spouses will be replicated as well. In any case, when people are allowed to freely determine their governing law, the logic of the market will generate mechanisms that refine the decision-making process. If a market of law takes root, certain individuals – legal practitioners – will specialize in foreign law and offer their services to customers interested in these new options. Specialized publications on the advantages and disadvantages of different legislation would emerge, as a response to the need for information.[566]

Indeed, the possibility to choose between the law of the nationality and the law of the habitual residence for marital issues has already encouraged many notaries to learn more about other legal rules on marriage law. Renowned

---

564 See: Mankowski (2017) 113.

565 Van den Bergh (2000) 438.

566 Expenses incurred by some when inquiring about the suitability of alternative legal systems will generate positive externalities for others. Paying an expert to investigate the positive features of a particular legal system generates gains for the couple, the expert and third parties, as this information can be used to advise further clients. The costs of making informed decisions about the features of foreign legal systems will drop, the more people are informed.

law firms in cosmopolitan cities already have experts on foreign law to advise clients, not only on contractual and corporate issues, but also on inheritance and marital matters. The current need for legal expertise on foreign law is something that not only concerns wealthy people. In order to cover the high demand for information about foreign family law, the Council of the Notariats of the European Union has opened a web portal with comprehensive information about the principal features of marriage law in force in all its Member States.[567] Questions about which goods are part of the common property, who is liable for debts incurred during the marriage or what the consequences are of a divorce or separation are answered in all the official languages of the European Union. Furthermore, if technical information is needed, there is a plenty of specialized literature in English and other languages with updated information about the specific contents of European and non-European legislation in family matters.[568]

2.2. RESPONSIVENESS ON THE SUPPLY SIDE

Some authors are very skeptical of the existence of any interest on the state side to participate in the law market.[569] Whereas in regular markets money pushes suppliers to offer products of good quality, it is not clear what the incentive for the states would be to offer laws of quality, or even to adapt them according to the desires of the people. That criticism is valid. The model of competition presented by Charles Tiebout is based on the idea that individuals pay taxes in the jurisdiction they are living in. Municipalities will then be encouraged to offer better public services, as that leads to an increase in their tax revenue. In the case of the market of law, that does not happen, as people do not pay royalties or fees to governments for using their law. There are, however, other gains that could motivate states to participate in the market of law. The interest of local politicians, as well as of those private individuals who obtain direct benefits from the export of domestic law could become a driver for changes in the national law in accordance with the preferences of the people.

2.2.1. Benefits of Allowing the Use of Foreign Law

At first glance, one might think that it is economically beneficial for states to ban the application of foreign law as this would save costs for the administration

567 See: <http://www.coupleseurope.eu>.

568 See for example: Basedow et al. (2017) vol. IV; Boele-Woelki et al. (2004); Boele-Woelki et al. (2009). See also: Bergmann et al. (1983–2021).

569 Carbonara & Parisi (2008) 349; Kieninger (2002a) 86; Vogenauer (2013) 28; Ott & Schäfer (2002) 215–216; Parisi & Ribstein (1998) 241.

of justice.[570] It is important to remember that costs of legal proceedings on family issues are partially assumed by the state.[571] Thus, if their domestic law is used, translations and opinions of experts will not be needed to resolve legal disputes. Furthermore, fewer errors and greater speed in the resolution of cases will be achieved because a well-known set of rules will be applied by national courts to the cases.[572] The application of the *lex fori* would be a way to reduce expenditure for the government and to increase the productivity of the administration of justice, as no extra costs would be incurred in the resolution of disputes with international components.[573]

However, this reasoning is not entirely correct. Indeed, the economic losses resulting from banning the application of foreign laws are like those from the implementation of protective measures aimed at banning the import of foreign products. On the one hand, this might represent a serious disadvantage for nationals involved in a relationship with a person from another country if those foreign courts use the same approach to resolve conflict of laws. On the other hand, the prohibition would also reduce the competitiveness of states *vis à vis* their peers because migrants of all kinds – including high-skilled ones – would be less ready to move there due to the unexpected changes their rights and obligations might suffer in the wake of the application of an unknown law. Allowing the application of foreign legal systems, in turn, might lead to a better situation of nationals in proceedings carried out abroad and make the jurisdiction more appealing to new residents.

2.2.1.1. Improving the Situation of Nationals in Legal Proceedings Conducted Abroad

Allowing the application of foreign law can be seen as a strategy used by states to encourage their peers to behave in a similar way.[574] The application of the *lex fori* is advantageous to save costs for the justice system, but in a situation where people constantly move from one country to another – a repeated game in the terms used by game theory scholars – these savings diminish if other states do the same. If states desire to maximize the gains from agreements concluded by their residents and nationals – including those abroad – they should allow the application of foreign laws by national courts to invite other states to do the same on the basis of reciprocity. In fact, this is the commonly adopted strategy by players in the above-mentioned prisoner's dilemma games:[575] acting in a

570 Ribstein & O'Hara (2009) 66; Schäfer & Lantermann (2006) 93.
571 See Chapter 1 Section 2.5.
572 Parisi (2007) 8.
573 Rühl (2006) 807; Rühl (2011) 274; Kirchner (2004) 615.
574 O'Hara & Ribstein (2000) 1225, 1228.
575 Kramer (1990) 339–344. See also: Stuart (2000) 291 et seqq.

manner that temporarily reduces their gains while increasing another person's gains, with the expectation that the other acts in a similar manner at a later time. Allowing the application of foreign law is no benevolent act, but is simply a rational behavior of states. In exchange for assuming the costs of the application of a foreign law in their jurisdiction, they benefit from cooperative agreements no matter the place where they occur or the personal characteristics of the individuals involved.[576]

In this context, there is no reason to ban the possibility of choosing any of the available foreign legal systems on the market. Quite the contrary, allowing the free determination of the applicable law would help states to reduce the costs arising from the applicable foreign law in their jurisdictions. As spouses will not be limited to selecting a legal system connected to their relationship, they will have the opportunity of choosing based on the quality of the options as their disposal. By stimulating the freedom of choice, the costs incurred by the administration of justice will be decreased, as people will tend to use only a limited number of legal systems – those with the most attractive features – among the whole wide menu of lawful dishes.

2.2.1.2. Increased Competitiveness to Attract Investments and Workers

The second advantage refers to the benefits derived from the arrival of newcomers. States compete with each other to attract workers, companies and investors to their jurisdiction. Taxable profits, as well as a financial injection into their internal markets are just some of the advantages that could prompt governments to draw persons to their territory.[577] The possibility to freely determine the law applicable to private relationships must then be understood as an investment by governments to look more attractive on the international labor market. It is a lure to encourage the arrival of companies that are interested in non-monetary benefits for their workers, as well as entrepreneurs looking for an appealing place from which they can operate their businesses. The use of foreign law could be understood as a plus offered by each country to entice people to its territory. It is one of the many public services that states should provide to compete with other jurisdictions in the international market of employment and services.[578]

576 In this regard it was said: "because states are locked in a relationship of infinite duration, dynamic game theory suggests that any outcome making all players better off than the noncooperative one is consistent with long-run self-interested behaviour". See Stuart (2000) 298. See also: Brilmayer (1991) Chapter IV; Kramer (1990) 341.

577 Kieninger (2002a) 87–88; Ogus (1999) 408.

578 Ogus (1999) 408; O'Hara & Ribstein (2000) 1161 et seqq.; Kirchner (2004) 612–614; Ribstein & O'Hara (2009) 7, 12, 60, 73; Vihanto (1992) 414.

2.2.2. *Benefits from Reforms in Accordance with the Demand*

Allowing the use of foreign law seems to be advantageous for jurisdictions despite the costs. That is confirmed by the growing number of countries that allow spouses the designation of the law of their country of origin or residence to govern their marriage.[579] However, efficiency is not reached by simply allowing the use of foreign legal systems by national courts. It is also necessary that lawmakers react to the competition by introducing reforms in accordance with the demand. Next, the forces pushing for adjustments in national legal systems as a response to the law choices made by people will be presented. Monetary gains for certain groups, as well as incentives for local representatives will be regarded as the main causes of competitive behavior of states. If barriers to party autonomy are eliminated, interesting economic and political incentives will emerge as a driver for the introduction of changes in local legal systems.

2.2.2.1. Profits for Certain Interest Groups

A push to introduce reforms in domestic legislation and compete with other jurisdictions in the law market might come from those groups that profit directly from the use of the domestic law within and beyond their own jurisdiction.[580] As mentioned above, lawyers would either be adversely affected by the use of foreign law, or would profit from exporting their own legislation. Maybe they should be actively concerned about the quality of their law.[581] The prevailing use of a legal system other than the domestic one lowers the value of their labor capabilities and forces them to make further investments into research to remain competitive on the market. The replacement of the national law in local cases not only means more costs for them to perform their professional activity; it also leads to the entry of rivals, which are able to offer cheaper services, as they already have the knowledge – expertise in foreign law – that is now required on the market. On the other side, the use of their domestic law abroad is beneficial for them: they will have more clients as their services will be in demand by more people.[582]

---

579 See Introduction. Except for Denmark, all Member States of the European Union are bound by the 2007 Hague Protocol on the Law Applicable to Maintenance Obligations, which allows people to choose the law of their residence or the law of their country of origin to govern questions about maintenance obligations between spouses. In 17 Member States, Council Regulation (EU) No. 1259/2010 is in force, and in 18 Member States Regulation EU 2016/1103. Both allow the choice of law for divorce and property regime issues.

580 Eidenmüller (2009) 643.

581 Ogus (1999) 408; O'Hara & Ribstein (2000) 1229; Kobayashi & Ribstein (2013) 540; Ribstein & O'Hara (2009) 28, 74–75. For evidence about the current participation of lawyers in law-drafting activities see: Kobayashi & Ribstein (2013) 539.

582 Cuniberti (2013) 488; Kobayashi & Ribstein (2011) 540; Ribstein & O'Hara (2009) 77, 167.

Having an export-quality product gives lawyers the opportunity to provide legal advice to spouses, law firms or courts abroad. Substantial economic gains can be derived from the preparation of reports and expert opinions. It follows that they will be better off if they promote improvements of their legal system, and conversely harmed by delays in the introduction of necessary changes. Thus, lawyers would have a direct incentive to investigate and propose reforms in line with the current preferences on the market.[583] Studies have traced the significant influence that lawyers' associations have had – for example – while drafting the statutes of corporate law.[584] The fact that lawyers are organized in bar associations, earn reputation from proposing reforms, and benefit from exporting their services to other jurisdictions, are good reasons for their active participation in law-making.[585] Although these studies are focused on business law, it should be noted that there are 40 million potential clients – all those couple involved in a marriage with international connotations[586] – just for issues related to marriage law in Europe.

Furthermore, other groups could – to a lesser extent – be interested in having a legal system of export quality.[587] Law schools for example would also be able to capture both monetary and non-monetary benefits from the law market, thanks to more students in their classrooms. Having an internationally successful law does not only lead to more revenue from university fees. The greater the demand, the greater the academic quality, as more rigorous filters could be used for the admission of new students. A greater demand for local education is, moreover, advantageous not only for the universities, but also for the internal economy of the place where it is situated. Even if educational institutions are primarily or totally funded by public resources, the arrival of more students is a strong financial incentive for the whole society and foremost for the city where they live.[588] For their part, legal scholars will also profit if their domestic law is used abroad often. The export of law leads to more publications in international journals, and more demand for their services as experts in legal proceedings and as specialists for legislative reforms in other countries.[589]

There are, then, interesting economic incentives for some people to organize themselves, investigate the specific reasons why people choose or reject

583 Ribstein (2004) 327; Macey & Miller (1986) 496; Ogus (1999) 412.

584 For evidence about the participation of lawyers in law-making see in detail: Ribstein (2004) 328 et seqq. See also: Kobayashi & Ribstein (2013); Macey & Miller (1986). See also: Ribstein & O'Hara (2009) 76.

585 Ribstein & O'Hara (2009) 76.

586 It was estimated that in 2007 of the approximately 122 million marriages in the EU, around 16.3% had some kind of international element. For more data about the number of individuals involved in a marriage with international connotations see Introduction Section 1.

587 Ogus (1999) 408.

588 For empirical evidence about the economic impact of universities on the economy of the region where they are located, see: Pellenbarg (2005) 35 et seqq.

589 Ogus (1999) 409; O'Hara & Ribstein (2000) 1183.

a certain legal system, and pressure their government to introduce corrections and innovations in their law. The law market offers opportunities for employment, especially for those countries specialized in the service sector. Likewise, just as representatives of powerful sectors – construction, banking, hospitality or any other industry – currently try to persuade their government to introduce legal measures that improve their competitive position at an international level, something similar could happen around the market of law: lawyers, universities and academics will advocate for reforms to make their law better in comparison to the ones in force in their competitors' countries.

2.2.2.2. Political Gains for Local Representatives

Potential gains from the export of national laws to other jurisdictions are not the only reason for changes in the law. People in a purely domestic relationship can also demand the introduction of reforms. The extension of the freedom of choice championed in this book is the same as that granted by modern conflict of laws systems to contractual parties,[590] so that spouses can determine the governing law freely only as long as the relationship has an international connotation. Couples involved in a pure domestic relationship are therefore not allowed to circumvent the national law *via* choice of law agreements.[591] As these individuals cannot opt out from the national law, they have no other option than demanding changes in the internal law. The elimination of inefficient requirements in the law, and the import of better legal rules can be used as a campaign promise by local representatives. Politicians will be encouraged to analyze international trends and propose changes in line with the preferences of their electors.[592] At this point, migration should be understood as a lubricant for the proper operation of the law market, as it facilitates the dispersion of information about good and bad aspects of other legal systems. The choices of law made by individuals from other societies let local people see the exact effects of the application of other legal provisions with their own eyes, and so assess the convenience of changes in their domestic law. The preferences of local electors, however, not only influence reforms, but they also limit proposals made by interest groups seeking to primarily appeal to an international market. This assures that the regulation of marriage does not solely respond to economic interests from the potential export of the law, but also to the real preferences of spouses living in this society.

---

590 For the extent of the party autonomy in the Rome I Regulation see: MANKOWSKI (2017) 87 et seqq.

591 Regarding the concept of internationality of the relationship as a condition for the conclusion of choice of law agreements in the Rome I Regulation, see: MANKOWSKI (2017).

592 OGUS (1999) 407.

3. EVIDENCE SUPPORTING THE PLAUSIBILITY OF LAW MARKET

As indicated above, there are some theoretical arguments that validate the plausibility of a regulatory competition. However, some verifiable data is necessary to lend more credibility to these arguments. Without any empirical evidence, doubts as to whether individuals would actually make use of the possibility to choose another law, and base their decision on the specific contents of these options, are reasonable.[593] The same applies to the assumption that states would respond to the demand for new laws by offering legislation according to the preferences of the people.[594]

As of today, there is unfortunately no conclusive study focused on answering these questions from an empirical perspective. On the one hand, as far as I know, no legal system in the world allows spouses to determine freely the law applicable to their marriage.[595] Most legislation applies the law of the court or the spouses' common nationality to legal questions arising from marriages with international connotations. Some countries – most of them located in Europe – allow the choice of law; however, party autonomy is only granted for certain aspects of the marriage and restricted to the law of the spouses' country of origin or their place of residence. In any case, party autonomy in marriage law was only recently introduced, which makes the compilation of enough data about the current behavior of spouses still unfeasible. On the other hand, there are also methodological difficulties with studies on the actual use of choice of law, as spouses are not obliged to make such agreements public or record them in a public register.[596] Moreover, contracts containing a choice of law decision are typically concluded before notaries who are subject to confidentiality clauses. Gathering information about the frequency or the motives behind the choice of law is very complicated.

Nevertheless, it is still possible to gain an idea of the consequences of the choice of law by way of an analogy to the current situation in commercial

593 Kieninger (2002a) 83; Tjiong (2002) 83; Vogenauer (2013) 19.

594 Kieninger (2002a) 86; Vogenauer (2013) 28; Ott & Schäfer (2002) 215–216; Parisi & Ribstein (1998) 241.

595 However, before Regulation 2016/1103 entered into force, the Austrian conflict of laws system did not include – at least expressly – restrictions on the freedom of choice granted to spouses to designate the law governing the marital property regime. According to Art. 19 of the Austrian Act on Private International Law: "*Das Ehegüterrecht ist nach dem Recht zu beurteilen, das die Parteien ausdrücklich bestimmen, mangels einer solchen Rechtswahl nach dem zur Zeit der Eheschließung für die persönlichen Rechtswirkungen der Ehe maßgebenden Recht* (Marital property law shall be judged according to the law expressly selected by the parties, and in the absence of such a contractual choice of law, according to the law governing the personal legal effects of the marriage at the time of entry into marriage. For a translation of the Austrian Act on Private International Law (Federal Statute of 15 June 1978 on Private International Law) see: Friedman (2017) 2951–2957."

596 About the difficulties to find empirical evidence of choice of law, see: Cuniberti (2013) 460.

contract law. Furthermore, some historic changes in marriage law could also shed some light on the possible responsiveness of states and people if spouses are allowed to choose the law governing their marriage.

3.1. CURRENT SITUATION

The freedom of choice in commercial contract law is granted by a large number of countries.[597] Based on that, studies have been conducted investigating the emergence of a law market in this area of law.[598] They do not conclude that the liberalization of the choice of law has led to a fierce regulatory competition among all legal systems. However, some elements point to the existence of a certain degree of competition, at least among a group of countries.[599] They have further shown that not only contractual parties make use of the choice of law, and base their decisions on specific features of a legislative scheme; some states also responded to this demand by advertising the use of their national legislation in international commerce.[600]

3.1.1. Evidence of a Response on the Demand Side

Commenting on the plausibility of a regulatory competition in contract law, some authors have suggested that not even sophisticated parties would be informed enough about the contents of all the laws available.[601] If so, it is quite dubious that ordinary people would venture to make use of the choice of law. It was further argued that in those situations where parties include a choice of law clause, they opt most frequently for their home law no matter whether this law actually meets their needs. There is even an expression – "champagne syndrome" – used by scholars on conflict of laws to describe the assumption that contractual parties usually regard the choice of law as an element without any real importance.[602] This perception is built on the fact that parties introduce such clauses only at the very end of the negotiations, at a moment where they have already agreed on all substantive matters of the contract. These arguments sound compelling. However, empirical data do not appear to support them.

---

597 With very few exceptions – e.g. Iran and Brazil – party autonomy is almost universally recognized. See: Mankowski (2017) 104. About the trend of convergence in United States and Europe in respect to the freedom of choice, see: Rühl (2007a) 155 et seqq. See also: Eidenmüller (2009) 642.

598 See: Ackerman (2011); Cuniberti (2013); Eisenberg & Miller (2009); Miller & Eisenberg (2009); Vogenauer, Stefan & Weatherill (2006); Vogenauer & Hodges (2010); Voigt (2008). For an analysis of the results, see: Rühl (2014b).

599 Rühl (2014b) 993.

600 Cuniberti (2013) 493 et seqq.; Rühl (2014b) 979.

601 Kieninger (2002a) 75 ff.; Kieninger (2002b); Mankowski (2017) 112–121.

602 Herbei (1999) 1, 8; Rühl (2014b) 978.

3.1.1.1. Actual Use of the Choice of Law by People

A study conducted in 2003 revealed that 82 per cent of all contracts submitted to the arbitration of the International Chamber of Commerce – ICC – contained a choice of law clause.[603] Another study focused on the period from 2007 to 2012 came to similar conclusions.[604] Furthermore, a survey made in 2004 about the opinions of businesspeople shows that 83 per cent considered the possibility of determining the governing law to be very important. 43 per cent of the interviewees had made use of the choice of law at least one time.[605] In 2008, the study was repeated, and the results were even clearer: 91 per cent regarded the choice of law as important or very important, and 85 per cent had at least occasionally chosen foreign law for their businesses.[606] Another survey conducted in the United States on 2,882 commercial contracts, revealed that 99.4 per cent of them contained a choice of law clause.[607]

Regarding the specific factors driving contractual parties to choose a certain legal system, the survey made in 2004 showed that for 79 per cent the predictability of the legal system was the most prominent reason to choose it. Fairness and flexibility of the law were also pointed out as very important for 78 per cent and 66 per cent of the responders respectively. 44 per cent of the interviewees had chosen foreign law at least occasionally, because they considered their national law not good enough to achieve the objectives pursued with their contracts.[608]

In the case of marriage, the numbers are less grandiose, but nonetheless interesting.[609] According to a study conducted in the Netherlands in 2014, 80 per cent of marriage contracts concluded before a notary contained a choice of law clause. This number may not mean much, but approximately 25 per cent of all married couples conclude a marital agreement in this country.[610] So, approximately one of every five couples in the Netherlands has made use of party autonomy to guarantee the governing law in at least one aspect of their marriage. This study does not dwell on the motives of the spouses for choosing one law. However, legal certainty may have played an important role, as the choice of law was mainly introduced as an accessory clause in contracts focused on specific obligations and rights of spouses in family law.[611]

There is no conclusive data about which legislative scheme or schemes are consistently preferred over others. As was said before, empirical studies are scarce due to the methodological limitations, as well as because in the past,

603 Voigt (2008) 9, fn. 7.
604 Cuniberti (2013) 468.
605 Vogenauer, Stefan & Weatherill (2006) 120–123.
606 Vogenauer & Hodges (2010) 13.
607 See Rühl (2014b) 981 analyzing data from: Eisenberg & Miller (2009) 1487.
608 Vogenauer, Stefan & Weatherill (2006) 121–122.
609 Wautelet (2018) 218.
610 Hoens & Schols (2014) 34, 43.
611 Wautelet (2018) 218.

many legal systems did not even allow the choice of law in matrimonial issues at all. However, in the area of contract law, where party autonomy has a longer history, it is possible to identify certain states' legislation as the most popular.[612] In a study focused on more than 4,400 international contracts concluded by approximately 12,000 parties, it was discovered that English and Swiss law are on average three times more often chosen than French law and almost five times more than German Law. This study also revealed that over a period of six years, more than 20 per cent of parties have agreed to subject their contracts to the law of a third state. This number rises to around 30 per cent if only the last four years are considered.[613] The fact that individuals are ready to choose the law of a third country shows that there is – at least for business contracts – a response of the parties to the offers on the international market for contract law.[614]

3.1.1.2. Specific Features of the Law as Reasons to be Chosen

According to the data, it seems that the people are making use of the possibility to choose a law. But do they pay attention to the contents of that law? There may be extrinsic factors that are driving people to choose certain legal systems. As most surveys cited only refer to contracts submitted to arbitration, one could think that the seat of arbitration might have influenced their decision more than the quality of the law. The success of Swiss law could be explained by the fact that many parties prefer this country as an arbitration venue. However, although France is designated as arbitration seat more frequently than Switzerland, its laws are chosen three times less often than the Swiss ones. Moreover, studies also confirm that Swiss law is consistently chosen as governing law, even in situations where Switzerland is not the venue for the arbitration.[615]

Language could also be a reason to select a certain legal system.[616] It is perfectly logical to assume that contractual parties would prefer legislation available in a language they understand. The fact that Swiss law – including much of the jurisprudence of higher appeal courts – is available in three languages could explain its success. The preference for the English law could then be the result of the dominance of the English language in international commerce. However, language alone cannot explain the preferences for these legal systems either.

612 Eidenmüller (2009) 645.

613 Cuniberti (2013) 472–475.

614 A similar dynamic also occurs within countries where different domestic legal systems coexist. For instance, although the law from the State of Delaware is the most popular for the internal regulation of corporations – according to recent studies approximately two-thirds of the Fortune 500 companies and more than four-fifths of all new US initial public offerings chose to incorporate in Delaware – the law of the State of New York is the law most widely used for contracts concluded by corporations. For data see: Eidenmüller (2009) 645; Gödker & Hornuf (2019) 1789.

615 Cuniberti (2013) 475 et seqq.

616 Schäfer & Lantermann (2006) 97.

On the one hand, although the Swiss legislation is available in three languages, German and Italian are spoken only by a limited number of people around the world. French in turn is a very widely spoken language, and remains the second language of international diplomacy. If the language were the crucial point, the Swiss law would owe its popularity to the large number of Francophone people. But why did the French law not benefit from that? Something similar happens in the case of English law. If the language explains its preference, why are Australian or US State laws not chosen? According to the study, Swiss and English laws are on average three times more attractive than, for example, French and all US State laws added together.[617]

Finally, it was also argued that because there are no significant differences in the laws in force in all of these countries, one cannot assume that the parties are actually interested in the contents of the legal provisions. The similarities are even more evident when analyzing German, French and Swiss legislation.[618] In my opinion, however, the fact that these legal systems are at the top of the wish list of contractual parties, instead of contradicting, rather confirms that people pay attention to the quality of the law. There is little doubt that all of them are characterized by their high legal certainty, foreseeability, jurisprudential development as well as the presence of leading scholars, who not only explain their contents in depth, but also constantly try to improve or innovate their law. It would be contrary to the expectations of a law market, if legal systems with no legal tradition were constantly picked by people. But legal systems whose quality can hardly be denied – English, Swiss, French, German and New York law – are chosen the most.

3.1.2. Evidence of a Response on the Supply Side

Some scholars doubt the existence of a real incentive on the supply side, encouraging states to offer improved laws to consumers.[619] There is a lack of clear benefits from the use of their law, and consequently no real interest in exporting domestic law. However, the appearance of advertising materials about the advantages of certain legislation makes me think otherwise.[620] The possibility to choose the law applicable to contracts has given rise to many publications explaining the advantages of one national legal system over another in the last years. These publications are mostly from private entities, generally law firms. But, in many cases they are not only financially supported by public organizations – chambers of notaries or bar associations – but also by national

617 Cuniberti (2013) 482 et seqq.

618 Cuniberti (2013) 497.

619 Kieninger (2002a) 86; Vogenauer (2013) 28; Ott & Schäfer (2002) 215–216; Parisi & Ribstein (1998) 241.

620 Eidenmüller (2009) 643; Rühl (2014b) 983.

governments. Detailed documentations and colorful brochures with the clear purpose of convincing individuals of the attractiveness of their legal system and its superiority over the competitors[621] are available. The Law Society of England and Wales, supported by the Ministry of Justice, has edited a brochure for the general public that – quote – "lets people know why it is in their own interest to use English law". They claim English law provides more predictable outcomes, legal certainty and even fairness compared to civil law legislation.[622] Transparency, flexibility and freedom are also pointed out as reasons to choose this law. In a clear reference to its competitors, it is even said that "English law is more flexible than many civil law systems, which rely on a more rigid and prescriptive civil code".[623]

Other countries did not want to stand for that. The so-called Alliance for German Law – supported by the German Minister of Justice – has also published documents listing a number of advantages of German Law *vis à vis* English and American Law.[624] There are even brochures supported by the German and the French Ministries of Justice jointly, addressing the superiority of Continental Law over Common Law.[625] Bar associations and private lawyers have not missed the opportunity to portray their national law in the best light. Swiss practitioners are very active here. They write on Swiss law in a variety of publications, speaking out in favor of the alleged neutrality of the Swiss law, its availability in several languages, consistency, as well as its relative accessibility. The superiority of the Swiss law has even been justified by the low number of mandatory rules in Swiss law.[626]

Admittedly, some of the arguments mentioned above are questionable. However, they certainly show the willingness of a group of people – lawyers, academics and governments – to promote the use of their law beyond their borders. The existence of information materials and individuals advocating for certain legal systems confirms – in a way comparable to regular markets with their marketing materials and sale teams – the existence of a real interest to be involved in the market for law. As far as I know, there is no advertising material focused on promoting the use of a specific marriage law. A quick search on the web, however, reveals an increasing number of internet pages advertising the user-friendliness of some legislation for – in particular – same-sex couples.

---

621 Cuniberti (2013) 493; Eidenmüller (2009) 641, 643.

622 Law Society of England and Wales (2008) 5.

623 Law Society of England and Wales (2008) 7–8. See also: Ministry of Justice (2011) 8.

624 According to their marketing material: "'Made in Germany' ist nicht nur ein Qualitätssiegel für deutsche Autos oder Maschinen, sondern auch für deutsches Recht. Faire Gesetze und eine leistungsfähige Justiz sind ein Garant für gesellschaftlichen Frieden, individuelle Freiheit und wirtschaftlichen Erfolg". See: Bundesnotarkammer et al. (2008) 2.

625 Rühl (2014b) 984.

626 In detail see: Cuniberti (2013) 494.

3.2. HISTORIC EVIDENCE RELATED TO THE EMERGENCE OF A LAW MARKET FOR MATRIMONIAL ISSUES

There are two well-documented historical episodes in the United States suggesting that a degree of regulatory competition existed in the area of marriage law. Even if that does not constitute irrefutable proof of a market of law, it shows a real interest of states to compete with each other by offering their new and improved marriage laws to interested people.

After gaining their independence, the former colonies continued to use English law to regulate their communities. This situation was detrimental to women, as common law not only restricted the exercise of their civil and political rights, but also imposed severe legal disadvantages on married women.[627] This legal situation began to change at the end of the nineteenth century. Movements led by a number of courageous women made the introduction of reforms for a higher degree of equality between males and females before the law possible.[628] However, it is interesting to note that even before the appearance of feminist movements, there were some significant changes in the law that improved the situation of married women substantially.[629] These reforms, however, did not happen in the whole country. They only occurred in jurisdictions located in specific regions of the territory – the Northeast and the American frontier. To better understand this phenomenon, the Tiebout-model was deployed.[630] With the premise that States can use their law to attract people to their jurisdiction, the desynchronization in the introduction of these reforms can be analyzed. With that in mind, constitutional amendments and the passage of the Married Women's Property Acts in the whole country during the period from 1788 until 1943 have been studied.

3.2.1. *The Case of the Northeast*

The first case study describes the legal situation of women in the northern part of the East Coast of the United States in the middle of the nineteenth century. In this region – as well as in the rest of the country – the English doctrine of "coverture" was in use.[631] In accordance with it, the legal existence of women was almost suspended once they got married. From this point on, women had no formal right to own property, nor to enter into contracts as independent persons. They were neither allowed to engage in formal business nor to stand

---

627 For the legal regulation of the marriage in England and the US at that time see: BLACKSTONE (1765) 421–433; HARTOG (2002) 137 et seqq.

628 BASCH (1986) 99.

629 BASCH (1986) 98 et seqq.

630 LEMKE (2016).

631 Sometimes spelled "couverture doctrine". See for example KUPER (2002).

in court alone.[632] This poor legal position clashed with the increasing economic development and the promising labor offers for women in the region. As the textile industry became the dominant industry in New England during the industrial revolution, employment opportunities for females sprung up, since physical strength was not required to do these jobs. Furthermore, shift work allowed them to combine these jobs with home chores.[633]

Many entrepreneurs saw the advantages of integrating women into the labor market. In order to seem more appealing – especially to the parents of girls – businessmen were prepared to introduce new labor practices.[634] Women-only accommodations or supervision by older female chaperones were offered to prospective mill girls. Furthermore, headhunters were contracted to go out into the rural areas of the United States – and even abroad – to promote the benefits of working in the textile industry.[635] Their offer was crowned by attractive salaries: according to some estimates, the bank balances of women working in the textile industry were in the hundreds and thousands of dollars.[636] However, this offer was still not good enough, as it was necessary to import workers from far-away places like Scotland or Ireland.[637] At a first glance, the reason for the shortage does not seem logical because a big number of women were already living in the region at that time. However, when taking into account the legal situation of those women, the mystery is solved.

According to the memoir written by a mill girl named Harriet,[638] many women were discouraged from accepting employment or even continuing to work. They feared that their husbands would find them and seize their personal earnings. Many mill women hid their faces from visitors, or used fake names to avoid that men could take advantage of their financial success.[639] The coverture doctrine allowed male spouses to unilaterally dispose of the property of their wives. It is then no surprise that few married women were actually tempted by those job offers. In this situation, there was obviously much interest in a women's property law reform. This, coupled with the benefits for the industrialists from the use of cheap labor, created an environment ripe for the introduction of changes in marriage law. So, the States in the Northeast were the first to pass

632 According to the judge William Blackstone – one of the most influential jurists in the UK and the US during the 18th century: "The very being or legal existence of a woman is suspended during the marriage, or at least is incorporated and consolidated into that of the husband". See: Blackstone (1765) 430.

633 Ginger (1954) 67 et seqq.; Robinson ([1898] 1976) 1–24; Abbott (1906) 460 et seqq.

634 Lemke (2016) 301. For the attitude toward women in the industry at that time see: Abbott (1906) et seqq.

635 Lemke (2016) 303.

636 Ginger (1954) 69.

637 Ginger (1954) 75; Lemke (2016) 301.

638 Robinson ([1898] 1976).

639 Robinson ([1898] 1976) 66–67.

separate earnings acts in favor of married women. During the 1850s, a number of legislative efforts tried to overrule the coverture doctrine. By 1860, in virtually all jurisdictions of New England, women were granted the right to have separate property from their husbands, as well as the possibility to buy and sell property without male consent. Those reforms happened despite women not having any political rights, with the exception of course of *voting with their feet*.[640]

3.2.2. The Case of the American Frontier

The second case study also examines a region trying to attract women to its jurisdictions: the American Old West. According to the first official census of California in 1850, 91.8 per cent of the population was male. In 1849, there were only 15 women in San Francisco while in Denver – a settlement of 1,000 people in those days – only five women were counted.[641] It is very difficult to imagine reasons that would have led women to go to these remote places. However, as in the case of the Northeast, there were also very attractive employment opportunities for female workers in the West. Restaurants were the first to see the economic potential of hiring women, in order to attract more customers to their locales. A restaurant chain called Hearvey's, for example, not only had the explicit policy of employing "women between 18 to 30 years of good character, attractive and intelligent"; it even opened an office in Chicago to recruit candidates and create publicity about the great labor opportunities for girls along the frontier.[642] Waitressing, however, was not the only opportunity for women. After the first settlements were established, there was also a great demand for female teachers, nurses and other professions typically undertaken by women at that time.

Similarly to the first case, these jurisdictions had also been suffering from unfavorable laws for women, and the disincentives arising from the use of the doctrine of coverture. It comes therefore as no surprise that legislative reforms during this period attempted to improve the situation of married women. California, Nevada and Colorado ruled out the doctrine of coverture in 1872, 1873 and 1861 respectively.[643] In States without the need to attract females to their jurisdictions, coverture remained a cherished tradition: in Texas, Louisiana, Tennessee, Alabama or Florida, the abolition of this doctrine was achieved only in 1913, 1916, 1919, 1920 and 1943 respectively.[644] A further analysis of the laws in all States during the period from 1788 until 1943 shows, that on average, the

640 Lemke (2016) 296.
641 Brown (1958) 16; Lemke (2016) 305.
642 Poling-Kempes (1989) 42.
643 Lemke (2016) 308.
644 Lemke (2016) 296.

Northeast took the lead in reforms, followed by the West.[645] At the tail end was the Southeast, whose politicians had no need to compete with anyone for the arrival of female migrants to their region.

3.3. FURTHER EVIDENCE

The case studies above confirm that if there are enough incentives for governments, they are willing to use their own law as a marketing tool, compete with other jurisdictions, and even copy successful reforms. Marriage law is no exception. There is evidence supporting the hypothesis that reforms in this area of the law in the nineteenth century were introduced, and later replicated, with the objective of attracting residents. In fact, a similar strategy was also used, but for the opposite purpose: the Nazi-regime enacted many repressive rules – some of them in marriage law – in order to push Jews out of Germany.[646] The aforementioned cases also show that people will respond to legal incentives, as long as the benefits outweigh the potential costs. Promising labor offers can influence the decisions of women to move to another jurisdiction. However, that alone is not enough, if it is not accompanied by a legal framework that guarantees the enjoyment of the fruits of their labor.

Now, the question has been asked before: how important is marriage law at the moment of actually taking this far-reaching decision? Are individuals generally concerned about the law applicable to their marriage? Would they make sacrifices for the sake of being allowed to use preferred legislation? Furthermore, could legislators be motivated to introduce reforms in marriage law based on only the potential economic gains of some interest groups? Responses to all these questions can be found in the development of the Nevada marriage law.[647] Although they do not prove regulatory competition, they do however support its plausibility, and shed more light on the possible reactions of both actors – States and spouses – in a situation where individuals are empowered – at least indirectly – to choose the law applicable to matrimonial issues.

Although nowadays Nevada – and especially Las Vegas – is world-famous for its quick marriages, in the past it was popular for the permissiveness of its divorce law. In fact, before the no-fault revolution in the seventies, Nevada had the reputation of being the "divorce heaven" for individuals in need of a fast

---

645 Lemke (2016) 298.

646 According to Article 1 of the Law for the Protection of the German Blood and the German Honor: "Marriages between Jews and subjects of the state of Germany or related blood are forbidden. Marriages nevertheless concluded are invalid, even if concluded abroad to circumvent this law". For an analysis of the *ratio* of this law See: Friedländer (2009) 50 et seqq.

647 See: Blake (1962) 153 et seqq.; White (2009) 882; Ribstein & O'Hara (2009) 172.

and uncomplicated dissolution of their marital bond.[648] The opportunity of this unique marriage law was quickly seized by groups who noticed its economic potential. Hostelry, for example, benefitted from the arrival of people staying for a while to formalize the dissolution of their marriage. Many other businesses such as restaurants, transportation companies, casinos[649] and – obviously – law firms[650] also gained from this situation.[651] By 1905, politicians were proudly supporting their legal rules and boasting about "the divorce capital of the world". At that time, the law in Nevada only required a period of residence of six months, to be able to demand a divorce in court, so it was not uncommon to find people from all over the world queueing before the family court.[652] For some people, going abroad was the only opportunity to get a divorce, as many national laws banned this possibility.[653]

There is no data about the exact number of outsiders that changed their residence to obtain a divorce in Nevada. However, the number was probably economically significant, so much so that in 1927 the residence period was reduced to only three months, as a response – in the words of a politician – "to a perceived threat to [Nevada's] divorce supremacy from France and Mexico".[654] Data shows that the reduction of the waiting period doubled the number of applications for divorce.[655] Four years later, the legislation was reformed again. From the year 1931 on, the law only required six weeks of residence to qualify for the application of Nevada's marriage law, and consequently to initiate a divorce proceeding. At this point, the divorce industry was clearly evident in the numerous arrivals, often housewives trapped in unhappy marriages.[656]

The reaction of the whole nation to the new policy of Nevada was notable. Some years later, the US Supreme Court supported the competition led by Nevada and followed by Indiana and the Dakotas, by ruling that all US States had to recognize divorces granted in other jurisdictions. The legal basis for this

---

648 Blake (1962) 159; Jacobson (1959) 103; Haussamen & Guitar (1960) 121; White (2009) 882.

649 "For wealthy divorce-seekers desirous of privacy or a vacation, a trip to Nevada could provide both a diversion and a divorce, particularly after the development of its casinos". White (2009) 882.

650 Several lawyers did relocate their practices to take advantage of these more liberal divorce laws. See: White (2009) 882.

651 Jacobson (1959) 104.

652 Blake (1962) 153; Jacobson (1959).

653 See in detail: Haussamen & Guitar (1960) 147–170.

654 See <http://renodivorcehistory.org/themes/law-of-the-land/residency-requirements/>.

655 See: Blake (1962) 157; Jacobson (1959) 103.

656 Ribstein & O'Hara (2009) 172. According to statistics, by the 1920s, the Nevada courts were granting about 1,000 divorces a year. In 1928, after the residence requirement was reduced, the number was about 2,500. After 1931, the rate again doubled, so that in this year there were 5,260 divorces. As was said, it is not possible to find out how many were individuals coming from other jurisdictions. Blake (1962) 157–158.

decision was Article IV, Section 1 of the United States Constitution: the Full Faith and Credit Clause.[657] This decision favored legal competition, and was probably the main reason for the subsequent standardization of the rules on divorce in the United States. The obligation to recognize divorces under any federal legal system ultimately led to a harmonization. As mentioned, the competitors of Nevada were not just other US States. Nevada's success showed that many individuals were ready to cross borders to start a proceeding for divorce. This led – according to Nevada's politicians – some countries to imitate what had happened in the United States, and capitalize on this new market opportunity.[658]

The aforementioned examples cannot be used as irrefutable proof of the rise of a regulatory competition as soon as people are allowed to freely determine the law applicable to their relationships. In fact, the only way to see the overall effects of a law on their behavior is to put it into practice. However, it cannot be denied that history reinforces the plausibility of a regulatory competition. A similar dynamic – individuals moving to specific jurisdictions to assure the application of their law; third parties profiting from this situation; and States introducing their own reforms after observing this phenomenon – can currently not only be observed in the *law market for same-sex marriages*.[659] Since the late 1990s, the United States have seen the advent of "covenant marriages" – that is, unions between two persons that can only be dissolved under very restrict conditions such as adultery, felony convictions or abuse.[660] In this area it was also detected that not only were outsiders profiting from this option, but also that other jurisdictions reacted by transplanting the concept of covenant marriage into their domestic law.[661]

4. LAW MARKET FAILURES

After reading arguments about the emergence of legal competition, it is now time to discuss the outcomes of such a dynamic. Until now, it was assumed that

---

657 See in detail Blake (1962) 173–188; White (2009) 882.

658 For the impact of the "migratory divorce" in France, Mexico, Cuba, the Virgin Islands and other US States, see: Jacobson (1959) 105–118.

659 For the economic incentives of legislators to recognize same-sex marriage based on the average amount spent on weddings, and increased retail revenue generated by tourism, see: Brown (1994). See also: O'Hara & Ribstein (2000) 1208; Ribstein & O'Hara (2009) 166–167.

660 Stark (2019) 33. Entering into a covenant marriage requires pre-marital counseling. Felkey (2011) 369; White (2009) 878.

661 Louisiana became the first State to pass a covenant marriage law in 1997; shortly afterwards, Arkansas and Arizona introduced this union into their legislation in 1998 and 2001 respectively. See: Felkey (2011) 369; Stark (2019) 33; White (2009) 883. For discussions regarding the development of a market for covenant marriages, see: Buckley & Ribstein (2001).

regulatory competition would induce a race to the top in law-making. However, market failures are always possible.[662] Could that also happen in the market for marriage law?

4.1. REGULATORY COMPETITION ACROSS HISTORY

There is nothing new about the coexistence of competing legal systems within one country or even community. Some historians have even suggested that the struggle among legal systems has been a distinctive characteristic of the Western legal tradition.[663] From medieval times well into the collapse of the *Ancient Régime*, the layman was subject to the ecclesiastical and secular laws, the latter in turn divided into royal law, feudal law, manorial law, urban law and mercantile law. In many cases the competences of courts were not clearly delimited, leading to situations where people could actively select the instance ultimately responsible to hear their case.[664] In England, for example, each court not only had its own judges and procedural rules, but also its own judicial precedents, and consequently distinct rules and principles to resolve legal disputes. In situations of overlapping competences, individuals could initiate proceedings in a specific jurisdiction and so guarantee the use of those rules and doctrines. They were able to indirectly choose the legal system applicable to their case, simply by selecting the court in which to sue the defendant.[665]

The outcome of this situation has been judged very differently among scholars. Some of them think that it provided incentives to create efficient legal rules, led to innovations, reduced delays in the proceedings, and even enhanced the impartiality of the justice system.[666] Adam Smith, for example, was of the opinion that jurisdictional competition produced better laws.[667] However, other scholars – most notably Jeremy Bentham[668] – were not as optimistic about the benefits. Until the early nineteenth century, judges were paid for each legal

---

662 For the concept of market failure and its application into the analysis of the law see Chapter 3.

663 Berman (1983) 10; Klerman (2007) 1181.

664 Berman (1983) 10; Guadagni (1998) 542; Parisi (2007) 2; Zywicki (2002) 1581–1582.

665 Zywicki (2002) 1582 et seqq. An interesting phenomenon relating to marriage law occurred in Africa as a result of Colonization. Natives were encouraged by missionaries to enter into a Christian marriage. If they accepted, the couple and their children became subject to European law in matters related to family and inheritance law, so that the local population was – to a certain extent – able to choose between domestic and foreign rules to govern their family relationships. See: Guadagni (1998) 542–543.

666 Baker (1990) 44, 52; Garoupa & Gomez (2011) 228 *in fine*; Zywicki (2002) 1552–1553, 1632. See also: Klerman (2007) 1184.

667 Smith ([1766] 1978) 281–282; 423–425; Smith ([1776] 1976) 241–242. See also: Klerman (2007) 1184.

668 Bentham ([1843] 1962) 199 et seqq.

proceeding they resolved, so the more cases they heard, the more fees they received.[669] As the competent court was frequently the one where the claim was first filed, judges might have competed with each other by developing case law more beneficial to plaintiffs.[670] Indeed, there is evidence of a bias in these courts in favor of those bringing the case into the court.[671]

4.2. RISKS LINKED TO THE MARKET OF LAW

The situation of the Courts of England in the nineteenth century shows that competition does not necessarily lead to an improvement in law-making. An efficient development of the law is by no means a matter of course. Quite the contrary, efficiency requires the fulfillment of certain conditions. Just like markets can fail and lead to a wrong allocation of goods and services, the freedom of choice in the market of law could also fail and deliver negative legal rules, not only for the spouses, but also for the rest of the people.[672] There is, for example, the risk that some states might not want to improve the situation of their people when enacting laws. In many cases, governments legislate with other objectives in mind than those based on promoting the maximization of the welfare of their society. Legal rules can be used to impose anachronistic visions of how the behavior of people should be, based on moral, religious or cultural traditions. The results could be racist, gender biased, or displaying any other type of discrimination. The market of law is understood as a process of trial and error, where the suitability of a legal system is discovered thanks to good and bad decisions of people. It is then not possible to rule out that some individuals will choose laws affecting seriously fundamental rights.

Furthermore, states could try to cater to the interests of only one of the contracting parties. That is expected in situations where only one of them can influence the choice of the applicable law.[673] If powerful interest groups profit from the use of their law, and only one of the contractual parties is empowered to select it, they might exert pressure on law-makers to tip the balance in favor of this side.[674] Think, for example, of consumer or employment contracts. If states are very keen to export their law, they could design legal systems that

---

669 Klerman (2007) 1182.

670 Klerman (2007) 1179.

671 Klerman (2007) 1185. Jeremy Bentham for example thought that competition might have negative effects, as it encouraged judges to create complicated procedures to increase their fees. See: Bentham ([1843] 1962) 199–201.

672 Garcimartín Alferéz (2002) 112, et seqq.; Klerman (2007); Rühl (2014b) 986; Van den Bergh (1998) 136–139. See also: Eidenmüller (2009) 648; Gatsios & Holmes (1998) 274; O'Hara & Ribstein (2000) 1163; Parisi (2007) 8; Van den Bergh (2000) 445.

673 Rühl (2014b) 990–992; Garcimartín (2008) 257.

674 O'Hara & Ribstein (2000) 1188–1189; Schäfer & Lantermann (2006) 101–102.

benefit traders and employers at the expense of the rights of consumers and employees. Biased legal rules could be written to skew their legislation in favor of the stronger party.[675] Aside from that, states might also generate externalities in third parties – individuals or other states – when enacting laws aimed at attracting investors into their country. Think, for example, of rules on responsibility for environmental contamination caused by extractive industries. In order to attract foreign industries to their territory, a government might favor factories by reducing pollution liability. In contexts where raw materials are located at the border of the country, the government will not respond to political pressures to change its liability enforcement. The strong desire to ensure the realization of certain activity will overshadow damage suffered by individuals without the right of participating in political life and the decision-making process.[676] In a context where countries desire to attract further industries they might also employ similar strategies such as reducing product liability for certain products – those destined for export – with the aim of leaving the door open to take advantage of foreign consumers. The same applies to employment law, where states can reduce working conditions in specific sectors – for example those covering airline personnel, truck drivers, etc. – to enable employers the application of favorable law regardless of the country of residence of the employees or the place where they performed their work. In situations where there is an imbalance in the bargaining power between parties the elimination of barriers to the freedom of choice might lead not only to damage to the weaker one, but also to a downward spiral, where states compete with each other to offer law detrimental for those individuals.

4.3. NORMATIVE IMPLICATIONS

From the above, it can be concluded that the law market should be promoted, but only to the extent that there are no failures that cause a deterioration of the law in the terms explained above. That does not mean abandoning legal competition as the guideline for the design of conflict of laws rules.[677] It only emphasizes the necessity of introducing corrections when market forces do not work appropriately.[678] Thus, if the freedom of choice – in a particular environment or even in a concrete case – leads to undesirable economic results,

675 Klerman (2007) 1187; Rühl (2014b) 987. For corporate law see: Bebchuk (1992) 1440; Bebchuk & Allen (1999) 1168 et seqq.; Eidenmüller (2009) 650; Trachtman (2000) 339.

676 Garcimartín Alferéz (2002) 113; Garcimartín (2008) 257–258; Van den Bergh (2000) 446. See also Ribstein & O'Hara (2009) 25.

677 For the role of competition law from an economic perspective see: Li & Li (2014) 47–48.

678 Garcimartín (2008) 258; Gatsios & Holmes (1998) 273–274; Kerber (2000) 87 et seqq.; Schäfer & Lantermann (2006) 93–94.

an intervention in the form of limitations on party autonomy is justified.[679] The selection of a legal system containing discriminatory rules can be considered an externality due to the adverse effects that enforcing these agreements might cause on the members of society of the jurisdiction where the court is located. However, in contrast to substantive private law, limitations on the freedom of choice in private international law should not only avoid spillovers on those directly or indirectly involved in the contractual relationship. They must also prevent other jurisdictions from trying to make use of these failures and so ensure the application of their own law regardless of the externalities it may cause to other individuals or even states.[680]

Therefore, if freedom of choice creates consistently and continuously wrong incentives in the market, a rule restricting the freedom of choice for this single situation must be introduced. Employment and consumer contracts are paradigmatic examples where a limitation is economically justified, since the characteristics of the contracting parties involved often lead to systematic imbalances in the relationship that can be harnessed by both: the strong party which might impose upon the other the application of a law beneficial for their own interests, and states which might try to enact law in favor of the strong party to assure the application of their law abroad and or to attract investors. In other cases, when a market failure is not recurrent in a specific environment, but it rather responds to the particular circumstances of a specific case, an intervention might still be justified. This however must not occur in the form of a rule, but on the merits of an escape clause allowing courts to analyze the particularities surrounding the case and so determine if an intervention is justified.[681] The regularity with which a particular failure occurs determines the proper course of action – i.e. the inclusion of a rule or the discretion of the court – to address undesirable effects of the party autonomy.

In the specific case of marriage law, an intervention might be needed, but not in the same form as is required in employment or consumer law, where the presence of a stronger and weaker party is the general rule. The avoidance of a failure – in particular the generation of externalities – will rather be achieved by resorting to the public policy of the forum. A specific limitation on the party autonomy of the spouses does not seem appropriate, since an imbalance in the relationship is not the general rule, but a situation that can occur likewise in any other contract.[682] There are certainly situations where the authority of the husband is uncontested, when he takes unilateral decisions affecting both spouses. Indeed, some societies not only tolerate but also promote ideas

---

679 Carrascosa (2011) 127; Eidenmüller (2009) 648, 65; Garcimartín Alferéz (2002) 112.

680 Eidenmüller (2009) 652; Garcimartín Alferéz (2002) 118; Rühl (2014b); Kerber (2000) 82–83; Kieninger, (2002b) 93 et seqq.

681 Rühl (2011) 317–318.

682 For another view, see: Wautelet (2018) 226.

asserting the superiority of men over women. Nevertheless, just because this happens, one must not conclude that the general rule is the imbalance of power between men and women to the point of claiming a special protection of the legal system as is the case in consumer or employment law.[683] Assuming that there are significant differences in bargaining power as a justification for a restriction on the party autonomy of spouses would make the imposition of limits necessary not only in international marriage law, but also in contract law in situations where women conclude contracts with men. This would not only be unconstitutional in most countries, but also ridiculous as a matter of common sense. Claiming inequalities in the bargaining powers between men and women as a reason to limit the party autonomy of spouses is by no means something new. This argument was already used in the past to justify the prohibition of women to dispose of their property, the need of the wife to require a permission of a court to take out a loan and even the ban on divorce. History, however, has shown that these concerns about women were unfounded.[684]

In sum, the *ordre public* clause and *loi d'application immédiate* are put forward as appropriate legal institutions to avoid inefficiencies arising from market failures in international marriage – in particular – to prevent externalities arising from the conclusion of choice of law agreements.[685] Situations where party autonomy is exercised abusively, or the application of foreign law compromises fundamental rights of one or both spouses will certainly not be tolerated. They will, however, not be combated thought a rule limiting the freedom of choice of all spouses, but by means of resorting the public policy of the forum.[686]

5. CONCLUDING REMARKS

This chapter was focused on the dynamic that would emerge if individuals were allowed to freely choose the law governing their marriage. It was argued that

683 Regarding binational couples, there is no pattern of dominance of men over women even when the latter lives in the country of origin of her husband. For the marital dynamic and the power balance in transnational marriages, see: Nowicka (2017) 134–136. One study confirms that women remain the key agents of sustaining or rejecting the national heritage and practices in the everyday life of binational couples, to the point that "the women determine the degree and shape of the intra-family cultural diffusion". See: Buler & Pustułka (2017) 37.

684 The case of Switzerland is illustrative here: Well documented are not only the discussions of Eugen Huber – the creator of the Swiss Civil Code – with legislators, but also with groups of women about the reasons for limits on the rights of married women. See: Gerber (1997) 480–493; Gerber & Kaufmann (1993) 178–220; Ryter (1997) 494–506. For the legal situation of married women in Europe in the 19th Century see: Gerhard (1995) 167–196; Gerhard (2013) 281–304; Sabean (1997) 460–479; Vogel (1988) 134–166; Weber-Will (1997) 452–459.

685 Eidenmüller (2009) 648; Ribstein & O'Hara (2009) 15, 62.

686 Schäfer & Lantermann (2006) 103–105.

in a situation without barriers for the choice of the applicable law, the behavior of individuals and states could be comparable to consumers and suppliers in regular markets. Individuals would have the opportunity to select a legal system that meets their needs. States would be encouraged to improve their laws according to the preferences of those people. The results of allowing the choice of law seem promising. On the one hand, it increases legal certainty and helps to better satisfy the preferences of the spouses, as they are empowered to choose the legal regulation they consider most convenient. On the other hand, party autonomy contributes to the improvement and innovation of the law, as it helps identify successful provisions in foreign legal systems and transplant them to other jurisdictions. However, the plausibility of a law market in the area of marriage law is far from a matter of course. Although theoretical arguments and historic events seem to confirm the hypothesis of the emergence of a market of law, verifiable evidence of the decisions that today's spouses actually take is still required to arrive at a definitive conclusion. What does seem clear is that rejecting party autonomy based entirely on economic arguments is short-sighted. As long as spouses behave as economic agents, the benefits from the choice of law would most likely outweigh the costs of the application of foreign laws, due to the gains for both – individuals and states – which the freedom of choice bestows. Furthermore, if some legal systems are systematically chosen more often, costs of the administration of justice will be reduced, as courts will apply these laws in the majority of cases. The *ordre public* clause will be used by courts to repeal undesirable situations such as, for example, cases where the chosen law affects fundamental rights of the spouses.

The law market is a powerful concept that changes our view of the law and the law-making process. It illustrates, from an original and fresh perspective, how different forces could shape the existence and contents of legal rules. The next chapter presents further advantages from the elimination of barriers to the freedom of choice in international marriage law.

CHAPTER 7

ADVANTAGES OF ALLOWING FREE DETERMINATION OF THE APPLICABLE LAW TO MATRIMONIAL ISSUES

Previously, the plausibility of the emergence of a market of law, as well as the conditions for its appropriate functioning, were discussed. The following lines now focus on showing that the freedom of choice is not only a means to promote regulatory competition in the area of marriage law, but also a tool to draw the maximum benefit for spouses from the existence of different legal systems in the international arena. Legal pluralism is not depicted as a problem, but rather as an opportunity to improve the situation of those involved in a marital relationship.

This chapter is divided into six sections. Each of them deals with one of the main advantages from the elimination of barriers to the freedom of choice: legal certainty; greater capacity to influence one's own well-being; safeguarding the rights of minorities; experimentation and innovation in law-making; tendency towards convergence; and incentives for the formalization of the relationship.

1. LEGAL CERTAINTY

It is widely accepted that the most straightforward benefit from the freedom of choice is the opportunity to organize the private sphere in a structured and orderly fashion.[687] Party autonomy allows reliable predictions about the outcomes of potential lawsuits, and the consequences of foreseeable or unforeseeable events like a marital crisis or the death of the partner. It lets spouses calibrate

[687] Predictability of the litigation's outcomes and the protection of the legitimate expectations of the people were put forward as the principal reasons to justify the harmonization of the conflict rules in the discussions about the international instruments dealing with marital issues. See: Bonomi/Explanatory Report (2013) 41; recital 9 Regulation 1259/2010; recital 15 Regulation 2016/1103; EPEC (2006) 48, 56; EPEC (2006) 185. See also: O'Hara & Ribstein (2000) 1189. See also Gray (2021) 42–51.

the amount of effort invested in the relationship, and make timely decisions that – if they do not improve their current situation – at least prevent further loses in the future.[688] An unforeseeable change in the governing law in turn renders any effort to plan one's life prudently moot, and creates a breeding ground for opportunistic behavior by either of the spouses. Legal certainty is definitely one of the biggest advantages of allowing individuals to determine the law governing their marriage themselves.[689]

1.1. CHOICE OF AMBIGUOUS RULES BY SPOUSES

But, should choice of law agreements appointing a legal system with ambiguous rules be enforced? If the objective of the choice of law is guaranteeing legal certainty, one could then arrive at the conclusion that arrangements selecting unpredictable substantive rules should not be protected by the law. This is based on the belief that the vaguer and more imprecise legal provisions are, the more common problems for the contractual parties become. However, that is not necessarily true. Studies have shown that contracts specifying the obligations and rights between parties in great detail can breed distrust,[690] lead to increased likelihood of litigation,[691] and even provoke an overly strict adherence to the letter of the law – work-to-rule – to the detriment of the main objective of the relationship.[692] Some authors have even suggested that a lack of specifications could encourage parties to find their own, individually negotiated solutions to avoid bringing a case to court.[693] The uncertainty about the outcomes of a legal proceeding might encourage them to resolve their problems by themselves, instead of taking their chances with a potentially unfavorable judicial decision. Think, for example, of a legal system whose provisions do not clearly indicate the criterion used by courts to allocate assets in the common property after a divorce. Although the uncertainty seems dangerous, the lack of precision could also motivate spouses to negotiate a judicious and even-handed solution before going to court. A degree of uncertainty about the outcomes of a legal proceeding can – under specific circumstances and for certain aspects of the relationship – be positive, as it makes the partners more predisposed to bargaining.[694]

In general, having clarity about the legal consequences of a marriage is advantageous, because it lets people calmly develop a course of action to follow

688 See Chapter 5 Section 3. See also: Neuhaus (1963) 795; Brosch (2019) 10; Ribstein & O'Hara (2009) 37, 164.

689 Bix (2002) 264.

690 Chou et al. (2011) 5; Epstein (2014) 309; Shur-Ofry & Tur-Sinai (2015) 412.

691 Shur-Ofry & Tur-Sinai (2015) 411, 415.

692 Epstein (2014) 309; Triantis (2002) 1072.

693 Chou et al. (2011) 22–23.

694 For bargaining in divorce from an economic perspective, see: Zelder (2002) 164–167.

during their relationships.[695] Still, some individuals might desire a certain degree of ambiguity in the effects of their relationship. These imprecisions can create a good climate for the development of endogenous extralegal mechanisms resolving disputes.[696] Thus, even if imprecise rules are applicable as a consequence of a choice of law agreement, the will of the spouses should still be respected. Choice of law agreements must be enforced, regardless of the specific content – in terms of predictability – of the law designated by the couple.

1.2. AMBIGUOUS RULES AND UNCERTAINTIES IN THE LAW GOVERNING THE RELATIONSHIP

To now generally conclude that unpredictability in the applicable law is desirable would be one step too far. The potential benefits of non-detailed contracts depend on the specific questions left open by the substantive law.[697] Sometimes vagueness about certain aspects can be positive. However, total ambiguity about the rules governing the whole relationship is quite different, as it brings about an unpredictability regarding not only some, but all obligations and rights of the spouses. The main advantage of the freedom of choice is not a perfect awareness of the legal consequences of any event during a partnership. It rather lies in the possibility of having a clear point of reference for the development of strategies to achieve personal goals. By making use of party autonomy, each spouse is able to know not only the benefits and costs, but also the risks – in terms of predictability – of their actions.

Some lacunas or ambiguities in the law are unavoidable. Courts require a margin of discretion to align a judicial decision with the situation of the spouses when resolving the dispute.[698] The choice of law, however, allows spouses to identify – before or after the conclusion of their marriage – the exact cases where they will encounter uncertainties. Based on this information, they can evaluate the suitability of the legal system and modify their behavior to accommodate the accuracy or inaccuracy of the provisions applicable to their relationship. Thanks to party autonomy, spouses are ultimately able to not only know, but also choose the specific gaps in the legal regulation of their relationship.

---

695 Chou et al. (2011) 7; Epstein (2014) 298–302. See also Chapter 5 Section 3.

696 For the concept of extralegal mechanisms and their importance in the marital dynamic, see: Chapter 2 Section 1.3.

697 Chou et al. (2011) 25; Epstein (2014) 312; Shur-Ofry & Tur-Sinai (2015) 416–417, 429 et seqq.

698 For a discussion about the margin of discretion that legal provisions should give to a court from a law and economics perspective, see: Ehrlich & Posner R. (1974); Schäfer (2001).

2. GREATER CAPACITY TO INFLUENCE ONE'S WELL-BEING

The market of law not only tolerates, but explicitly supports a situation where different law-makers have the power to enact substantive laws and introduce subsequent variations anticipating the preferences of the group of people they represent. Its functioning rests on the idea that legislators are able to differentiate their product from others provided by the competition and appeal to "clients" located within – and sometimes even outside – their jurisdiction.[699] The possibility to freely choose the law governing a marriage is essential to capitalize on this tempting variety. Having more options is positive, since it offers individuals a greater chance to find the alternative that best fits their needs.[700] The more alternatives people have, the bigger the spouses' margin to maneuver is, and therefore the greater their capacity to shape their future.[701]

2.1. BOUNDED RATIONALITY AS JUSTIFICATION TO RESTRICT THE NUMBER OF OPTIONS

Against the aforementioned, one can argue that having a greater number of alternatives is pointless, as individuals do not appear to be cognitively able to draw on the wide range of options.[702] Intuitively, one expects that the benefits of legal diversity can only be enjoyed if people are able to: gain access to all the legal provisions of the offered legislative schemes; understand their contents fully; analyze the pros and cons of each set of rules; and determine on the basis of their own particular goals the one that best fits their preferences.[703] Empirical data, however, has shown that, as a general rule, people do not behave in such a way, not even when they take decisions with long-lasting effects.[704]

---

699 See Chapter 6 Section 2.2.

700 Bix (2002) 263. See also: Gabor (2013) 5; Gatsios & Holmes (1998) 273; Kirchner (2004) 615–616; Rühl (2011) 198–199, 437–438; Van den Bergh (2000) 437–338; Whincop & Keynes (2001) 39.

701 See for all: Ribstein & O'Hara (2009) 28.

702 Rühl (2011) 202–204; Eidenmüller (2009) 651.

703 The earliest economic models analyzing the marital dynamic assumed such behavior. See: Becker (1973); Becker (1974); Mortensen (1988). For criticism of such models, see: Gigerenzer & Todd (1999) 3, 5 et seqq.

704 A selection of articles about cognitive bias and errors in judgement can be found in Kahneman & Tversky (2009); Gilovich et al. (2002); Gigerenzer et al. (1999). For the application of psychological insights in the analysis of the behavior of individuals *vis à vis* the law, see: Sunstein (2000), Parisi & Smith (2005), Gigerenzer & Engel (2006). For an analysis exclusively focused on cognitive bias affecting prospective spouses selecting a partner, see Frey & Eichenberger (1996). For biases related directly to private autonomy in private international law see: Rühl (2011) 202 et seqq.; Eidenmüller (2009) 651, et seqq.

Instead of analyzing the options at stake in detail, they rather use cognitive shortcuts – also called heuristics – when confronted with multiple options.[705] It was demonstrated that individuals do not behave "rationally", or at least not in the terms of the rational choice theory when confronted with different options. Rather than paying attention to all the alternatives and the information they have, people rely on simplified methods to process information, value the options and decide. They base their decisions on a reduced number of cues that are seemingly good enough for their personal purposes. Furthermore, in order to have a manageable number of options or in case their cues are not clear enough, they use considerations without a logical correlation to the issue at stake. The bigger the number of options or features assessed, the stronger the tendency to disregard information and even greater the predisposition to concentrate on just one reason – or a couple of reasons – at the moment of taking decisions.[706]

According to these studies, individuals do not conscientiously analyze all the features of the options they have at their disposal. They rather establish a finite and often very small number of attributes – priorities – and order them hierarchically according to their subjective importance.[707] Among all these alternatives, the one that fulfills the attribute they regard as the most important is chosen without considering further down-sides in comparison with other alternatives. Thus, once one of the options satisfies the requirement considered to be the most important, the rest are automatically ruled out regardless of other advantages they might have.[708] Allegedly, human reasoning functions similarly to a decision tree: individuals choose an option based on a single reason and use another reason only if there is a tie between them.[709] It was also shown that if many alternatives meet their requirements or when individuals simply lack enough information to see whether any one of them actually meets their preferences, people rely on attributes that are – apparently – not related to the discussed option at all.[710] For example, alternatives that are more familiar – those whose name comes easily to the mind in a specific context – are consistently preferred over the rest, to the detriment of unfamiliar ones which are immediately discarded.[711] In fact, marketing experts are very aware of this phenomenon; for

---

705 See: Bettman et al. (1998); Bröder (2000); Dieckmann et al. (2009), Ford et al. (1989); Gigerenzer & Goldstein (1996); Kurtz-Milcke & Gigerenzer (2006); Martignon & Hoffrage (2002); Yet et al. (2007).

706 Ford et al. (1989) 75; Rieskamp & Hoffrage (1999) 165; Kurtz-Milcke & Gigerenzer (2006) 48.

707 Gigerenzer & Goldstein (1999) 75, et seqq. Kurtz-Milcke & Gigerenzer (2006) 49; Gigerenzer & Todd (1999) 15. See also: Simon (1990) 9.

708 Kurtz-Milcke & Gigerenzer (2006) 50; Gigerenzer & Todd (1999) 14.

709 Kurtz-Milcke & Gigerenzer (2006) 52; Gigerenzer & Todd (1999) 4, 14 et seqq.

710 For a detailed discussion see: Gigerenzer & Goldstein (1999) 75 et seqq.

711 In psychological literature, such a shortcut is called recognition heuristic. Goldstein & Gigerenzer (1999) 50; Kurtz-Milcke & Gigerenzer (2006) 50.

this reason many advertising campaigns focus mainly on popularizing the brand name of the product instead of praising its quality.[712]

For the matter at hand – party autonomy in international marriage law – these findings suggest that spouses will not undertake an intricate analysis of the contents of a law.[713] They will only pay attention to the regulation of one, or at the very best a few, aspects of their relationship – only those that they regard as the most important. The reasons to choose a certain legal system will then not be the total benefits from its application, but rather the advantages of a sole provision dealing with a specific issue of the marriage. As a result, a single legal rule referring exclusively to – for example – the time to wait for a divorce, maintenance allowances or the principle of joint ownership between spouses could be decisive. At the very best, maybe two or three further provisions will steer their choice of legislation; the rest will simply be ignored. Moreover, to have a manageable number of alternatives – or if two or more legal systems match their wishes – the "playoff" will be resolved on the basis of unconnected reasons, such as for example the trust generated by the name of the country where the law comes from.

If that is human nature, offering a kaleidoscope of options would not make much sense, since people are not able to profit from such a large range of possibilities. Furthermore, as their analysis is shallow, choosing a set of rules that harms their interests is very likely. A paternalistic approach, to protect them from themselves, could be justified, as people do not seem to be capable of taking informed decisions.[714] Imposing restrictions on the choice of law would then be seen as a positive, since overexposure to information prompts the use of "irrational" strategies.

2.2. ACCURACY OF HEURISTICS IN DECISION-MAKING: THE LESS-IS-MORE EFFECT

Notwithstanding the above, the fact that people do not analyze exhaustively all the alternatives does not mean that they will make irremediable mistakes

---

712 Consider for example *Benetton*'s controversial but successful advertising campaigns. The strategy juxtaposed the company's logo with shocking images to grab the public's attention, but without ever showing the products offered by the company. According to Oliviero Toscani – the man behind the campaign – although he did not convey anything about the products, the strategy vaulted *Benetton*'s brand recognition higher than *Chanel*'s and placed it among the top five brands in the world. See: Goldstein & Gigerenzer (1999) 56.

713 For comments about the effects of bounded rationality on the choice of the governing law, see: Eidenmüller (2009) 651; Rühl (2011) 102 et seqq.

714 For reasons for restrictions on party autonomy based on their bounded rationality, see: Wautelet (2018) 230. For issues related to bounded rationality and the freedom of choice in private international law, see: Rühl (2011) 3202–3204; Whincop & Keynes (2001) 44–45.

when confronted with multiple options. Empirical data has also showed that weighing the features of all options, adding the values of each alternative, and choosing the one with the highest overall value does not yield better results than simple heuristics.[715] Many studies have demonstrated that cognitive shortcuts are capable of successfully performing in real-world situations, although they do not satisfy the classical norms of rational inference.[716] In fact, when a great number of factors could influence the final result of an event, it becomes impossible – even for computers – to decide how information must be weighed to predict the future accurately and so choose the best option. These studies conclude that the more complex a task is, the more reliable the use of shortcuts in decision-making becomes. Focusing on only a few attributes, or even just one, is better when many circumstances – some of them impossible to foresee in the present, such as for example the needs or problems of the future household – could influence the result of the analysis decisively.[717]

An interesting experiment carried out in 2004 illustrates the effectiveness of using the heuristics of concentrating on just one good reason.[718] It shows in a simple way how this strategy can yield better results in comparison to sophisticated analytical methods using all available information:

A group of amateur tennis players were asked which of the names of the Wimbledon contestants they recognized. From these mentions – only from the recognition of the name – they predicted which player would reach the final rounds of the tournament. The player that was recognized more often by the participants was forecast as the winner of each duel. Other predictions were also made, one with the aid of the database of the official ATP Champions Race ranking (ATP-CR) and another with the ATP Entry ranking (ATP-ER) that is, with information generated from the analysis of the performances of each player during the calendar year according to two complex mathematical models. The better ranked player was presumed to be the winner of each game. As an additional standard of comparison, the Wimbledon seeding – ranking determined by an official committee of experts that evaluates the abilities of the players to perform on the rye grass of Wimbledon – was also included.

The results were astonishing; predictions based on the sole recognition of the name were correct for 72 per cent of all matches. This degree of accuracy was higher than the predictions based on the official rankings – 66 per cent

715 Czerlinski & Gigerenzer (1999) 98, et seqq.; Gigerenzer & Todd (1999) 21, et seqq.; Goldstein & Gigerenzer (1999) 44.

716 For a selection of some of these studies see: Gigerenzer & Todd (1999); Gigerenzer et al. (2011).

717 Goldstein & Gigerenzer (1999) 38, 45 et seqq. See also: Dieckmann et al. (2009) 210.

718 Serwe & Frings (2006).

and 68 per cent for ATP-CR and ATP-ER respectively – and the forecasts made by experts (69 per cent).[719] Another study carried out later drew similar conclusions for the results of Wimbledon 2005.[720] Subsequently, similar experiments have been made in different contexts, such as predicting elections[721] and investments in stock markets.[722] In those and many others,[723] the conclusion is the same: in situations of high uncertainty, forecasts based on a reduced number of clues yield results that are at least as good as those based on predictions made by experts or sophisticated algorithms.[724] Basing a decision on just one reason and disregarding the rest of the information could be regarded as illogical or even *naïve*, as the positive and negative sides of each option are not considered carefully and not all available knowledge is used.[725] However, such a strategy does work very well in reality in comparison with other available methods of prediction.[726]

The aforementioned should not encourage people to take decisions lightly; it simply confirms that using the whole of the information an individual – or computer – might have is not necessary to select an optimal alternative. Basing the choice of law on only one or just a couple of aspects of the substantive regulation must not be regarded as flawed. Quite the contrary, in a context of uncertainty about which legal provision will actually matter in a subsequent legal proceeding, ignoring parts of the available information and only focusing on one or two relevant aspects seems to be the best strategy.[727] It is in such

---

719 Serwe & Frings (2006) 327.

720 Scheibehenne & Bröder (2007).

721 Gaissmaier & Marewski (2011).

722 The performance of recognition-based portfolios could be like those managed by experts. According to Ortmann et al. (2008), sometimes they even outperform them.

723 For more studies on the performance of the recognition heuristic, see: Gigerenzer & Gaissmaier (2011) 460 et seqq.; Rieskamp & Hoffrage (1999) 149, 155.

724 Gigerenzer & Gaissmaier 461; Gigerenzer & Goldstein (1999) 83 et seqq.

725 These authors say that the strategies used by people are not only *naïve* and simple, but they would not even pass a test of basic reasonableness. See: Keeney & Raiffa (1993) 77–78.

726 I do not suggest that people should take decisions without taking into consideration the pros and cons in all spheres of life. The suitability of the type of heuristic used depends strongly on the task. The mind is equipped with a "toolbox" of heuristics, a collection of decision-making strategies that help individuals resolve problems fast and with good-enough accuracy. Heuristics are composed of building blocks that specify how information is acquired, when the search should be stopped, and how this information is integrated into a decision-making process (see: Torsten & Rieskamp (2007) 346). In general, the selection of the right strategy is a result of the experience of how accurate all available heuristics are in this specific context. The more experience the decision-maker has, the higher the probability of success, since they will select the strategy that best fits the task and the environment. However, more expertise does not necessarily mean higher complexity, as many experiments have shown, very simple strategies can often beat very complex ones. See: Marewski & Schooler (2011) 394. See in detail: Gigerenzer & Todd (1999).

727 Martignon & Hoffrage (1999).

an environment where – according to recent advances in psychology – less is more.[728]

2.3. BRAND NAMES AND CHOICE OF LAW

A brand can be a name, symbol, design, or any combination thereof which identifies assets produced by a particular organization as having special characteristics that differentiate them from the rest.[729] Although products traded in regular markets are the first that spring to mind when thinking of brand names, there is no reason why the quality of a law cannot be associated with the name of the country where it is discussed, passed and – as a general rule – applied.[730] Based on the fact that people tend to use the trademark of a product as conveyer of information about its quality, the features of a set of rules could be linked with the name of the country where it originates. So, just as the appellation of origin – *denominación de origen* – helps when judging the quality of goods like wine,[731] the place where the "factory" of that law is located could also be a criterion for a choice of law.

It is foreseeable that people would – at least in the beginning – be reluctant to use the law of a country they do not feel familiar with, in particular if they do not personally know people from this jurisdiction. This is not only because of the natural tendency to prefer the current state of affairs – the so-called *endowment effect*[732] – but also the natural mistrust people have of what is perceived as foreign. But that happens to every new and innovative product when is launched. Over time, however, the reticence tends to disappear and little by little customers

728 The academic work cited here refers to seminal papers and those easy to understand for laymen in psychology. For more modern and specialized literature about the accuracy of heuristics, consult publications of The Center for Adaptive Behavior and Cognition and the Max-Planck-Institut für Bildungsforschung.

729 De Chernatony (2003) 412.

730 De Chernatony (2008) 16–17.

731 On the appellation of origin, see: Marewski & Schooler (2011) 393.

732 The endowment effect – also called *status quo* bias – refers to the tendency of people to value things more highly merely because they already have them. To understand the implications of the endowment effect when designing legal rules, consider the percentage of organ donors in Germany and Austria – two neighboring countries with a similar culture, ethnic heritage, comparable levels of education and the same language. In Germany, less than 15% were potential donors, in Austria more than 98%. What caused such a massive difference? The default rule in Germany was to opt-in to be a potential donor, in Austria the opposite: individuals are regarded as donors unless they refuse explicitly. See: Gigerenzer (2007) 182. Richard Thaler coined the term "endowment effect" after observing in several experiments that people demand much more money to give up an owned object than what they would be willing to pay before having this object in the first place. See: Thaler (1980) 43. Experiments with real transactions were conducted some years later. See: Knetch and Sinden (1984) 509, et seqq.

begin to see the benefits of using the new product after the early adopters popularize its advantages. Wrong decisions are unavoidable, as are right ones. Thus, through a process of trial and error, the best legal systems will sooner or later come to light.[733] Once the market stabilizes and a set of legislation has emerged as the most popular laws, people can use the name of the country to convey reliable information about its characteristics. The prevailing selection of some legal systems by individuals with similar tastes will be used as a rule of thumb to choose among a manageable number of options. It is not necessary to be exhaustively informed about the contents of all the legal provisions in one law. The name of the country signals quickly which option to take, and which to disregard, in an easy and frugal way.

Individuals use brand names all the time to make transactions of minor and major importance in regular markets.[734] They are a big help when purchasing computers, vehicles or medicines. The same applies to decisions involving services, such as for example choosing a hospital, an insurance company or a pension fund. States, for their part, foster the use and protect holders of trademarks, and so recognize the advantages from the use of brand names. Why not tolerate or even support this dynamic in the context of the choice of law?

3. SAFEGUARDING THE RIGHTS OF MINORITIES

In some jurisdictions, the legal regulation of the marriage is directly derived from religious precepts or ancestral practices that – to a greater or lesser extent – reflect the views of the society about how the marital relationship ought to be organized. The family law in force in most Islamic countries[735] – for example – stems from the interpretation of two fundamental sources of the law: the *Quran* and the *Sunnah*.[736] Only in the absence of concrete answers

---

733 Kerber (2000) 71.

734 Goldstein & Gigerenzer (1999) 56; Kurtz-Milcke & Gigerenzer (2006) 48, et seqq.

735 Within Islam, there are different subgroups that operate under a common name, tradition and identity. Based on the number of followers, the principal branches of Islam are the *Sunni*, *Shia*, *Ahmadiyya* and *Abadi*. They differ not only in doctrine, ritual, theology, and religious organization, but also in their understanding of family organization, and thereby in the interpretation of family law. Furthermore, in each branch there is a variety of *madhahib* – schools of thought of religious jurisprudence – which have the authority to interpret the law. The most prominent ones in the *Sunni* tradition are the *Hanafi*, *Maliki*, *Shafi'i* and *Hanbali*. The principal *Shia* schools are the *Ja'fari*, *Zaidi*. There are however other schools of thought, such as the *Ibadi* and the *Zahiri*. For the diversity of interpretations, see: Kamali (2003) 325 et seqq. See also: Ibrahim (2008) 112. See also: Arshad (2010) 12.

736 Rafeeq (2010) 117–118. For information about the sources of law in Islamic countries see: Arshad (2010) 15–20; Rehman (2007) 111; Coulson (1964) 22.

can jurists look for analogous situations in other sources.[737] On the whole, trained scholars – not the parliament – have the authority to interpret and articulate legal principles from these sources of the law.[738] Adaptations of the law in Islamic countries are possible, but only via the interpretation of existing sources of law, which in practice makes its modernization difficult.[739]

At a first glance, these obstacles seem inefficient. This inflexibility impedes the adaptation of the law to accommodate a modern reality so that it might adequately respond to the current needs of the people. However, this immutability also allows a better access to its content, since the law reflects ancient traditions that are well-known by all the members of the society where they come from. Additionally, using the same law from generation to generation establishes a wide range of – legal or extra-legal – practices and strategies to better meet the current needs of the spouses. In Islamic law, for example, maintenance payments are usually granted up to a period of only three months after the dissolution of the marital union.[740] To mitigate this issue, it is not uncommon[741] to conclude a marital agreement where prospective spouses – or their legal representatives – agree on a payment in the form of money or possessions to the woman in the event of a dissolution of the marriage.[742] Despite having a different legal nature,

---

737 In this process, they rely on secondary sources like the *Ijma* – the consensus of scholars within the jurisprudence – and the *Qiyas* – a process of deductive analogy where different interpretations are contrasted to arrive at concrete solutions. See: Arshad (2010) 20 et seqq.; Rehman (2007) 112, Kamali (2003) 12, et seqq.

738 Rafeeq (2010) 118. Legal systems in former colonial countries are significantly influenced by Western traditions of law. Marriage law in lusophone (Portuguese-speaking), francophone and Arabic-speaking Islamic countries is generally set out in systematic collections of law, whose prescriptions are strongly inspired by the civil code of the metropolises. By the same token, common law has also had a great influence in former British Colonies (see: Rafeeq (2010) 119). However, despite the similarities with Western legal systems, secular authorities rarely have much influence on the content of their marriage law. The legislative organ of an Islamic state cannot in any case abrogate the *Quran* or the *Sunnah*. See: Kamali (2003) 16.

739 In the last couple of years, some Islamic countries have specifically selected the most appealing doctrine for the current generation among the existing Islamic schools. Their objective was to reach a greater degree of gender equality in the application of law in their jurisdictions. This approach has limited archaic practices that are contrary to principles widely accepted in modern democratic societies, and banned practices like polygyny in countries like Pakistan, Syria or Iraq. In Tunisia, via interpretation of sources of the law, the abolition of polygamy was reached. See: Pakistani Muslim Family Law Ordinance (1961); Article 17 of Syrian Law of Personal Status 1953 (Decree No. 59 of 1953); Article 3 of Iraqi Law of Personal Status 1959; and Article 18, Tunisian Code of Personal Status 1956. See also: Yassari (2014) 106–109.

740 Arshad (2010) 98, 128. See in detail: Yassari (2014) 211.

741 Arshad (2010) 89.

742 See: Arshad (2010) 95; Sportel (2013) 1094 et seqq. See for German case law: Kammergericht Berlin, 3 February 2017–16 UF 77/16 (discussing the validity of an agreement by which the husband has to pay 135 000 € to his wife in case of divorce. The spouses concluded a contract in which they designated German law as the applicable law); Oberlandesgericht Hamm, 22 April 2016 – II-3 UF 262/15.

this contractual obligation plays the role of alimony,[743] but with an interesting difference: neither the financial situation of the creditor nor the needs of the debtor are subject to scrutiny when establishing the amount. It is automatically due after the divorce is granted, in the terms agreed on, which – ultimately – might be advantageous for the beneficiary of the payment.[744]

I do not suggest that legal systems strongly influenced by religion are better or worse than secular ones, but simply point out that the suitability of a law is subjective. The convenience of a given set of rules ultimately depends on the specific life-plan each individual has and – in particular – on knowing the appropriate remedies to tailor the legal provisions to one's interests. A legal system – regardless of its lack of dynamism – could then be suitable for some people, if they already have a particular strategy – such as for example the conclusion of a marital contract with specific clauses – that makes it possible to fit the law to their preferences and needs.

3.1. BENEFITS OF ALLOWING CHOICE OF LAW FROM THE PERSPECTIVE OF MINORITIES

The general rule in most Western countries is very different from the ones mentioned above.[745] Although family law is certainly shaped by the traditions of a society, legal provisions can be amended and abolished at any time, if the members of a society deem it appropriate. The constitution and obligations of international nature restrain the power of domestic law-makers, but these limits still grant enough margin of discretion – in comparison with religious legal systems – to adapt the law to the current needs of a society. In most countries the legislation on marriage law is enacted according to democratic principles. This means that – at least by and large – the rights and obligations arising from a marriage reflect the preferences of the majority. This majority, however, not only decides on the contents of the law; it also sets the requirements needed to participate in the collective process of decision-making. Some of these requirements – e.g. being of a certain age to take part in the political process – guarantee rules that increase the welfare of a society in aggregate terms.

---

743 For the economic function of the *mahr* see in detail: Yassari (2014) 262–266. It is important to stress that maintenance obligations and *mahr* have a different legal nature. For the regulation of maintenance obligations in Islamic law, see: Yassari (2014) 211 et seqq.

744 Yassari (2014) 262. For the so called *mahr al-musamma* see: Arshad (2010) 53.

745 A notable exception is Vatican City State which, along with the Philippines, is the only jurisdiction whose marriage law does not allows spouses to get divorced.

However, there is one requirement – possession of the relevant nationality – that despite being laid down in virtually all countries,[746] leads to a paradoxical situation in terms of legitimacy.

Given people's ever-increasing mobility, the requirement of having nationality to vote excludes many from directly influencing the creation, modification or suppression of legal provisions applicable to *inter alia* their marriage. Even though these individuals are targets of that legislation, residents of the country and subject to taxation, they have no say in this matter.[747] Thus – *prima facie* – only nationals of the country decide over the extent of rights and obligations for foreigners.[748] Allowing those people to opt out from the domestic legal regulations simply recognizes the inherent limits of our system of government.[749] The choice of law gives foreigners a space to express their diversity by giving them an opportunity to govern their personal sphere according to the way they deem the most appropriate.[750] It also allows them to be more informed about the rights and obligations arising from a marriage while at same time permitting them to use familiar strategies – for example the conclusion of marital contracts – to achieve their personal goals.[751] In many cases, migrants do not know beforehand where they will end up. Refugees are frequently obliged by their circumstances – or by the law – to apply for

746 There are at least five countries – New Zealand (see: Earnest (2003) 18), Malawi (Art. 77 para. 2 sub-para. C Malawian Constitution), Uruguay (Art. 78 Uruguayan Constitution), Chile (Art. 14 Chilean Constitution) and Ecuador (Art. 11 Ley Orgánica Código de la Democracia published in Registro Oficial Suplemento 578 on 27 April 2009) – that allow foreigners of any nationality to elect regional and national representatives with the power to enact, modify and derogate from law in civil issues. In general, however, having the nationality of the country is an unavoidable precondition to exercise the right to vote in government elections and consequently to actually be heard in the process of law-making in civil issues. Some states grant the right to vote to nationals of specific countries. In Brazil – for example – Portuguese people permanently residing in the country can vote. See Art. 12 s.1 of the Brazilian Constitution. See also: Earnest (2003) 18. In other countries – for example Spain – foreigners have the right to elect representatives with the power to enact law in civil issues, but with only local effects in certain areas.

747 With exception of "voting with their feet". See also: Chapter 6 Section 1.

748 The situation is even more complicated considering that in many countries, populist right-wing parties constantly try to make it more difficult for foreigners to acquire the citizenship of their country of residence. As stated by one commentator: "citizenship functions as a mechanism of social exclusion rather than one of inclusion [...], citizenship regulations are used with the aim to separate foreign populations from the national community on a legal basis". See: Achermann et al. (2010) 3.

749 Democracy is said to be the best option in comparison with all the other types of government, but it is not perfect, as it inevitably leaves aside the preferences of some people. In the famous words of Winston Churchill, "Democracy is the worst form of government, except for all the others". See: Atkinson & Wade (2014) 53.

750 Carrascosa (2011) 117; Mak (2020) 62–63; Ribstein & O'Hara (2009) 15.

751 Carrascosa (2011) 179.

asylum in one state regardless of whether this actually is their destination.[752] Something similar might happen to other kinds of expats – for example those working for international companies – who unexpectedly have to take up a position abroad following their employer's orders. Migrants in general run a high risk of succumbing not only to unknown legal provisions, but also to laws contrary to their sense of justice.[753] The choice of law solves this problem, as it guarantees that people belonging to another culture are not forced to abandon their own traditions to blend into a foreign society, especially if they might only reside there temporarily.

More often than not, national pride lets people assume that the law they claim as their own is suitable not only for them, but for any other person. However, the suitability of any body of rules does not depend on subjective elucidations or parochial beliefs. It simply depends on the particular interests of its addressees, and the specific strategies they plan to use to achieve their personal goals. The freedom of choice allows the development of a minority culture, a contemporary expression of an identity, without jeopardizing the values that underpin the operation of legal systems of the state where the foreign law is applied. As choice of law agreements are limited by the public policy clause, the respect of fundamental principles like non-discrimination based on gender is guaranteed.[754] What is more, interpretations made by courts to adapt foreign law to fundamental rights could further be applied in other countries when this legal system is applied in similar cases, so that not only the domestic law, but also domestic interpretations of foreign law can be "exported" to other

752 See: Articles 3, 8–17 of Regulation (EU) No 604/2013 of the European Parliament and of the Council of 26 June 2013 establishing the criteria and mechanisms for determining the Member State responsible for examining an application for international protection lodged in one of the Member States by a third-country national or a stateless person.

753 Regarding the situation of refugees, two issues should be taken into consideration: While there may be the wish to have no further relations with the state of origin, it does not necessarily mean the desire to break with their customs and traditions, but rather with the political system or the group in power. And, although in many cases the refugee or stateless person wants to remain in the host country, there are also cases in which the individual prefers to return to their country of origin once the conflict is over.

754 Periods of civil war, persecution or general lawlessness are no indication of the quality or modernity of local laws. Iraq's family law, for example, was enacted in 1959 and continues to be valid to this day, despite the climate of violence and oppression in the last 35 years. In Syria, there were no changes in the legislation in the area of marriage law during the civil war. See: Welchman (2007) 25. That does not mean that there is no discriminatory law in force in Iraq, Syria or any other country from which people are fleeing. The legal situation of certain groups of people is certainly due to the existence of provisions against fundamental rights – especially for women – in those jurisdictions. However, it is important to highlight that the existence of discriminatory laws is not necessarily a characteristic of countries in a situation of internal conflict. There are many peaceful countries with discriminatory rules from which no refugees typically flee. And conversely, countries with numerous refugees like Cuba, the Ukraine or former Yugoslavia did not have discriminatory rules in the area of family law.

jurisdictions. The market of law becomes thus an interesting tool to introduce necessary reforms into all those foreign legal systems whose ossified structures make their modernization difficult, when applied outside their country of origin.

3.2. BENEFITS OF ALLOWING CHOICE OF LAW FROM THE PERSPECTIVE OF THE MAJORITY

The choice of law creates a climate of mutual respect towards other ways of seeing the world. It guarantees a space to maintain and protect one's identity, being or just feeling different *vis à vis* other people. As mentioned before, in many societies the rules of marriage law are based on ancestral customs or religious beliefs. This law may for some individuals be inseparable from an ingrained sense of justice and morals[755] From an economic perspective, if it is aligned with fundamental rights, there is no reason to force them to change their view.[756] Allowing people the use of their own law stands for respect and tolerance towards a different way of organizing private life. Such a climate would be helpful for a very important objective of any country nowadays: the integration of foreigners into a host society. Allowing individuals to live their lives according to their own customs, and regulate their personal relationships according their own traditions may be one of the keys to a successful integration policy.[757] Furthermore, the use of foreign law could also be a mechanism to discover regulations that might meet the preferences of the members of the host society as well.[758] As said before, right after the opening up of the law market, prospective spouses are likely reluctant to use a law different from their own. That is perfectly understandable, due to the cost of gathering information. However, permitting minorities to use foreign law would accelerate the dispersion of information about the quality of foreign legal systems. Their choice of law would serve as a lubricant for the proper operation of the market of law. It would facilitate an easier assessment of the characteristics of the offered products.

755 De Hart et al. (2013) 996–999; Sportel (2013) 1098–1104.

756 For a definition of assimilation in the context of the protection of the rights of minorities, see: Advisory Committee on the Framework Convention for the Protection of National Minorities (2016) 18.

757 "[I]ntegration is a process of give-and-take and affects a society as a whole. Efforts cannot therefore be expected only from persons belonging to minority communities, but they must also be made by members of the majority population". See: Advisory Committee on the Framework Convention for the Protection of National Minorities (2016) 18.

758 For the idea of competition as an incentive for innovation – *Entdeckungsverfahren* – see: Hayek (1948a); Hayek (1948b); Hayek (1969); Hayek (1948d). See also: Vihanto (1992) 412, 418.

Permitting the choice of law in multicultural societies means the coexistence of a wide range of substitutive bodies of rules: different products sculpted in accordance to the needs, beliefs and requirements of distinct groups of people.[759] Observing how these products work in reality improves the situation of every person in that society, because it allows the testing of the actual quality of the domestic law in comparison to others. The freedom of choice might then lead to a *yardstick competition*[760] – the demand for reforms in local laws based on the attractive features of foreign legal provisions. In sum, not only minorities but also the majority stands to gain from permitting the choice of the applicable law to marriage.

4. EXPERIMENTATION AND INNOVATION IN LAW-MAKING

The criticism leveled at the legal fragmentation of the private law in Europe is nothing new. More than 200 years ago, François-Marie Arouet – Voltaire – described as an *étrange barbarie* the fact that for travelers in Europe, together with their horse, the law applicable to civil matters must also change at almost every postal station.[761] In recent times, however, the mechanisms offered by the European Union – most notably the procedure known as enhanced cooperation – have encouraged some scholars to go a step further and so conceptualize a complete set of principles of European family law[762] with a view to an eventual harmonization of the substantive law.[763] Whether a

759 Kerber (2000) 73.

760 The term *yardstick competition* refers to a competition of parallel monopolistic entities that takes place merely through the free flow of information. See: Gabor (2013) 12; Shleifer (1985).

761 Voltaire (1966) 10. The process of codification resolved the problems generated by legal pluralism within countries in Europe, as it applied a single body of rules – the civil code – at a national level. Some comparative law scholars of the early 20th century were convinced that the codification movement of the 19th century would sooner or later prompt the unification of the civil law in all of Europe. See: Kötz (1986) 1–2. The International Institute for the Unification of Private Law – UNIDROIT – was set up in 1926 precisely with the very purpose of studying methods for modernizing and harmonizing the private law of its members. See: Kronke (2001) 1149.

762 There is a Model Family Code, developed from a global rather than a European perspective, see: Schwenzer (2006).

763 Most authors recognize the lack of competence of the EU to lead a harmonization of substantive law in family law. For arguments for the unification and harmonization of family law in Europe, see: Dethloff (2003); Meulders-Klein (2003). For harmonization in the United States: Ryznar & Stępień-Sporek (2011). See also: Antokolskaia (2006) 512; Antokolskaia (2010) 398–399; Boele-Woelki et al. (2013) 2; Meulders-Klein (2007) 278.

"European Marriage Law" would replace national legislation, or rather be just an option – an alternative beside the domestic law in the form of an optional family law – is not entirely clear, as this initiative is still of a strictly academic nature.[764] Be that as it may, the growing number of studies in this regard[765] begs the question whether initiatives seeking a uniform law should be preferred to those supporting the competition of *diverse* legal systems. First, the advantages – in terms of efficiency – of the law market *vis à vis* a harmonization of substantive law are presented.[766] Afterwards, the principal drawbacks of drawing up an optional instrument on substantive marriage law for Europe are discussed.

4.1. DETECTING THE PEOPLE'S PREFERENCES EASILY

If spouses are allowed to choose foreign laws based on their advantageous features, law-makers will be able to detect aspects that could be improved. The market of law then becomes a mechanism not only to discover the preferences

---

764 The already codified rules of international law in family matters – international conventions; EU legislation; and case law of the European Court of Human Rights and the European Court of Justice – are regarded by some scholars as proof of the existence of a European Family Law that, although still unsystematically, could be used as a basis for the creation of a common body of rules. See: ANTOKOLSKAIA (2010) 409; MARTINY (1995) 424; SCHERPE (2016) 6–32.

765 Among the academic projects dealing with the harmonization of private law in Europe, one can cite: The Study Group on a European Civil Code (1998); the UNIDROIT Commission for the Principles for International Contracts (1980); the Lando Commission on European Contract Law (1982); the European Group on Tort Law (1992); The Common Core of European Private Law (1992), The Ius Commune Casebook for Common Law of Europe (1994); and The Commission on European Family Law CEFL (2001). See: ANTOKOLSKAIA (2006) 21. See also: Preliminary Draft of Uniform Rules on International Financial Leasing adopted in 1984; Preliminary Draft of Uniform Rules on Certain Aspects of International Factoring approved in 1982; European Convention on Product Liability in Regard to Personal Injury and Death of 1977; or Council Directive 85/374/EEC of 25 July 1985 on the Approximation of the Laws, Regulations and Administrative Provisions of the Member States concerning Liability for Defective Products. See: ANTOKOLSKAIA (2010) 398; KÖTZ (1986) 4–5.

766 Throughout this book the term "efficient rules" refers to legal provisions – or any other legal measure taken by governments – that facilitate the emergence of cooperative dynamics between people. Legal provisions that eliminate barriers to the conclusion of contracts – or any other kind of voluntary agreement – are regarded as efficient as contract are the typical means used to depict the terms in which such dynamics will be carried out. This is based on the idea that the constant conclusion of voluntary agreements between people – i.e. the engagement in cooperative dynamics – allows the existing resources to end up in the hands of those that value them the most. See: Chapter 1 Section 1.1 and Section 1.2. *in fine*. For situations meriting the imposition of restrictions on the freedom to conclude voluntary agreements – externalities, asymmetry of information, constraints affecting decision-making and monopolistic positions – see Chapter 3 Section 1.

of spouses, but also to monitor the development of the people's tastes based on changes in their choices over time.[767] Rather than being seen as a punishment, opting out indicates to national legislators that there is room for improvement. It is constructive feedback – a signal pointing out that reforms may be required or that those already introduced did not work as expected.[768]

Promoting initiatives seeking a convergence of national law with a top-down approach – like those guided by a central higher authority such as the European Union – may seem appealing, as this way forward permits a rapid introduction of amendments in the law that in other circumstances would take much longer. However, in the long run the diversity encourages a better utilization of information because it allows political players to obtain gains from legal reforms.[769] If the substantive law is not harmonized, but there is a variety of laws, local politicians are motivated to pay attention to the needs of the people living in their jurisdiction, to be interested in solutions implemented abroad, and to propose changes in accordance with what is occurring in other countries. In contrast to harmonization, decentralizing the law-making creates incentives to constantly monitor the match between the preferences of people and contents of the law.[770] The immediate reward political agents will obtain in the form of votes motivates them to regularly keep an eye in what their peers are doing abroad and to try fresh ideas.[771] In terms of efficiency, fostering legal diversity is promising because local politicians know the needs of the local populace better than the central higher – and distant – authority.[772]

It is to be expected that if a top-down harmonization is reached, supranational law-makers might also try to obtain information from lower-level agents and pay attention to the ideas and initiatives proposed by them to improve the (supranational) legal system. However, the introduction of reforms would be considerably slower, as international legislators are compelled to reconcile all the demands of all jurisdictions and try to create a balanced compromise.[773] In a decentralized system, national law-makers have much more liberty to act according to what they consider more appropriate for themselves. The legal diversity leads to greater agility in the introduction of legal amendments not

---

767 Carrascosa (2011) 125; Eidenmüller (2009) 648; Ogus (1999) 409. See also Carbonara & Parisi (2008) 342, 346; Gabor (2013) 6.

768 Vihanto (1992) 432.

769 Vihanto (1992) 419. Mak (2020) 62.

770 It is assumed that political agents, just like any other individual, strive for direct personal benefits like power, reputation, or wealth. They will be interested in proposing reforms in line with the preferences of the people, as they want to keep their position, i.e. be re-elected. See: Gerken (1995) 10.

771 Ogus (1999) 407.

772 Kerber (2000) 85.

773 Eidenmüller (2009) 652; Mak (2020) 61.

only in their own jurisdiction, but also abroad, as legislators of other countries have the opportunity to learn from such reforms and to replicate them if they prove to be successful or – of course – to reject those amendments if they do not work as expected.[774]

4.2. DISCOVERING UNFORESEEABLE IMPROVEMENTS: STATES AS RESEARCH CENTERS

Individuals – electors as well as their representatives – know different things, as each person lives in different conditions that influence the amount of information they have and the way it is processed. Even in the imaginary case of two individuals that have been exposed to the exact same reality, each of them will have different knowledge due to the different capacity persons have to learn and interpret facts in general.[775] Being so, one can expect that the combined knowledge of people will be better utilized if they work individually or in separated groups rather than subordinated to a single leading head – a central higher authority – empowered to decide the best solution for the whole population. No matter how high the intellectual capacities of this central head are, as long as the leading actor is a human being, his knowledge will never match that which all persons possess as a whole.[776] In these terms can also be explained the superiority of a decentralized system of decision-making: Legislatures will arrive at different solutions to a certain problem due to the inherent differences in knowledge that individuals living in different jurisdictions have when compared to each other.[777] Allowing states to create their own substantive marriage law leads to the coexistence of a variety of proposals aimed at striking the same objective: the designing of a group of legal rules that enhance the profits derived from the marital union. The more the proposals, the better also for law-makers as this situation increases the possibilities to find out the most suitable regulation in order to subsequently be replicated it in the own jurisdiction.[778]

Sometimes the arrival at an efficient solution is not necessarily the result of a systematic observation, measurement or experiment. Good ideas do not only emerge from an inductive or deductive process where the validity of a hypothesis is tested; in many cases, suitable solutions happen by accident, that is, in a way that is not a consequence of an attempt to execute an original plan.[779]

774 Kerber (2000) 72; Vihanto (1992) 432. See also Mak (2020) 45–46.
775 Vihanto (1992) 415.
776 Van den Bergh (2000) 438; Vihanto (1992) 417; Hayek (1948d) 14.
777 Kerber (2000) 74.
778 Eidenmüller (2009) 648; Kerber (2000) 72; Ribstein & O'Hara (2009) 168; Streit (1996) 13–14.
779 Hayek (1948a) 52; Kerber (2000) 68–69; Oates (1990) 52; Vihanto (1992) 416.

As the full effects of a regulation can be known only when it is put into practice, it can occur that ideas previously discarded have better results than expected. It could also happen that when facing an imminent failure, law-makers are pressured to slightly alter their original plan and so arrive at novel solutions very difficult to assess in theory. Moreover, solutions that at the first moment appear to be inappropriate could subsequently become suitable due to changes in the preferences and needs of societies. Whatever the reason, the coexistence of a variety of legislation can be seen as a process of gradual experimentation – a source of unpredictable and surprising discoveries even for the promotors of the laws themselves.[780]

The choice of law, for its part, assures that the costs generated by inefficient laws will be lessened as people are able to opt out from legal systems of lower quality. It not only obligates law-makers to assume the costs in political terms of enacting unsuitable laws or waiting too much for reforms,[781] but also creates an innovative environment, as political agents are encouraged to use their entrepreneurial talent in the search for problems in the legal system and the discovery of innovations: they will be elected or re-elected if they present clever changes in the law. The stimuli created by the competition at a state level offer the most favorable conditions for new ideas and discoveries to emerge.[782] In sum, jurisdictions competing with each other become innovative law laboratories where different alternatives – sometimes opposing ones, in other cases complementary – are put through the mill.[783] Legislators serve as "law scientists", who by trying to improve their own environment could generate positive externalities for the rest of the society, since their discoveries could subsequently be transplanted elsewhere.[784] Through the choice of law, individuals will be the judges in charge of assessing the quality of the invention offered by the experimenters without greater risk. Failed experiments would have less impact on the well-being of the society, since people would have the opportunity to opt out from the law if they perceived it as unsuitable.

4.3. REDUCTION OF TESTING COSTS

Testing and evaluating different provisions increases the probability of finding undesirable rules and, more importantly, other provisions that could replace

780 For the idea of competition as an incentive for innovation – *Entdeckungsverfahren* – see: Hayek (1948a); Hayek (1948b); Hayek (1969); Hayek (1948d). See also: Vihanto (1992) 416.

781 O'Hara & Ribstein (2000) 1161–1162.

782 Vihanto (1992) 416–417; Ribstein & O'Hara (2009) 32.

783 Oates (1990) 52.

784 Gatsios & Holmes (1998) 273; Kerber (2000) 80; Vanberg (1996) 86, 89–92.

them. However, innovations in the law not only require time and money to detect the people's needs, they also mean assuming the responsibility for errors if those changes do not work as expected.[785] Before undertaking major reforms – think, for example, of the introduction of the no-fault divorce 40 years ago, or what is currently happening with same-sex marriage – there are always risks many legislators are not willing to take. The fear of having to foot the bill for unexpected side effects makes politicians reluctant to introduce reforms, even more so if they are unpopular in parts of the society.

Legal pluralism reduces these risk costs, as it allows for parallel experimentation in law-making. It is not necessary to take all the risks as the effects of reforms can be observed elsewhere without the need to bear the political cost. Politicians have the opportunity to examine the repercussions of the same reform in different realities and of different reforms in similar realities.[786] Furthermore, as changes are often introduced step-by-step, they can "kick the can down the road" and only copy the law after some corrections to the new law in force in other jurisdictions have been made. At the end of the day, fewer investments are required to arrive at good solutions. Think, for example, of the case of those countries that have waited before regulating the legal status of same-sex couples. At first glance one can think that delays in the introduction of reforms are detrimental for the LGBT community. However, in the case of countries such as, for example, Argentina that was not so. The time delay allowed certain fears of the society to be assuaged, as they had the opportunity to observe that the introduction of same-sex marriage caused no disruption in other jurisdictions. Unlike the case of Uruguay that included civil union in 2007,[787] the reform adopted in Argentina in 2010 did not need to include intermediate forms like civil unions or registered partnerships as in its original proposal.[788] It rather granted from the outset, at a federal level, fully equal rights to homosexual and heterosexual couples to enter into marriage.

The coexistence of a variety of legal systems at an international level is positive from the point of view of testing and observing the laws of other countries, since the costs of finding an appropriate law will be lower or sometimes even free. The law market could thus be understood as a cheap mechanism whereby facts are discovered to then introduce changes with greater confidence in a legal system:[789] Allowing choice of law and promoting competition between jurisdictions can be seen as a safe and low-cost voyage of exploration into the unknown.[790]

785 Rühl (2011) 64.
786 Kerber (2000) 71; Neuhaus & Kropholler (1981) 81; Kerber (2000) 73–74; Van den Bergh (2000) 438.
787 Ley Nº 18.246 issued 27 December 2007.
788 Ley 26.618 Boletin Oficial de la Republica Argentina, Año CXVIII, Número 31.949 (Amendment to the Argentinian Civil Code of July 2010).
789 Hayek (1969) 251.
790 Hayek (1948b) 101; Vihanto (1992) 418.

New and original ways of doing things that have never been done before in the law can be discovered.[791] As long as one does not believe that everything possible has been said about marriage law – and rather thinks that there is still room for improvement – diversity is preferred over harmonization.

4.4. WHAT ABOUT AN OPTIONAL SUBSTANTIVE MARRIAGE LAW FOR EUROPE OR ELSEWHERE?

In principle, the creation of an optional code with substantive legal provisions on marriage law is – from an economic point of view – positive, as it offers more alternatives to choose from. The more options, the better it is for people as this means a greater chance to regulate a relationship according to what they deem most convenient.[792] Notwithstanding this, as any political initiative always entails costs – effort, time and money – it is also important to consider the downsides, specifically, to what extent one additional option is really necessary when there are already so many alternatives to choose from.

Although there will be no shortage of experts ready to work on the draft of an optional code, at the end of the day politicians ultimately decide about the adoption of a text.[793] This often means that the final results will not be the best in terms of legal technique and coherence, because the approval of common rules requires negotiations with representatives of different jurisdictions – each of them interested in imposing their own vision of the regulation of the marital union.[794] The lack of a consensus might ultimately be resolved by introducing ambiguous legal provisions, whose degree of vagueness allows the various groups to interpret the law according to their own liking.[795] It is also to be expected that provisions imported from different legal systems and having different rationales will be included.

The problems, however, go beyond the creation of a "legal Frankenstein" – a misshapen body of rules – as future reforms will also need to indulge the politicians representing societies whose preferences have developed

791 Hayek (1948a) 101.

792 Gabor (2013) 5; Ribstein & O'Hara (2009) 28. See also in this chapter Section 2.2.

793 Neuhaus & Kropholler (1981) 78–79.

794 Neuhaus & Kropholler (1981) 79, 80, 82. Such behavior could also be explained by the costs incurred in the administration of justice needed for the implementation of new rules. See: Carbonara & Parisi (2008) 344; Smits (1998) 338.

795 See: Neuhaus & Kropholler (1981) 79–80; Mertens (1992) 222. Some experts with experience from prior international conventions warn that the negotiations in an international context are often carried out by individuals – diplomatic or political representatives – with little technical expertise to understand and foresee the consequences of the legal prescriptions they are discussing. See: Neuhaus & Kropholler (1981) 76; Mertens (1992) 221.

asynchronously.[796] The more countries are represented in an international law-making body, the more dissimilar the ways to perceive reality among its members are.[797] Problems that seem urgent in some countries might be irrelevant in others, due to social, cultural and economic differences between them.[798] Slowness, stiffening and a possible paralysis in the introduction of reforms in the legal system would then be the price to pay for a harmonization carried out from the top down.[799] Progressive reforms that in the long or even short term would be beneficial for the whole society would run the risk of being delayed. They could even never come about due to the opposition of groups that do not see the need from the view of the society they represent.[800]

A top-down harmonization might also significantly slow the clarification of the contents of a law due to the high costs of bringing the case to higher instance courts in order to create uniformed interpretations of the law.[801] Regardless of whether there is a specialized authority competent to harmonize judicial decisions, reaching this point in the appeals process for common people would be very costly and this would impede the clarification of the extent, scope and meaning of the legal provisions within reasonable period of time. The transitional interval of legal uncertainty after the introduction of any new law will tend to be longer due to the costs of reaching courts of higher instance that make the harmonization of the interpretation of the law valid in all jurisdictions.[802] The lack of case law and the consequent uncertainty arising from the creation – from scratch – of a set of rules in marriage law might then finally lead this set of rules to suffer the same fate as Esperanto.

Besides, another major risk of supporting an initiative to create an optional code is that it might be used as a Trojan horse to prevent the elimination of barriers for the free choice of the applicable law. In general, I am not opposed to the creation of a European family law, as long as it will compete on its merits with all other legal systems on the market of law. The creation of a harmonized set of common substantive rules would probably lead to the putting aside of

796 Hayek (1948c) 263.

797 Neuhaus & Kropholler (1981) 79.

798 Kerber (2000) 73; Kötz (1986) 11.

799 Kötz (1986) 11; Neuhaus & Kropholler (1981) 81. It is important to differentiate between top-down and bottom-up harmonization. The first refers to a centralized method of obtaining a greater degree of legal uniformity, imposed by a higher authority. The second type results from a spontaneous development in the legal systems which lets the legal rules in force in different jurisdiction ultimately converge. The criticism in this section is leveled solely at the first one. See: Antokolskaia (2010) 400; Martiny (1995) 422.

800 Neuhaus & Kropholler (1981) 80; Smits (1998) 338.

801 Kötz (1986) 8. Any legal provision needs to be interpreted before it is applied, regardless of how apparently precise the wording of the law seems. See: de Molina (2012) 825.

802 For this problem, see: Neuhaus & Kropholler (1981) 82; Kötz (1986) 12.

proposals aimed at equalizing the freedom of choice in marriage with that granted in contract law.

However, one can go even further. Until now it has been assumed that legislators act faithfully; that they are serving the interests of their electors. But what if this is not the case? Whether we like or not, one should take into consideration that not only national, but also international law-makers might act on behalf of specific interest groups or follow their own self-interests.[803] Legislators can enact norms that respond to the needs of a specific lobby with important socioeconomic power rather than those of the society they represent.[804] One of the lessons that can be learned from the public choice literature[805] is that a number of inefficiencies in the law are caused by legislators trying to primarily transfer wealth from one group to another in exchange for campaign contributions or other kinds of "rents".[806] Thus, certain interest groups may achieve redistributive goals or impose their own vision of the world by altering the provisions of private law. In the same way as a software engineer lobby could advocate for extending the patent protection period related to their products, it could also happen that religious communities, whole churches or any other conservative organization would try to impose a traditional model of family on marriage law through lobbying for introduction of certain mandatory rules in the area of family law.[807] The slowness in the introduction of same-sex-marriages in many countries shows the actual power of interest groups – in particular religious organizations – to influence the law-making in family issues.

I do not reject any initiative aimed at the creation of supranational rules. There are of course many cases in which the harmonization of substantive law is not only positive, but even necessary to increase the welfare of the whole society. What I try to point out are some of the drawbacks of the uniformization from an institutional perspective. The factual power that some interest groups have in parliaments is one more argument in favor of the law market. Freedom of choice not only motivates legislators to introduce reforms, but also

803 Ribstein & O'Hara (2009) 14, 21–23; Becker (1983) 374, 392. See also: Van den Bergh (2000) 436.

804 O'Hara (2000) 1578.

805 O'Hara (2000) 1576. For a general discussion about the effectiveness of small groups exercising political influence, see: Olson (1971) 53–56.

806 Influential interest groups "are typically those who can organize most cheaply and effectively to raise and spend money, or to mobilize votes and other political resources. Successful interest groups tend to be those that are best able to prevent some members from free riding off expenditures and additional political efforts by others. Because relatively small, homogeneous groups often can more effectively contain free riding, resulting legislation may fail to serve the interests of even a majority of voters". See: O'Hara & Ribstein (2000a) 1157.

807 Ribstein & O'Hara (2009) 162.

disciplines them.[808] It diminishes the incentives to succumb to the offers made by lobbyists and makes the manipulation of the law in domestic jurisdictions less attractive due to the possibility to evade their manipulated rules.[809] To cite one example, thanks to legal diversity – and the recognition of decisions rendered abroad – same-sex couples who are from countries where such unions are not allowed can now live their life according to their preferences. Thanks to legal diversity they can also show the rest of the people back home that there is no reason to object to such a change. The choice of law helps them to challenge arguments adduced by representatives of interest groups as it permits to see with the own eyes the effects of changes in the law.

In sum, creating an optional code is welcome, but only to the extent that it does not stop initiatives to eliminate barriers to the freedom of choice. Whether these new common rules would indeed be a major contribution is not entirely clear due to the lack of coherence or consistency this set of rules might have; the risk of petrification of its provisions caused by the difficulties of introducing reforms;[810] the shortage of case law and scholarly texts interpreting the legal provisions; and the current existence of several solid legal systems at the disposal of the people. It seems, however, clear that giving up the freedom of choice in exchange of a common set of substantive rules in marriage law is not a good option for Europe or elsewhere from an economic point of view.

5. TENDENCY TOWARDS A CONVERGENCE

It was argued that laws become more efficient when the competence to legislate is divided into sub-units.[811] The choice of law plays a key role, as it shows the preferences of the people and incentivizes states to undertake the necessary reforms in their law. At first glance, this development appears to suggest the convergence into a single efficient regulation for marriage.[812] The point of equilibrium would be reached when all the legislators replicate the most successful legal product in their own jurisdiction. One could even conclude that regulatory competition in marriage law would lead to a single efficient legal system – "the perfect law". However, finding such a law is not possible. The differences between societies, and the changes in the requirements of the members of any given society over time make this objective unattainable. Law

808 Regulatory competition has "the positive effect of restraining the Leviathan state". See Gabor (2013) 6.

809 O'Hara & Ribstein (2000) 1186.

810 Kötz (1986) 11, 12; Neuhaus & Kropholler (1981) 80.

811 See Section 4 in this chapter.

812 Carbonara & Parisi (2008) 342; Smits (1998) 337; Van den Bergh (2000) 439.

should rather be regarded as an incomplete public good, a product that needs to be constantly improved by law-makers according to the needs and preferences in a specific place and moment.[813] Promoting competition between legal systems will not lead to the perfect law for marriage issues. But it does create appropriate conditions for initiatives in this direction. In fact, the establishment of a single marriage law is not desirable, as it assumes that individuals have equal preferences and pursue the same objectives.[814]

One can, however, assume that the dynamic generated by the law market would lead to more similarities between national legal systems. As states are encouraged to adopt successful rules from other jurisdictions, a not insignificant degree of standardization will occur as a consequence of this process.[815] The transplantation of legal rules, foreign doctrines or even entire legal systems is by no means a novelty in comparative law. Such a phenomenon took place in Europe predominantly during the 18th and 19th century and later in other parts of the world, where European civil legislation on family law were used as a model or even fully replicated.[816] Nowadays this phenomenon occurs in the opposite direction with the introduction of foreign legal institutions – especially those used in American law – into European civil codes.[817] The law market stimulates and accelerates such a dialogue between different legal systems. Thanks to it, the convergence will not be imposed but rather the result of the decisions made by the addresses of the law – the spouses. It also assures that the harmonization only comes about in those aspects of the relationship – and in general areas of the law – where it is really needed.[818] The reform introduced in the Netherlands in 2018 by which the default property regime was changed – from a statutory community of property to limited community of property – is a tangible evidence of the similarity that European national laws are actually reaching.[819]

---

813 Garcimartín (2008) 254; Kerber (2000) 73.

814 Competition is viewed as a process of creative destruction – Schumpeter ([1911] 1993 110–139, 334–348) – that is, a process "in which innovation is induced by creative entrepreneurs who invent new products or production techniques. This destroys a possibly existing economic equilibrium again and again, leading to a cyclical succession of innovation and imitation" – Gerken (1995) 5. For the process of creative destruction, see also Vihanto (1992) 416; Garoupa & Gomez (2011) 229–231.

815 Carbonara & Parisi (2008) 347; Eidenmüller (2009) 647; Ogus (1999) 409; Smits (2002) 89–90.

816 As it is well known, the French Civil Code – the Napoleon Code – was far into the twentieth century in force in several European States. Outside Europe one can mention the cases of Tukey and Japan, which adopted the entire Swiss and German Civil Code respectively.

817 Eidenmüller (2009) 647; Smits (1998) 335–336; Smits (2002) 96. For examples of legal transplantation in the course of legal history, see: Carbonara & Parisi (2007) 368.

818 Smits (2002) 96; Smits (1998) 338.

819 From 1 January 2018 onwards, unless otherwise stipulated by prenuptial agreement, a limited community of property regime applies to all marriages concluded in the Netherlands (see: new Art. 1:94 Dutch Civil Code).

It – the Dutch marriage law – illustrates the spontaneous harmonization and the reciprocal influence, as the Netherlands were precisely the first country that allowed same-sex couples to get legally married.[820]

6. INCENTIVES FOR THE FORMALIZATION OF THE RELATIONSHIP

Every lawmaker – whether legislator, judge, parent or spiritual leader – must consider the possibility that his subjects are able to elude his grasp and assess the potential damage. History is full of examples where the cost of banning one activity is higher than the damage it caused in the first place. Even fierce defenders of certain prohibitions had to give in and accept, that tolerating some activities is preferable to supporting the collateral damage of a ban. High rates of evasion and the creation of a black market should be considered before imposing mandatory rules.[821] The failure of imposing limits on rental prices of housing or prohibitions over alcohol or gambling are examples of cases in which attempts to control certain activities have created incentives that caused more harm than what they sought to avoid.[822] I do not pretend to affirm that every ban or limitation of certain activities has to be rejected, but in order to determine the real appropriateness of a measure, its benefits must be contrasted with the costs needed to contain the undesirable activity and those caused by individuals trying – or managing – to circumvent the law.[823] The lower the cost of eliminating or containing evasion, the more successful will the regulator's efforts be.[824]

Think for example of a society whose legal system allows for a unilateral divorce, but only in very specific and exceptional cases. Even if such a regulation met the preferences of the majority, it is inevitable that some people would

820 The Netherlands was the first country in the world to legalize same-sex marriage. The bill was presented by the Government on 8 July 1999, passed by the Lower House on 12 September 2000, passed by the Upper House on 19 December 2000, and signed into law by Queen Beatrix on 21 December 2000. The law came into effect on 1 April 2001. See: De Groot D.A.J.G. (2021) 236 et seqq.; Waaldijk (2001) 437.

821 O'Hara (2000) 1552–1553.

822 There was – for example – a significant increase of violence associated with the production, distribution, and sale of alcohol during the Prohibition Era in the United States. This declined when the prohibition ended: "In 1933, the last year of Prohibition, there were 12,124 homicides – 7,863 resulted from assaults with firearms and explosives. By 1941 these figures had declined to 8,048 and 4,525 respectively". See: Ostrowski (1989) 641–642.

823 Significant problem for the whole society could also be provoked when mandatory rules are addressed at a small number of individuals. In the United States – for example – the obligation imposed to landowners to take measures to preserve endangered species prompted them to preemptively destroy habitats located on their property. See: O'Hara (2000) 1553; Thompson (1999) 1153–1154.

824 O'Hara (2000) 1553.

dislike this limitation. Some of these detractors could even reject marriage at all, because it is too restrictive to get out of. If the reason behind the rigidity of the divorce rules is protecting one spouse from economic losses, banning any possibility to bypass the domestic law would be counterproductive. Not only the costs of a premature dissolution of a relationship have to be factored in, but also the losses if marriage is much less commonly celebrated, due the difficulty of obtaining a divorce.

In the face of this, the choice of law can be seen as a strategy to deal with the rejection of specific provisions by some groups without the need to change the whole system. As choice of law agreements cannot contravene overriding mandatory rules, or the public policy of the jurisdiction, states continue to have the power to ban negative conducts. A choice of law clause does not mean that spouses can avoid any regulation of their marriage at all. It only represents the choice of an alternative law, which also contains mandatory rules that control – only with a different intensity – the conduct of people.[825] Furthermore, as it was mentioned above, it also permits to see to which extent certain fears of uncommon activities are actually justified. Do not forget that until recently,[826] the conclusion of contracts between spouses, divorce and most recently same-sex marriages[827] were banned in most legal systems. As long as the chosen law does not contravene fundamental values such as equality or impartiality, allowing the use of foreign law is nothing more than calling into question – under the limits imposed by the *ordre public* – the current domestic prescriptions.

7. CONCLUDING REMARKS

Possessive and transactional security is a major improvement from the introduction of the party autonomy in international marriage law. But the gains go beyond benefits for the spouses, and include the rest of the society as well. The freedom of choice increases the legal certainty, by clarifying – from the very beginning – the exact rights and obligations created by a marriage, as well as the lacunas left by the chosen law. It consequently allows people to organize their private sphere in a more orderly fashion, calculate the degree of effort invested in the marriage, and take decisions on time that – if they do not improve their situation – at least prevent serious harm in the future. Party autonomy also

825 O'Hara & Ribstein (2000) 1192.

826 The Netherlands was the first country in the world to legalize same-sex marriage. The bill was presented by the Government on 8 July 1999, passed by the Lower House on 12 September 2000, passed by the Upper House on 19 December 2000, and signed into law by Queen Beatrix on 21 December 2000. The law came into effect on 1 April 2001. See: De Groot D.A.J.G. (2021) 235; Waaldijk (2001) 437.

827 For an outstanding historical analysis of the legal recognition of same-sex marriages in Europe see: De Groot D.A.J.G. (2021) 233 et seqq.

capitalizes from the legal pluralism as it put at disposal of people many options to find a legal framework matching the individual preferences and needs, they might have. The attainment of benefits arising from the variety does not require that spouses are fully aware of the content of all legal provisions contained in the wide offer. They are capable of quickly discarding unsuited alternatives and choosing an optimal option without analyzing all the available data at their disposal, but with the aid of heuristics. Spouses can behave in a similar way as people do with brand names in regular markets. They can use the name of the country of precedence of a law to have a manageable number of options and subsequently base their decisions on those specific aspects they consider the most important.

The party autonomy also ensures foreigners – and in general any minority group – a space to express their own identity, as they can designate a legal system reflecting their special values, culture and traditions. It gives them the opportunity to govern their personal sphere according to their way of life; be much more informed about the rights and obligations arising from their marriage; and use familiar strategies to achieve personal goals. As choice of law agreements are limited by the *ordre public*, the freedom of choice does not pose a serious danger in case a detrimental law is chosen. Selecting a legal system containing provisions against fundamental rights might rather lead to its adaptation to values recognized as having universal validity. Indeed, not only national legal provisions, but also case law dealing with the accommodation of foreign law to fundamental rights can be exported to other jurisdictions within the framework of the law market.

The use of a foreign legal system shows residents alternative approaches to resolve disputes between partners. They can evaluate the quality of their domestic law in comparison with other laws, and so accelerate the dispersion of information about the adequacy of a specific legal rule – or set of rules – originating from other countries. The freedom of choice exercised by outsiders becomes a lubricant for the proper operation of the market of law, it dissuades fears of new and alien rules and helps to look at the domestic rules with more critical eyes. The existence of different legal systems and the possibility to choose freely among them creates a conducive environment for experimentation and innovation in law-making. Domestic political representatives can more easily detect the preferences of the people, propose amendments, monitor trends and anticipate future needs. States become laboratories where different regulations – sometimes opposing, in other cases complementary – are put to the test. The more legal systems coexist, the better for law-makers, as they can find good legal provisions to subsequently replicate in their own jurisdictions. The legal diversity reduces testing costs, as it assesses the effects of the application of the same provision in different realities as well as different provisions in similar realities. The dynamic generated by the law market would lead to more similarities between national legal systems. As states are encouraged to adopt successful rules from other jurisdictions, not a full, but a significant degree of standardization would occur as a consequence of this process. As a corollary, the possibility of opting out from the domestic law would encourage more people to formalize their relationship, and so reinforce the trust between them to invest more efforts and so obtain greater benefits from their mutual cooperation. In sum, legal certainty; greater capacity to influence one's own well-being; safeguarding the rights of minorities; experimentation and innovation in lawmaking; tendency towards a convergence; and incentives for the formalization of relationships are the principal arguments in favor of the elimination of barriers on the party autonomy from an economic perspective.

CHAPTER 8

APPLICABLE LAW IN ABSENCE OF A CHOICE OF LAW AGREEMENT

Applying foreign law entails costs for spouses and the administration of justice. Misinterpretations and the investment of more resources are expected in cases involving foreign legal provisions in comparison to domestic law. However, granting individuals the possibility to select the law governing their relationships also brings forth a number of advantages. Whether such benefits outweigh the costs is difficult to measure. But the fact that the number of states allowing the conclusion of choice of law agreements consistently grows, speaks volumes. The introduction of party autonomy in international contract and marriage law[828] is probably the most prominent feature of modern national and international conflict of laws regulations.[829]

Now it is time to discuss the applicable law in situations where the spouses have not made use of their freedom of choice. All arguments in the chapters above were praising the merits of party autonomy. However, no precise method

---

828 By way of example, the following countries allow the determination of the law applicable to at least one aspect of the relationship: *Albania*: Art. 24 Private International Law Act; *Argentina*: Art. 2630 Civil and Commercial Code; *China*: Art. 24 Law of the Peoples's Republic of China on the Application of Laws to Civil Relationships; *Dominican Republic*: Art. 44 Private International Law Act; *Korea*: Art. 38 Private International Law Act; *Lichtenstein*: Art. 20 Statute on Private International Law; *Norway*: Cordero-Moss (2017) 2396; *Russia*: Art. 161(2) Russian Family Code; *Serbia*: Arts. 74, 79 Draft of Private International Law Act; *Switzerland*: Art. 52 Private International Law Act; *Thailand*: Art. 25 Private International Law Act; *Turkey*: Art. 15 Private International Law Code. To this list one has to add those countries that are part of The 2007 Hague Protocol on the Law Applicable to Maintenance Obligations: *Austria, Belgium, Brazil, Bulgaria, Croatia, Cyprus, Czech Republic, Estonia, Finland, France, Germany, Greece, Hungary, Ireland, Italy, Kazakhstan, Latvia, Lithuania, Luxembourg, Malta, Netherlands, Poland, Portugal, Romania, Serbia, Slovakia, Slovenia, Spain, Sweden, Ukraine*. For an updated list of contracting parties to the Hague Protocol, see: <https://www.hcch.net/en/instruments/conventions/status-table/?cid=133>.

829 Corneloup (2013) 15; Brosch (2019) 1. For the regulation of party autonomy in family issues in the EU see in detail: Brosch (2019) 15 et seqq. For contract law, see: Basedow (2006a) 66; Basedow (2006b) 241.

to determine the applicable law in absence of a choice of law agreement was mentioned. This chapter is entirely devoted to this issue. First, some specifics about the goals pursued by gap-filling rules, and the conflict of laws provisions in general, are discussed. After that, the costs encountered by individuals involved in a relationship with an international element are analyzed. In this second section it is concluded that conflict rules – like default rules in substantive law – should also allocate transaction costs in a way that maximizes the surplus from the cooperation. The third and fourth sections are focused on the connecting factors applicable to contracts and marriages. After explaining the economic rationale behind the conflict rules, it is argued that the spouses' first place of residence is the most appropriate connecting factor for the marriage, as it not only provides a high degree of legal certainty, but also reduces costs needed to get information about the content of the applicable law. The law of the place of conclusion of the marriage will be put forward as the subsidiary connecting factor for those rare cases where spouses have never had a common place of residence.

1. ECONOMIC RATIONALE BEHIND DEFAULT LEGAL PROVISIONS IN CONFLICT OF LAWS

Default rules in substantive contract law fill the gaps left by the parties about the specific manner in which the principal obligations should be performed. These rules provide solutions for predictable and unpredictable contingencies that might affect the normal unfolding of the relationship.[830] They are not conceived to supersede the wills of the parties, but rather to complement them, as they only cover issues the parties have not provided a specific solution for.[831] Legal systems should let individuals determine by themselves the law governing their legal relationships.[832] The lack of a choice of law agreement can hence be considered a lacuna left by the contractual parties that has to be filled like any other loophole in a contract.[833] The same approach used in substantive law to address gaps in contracts will now be applied in private international law to design a general rule indicating the governing law of the relationship in absence of a choice

830 Ayres & Gertner (1989) 93; Coleman et al. (1989) 640, 673; Cooter & Ulen (2016) 293; Schäfer & Ott (2012) 433.
831 See Chapter 3 Section 2.2.
832 See Chapter 7.
833 Michael Whincop and Mary Keyes – Whincop & Keynes (2001) 43 – used the term "metadefault rules" for those provisions indicating the applicable law in absence of a choice of law agreement. Jürgen Basedow – Basedow (2008) 714 – have employed the term "dispositive rules". In following, the terms default or gap-filling rules will be used interchangeably.

of law agreement.[834] Before going through the analysis of the conflict of laws rules, let us first recapitulate the economic logic underlying default provisions in substantive law, as well as the attributes of private international law provisions required to maximize the number of cross-border transactions.

1.1. HYPOTHETICAL WILL OF THE PARTIES IN SUBSTANTIVE LAW

Default rules in contract law are regarded as efficient,[835] if they reflect the solutions at which contractual parties would have arrived if they had bargained over a disputed issue at the moment of the contract's conclusion.[836] By supplying legal provisions that mirror the will of the contractual parties, the legal system facilitates the realization of exchanges, as people do not need to spend time on imagining every possible event that could affect the performance of their obligations and negotiating a specific solution for those contingencies.[837]

The function of default rules is making the conclusion of contracts as simple as possible, to the point that it is only necessary to focus on the most basic and important elements of the relationship – e.g. price and object in a sale contract; love and respect in the case of marriage. Based on this, default rules should reflect what most individuals would have agreed on if they had had the opportunity to discuss the allocation of all responsibilities between them. In order to concretize the hypothetical will of the parties, it is assumed that solutions that maximize the surplus created by contracts are the ones preferred by people. Previously, it was shown that the cheapest-cost-avoider achieves this goal.[838] According to this criterion, the contractual party that could avert or mitigate a risk at the lowest cost, should be the one to do so. The term "cost" should not be

---

834 Gunst (1994) 158–159.

835 Throughout this book the term "efficient rules" refers to legal provisions – or any other legal measure taken by governments – that facilitate the emergence of cooperative dynamics between people. Legal provisions that eliminate barriers to the conclusion of contracts – or any other kind of voluntary agreement – are regarded as efficient as contracts are the typical means used to depict the terms in which such dynamics will be carried out. This is based on the idea that the constant conclusion of voluntary agreements between people – i.e. the engagement in cooperative dynamics – allows the existing resources to end up in the hands of those that value them the most. See: Chapter 1 Section 1.1 and Section 1.2. *in fine*. For situations meriting the imposition of restrictions on the freedom to conclude voluntary agreements – externalities, asymmetry of information, constraints affecting decision-making and monopolistic positions – see Chapter 3 Section 1.

836 Ayres (1998) 586. See also: Cohen G. (2000) 82; Coleman et al. (1989) 641; Posner E. (2005) 585; Posner R. (2005) 1585; Posner & Rosenfield (1977) 88; Scott & Scott (1998) 1306; Schäfer & Ott (2012) 455–457; Veljanovski (2007) 123.

837 Craswell (2000) 4; Whincop & Keynes (2001) 34–35.

838 See Chapter 3 Section 2.3.

understood as just the expenditure needed to avoid the contingency, but as the result achieved by adding and subtracting expenses and also gains from the risk-avoiding investment. As will be shown later, the realization of this investment can generate extra benefits that should be factored in when determining the cheapest-cost-avoider.[839]

1.2. HYPOTHETICAL WILL OF THE PARTIES IN PRIVATE INTERNATIONAL LAW

The aforementioned logic applies now to private international law, so that the conflict rule should also mirror the solution parties would agree on if they had negotiated.[840] However, whereas in substantive law, gap-filling rules avoid the need to bargain over any contingency affecting the relationship, in private international law the default rule is intended to avoid the negotiation of one single provision: the choice of law clause.[841] At first glance, a single stipulation of the contract seems of little importance. But looking more closely, the relevance of that default rule as a booster of cooperative dynamics between people becomes obvious.

The choice of law clause is crucial, as all the contract's stipulations depend on the law governing the relationship. It determines the application of mandatory and default rules, and the validity and enforceability of any obligation agreed on expressly or tacitly by the parties. Clarity about such an essential matter – regardless of whether it was discussed or not by the parties – is crucial to the quest of encouraging people to enter any contractual relationship with international connotations. Negotiations in an international arena can be very complicated, not only because the contractual parties might not share the same practices, culture or even language; they are also usually located far apart before, during and sometimes even after the conclusion of the contract.[842] The default rule is of key significance when negotiating under these conditions, as people have the opportunity to opt for the default rules, instead of struggling to explain themselves and to understand the position of the other side. Even when transaction costs are low – parties share the same preference, have the same culture, speak the same language, and are consequently well prepared to discuss the terms of their contract – gap-filling rules are still useful. The default provisions can be a point of departure when negotiating bespoke

---

839 See in this chapter Section 3.3.2.

840 Basedow (2006a) 69; Basedow (2006b) 245; Carrascosa (2011) 67 et seqq.; Garcimartín (2002) 134; O'Hara & Ribstein (2000) 1151–1152, 1190–1191; Rühl (2011) 374, 517; Schäfer & Lantermann (2006) 97–98; Whincop & Keynes (2001) 35–37, 453–45.

841 See in detail: Rühl (2011) 362, 543.

842 Kronman (1985) 9–10; Rühl (2011) 36–37.

terms of the contract. One side could, for example, propose the application of another legal system – overriding the rule – in exchange for a greater investment in the relationship or paying a greater price. When parties have the opportunity to negotiate, the relevance of the default rule lies in serving as clear base-line for attempting to haggle for more favorable legal conditions in return for compensation to the counterpart. The default rule in private international law is finally of key importance in situations where: a contract becomes inadvertently international after its conclusion; parties were not aware of the cross-border connotations of their relationship at the moment of its conclusion; or any of the partners did not even think of the problems arising from legal pluralism.[843] In these cases, the default rules allow people to consult *ex post* – after the conclusion of the contract – the legal provisions and adjust their behavior and so maximize their benefits or – at least – reduce losses.[844] The mere existence of default rules encourages the realization of transactions, as people can rely on the fact that the legal system provides a solution when they themselves have – for any reason – not paid attention to a looming conflict between different legal systems.

However, default rules must not only be seen as a "rearguard-law",[845] a kind of life-belt for situations the contractual parties have not thought of. They must also be understood as enablers of fast and easy transactions if they effectively mirror the preferences of the majority.[846] People often simply rely on the dispositive rules and plan their life from the very beginning based on the default regulation. Just by paying attention to the default rule, each person can calculate the expected value of the legal relationship even before a proposal is made. It follows, that default provisions causing unforeseeable changes in the rights and obligations arising from a marriage are detrimental. They would cause damage to those who have diligently planned a course of life based on one law. The immutability of the governing law is even advantageous for oblivious persons, as they can ascertain whether any of the decisions taken in the past were correct – according to the current demeanor of the partner – and if not, change their behavior. As it is impossible for law-makers to know exactly when their subjects will be interested in consulting the law, the conflict rule must convey certainty about the governing law as early as possible. The applicable law must be simple, predictable as well as stable; it must not be subject to variations from the change of circumstances after the conclusion of the marriage unless – of course – otherwise arranged in a choice of law agreement.[847]

---

843 Carrascosa (2011) 132.

844 See in detail Chapter 5 Section 3.

845 In the words of Basedow's translator "*un ordenamiento de rataguardia*". See: Basedow (2010) 19.

846 Basedow (2006a) 69; Basedow (2006b) 245; Carrascosa (2011) 67 et seqq.; Garcimartín (2002) 134; O'Hara & Ribstein (2000) 1151–1152, 1190–1191; Schäfer & Lantermann (2006) 97–98; Rühl (2011) 374, 517; Whincop & Keynes (2001) 35–37, 453–445.

847 See Chapter 5 Section 3.

However, predictability and stability of the outcomes are not the only features default rules should have in order to ensure the maximum possible cooperative dynamics at an international level. The accuracy, uniformity, consistency, and simplicity of the conflict rule also play a key role. The default rule must be precise; the connecting factor used to link the case with a law should avoid ambiguities and guarantee the application of a single legal system to the relationship. It must also be widely used by many jurisdictions, which depends on its ability to respond to the needs of the majority, but without losing sight of its cost of implementation. A default rule must also encompass most situations within the statements of facts – within the *Tatbestand* – to assure the application of only one set of rules to the major aspects of the relationship. Finally, the structure and content of the conflict rule must not be overly complicated. The connecting factor should also link the relationship with a legal system to which access – in terms of costs of information – is the least onerous for the parties.[848] At the moment of designing the default conflict provision, it will be then assumed that the hypothetical will of the parties corresponds to a rule with those attributes: predictability, stability, accuracy, uniformity, consistency and simplicity. For the content of the default rule, a distinctive feature of cross-border relationships in comparison with domestic ones must also be remembered: the costs of internationality.[849] Various conflict rules might possess the aforementioned attributes. But few also allocate these costs to the party in the better position to bear them.[850]

2. ACCESS TO INFORMATION AS STARTING POINT TO DESIGN CONFLICT RULES

In this section, the nature of the costs surrounding the conclusion of arrangements connected with different legal systems will be discussed. Based on the incidence of these costs, a criterion for the determination of the applicable law will be presented.

2.1. COSTS OF INTERNATIONALITY

At an international level, the utility of the law diminishes due to the existence of other legal systems containing different and – in many cases – contradictory legal provisions about the terms and conditions of agreements. A system of

848 See Chapter 5 Section 2.
849 Garcimartín (2002) 131–132. See also: Chapter 5 Section 1.1.2.
850 Garcimartín (2002) 134–135, 154; Gunst (1994) 159, 164; Roth (1985) 383–385.

conflict of laws restores the utility of the law, by specifying which set of rules is applicable to a relationship. However, in doing so, this system creates additional costs – costs of internationality – because the selection of a specific law requires one party to gather information about a law whose content might be partially or totally unknown. This individual must make further investments to be aware of the terms and conditions of the relationship established by a – in his view – foreign law.[851]

Think, for example, of these two cases: Two individuals located in different countries agree to buy and sell – respectively – a product; and two young people residing in different countries want to get married. In both instances, one side will be prejudiced by the application of a foreign and unknown legal system. This person would have a harder time to assess the convenience – benefits and drawbacks – of concluding their contract or celebrating a marriage respectively. The establishment of a specific legal system governing the relationship might then end up penalizing at least one party if – from his perspective – an unfamiliar set of rules is chosen by the default rule. This party is pushed to invest further resources to know the particular obligations assumed as well as the specific rights arising from the relationship. The term "costs of internationality" can be defined as all those expenses necessary to obtain possessive and transactional security as a consequence of the application of a law different from one's "own law". Such costs refer to the time, money and any other effort needed to be aware of the specific rights and obligations derived from the conclusion of a contract, and the need to adapt goals and demeanor to the foreign law.[852] Irrespective of whether or not the law-makers intended that, conflict rules allocate these costs between the parties when using a connecting factor for the determination of the law governing a relationship.[853]

2.2. LAW OF THE COUNTRY OF RESIDENCE AS THE "OWN LAW"

The application of a familiar legal system is advantageous. Not only is the scope of the rights and obligations arising from a contract better known, this expertise also permits one to propose changes in the substantive default rules to adapt the terms of the relationship to accommodate their own preferences and needs. Maximizing the expected gains of a contract becomes much easier when one knows the content of the governing law inside out.[854] It is, however,

851 Garcimartín (2002) 131.
852 See Chapter 5 Section 1.2.
853 Garcimartín (2002) 131–132; Gunst (1994) 137; Roth (1985) 318.
854 Carrascosa (2011) 87.

not possible to establish *in abstracto* the legal system that an individual is actually more or less informed about. One can safely assume that a person with Dutch nationality living in Spain, who concludes a contract in France to be performed in Germany, will have a disadvantage if the laws of Peru, Tuvalu or Botswana apply to the contract. The proximity of the person – or the contract – to a country can be used as a cue to estimate the amount of information a contractual party might have about the content of a law.[855] Legal systems linked in some way with the relationship or the parties, are presumably more well-known than others. However, it is not possible to determine objectively which – among all those in some way connected with the relationship – is the law the person is most informed about. Neither the nationality, country of performance, place of conclusion, or the country of residence guarantees a higher degree of knowledge a person might actually have about the content of the law. The same applies to spouses: the fact that a person has a particular nationality, celebrates the marriage in a specific jurisdiction, lives in one country or wants to move to another right after the marriage does not tell us by itself anything conclusive about their knowledge. There is no objective reason to assume that one or the other spouse is more or less informed about the marriage law of a state based on any of those circumstances.[856]

As it is not possible to determine the legal system about which a contractual party is consistently better informed; the determination of the law favorable to one party – "the own law" – cannot be founded on the basis of the knowledge this person actually has about the content of the law. That, however, does not preclude us from identifying the law most favorable for a party, as the advantage of using one or another set of rules can be estimated by reference to the costs this person must incur to make informed decisions. The determination of the law favorable to one party – "the own law" – will thus not be settled on the basis of knowledge this person already has, but on the costs this person would have to invest, to get information about the contents of a law.[857] One cannot forecast the specific knowledge an individual has about a legal system. One can, however, predict the degree of difficulty a person will encounter when trying to obtain such knowledge.

The determination of the costs of internationality will thus be based on the difficulties people have to find information at the moment of the conclusion of the contract or celebration of the marriage respectively.[858] The application of a law different from the one in force in the country of residence will be regarded as less favorable, as learning about the rights and obligations created

855 Carrascosa (2011) 67, 71; Dutta (2017) 558.
856 Carrascosa (2011) 93.
857 Garcimartín (2002) 137; Carrascosa (2011) 72.
858 Garcimartín (2002) 147.

by the relationship requires the investment of more resources.[859] On the other side, the application of the law where the person is living is economically more advantageous because fewer – or even no – resources are needed to determine the content of this law. Researching legal sources or consulting an expert will be easier and cheaper because – *inter alia* – no translation of the legislation is needed and arranging a personal appointment is simpler.

3. DETERMINATION OF THE APPLICABLE LAW WHEN PARTNERS RESIDE IN THE SAME JURISDICTION

The application of a law other than the one of the jurisdiction where a person lives is – in most cases – adverse due to the costs needed to make informed decisions. The use of the law of the place of residence, on the other hand, is advantageous, as getting information about its contents – in general – requires less effort. It is not about conjecturing whether people like the contents of a certain law better, but they should prefer a law that is known or can easily be learned.[860] After all, only with this information can a person decide whether a different legal system – via a choice of law agreement – would better meet their interests. Thus, if contractual parties reside in the same jurisdiction, the law governing arrangements in absence of a choice of law agreement should be the law of the common place of residence of the parties at the moment of the conclusion of the contract.[861] This solution mirrors the general rule used by most conflict of laws systems in Europe for contracts.[862] They apply the legal system in force in the country of residence of the performer of the characteristic performance. If both live in the same jurisdiction at the moment of concluding the contract, the solution here defended will then apply.

Regarding the legal situation of spouses, the solution suggested here seems to contradict the international instruments dealing with the effects of marriage, as none include the common residence of the spouses at the moment of the celebration of marriage as the prime or subsidiary connecting factor. However, that is not entirely correct, as one instrument[863] – Regulation 2016/1103 about

859 Mankowski (2010) 456.

860 Mankowski (2010) 456–457.

861 As explained in the Preface, the definition and extension of concepts like habitual residence are excluded from the scope of this book. For issues related to the determination of the habitual residence of a person, see: Baetge (2012) 813–815; Dutta (2017) 555–556.

862 Cf. Art. 4 Rome I Regulation.

863 Before Regulation 2016/1103 entered into force, France, Luxembourg, and the Netherlands already used the first place of residence as the primary connecting factor for issues related to the property regime. See: Art. 4.1. Convention of 14 March 1978 on the Law Applicable to Matrimonial Property Regimes.

the property regime – uses the first place of residence of the couple after their marriage. This law in practice corresponds with the law of the country where both live when and at least shortly after getting married.[864] The prime connecting factor applicable to issues related to the property regime of the couple – the place of their first common residence – actually delivers efficient outcomes if the couple lives together at the time of their marriage.[865] Whether this connecting factor is also appropriate if partners reside in different countries will be discussed next.

4. DETERMINATION OF THE APPLICABLE LAW WHEN PARTNERS RESIDE IN DIFFERENT JURISDICTIONS

At first glance one can think that the designation of the law of a third country – a neutral law – could be an appropriate solution for contracts concluded by two individuals living in separate jurisdictions.[866] However, such a solution only seems "fair" on the surface. The application of a neutral law does not distribute the costs of internationality between the partners, but simply duplicates them. Both individuals must invest resources to be informed about the contents of this law. Both of the parties would then subtract these costs from their expected gains, which reduces – twice over – the surplus of the contract.[867] On the whole, an efficient solution – one that maximizes the benefits of the cooperation – allocates the costs of internationality to only one party, as described before, to the individual that can more easily bear the application of a foreign law. As long as these costs are different for each partner, the default rule should place the burden on the cheapest-cost-avoider; that is, on the party that needs to invest fewer resources to bear these costs.[868] The law of the country where the other party lives will then be used by the courts to resolve the case – unless of course the partners make a choice of law.

The designation of a legal system different to the one in force in the place of residence of any of the parties must, however, not entirely be ruled out.[869] The nature of some rights and obligations, as well as circumstances surrounding certain relationships might favor another legal system for some aspects or

---

864 Coester-Waltjen (2018) 203. As recital 49 of Regulation 2016/1103 states, "[t]he first common habitual residence of the spouses *shortly after* marriage should constitute the first criterion" (emphasis added). However, it is important to note that some authors consider that spouses should be able to establish their common residence within a period of up to six or eight months, to regard it as their first common residence. See: Coester-Waltjen (2018) 203; Hausmann (2018) 234; Looschelders (2018) 843.

865 With a similar view see: Carrascosa (2011) 90.

866 For some arguments in favor of the application of a neutral law, see: Carrascosa (2011) 175.

867 Rühl (2011) 534.

868 Carrascosa (2011) 140; Garcimartín (2002) 134–135.

869 See in detail Chapter 5 Section 2.3.

even the whole contract.[870] Rights *in rem* relating to a property or agreements creating a legal entity – in particular when the contract is concluded by three or more parties – might require a different treatment by the conflict of laws system. As explained above, the hypothetical will of the parties corresponds to rules with certain attributes: predictability, stability, accuracy, uniformity, consistency and simplicity. If reasons of practicability clearly indicate advantages of the application of a law different from the place of residence of the parties, the cheapest-cost-avoider criterion can be put aside. The same occurs in situations where the party in a better position to bear the costs of internationality is too difficult – or impossible – to determine. A legal provision that allocates the costs of internationality according to the cheapest-cost-avoider is desirable, but only to the extent that it does not generate unforeseeability, imprecision, ambiguities, incoherencies or intricacies in its interpretation and application.[871]

The cheapest-cost-avoider, however, does afford an adequate solution for the determination of governing law in the vast majority of arrangements involving monetary and non-monetary transactions. It indicates the general connecting factor of the most common contracts, such as for example sale, rent, loan or service provision contracts. It also provides a practical and straightforward solution for other legal transactions – e.g. barters or exchange of foreign currency – where determination of the applicable law is often difficult. For the purposes of this book, the cheapest-cost-avoider is of the utmost importance as it will guide the design of an efficient conflict rule in the context of a marital relationship. Let us analyze to what extent the approach used in contract law allocates the cost of internationality efficiently if the parties reside in different jurisdictions. Later on, the default rule applicable to marriage and the special situation of spouses will be looked at.

4.1. DEFAULT CONFLICT RULE IN INTERNATIONAL CONTRACT LAW

The concept of the characteristic performance has gradually been accepted as the point of departure to establish a rule – or legal presumption – for the determination of the applicable law to contracts.[872] This concept is currently used as guiding principle in practically all European countries, as well as in a number of jurisdictions in the United States and other parts of the world.[873]

870 Basedow (2006a) 59–60; Rühl (2011) 406–407. See also: O'Hara & Ribstein (2000) 1192–1194.

871 In this line, see Basedow (2006a) 60.

872 See: Mankowski (2010) 435, 441 et seqq.

873 Rühl (2011) 542.

It is tacitly included in the Restatement (second) of Conflict of Law for Purchase of Movable Goods and Contracts on Provision of Services as well as expressly set out in the Rome I Regulation.[874] It is further present in a variety of national codifications on private international law such as the Swiss,[875] Japanese,[876] Chinese,[877] Argentinian[878] and Russian[879] ones. Although exceptions and specific conflict rules for certain types of contracts exist – most notably for contracts involving immovable property, workers and consumers – currently the characteristic performance rule is playing a key role in modern international contract law.[880]

From an economic perspective, its use is welcome as it entails the application of a single legal system to a relationship and allows a fast and simple determination of the applicable law in most cases.[881] Thanks to its incorporation into judicial practice, not only judges and lawyers, but also lay people can ascertain the law governing a relationship without complications. It is only

874 The principle is expressly mentioned in Art. 4 para. 2 as the default rule when a legal transaction does not fall under one of the contract types listed in Art. 4 para. 1. The catalogue of connecting factors contained in paragraph 1 is, however, no more than a concretization of the principle of the characteristic performance. See: Magnus (2017) 227, 309.

875 Art. 117 of the Swiss Private International Law Act. See also: Decision of 12 February 1952, *Chevalley*, ATF 78 II 74.

876 According to Art. 8(1) of the Japanese Act on General Rules for Application of Laws (*Hō no Tekiyō ni kansuru Tsūsoku-hō*), the effects of the contract are governed by the law of the state with which it is most closely connected. "The most closely connected law is presumed to be the law of the place in which the party performing the characteristic obligation is habitually resident". See: Toshiyuki (2017) 2223; Nishitani (2021) 552–553.

877 According to Art. 41 of the Law on the Application of Laws to Civil Relationships Involving a Foreign Element of the People's Republic of China, "a contract is governed by the law chosen by the parties. Absent party choice, the contract is governed by the law of the place of habitual residence of the party whose performance of obligations can be most characteristic of the contract". See: Chen (2017) 1977; He (2021) 446.

878 According to Art. 2652 sentence 1 of the new and unified Civil and Commercial Code of Argentina, in the absence of a choice of law agreement, the contract is governed by the laws of the place of performance. However, according to the sentence 2, if there is no place of performance stipulated in the contract or it cannot be determined according to the nature of the relationship, the contract is governed by the law of the domicile of the party required to perform the most characteristic obligation of the contract. See: Dreyzen de Klor (2017) 1875; All (2021) 967.

879 According to Art. 1211(1) of the Russian Civil Code, the contract shall be subject to the law of the country with which the contract has the closest relation. However, paragraph 2 establishes that "the law of the country with which a contract has the closest relation shall be deemed the law of the country where the party responsible for the performance under the contract of crucial significance for the content of the contract has its place of residence". See: Asoskov (2017) 2459; Karayanidi (2021) 836–837.

880 It was the merit of Adolf Schnitzer to have first clearly formulated and systematized the concept of characteristic performance. See: Schnitzer (1958) 639–646; Schnitzer (1969) 20–24; Vischer (1996) 503. See also: Vischer (1962) 108–111; Lipstein (1981) 403–409. For a harsh criticism of Schnitzer's approach, see: D'Oliveira (1977).

881 Rühl (2011) 533; Mankowski (2010) 437; Schäfer & Lantermann (2006) 99 *in fine*.

necessary to identify the obligation that is not money, to quickly see the characteristic performance of the contract.[882] On the whole, this rule fulfills the formal features – predictability, stability, accuracy, uniformity, consistency and simplicity – required to encourage the realization of transactions in the international arena. Concerns arise, however, when analyzing the different manifestations of the doctrine of the characteristic performance. Whereas in some jurisdictions the law of the person owing the characteristic performance governs the relationship, in others the connecting factor looks to the place where the characteristic performance is to occur. In practically all European countries – as well as in those whose conflict of laws systems were inspired by the Rome Convention or the Rome Regulation – the governing law of the contract is the law in force in the place of residence of the performer. In contrast, in a number of jurisdictions located in the United States – those following the Restatement (second) – rather the place of delivery of the characteristic performance is decisive.[883] The difference between the two approaches is important from an economic point of view, as the costs of internationality are distributed differently.[884] Whereas the solution used in the United States seems neutral, the European approach clearly favors the party owing the characteristic performance, as their law – the one to which they have easy access – will govern the relationship.[885]

Is there an economic reason to favor one party over the other? Would the surplus of the contract be increased by applying the law of the party owing the characteristic performance? Is one manifestation of the doctrine more adequate than the other? These questions will be answered next.

4.1.1. *Creditor of the Characteristic Performance as Cheapest-Cost-Avoider*

Although particular circumstances surrounding a relationship could lead to a different outcome, in general the creditor of the characteristic performance is able to determine who the seller or provider of the product or service is, even without getting in contact with the potential partner. That occurs because this contractual party was formerly the addressee of proposals put forward by recognizable organizations or individuals in the market. Creditors of the characteristic performance can easily weigh the convenience of a transaction; they only need a single piece of information – the origin of the proposal to contract – to determine the convenience of the contract.[886] In contrast to

[882] Mankowski (2010) 437.

[883] See: Solomon (2007) 1714. See also: Basedow (2006a) 68; Basedow (2006b) 244. In practice, however, the law of the place of residence of the beneficiary of the performance applies in jurisdictions following the Restatement (second). See for example: Rühl (2011) 533.

[884] Schäfer & Lantermann (2006) 98.

[885] Mankowski (2010) 436–437.

[886] Schäfer & Lantermann (2006) 99.

sellers – who in general ignore the person that will accept his offer – buyers are able to know in advance who will be their partner, and consequently the exact rights, duties and risks of the conclusion of the contract, if the law of their counterpart applies.[887] Creditors of the characteristic performance are in most cases in a better position to bear the application of a foreign law, as they can obtain possessive and transactional security with less effort.[888] Let us see an example to better appreciate the suitability of using the law of the place of residence of the debtor of the characteristic obligation:

> The day she celebrated her first wedding anniversary, Maria Elisabet – a woman living in Spain – had to take the sad decision to sell her wedding dress to pay off the debts of her marriage party. The price she has in mind for the bridal gown is 9,000 euros, exactly the sum she needs to avoid repossession of some personal belongings by the bank. She is convinced that the price is fair, as the dress not only includes 25 crystals, but was also designed by Joan Caríssim himself, a reputed fashion designer. In order to accelerate the sale, she put an ad on the Internet portal ePay Global. She is not interested in holding an auction. For her, it is enough that somebody – no matter from where – pays the required sum as soon as possible to avoid the seizure of her assets.

If the law governing the contract were the law of the place of residence of the purchaser, Maria Elisabet – or any other person trying to sell a product internationally – would have serious problems at the moment of making the offer to sell. Due to the practical impossibility to predict who will ultimately be the buyer, sellers in general cannot establish a price reflecting the costs of the application of a foreign legal system to this relationship. The use of a law different than their own is adverse for any person – seller or buyer – as it is necessary to incur extra costs to get information about important questions like the reasons allowing a return of the product; the degree of responsibility for a deterioration in the goods during shipping; who must pay the transportation costs; and many other issues affecting the subjective gains of the transaction directly. However, the situation of the seller in our example – and in general in any purchase contract – is more problematic, as she has to get information about not just one, but all the jurisdictions reached by the offer, in this case all countries accessing the ePay Global website.[889] That not only leads to a lopsided rise of the selling price, but it might also outright discourage her from selling

---

887 Garcimartín (2002) 150–151; Rühl (2011) 538.

888 It is important to note that the application of the law of the debtor does not force creditors of the performance to tolerate the application of a foreign law, if information about the place of residence of the counterpart is unavailable. They can always refuse the conclusion of the contract if this information is not provided.

889 Garcimartín (2002) 151.

her product in jurisdictions with few potential customers – due to the smaller probability of finding a buyer there. She might even refuse to sell abroad at all.[890]

The application of the law of the buyer is negative by itself, not only due to the reduction in supply and the higher price caused by the inclusion of the costs of getting information about many laws.[891] It would also lead to a further distortion of the price caused by overlapping obligations in the legal systems involved.[892] As each of these legislative schemes might include different duties for those responsible for the characteristic performance, sellers will have to take into consideration these costs as well. By way of our example, regardless of whether only one country imposes on Maria Elisabet the obligation to assume the delivery costs, and another country the obligation to give a full refund if requested, she must include these costs in the price, as she cannot foresee if somebody from those places will finally buy her product. Thus, far for being an advantage for buyers, the use of their own law is counterproductive; the price could include costs from legal obligations that do not even exist in the law that will finally govern the relationship.[893] In contrast, in a situation where the law of the seller applies, the incidence of the costs of internationality is different. To calculate the subjective value of a given transaction, buyers must spend resources to get information about the applicable set of rules just once. As creditors of the obligation know who their counterpart is, they can determine precisely to what extent the transaction meets their preferences.

The economic advantage of using the law of the place of residence of the performer is not related to the need of finding the law most closely connected, or the seat of the relationship.[894] It rather lies with the objective of reducing information costs and so maximizing the surplus generated by the contract. By assuming that the hypothetical will of parties is the highest possible gains from the transaction, the conclusion is that they would choose the law of the characteristic obligation's performer. The rationale behind such a conflict rule does not follow a complex deliberation, it simply refers to the assumption that most people would prefer the application of a law that sets a price that is not only lower, but also reflects accurately the costs of making the transaction.

4.1.2. *Further Advantages of Applying the Law of the Performer of the Characteristic Performance*

Against the use of the law of the characteristic obligation's performer one can argue that it is only valid in situations where sellers – or providers of a service –

---

890 Schäfer & Lantermann (2006) 99.

891 For another view, see: Mankowski (2010) 460.

892 Rühl (2011) 535, 538; Garcimartín (2002) 151.

893 Rühl (2011) 535.

894 Rühl (2011) 516; Gunst (1994) 138.

make offers to many countries simultaneously. If a proposal were addressed to just one jurisdiction, the cost of information would be the same for any of the parties. Allocating the costs to either party would have no economic effect, as the surplus – the sum of the gains of each party – remains unchanged regardless of which party bears the cost of internationality.

This observation is accurate. However, when establishing the advantages of using the performer's law one should take into account the effects of the general rule on those individuals eager to place their products in different countries. As the rule would indiscriminately apply to all contracts, the use of the law of the creditor would harm those that desire to offer a product in many jurisdictions in the first place. Using the law of the performer avoids that individuals whose offers reach a variety of countries need to change their default rule.[895] Furthermore, it is also important to consider the risks of bringing a product into a single market. Placing an advert does not guarantee that a buyer will conclude the transaction. Sometimes it is necessary to change the place where the product is initially offered to find success. The use of the law of the beneficiary of the characteristic performance would be unfavorable in situations when after an unsuccessful first try, the performer moves his offer to another jurisdiction.

Continuing the example from above, suppose now that before advertising her dress, a friend of Maria Elisabet suggests offering it in Switzerland, as this is a country with the most exquisite tastes – and deepest pockets – in terms of fashion for brides. Her friend not only has a Spanish law degree, but he has also recently finished an extraordinary dissertation on private international law at a Bernese university. This being so, he offers her legal advice for the low price of 300 €, to avoid unpleasant surprises regarding her obligations as a seller. After having paid this sum and being informed that there is no significant difference between the Spanish and Swiss substantive laws, she puts an ad on a Swiss website, but this time with a price of 9,300 €. Against all odds, nobody bought the dress after several weeks.

Most likely Maria Elisabet will not run the risk of trying to sell the dress in another jurisdiction later. Each attempt to do so would cost her an additional 300 €, which once added to the price reduces the probability of selling the gown even more. The costs of gathering information about the law would discourage her not only from trying in another country, but also from selling in small jurisdictions. As explained above, if the number of attempts is reduced due to the information costs, it is expected that people prefer making proposals in jurisdictions with larger populations rather than in small ones. The advantage of using the law of the performer not only eliminates obstacles to bringing an

895 Rühl (2011) 539.

offer to other markets, but it also avoids that sellers will skip jurisdictions based on their size.[896]

4.1.3. Inclusion of a Different Conflict of Law Rule in Situations Involving Consumers

The efficiency of using the law of the characteristic performance's debtor (e.g. that of the habitual residence of the seller) as the default rule can – rightly – be called into question in a number of cases where the seller – or provider of a service – is not a person like the woman in our example. More often than not, the vendor is a business that offers not one, but many products to a variety of individuals in differing jurisdictions who acquire a product only once in their life. Under these conditions, allocating the costs of internationality to the debtor of the characteristic performance – and consequently applying the law of the buyer or beneficiary of a service – would increase the surplus of the contract, as the performer is able to offset the costs of information with the volume of their turnover. The incidence of the costs of internationality are different for entrepreneurs, as they can use their information about foreign laws not just once, but each time they make a deal with a consumer there. For consumers, the impact of these costs is far greater, because the information becomes useless afterwards, as they do not carry out repeated commercial activities.[897] Let us run another example:

> Assume now, that the board of directors of Joan Carissim S.A. – a firm located in Barcelona that sells wedding dresses – have decided to expand their operation to Switzerland, and two further countries in Europe (in total three jurisdictions). Thus, the seller does not offer just one, but an extensive catalogue of bridal gowns to a handful of countries selected beforehand by the board. Let's further assume that until the day of Joan's tragic death, the business was able to sell 100 dresses abroad.

In this constellation, the parties would prefer the application of the law of the consumer, as the surplus of each contract would increase. The costs of information about the contents of the law in each jurisdiction are the result of dividing them by all the contracts concluded by Joan Carissim S.A. in foreign markets. If 300 € is the cost of being informed about the law in force in each jurisdiction, the transaction cost for each of the 100 dresses sold would then only be 9 € (= 300 x 3 / 100) per contract concluded.[898] The application of the

---

896 For an economic analysis of the application of the seller's law see: Basedow (2006a) 70; Basedow (2006b) 246–247.

897 Garcimartín (2002) 138.

898 According to the example three jurisdictions are at stake.

law of the creditor is consequently more advisable, as it improves the use of the information. By applying the law of the beneficiary of the obligation, fewer expenses per contract will be necessary to overcome the cross-border risk in each jurisdiction where the products are offered. A contrary solution would be problematic, as each buyer would be obliged to spend additional resources – let's say 300 euros – each time a contact is concluded.[899] This situation would lead to a reduction of the willingness to buy and so fewer overall transactions.

This consumer-supplier case is certainly important when designing a conflict of laws system. However, it should not overshadow the use of the performer's law as the general rule, but rather support the inclusion of special conflict of laws provisions for contracts concluded in the framework of a business-to-consumer activity. Practically all jurisdictions that use the residence of the performer as the general rule include an exception for cases involving consumers. As explained above,[900] in the case of consumer contracts the freedom to determine the law governing the relationship must be constrained in order to avoid an economic race to the bottom. However, economic arguments not only support a restriction of the freedom of choice, they also demonstrate the efficiency of applying the buyer's law as the default rule.

In the end, both connecting factors – the one used for contracts in general and the one used for consumer contracts – in force in most countries in Europe, allocate the costs of internationality efficiently.[901]

4.1.4. Promoter of the Transaction and Determination of the Applicable Law

Previously, it was said that the application of the law of the characteristic performance's debtor – e.g. the law of the seller – reduces transaction costs. Excluding consumer contracts, this solution allows the allocation of the costs of internationality to the party in the better position to bear them. However – as you might have already noticed – the reason why the performer is in a worse position is not related to the features of the obligation. The true reason lies in his action: the fact that the debtors of the characteristic performance – sellers, service providers, etc. – are the ones who usually bring the proposal for a transaction into the market. Making an offer in an international arena without knowing the residence of the person who will accept it causes further costs. Let us modify the previous example again:

> Now imagine a bride dreaming of a beautiful dress for her wedding day. Her greatest wish is a bridal gown decorated with crystals and – naturally – designed by the late Joan Carissim. She knows she cannot afford a new one. So, she decides to buy a

[899] Rühl (2011) 541; Roth (1985) 332.
[900] See Chapter 6 Section 4.3.
[901] Rühl (2011) 540–541, 542.

> dress *d'occasion*. In order to live out her dream, she places an advert on ePay Global offering 9,500 euros for a dress that matches her expectations. After a couple of hours, she receives an email from a Spanish woman accepting the deal and assuring that having read her offer certainly made this day the happiest one in her entire life. Well then, who is now the cheapest-cost-avoider?

The answer is not the buyer, as she cannot predict the person who will finally accept her offer. The seller on the other hand can identify the origin of the offer and the corresponding foreign law. The surplus created by the contract would be maximized if the law of the seller applied.[902] The economic efficiency of the doctrine of the characteristic performance lies, then, in favoring the mover or "motor" of the transaction – here called the promoter of the transaction – that is, the individual from whom the initiative to make the transaction usually comes. Having to make the first step puts this party in an adverse position to bear the costs of internationality. The economic rationale of a general conflict of laws rule cannot simply be based on the nature of the performance. Whether one of the parties makes a payment of money or delivers an obligation is only tangential when determining the cheapest-cost-avoider. More important is who made the invitation to perform the exchange; this first step directly influences the effort necessary to be informed about the law applicable to the relationship.

In most instances determining the promoter of the transaction is not a complicated issue. It is sufficient to identify the individual who has submitted for consideration the possibility of being involved in a contractual relationship to the other. It does not matter whether the addressee of the proposal is known in advance by the offeror, or whether, as a consequence of an eventual negotiation, the original conditions of the proposal change. What is important is rather singling out the party who puts at the disposal of the future partner an offer, or invitation to offer, as this first move is what puts the other party in a better position to bear the cost of internationality.

The promoter of the transaction must, however, not be confused with the person who sends an offer to another party to purchase an asset that has already been publicly placed on the market. Sending an offer to another person does not automatically turn an individual into the transaction's promoter. The decisive factor is which of the parties has awakened the interest in the other of being involved in a relationship by promoting the possibility of an exchange, even if that initial offer is addressed to the public at large. Thus, the promoter of the transaction is not the person who communicates his desire to buy a product at a certain price after reading an advertisement about it. The promoter is rather the person who has published the ad, as without it the purchaser could never have thought of sending an order to buy the product.

---

902 Rühl (2011) 542.

The criterion of the cheapest-cost-avoider can be concretized in private international law by prescribing the application of the law of the party who creates the opportunity for a voluntary exchange. The doctrine of the characteristic performance – as it is applied in most European countries – delivers efficient outcomes because it leads – in most cases – to the application of the law of the promoter of the transaction; that is, the law of the person from whom the initiative to enter into a legal relationship comes.

4.1.5. Promoter of the Transaction as Residual Connecting Factor

Focusing on finding the promoter of a transaction allows the determination of the cheapest-cost-avoider accurately. Its use in the conflict of laws allocates the risks surrounding the realization of a transaction with international connotations in an economically suitable form; that is, in a way that maximizes the surplus from the cooperation. However, the efficiency of a legal rule relies not only on the results that are achieved with it in theory, but on the results delivered once it is applied in reality. The use of the promoter of the transaction might cause difficulties in the eyes of a third person – an arbitrator, judge or any other authority – when determining *ex post* the governing law of a relationship. Offers are often made in an informal and casual atmosphere – business dinners, telephone calls, video conferences, etc. – so that finding proof of the identity of the promoter might be very complicated.[903] Furthermore, even assuming that parties provide the necessary proofs and show what had actually happened, a certain margin of discretion is unavoidable when identifying the individual who made the first step for the conclusion of the transaction. Although such leeway is not *per se* a problem, it makes the outcomes highly dependent on the capabilities of the individual called to resolve the case. When designing a conflict of laws rule, it should not be forgotten that judges are human beings who make mistakes, owing to stress caused by work overload, time pressure or personal issues. They can also use their margin of discretion to favor one of the parties unduly. The simpler, plainer and more transparent the way of determining the applicable law is the better one for the people, as that assures a greater degree of predictability and certainty about the results of a proceeding.[904]

As a matter of principle, the allocation of the costs to the individual in a better position to bear them is the solution contractual parties would prefer. However, if this method creates unforeseeability or incentivizes opportunistic behavior, the appeal is lost. Using the promoter of the transaction as the general rule for the determination of the applicable law might then have the opposite effect of forcing people to resort to choice of law agreements to gain certainty about the

[903] Garcimartín (2002) 148.

[904] Schäfer (2001) 5–8.

governing law. In contrast, the principle of the characteristic performance – as it is applied in most European countries – although not delivering efficient outcomes in all cases, provides greater certainty due to the objectivity on which it is based. Although this criterion has the disadvantage of not always allocating the cost of internationality correctly – e.g. in situations when the offer to contract stems from the buyer rather than from the seller – this down-side can be compensated for by the high degree of predictability in the rest of the cases. Summarizing, one concludes that the habitual residence of the debtor of the characteristic performance is a suitable connecting factor for the determination of the governing law of contracts.

That does not mean that the promoter of the transaction is not a useful criterion. Quite the contrary, it can be used to resolve situations where it is not possible to identify a characteristic obligation of the contract. The determination of the law applicable to contracts such as barters, swaps, foreign exchanges, cryptocurrency exchanges or any other type that cannot be resolved by applying the doctrine of the characteristic performance can be done in an efficient – and more predictable – manner compared with the methods commonly used by courts. Situations that were resolved by the law most closely connected with the relationship can be handled efficiently through the application of the law of the party that made the first step in the terms explained above.

4.2. DEFAULT CONFLICT RULE IN INTERNATIONAL MARRIAGE LAW

As discussed in Part I of this book, the subject matter of the marital relationship does not consist of one or two, but rather of a great number of complex, multifarious and changeable obligations that do not at all resemble the payment of money.[905] The doctrine of the characteristic performance is consequently not very helpful, because there is no debtor or creditor of the characteristic performance. Although this doctrine might indicate the applicable law for some disputes between spouses or ex-spouses – e.g. those related to maintenance obligations – it cannot be used to determine the applicable law to further aspects of a marriage.

From the above it should not be inferred, either, that the determination of the applicable law depends on the law of the person who made the marriage proposal. The idea of the promoter of the transaction is helpful for the allocation of the cost of internationality in contracts concluded in regular markets when the characteristic performance cannot be determined. As in markets the offers are mostly addressed to a wide audience of people, favoring the promoter of

[905] See Chapter 1 Section 2.3.

the transaction leads to an increase of the contract's surplus. However, this criterion cannot be used in the context of a marriage, as proposals do not target the public, but a single person that is fully known before the marriage proposal. There are certainly cases where it is possible to identify one of the partners as the motor of the relationship. In the case of arranged marriages – for example – the person – or family – who made the first step for the conclusion of the marriage could be determined.[906] However, in most cases the idea of getting married tends to arise spontaneously in both individuals as a consequence of an interplay within the framework of an amicable or sentimental relationship. In general, the decision is the result of a process where little by little lovers not only discover the appropriateness of the other as a partner, but also their own interest in marriage.[907] Thus, although at some point one of the partners asks for the other's hand, this action does not necessarily indicate this individual's initiative.[908] The proposal might be driven by previous actions of the other eliciting it on the sly – but sometime not at all covertly – to strengthen the relationship they already have.

Still, the rationale behind the conflict rule for contracts can be used to draft a rule applicable to the relationship between spouses. The insight that not so much the expenditure needed to obtain information about foreign a law, but certainly the gains from this information are different for each partner, will be the key in the design of this conflict rule.

4.2.1. Cohabitation as Characteristic Feature of Married Couples

As mentioned earlier, using the characteristic performance for the determination of the applicable law to contracts concluded in regular markets is efficient, as it allocates – in most cases – the costs of internationality to the cheapest-cost-avoider.[909] That is so because in general, the offers – or invitations to offer – stem from individuals having the position of debtor of the characteristic performance in the relationship. The suitability of this connecting factor is then not based on purely theoretical reasons, but rather on the fact that in the vast majority of cases

906 For forced and arranged marriages in Arabic countries, see: Arshad (2010) 67. The idea that arranged marriages are something occurring mostly in developing countries is not true. According to a study published in the 1990s, 25–30% of all marriages in Japan were arranged marriages. See: Applbaum (1995) 37.

907 According to a study focused on binational couples, for the most part these relationships spark a process of reflection in the spouses about their life plans, and raise the question whether they want to permanently move to another country. See: Riaño (2015) 46.

908 According to a study made in the United States, when couples spoke of their marriage proposal and who initiated it, 41% indicated that both were involved, 35% said that the husband had more control and 21% thought that the wife had more control. See: Orbuch et al. (1993) 821.

909 See in this chapter Section 4.1.5.

the individual who makes the first step for the realization of a transaction is the performer of the obligation in kind – the seller, provider of a service, etc.

Likewise, the default rule for marriage can also resort to the normal way in which a relationship takes place to reflect the arrangement which spouses would prefer if they had discussed the governing law of their relationship. For this purpose two simple, but very plausible assumptions about the behavior of married persons will be made. First, in most cases spouses already know the place where they will live together immediately after the marriage – if not the exact address then at least the country – at the moment of celebrating their matrimony.[910] Second, if spouses did not live in the same jurisdiction beforehand, they will tend to choose the country of one of them as their first place of common residence.[911]

It can certainly happen – particularly in cases involving refugees – that neither of the spouses knows the country where they will live after the wedding.[912] It can also occur that after having a long-distance relationship, they decide to move to a third country immediately after the conclusion of their marriage. It can even come about that spouses never live together during their whole relationship. However, when drafting the conflict rule, one cannot rely on exceptional situations, but rather on the normal unfolding of a relationship. Efficient rules are those that deliver the best outcome in most cases.[913] Based on the aforementioned assumptions, it will be shown that the use of the law of the place of their first common residence should be the prime connecting factor, because it maximizes the surplus from a marital relationship. The law of the place of conclusion shall in turn be the residual connecting factor for those rare cases where spouses never had a common residence during their whole relationship.[914]

---

910 The UNHCR has reported cases of individuals who got married before fleeing from their country of origin, and then asked for asylum in different countries with the hope of obtaining protection in one of them. However, such situations are not the common case. See: UNHCR (2018) 64–70.

911 This assumption is based on the monetary and non-monetary benefits that starting a family in a place where at least one of them is already established offers. A study focused on bi-national couples affirms that the place of residence depends in general on the financial advantages it entails for them. See: Nowicka (2017) 119–120.

912 The 1951 Convention and the 1954 Convention contain a conflict rule applicable to the personal relationships of refugees and stateless persons. Art. 12 of both conventions establish that: "The personal status of a refugee/stateless person should be governed by the law of the country of his domicile, or, if he has no domicile, by the law of the country of his residence". The expression "shall be governed by the law" is understood as a modifier of domestic conflict of laws rules in force in the forum. In practice this means that the applicable law to the personal relationships of those individuals is the law in force in the place of the new domicile. For an interpretation of this article, see in detail: Lass (1995) 108; Metzger (2011) 875.

913 For the concept of majoritarian default rules, see: Chapter 3 Section 2.2.1.

914 The determination of the applicable law in situations where the *lex causae* contravenes the *ordre public* is outside the scope of this book. Thus, questions such as whether – from an

4.2.2. Allocation of Costs between Spouses

The idea of allocating the costs to the individual in a better position to bear them was theorized by Ronald Coase over 50 years ago.[915] According to him: when people are fully aware of the consequences of their actions in terms of benefits and externalities they might generate; when they do not behave opportunistically; when there are no barriers to discussing solutions; and when there are not further transaction costs to conclude an agreement; then it does not matter how the law allocates responsibilities in a legal relationship. The motivation to improve their own situation will push people to cooperate and find a solution beneficial for the bottom line of both of them.[916] However, as real-world transaction costs are rarely low enough to allow frictionless bargaining, the intervention of the state is needed. It has to provide legal provisions that reflect the solution at which individuals would have arrived if they had negotiated.[917] Two decades later, the ideas of Coase were summarized in a single example by another renowned researcher of economic analysis of law, A. Mitchell Polinsky:

> One of the central ideas in the economic analysis of law was developed in an article by Ronald H. Coase in 1960. This idea, which has since been named the Coase Theorem, is most easily described by an example. Consider a factory whose smoke causes damage to the laundry hung outdoors by five nearby residents. In the absence of any corrective action each resident would suffer $75 in damages, a total of $375. The smoke damage can be eliminated by either of two ways: A smokescreen can be installed on the factory's chimney, at a cost of $150, or each resident can be provided an electric dryer, at a cost of $50 per resident. The efficient solution is clearly to install the smokescreen because it eliminates total damages of $375 for an outlay of only $150, and it is cheaper than purchasing five dryers for $250.[918]

According to the Coase Theorem – in a world without transaction costs – it is irrelevant who has the lawful right to enforce their interests, because individuals would arrive at the most efficient solution by themselves. If the law gives preference to the neighbors' right to enjoy clear air, the factory will install the smokescreen. On the other hand, if the law grants the right to pollute – e.g. the factory is located in an industrial area – neighbors will not buy electric dryers, but rather pay for the smokescreen themselves, as this is the cheaper

economic view – the *lex fori* should apply directly or the subsidiary connecting factor should be used to designate the applicable law are left open. For the scope of the analysis of the book see the Preface.

915 Coase (1960).
916 Coase (1960) 15.
917 Coase (1960) 15 et seqq.
918 Polinsky (1983) 11.

option to resolve the problem. The cheaper option will convince all the affected individuals to come to terms with it and choose the most suitable alternative from an economic point of view – the one that avoids wasting resources.[919] However, it is very difficult for the second scenario to actually happen, as an unrealistic number of conditions must be met, *inter alia*:

- Neighbors must know what exactly a smokescreen is and that it can solve their problem.
- They must also be aware of the benefits in terms of costs that buying it brings in comparison with the electric dryers.
- All of them must know each other and be ready to look together for a solution to their common problem.
- Everyone must be genuinely ready to solve the problem and assume the costs without attempting to profit unduly – no free-riding.
- All involved must agree on a fair distribution of the costs of the smokescreen.
- They have to convince the factory to accept their proposal.

There are just too many conditions, making it very difficult for the neighbors to actually purchase the smokescreen. It is then more likely that they will simply buy the electric dryers, despite this solution being more expensive. According to the theory, people should choose the solution costing the least amount of resources to resolve a problem, but transaction costs will in reality bar them from this option. The allocation of the costs made by the law is then not irrelevant; quite the contrary, it is of the utmost importance as it must replace the ideal scenario and call for an appropriate use of resources. In this concrete case, the legal provisions should establish the prevalence of the rights of the neighbors over the interests of the factory, as – according to the data – this is the party in the better position to resolve the issue at stake efficiently.[920]

So far, the Coase Theorem is in line with our thoughts in this chapter, as the solution allocates the costs to the cheapest-cost-avoider. Notwithstanding this, there is something in this reasoning that – probably because it is too obvious – could easily be overlooked when designing a default rule. There is no doubt that the efficient solution is the one that allocates the responsibilities to the party that has to invest the least in order to avoid the occurrence of an event. However, one should not only take the actual expenses into account for each party, but also the potential benefits – if they exist – that bearing those costs can generate.

---

919 Cooter & Ulen (2016) 82–83; Friedman (2000) 39; Polinsky (1983) 12; Schäfer & Ott (2012) 74.

920 Cooter & Ulen (2016) 84; Friedman (2000) 39–40 Polinsky (1983); Schäfer & Ott (2012) 78. See also: Rühl (2011) 360.

If the investment in avoiding an unwanted contingency provides advantages beyond its primary function, this party can deduct them from the expenditure. Regardless of the initial assessment declaring one side the cheapest-cost-avoider, the other might then be in a better position to bear the costs if through the investment they get further benefits that compensate them.

Assume now that the purchase of a dryer not only avoids the damage caused by the factory, but also reduces the drying time of the laundry from 15 hours to only 45 minutes. Let us also assume that this advantage – which is particularly useful on rainy days and in winter – has a total value of $25 for each of the families.

In this scenario, the agreement at which they would arrive in the absence of transaction costs would not be installing the smokescreen, so that the law must not allocate the costs of prevention to the factory, when transaction costs preclude negotiations. The costs are smaller for the neighbors, due to the benefits derived from the purchase of the electric dryers. Under these circumstances, the determination of the cheapest-cost-avoider should be carried out differently; the subjective value of the electric dryers must be deducted from the price to arrive at the solution that maximizes the benefit for all involved:

$$150 \text{ in comparison with } [250 - (25 \times 5)]$$

$$\rightarrow 150 > 125$$

(total cost of the chimney filter vs. total costs of the dryers)

An efficient solution would then absolve the factory of their responsibility for the damage caused by their business activity. This solution allocates the costs to the party in the better position to bear them, as the investment generates further benefits for the neighbors that compensate – to a certain extent – for the cost needed to avoid the contingency.

The point here is not claiming that factories should not be liable for the pollution they cause, or for any other harm to third parties. The data here is imaginary and used only for the sake of a simple and clear explanation. In real life, not only does the number of people affected by emissions tend to be higher, but also the damage they do is more severe, especially when people's health is compromised. Thus, in real-life scenarios, factories – as a general rule – are the party in a better position to bear the costs, so they should be liable for damage caused by their activity.

What I want to point out, is that at the moment of determining the individual in a better position to bear the cost of avoiding the occurrence of events – and so the agreement at which they would arrive – not only the immediate expenditure needed to avoid them, but also the gains derived from the investment should be taken into account by the law-maker. This insight – although small – is of key importance when drafting a conflict rule for the law applicable to the marriage.

4.2.3. *First Place of Residence as the Prime Connecting Factor*

Based on the above, a case-by-case analysis of the circumstances of the spouses at their wedding seems to be required to allocate the costs of internationality.[921] However, this would be counterproductive due to the many facts that have to be considered when analyzing a concrete case. A legal provision granting a great margin of discretion to the court causes a high degree of unpredictability.[922] For this reason, considerations about the actual expenditure needed to get information about a foreign law before the proposal will be set aside. It will be assumed that they are similar for spouses residing in different countries. The analysis will rather be focused on what happens after they express their desire to be engaged in a long-term relationship. It is at this moment that – if they are not currently living together – they have to establish their future place of residence, a decision with direct repercussions not only on the expenses necessary to obtain information about the content of the law, but also on the value placed by each spouse on this information.

Sometimes the first common residence is determined by extrinsic factors or even by chance. However, in most cases this decision is rarely taken lightly,[923] and also responds to their sincere desire of maximizing the benefits from their marriage.[924] Issues like the labor opportunities each of them has abroad;[925] the presence of relatives in their future place of residence; the support of parents, siblings or friends to raise the children; and generally keeping a degree of stability when starting a family[926] do indeed play a major role at the moment of deciding about the place to live after the marriage.[927] It does not then seem at all

921 O'Hara & Ribstein (2000) 1188; Rühl (2006) 833 et seqq.; Rühl (2011) 522, 526–527; Schäfer & Lantermann (2006) 89–92; Whincop & Keynes (2001) 43.

922 Dutta (2017) 558; O'Hara & Ribstein (2000) 1188; Rühl (2006) 833 et seqq.; Rühl (2011) 522, 526–527; Schäfer & Lantermann (2006) 89–92; Whincop & Keynes (2001) 43.

923 According to a study focused on bi-national couples, only a third of the women changed their country of residence instantly after formalizing the relationship, whereas the other two-thirds moved back and forth for a long period of time before finally settling in the country of their partner. Riaño (2015) 46–47.

924 That involves not just monetary gains, but also stability, presence of relatives, etc. See Nowicka (2017) 120.

925 A better work opportunity for the spouse in their original country of residence was one of the principal reasons that motivated the other to change their residence. See: Riaño (2015) 51–52.

926 Riaño (2015) 53.

927 A study of transnational marriages published in 2017 confirms that although at times the reason for moving from one country to another was a troubling political situation, in general it depends on the potential financial standing of the family. See: Nowicka (2017) 119–120.

unreasonable affirming that in a situation where spouses do not live in the same country, they will tend to choose the place of residence of one of them as the first common one. This, not only due to the aforementioned reasons, but also because such a decision would help them to bear together the actual costs entailed for any person moving from one place to another with the intention of setting in a new location.

In this context the question which law would be chosen by the spouses if they had negotiated the law governing their relationship can then be reduced to: the legislation that corresponds to the law of only one of them, or the legislation that in addition will become the law of the other as a result of their change of residence? At the moment of answering this question it will be taken into account that the information about the foreign law has extra value for the immigrating spouse, as from then on this legal system will apply to a variety of legal situations in which this person will be involved. In this respect it is important not to overlook that the relevant marriage law is inscribed within the wider family law, which includes legal provisions covering not only the relationship between spouses, but also many other relationships of contractual and non-contractual nature with further individuals as heirs and underage children living in the same jurisdiction. Thus, whereas the investment of one party to get information about a foreign law can only be used for the relationship with their spouse, the other profits further, as this law will govern other matters of a family nature in which this person gets involved during the time he or she stays there.[928] If in addition one considers that in general the law of the new place of residence also applies to contracts concluded by the person, the benefits of the application of the law of the first place of residence are even more obvious: greater coherence from the perspective of the household will be achieved as a result of the application of the law of the spouses' common place of residence to all those legal relationships.[929] Thus, based on the additional gains derived from the investment to bear the costs of internationality, the individual who changes his or her place of residence will be regarded as the cheapest-cost-avoider. The law of the first common residence of the couple will be regarded as the law that they would have chosen if they had negotiated over the applicable law to their marriage. At the end of the day, this solution entails not only predictability and legal certainty but also an efficient allocation of costs between spouses.

The main connecting factor of Regulation 2016/1103 and a handful of national laws as principal connecting factor for certain aspects of the marriage –

928 Dutta (2017) 559.

929 The advantages derived from the application of the law of the person's environment have been constantly cited as one of the principal reasons for favoring the use of the habitual residence of a person as connecting factor. See for all: Kropholler (2006) 292.

Argentina,[930] Dominican Republic,[931] Iceland,[932] Norway,[933] Peru,[934] Québec,[935] Uruguay[936] – is adequate from an economic point of view.

4.2.4. Place of Celebration of the Marriage as Residual Connecting Factor

It can occur that after the marriage the spouses never have the opportunity to live together.[937] The denial of a residence permit, the death of one of them right after the ceremony or simply the desire to live separately during their relationship would require another conflict rule. For those and other – unusual, but possible – cases a subsidiary connecting factor is necessary.[938] When talking about the economic advantages of the cheapest-cost-avoider criterion in substantive law, it was admitted that sometimes the complexity of a situation makes the determination of the individual in the better position to bear the costs difficult, if not impossible. For those cases it was suggested to take the cost of implementation of a legal provision into consideration, when filling lacunas left in the contract. Rules known by the adjudicating authority – e.g. national customs, case law or in general the legal provisions hitherto used – will be preferable as they allow for a rapid settlement of the disputes and a lower incidence of errors.[939] This, however, does not mean that states can just continue using their (inefficient) domestic conflict rule when the common residence of the spouses cannot be ascertained. Law-makers should rather analyze all available solutions – including those used in other jurisdictions – and select among them the most adequate.[940] In this respect, it is important to remember

[930] Art. 2625 Argentine Civil and Commercial Code (for matrimonial property).

[931] Art. 43 Dominican Private International Law Act (for maintenance and matrimonial property).

[932] See: Bahner (2014) 14 (for matrimonial property).

[933] See: Cordero-Moss (2017) 2396 (for matrimonial property).

[934] Art. 2078 Peruvian Civil Code (for matrimonial property).

[935] Art. 3123 Quebec Civil Code (for matrimonial regime).

[936] Art. 25 para. 2 Uruguayan Act on Private International Law (for matrimonial property).

[937] See for example Tribunale di Roma, 6 June 2018 (case involving a woman with US nationality living in her country of origin and a man with Indian nationality who moved to Italy after the celebration of the marriage. They met via Facebook and had no opportunity to reside in the same country before or after the marriage. One year after the celebration of the marriage the husband filed for divorce in Italy since the wife refused to live with him, in order to keep her job as a physician in the United States. Summary available at: http://www2.ipr.uni-heidelberg.de/eufams/index.php?site=entscheidungsdatenbank&lang=en> EUFAMS code ITF20180606a).

[938] The determination of the applicable law in situations where the *lex causae* contravenes the *ordre public* is outside the scope of this book. Thus, the questions whether – from an economic view – the *lex fori* should apply directly or the subsidiary connecting factor should be used is left open. For the scope of this analysis, see: Preface, Section 2.

[939] See: Chapter 3 Section 2.4.

[940] See: Chapter 5 Section 2.2.

that the economic suitability of a conflict of laws provision depends not only on the way the costs of internationality are allocated between the parties, but also on certain attributes of the rule: predictability, stability, accuracy, uniformity, consistency and simplicity. Conflict provisions that satisfy these criteria should be preferred.

The following analysis focuses on the main connecting factors[941] used in Member States of the European Union and the domestic legislation of 50 other jurisdictions dealing with the applicable law to maintenance obligations, divorce or the matrimonial property regime.[942] In total, the prime connecting factors from over 70 jurisdictions are compared in order to determine which one fulfills the aforementioned attributes of the rule. Connecting factors like the common domicile[943] or common residence at the time of the beginning of the proceeding;[944] last common residence;[945] common residence at the time of the marriage;[946] and common domicile of the couple before the marriage are not considered, as the objective is finding a connecting factor for situations where spouses have not lived together.[947] Thus, the following connecting factors will be considered: the law most closely connected with the relationship;[948]

---

941 Subsidiary connecting factors are not included in the analysis.

942 *Albania, Angola, Argentina, Australia, Belarus, Bosnia and Herzegovina, Brazil, Bulgaria, Canada, Chile, China, Colombia, Croatia, Cuba, the Czech Republic, the Dominican Republic, Ecuador, Egypt, Estonia, Finland, Ghana, Iceland, India, Ireland, Israel, Korea, Lebanon, Lichtenstein, Macedonia, Malta, Mexico, Mozambique, New Zealand, Nigeria, Norway, Paraguay, Peru, Québec (Canada), Russia, Saudi Arabia, Serbia, South Africa, Switzerland, Thailand, Tunisia, Turkey, the United Kingdom* (post-Brexit), *the United States, Uruguay* and *Venezuela*. For an English translation of the set of conflict rules in force in most of these countries and/or a report of experts about these provisions, see: Basedow et al. (2017).

943 *Australia*: Mills (2017) 1882 (marital issues); *Ireland*: Coester-Waltjen & Jacob (1999) 18–19 (marital issues); *South Africa*: Schoeman (2017b) 2520 (alimony); *Uruguay*: Art. 26 Act on Private International Law (divorce). For a translation of the cited legal provisions, see: Basedow et al. (2017).

944 *China*: Art. 24 Law of the People's Republic of China on the Application of Laws to Civil Relationships (matrimonial property); *Dominican Republic*: Art. 47 Private International Law Act (divorce); *Estonia*: s. 58 Act on Private International Law (matrimonial property); *Finland*: s. 128 Marriage Act (divorce); *Paraguay*: Art. 166 Civil Code. For a translation of the cited legal provisions seee: Basedow et al. (2017).

945 *EU*: Article 8(b) Regulation 1259/2010 (for divorce); *Argentina*: Art. 2626 Civil and Commercial Code (divorce): *Canada*: see: Blom (2017) 1957 (matrimonial property); *Peru*: Art. 2077 Civil Code, Söhngen (2006) 94 (divorce/alimony); *Russia*: Art. 161 (1) Russian Family Code (matrimonial property); *Switzerland*: Art. 54 Act on Private International Law (matrimonial property); *Venezuela*: Art. 22 Act on Private International Law (alimony, matrimonial property). For a translation of the cited legal provisions see: Basedow et al. (2017).

946 *Israel*: Assan (2012) 35 (matrimonial property); *Lichtenstein*: Art. 20/art 21 Statute on Private International Law (matrimonial property/divorce). For a translation of the cited legal provisions see: Basedow et al. (2017).

947 *Brazil*: Art. 7.4. Introductory Act to the Norms of Brazilian Law (matrimonial property). For a translation of the cited legal provisions see: Basedow et al. (2017).

948 Art. 5 Hague Protocol of 2007.

the *lex fori*;[949] the law of the person who initiates the proceeding;[950] the law of the husband;[951] the law of the place of residence of the creditor[952] or the debtor[953] of a monetary obligation; the religion of the couple;[954] the law of the common nationality of the spouses;[955] and the law of the place of celebration.[956]

---

949 *Belarus*: Danilevich (2017) (marital issues); *Canada*: Blom (2017) 1957 (divorce/maintenance); *Chile*: Art. 14 Civil Code/Art. 82 Law on Civil Matrimony (marital issues, subject to conditions); *Colombia*: Art. 19 Civil Code (marital issues); *Croatia*: Art. 35/Art. 36 Private International Law Act (divorce/alimony); *Cuba*: Third Special Provision of the Civil Code (marital issues); *Denmark*: Fogt (2017) 2033–2034 (divorce/alimony); *Ecuador*: see: Pérez (2017) 2049 (marital issues); *Ghana*: see: Oppong (2017a) 2116 (marital issues); *Iceland*: see: Bahner (2014) 14 (divorce); *India*: see: Biswas (2017) 2160–2161 (marital issues); *Malta*: Cachia (2017) 2330–2331 (marital issues); *Mexico*: Albornoz (2017) 2344 (marital issues); *Mozambique*: Art. 52 (marital issues); *New Zealand*: Schoeman (2017b) 2375–2376 (marital issues); *Nigeria*: Oppong (2017a) 2382 (marital issues); *Russia*: Art. 160(1) Russian Family Code (divorce); *Saudi Arabia*: Krüger (2017) 2463 (marital issues); *South Africa*: Schoeman (2017b) 2520 (divorce); *Switzerland*: Art. 61 (divorce); *United Kingdom*: Dickinson (2017) 2624 (alimony, divorce, matrimonial property); *United States*: Silberman (2017b) 2645 (divorce issues, including division of matrimonial assets). See in detail: Basedow et al. (2017).

950 *Venezuela*: Art. 23 Act on Private International Law (divorce). See in detail: Basedow et al. (2017).

951 *Denmark*: see: Fogt (2017) 2034 (matrimonial property); *Egypt*: Art. 13 para. 1/Art. 13 para. 2 Civil Code (matrimonial property subject to certain conditions/dissolution of marriage); *Iran*: Art. 963 Civil Code (marital issues); *South Africa*: Schoeman (2017b) 2520 (matrimonial property); *Thailand*: Arts. 22, 23 Private International Law Act (marital issues). See in detail: Basedow et al. (2017).

952 *EU*: Article 3 Hague Protocol of 2007 (alimony); Art. 4 Hague Convention 1973 (alimony for married persons); *Albania*: Art. 25.1. Private International Law Act – Law No 10.428 of 2011 (alimony); *Argentina*: Art. 2630 Civil and Commercial Code (alimony); *Brazil*: See: Lima et al. (1937) (alimony).

953 *Egypt*: Art. 15 Civil Code (alimony); *Israel*: Assan (2012) 35 (alimony). See in detail: Basedow et al. (2017).

954 *Israel*: Assan (2012) 35 (divorce); *Lebanon*: Najm (2017) 2271 (marital issues). See in detail: Basedow et al. (2017).

955 *Albania*: Art. 24.1/25.1. Private International Law Act – Law No 10.428 of 2011 – (property regime/divorce); *Angola*: Art. 52 Civil Code (relations between spouses); *Bosnia and Herzegovina*: Art. 36 Act Concerning the Resolution of Conflicts of Laws (matrimonial property); *Bulgaria*: Art. Private International Law Code Art. 82 para. 1 (divorce); *Czech Republic*: s. 50 Private International Law Act; *Korea*: Art. 38/Art. 39 Private International Law Act (marital property/divorce); *Macedonia*: Art. 41/Art. 42 Private International Law Act (divorce/matrimonial property); *Serbia*: Art. 75 Draft of Private International Law Act of Republic of Serbia (marital issues); *Tunisia*: Art. 47/Art. 48/Art. 49 Private International Law Act (alimony/divorce/matrimonial property); *Turkey*: Art. 14/Art.15 Private International Law Code (divorce/matrimonial property). One jurisdiction applies cumulatively the law of nationality of both spouses. See: *Bosnia and Herzegovina*: Art. 35 Act Concerning the Resolution of Conflicts of Laws (divorce). See in detail: Basedow et al. (2017).

956 According to the consulted sources, no country uses the place of conclusion as the main connecting factor for alimony, divorce or matrimonial property. It is, however, of widespread use in many countries for the determinination of the law applicable to the validity of the marriage. See for example: *Argentina*: Art. 2622 Civil and Commercial Code; *Colombia*: 1940 Montevideo Treaties on International Civil Law; *Croatia*: Art. 33 Private International

The inherent unpredictability advises against the use of the closest connection as the criterion to determine the applicable law to a case. Its instability – in concrete terms, the possibility that the governing law might suddenly change as well as the difficulty to know the law that will finally apply – makes this connecting factor suboptimal. It is even more inaccurate when spouses have never lived together during their relationship, as this marriage would inevitably be linked with at least two legal systems – the place of residence of each spouse – making the law that will ultimately be applied by the authority unpredictable – even right before the beginning of the proceeding. The application of the *lex fori* or the law of the person who initiates the proceeding not only has the same problems in terms of unpredictability, but also creates a breeding ground for opportunistic behavior. If the couple has never had a common place of residence, it is highly probable that the courts of the countries where each spouse lives are competent to decide over the case. The use of these connecting factors would then encourage spouses to try to initiate a proceeding in a favorable jurisdiction for their interests. The governing law would only be known after one of them has filed the claim.

Uniformity demands that the default provision should be used in as many systems of conflict of laws as possible. Although diversity is positive, as it promotes experimentation, if each state employs a different conflict rule it erodes the possessive and transactional security of international transactions. The goal of achieving a harmonization of the private international law should always be in the mind of the law-maker. Consequently, they should disregard options with little or no chance of being used in other jurisdictions. The use of the law of the husband should be ruled out, as such a provision would be regarded as contrary to the principle of gender equality in practically all modern legal systems.[957] Consistency, for its part, demands a single rule covering most aspects of a marriage. The use of a single law reduces the costs of internationality, as it is necessary to gather information about the content of only one law. The connecting factor of the place of residence of the creditor is problematic, as it cannot be used to resolve disputes about the divorce or the division of assets,

---

Law Act; *Denmark*: Fogt (2017) 2034; *Dominican Republic*: Art. 41 Private International Law Act; *Ghana*: see: Oppong (2017a) 2116; *Israel*: Assan (2012) 35: *Lebanon*: Najm (2017) 2271; *North Macedonia*: Art. 39 Private International Law Act; *Mozambique*: Art. 50 Civil Code; *New Zealand*: see: Schoeman (2017a) 2375; *Paraguay*: Art. 132 Civil Code; *Peru*: Art. 2076 Civil Code; *South Africa*: Schoeman (2017b) 2520; *United Kingdom*: Dickinson (2017) 2623; *Uruguay*: Art. 22 Act on Private International Law; *United States*: s. 121 Restatement (First) of Conflict of Laws/ s. 283 Restatement (Second) of Conflict of Laws. For a translation of the cited legal provisions see: Basedow et al. (2017).

957 For the application in Denmark of the law of the residence of the husband at the moment of the conclusion of the marriage for issues related to the matrimonial property of the couple, see: Fogt (2017) 2034.

because for these aspects of the marriage neither of the spouses can be regarded as the creditor or the debtor of any characteristic performance. Finally, reasons of simplicity rule out connecting factors like the common religion of the couple, common nationality of the spouses, or the place of residence of the couple before the marriage. As explained before, simplicity entails not only the avoidance of an unnecessary legal lucubration in the wording of the provision, but also the reduction of the number of statements of facts – within the *Tatbestand* – and legal consequences – within the *Rechtsfolge* – in the structure of the conflict rule. At the moment of determining the most appropriate subsidiary connecting factor, one should try to encompass the greatest possible number of cases to avoid the need to include further provisions and so complicate the legal provision. As it can certainly happen that spouses do not have the same religion or nationality or that they have never lived together in the same jurisdiction before their marriage, those factors should then be set aside in favor of another connecting factor that can be applied in most cases.[958] Regarding the application of the law of common nationality, one should also consider that some countries do not have uniform inter-local conflict rules although they are comprised of different territorial units – each having its own marriage law.[959] The use of connecting factors such as the common nationality of the spouses can under these circumstances generate significant uncertainties even if both spouses have the same nationality, when they come from different territorial units.

Among all the candidates, the place of celebration of the marriage seems to be the most appropriate connecting factor, as it assures predictability, stability, precision, uniformity, consistency and simplicity. Furthermore, it resolves outright situations where even though the spouses lived together, the law of the first place of residence cannot be applied to the case, such as for example when a same-sex couple have as their first place of residence a country that prohibits such unions. Finally, the use of the place of celebration of the marriage does not represent a significant change of approach in the conflict of laws system in most countries, as it is – or was – applied as connecting factor for the determination of the validity of a marriage in a number of jurisdictions. It is true that the place of celebration might duplicate the costs of internationality, as it could be the law of a country where neither of them lives at the moment of the marriage, or it might not have a connection at all with either of the spouses. But the application of the place of celebration is intended for exceptional cases, as in general spouses end up living together at some point during their relationship.

---

958 It is also important to take into consideration that in some cases – especially in those involving refugees – it is not possible to determine the nationality of the individuals. See for example Tibunale di Roma, 2 March 2018 (case involving a husband and a wife with unknown nationality).

959 See in detail: Eichel (2016) 275–276, 284–286.

Furthermore, although some couples might get married in exotic locations – e.g. Las Vegas, Seychelles, etc. – there certainly are individuals preferring familiar places to get married in order to guarantee that friends and family can come to celebrate this momentous day in their life.[960] A situation where spouses do not live together at the time or after the marriage is unusual. A scenario where they – still – do not have a common place of residence after the marriage is atypical. A constellation in which they – furthermore – get married in a country where neither of them resides is possible, but even much more exceptional. For those cases[961] the conclusion of a choice of law agreement would be the best option at their disposal to reduce the cost of internationality.

5. CONCLUDING REMARKS

When designing a default conflict of laws rule, law-makers should bear in mind the presence of certain attributes in the conflict rule: predictability, stability, accuracy, uniformity, consistency and simplicity. As different rules might meet these requirements, the one that allocates the costs surrounding a relationship with international connotations in a way that reduces the surplus generated by the contract the least, should be preferred. These costs are called costs of internationality and refer to the expenses required to obtain possessive and transactional security as a consequence of the looming application of a law other than the party's own. The own law is in turn defined taking into consideration the efforts necessary to get information about the existence and extension of any right and obligation arising from a relationship. Based there on, the legal system in force in the place of residence of a person at the moment of concluding a contract is regarded as their own law.

It follows that if individuals living in the same country conclude a contract, the law in force there should govern the legal effects of their relationship. For the special case of the matrimony, the use of the law of the first common residence of the couple does deliver efficient outcomes, as in practice this corresponds with the law of the common residence at the moment of getting married. It is not about conjecturing that people like better the content of a certain law, but

960 See: EPEC (2010) 231, 238, 246.

961 See for example Tribunale di Roma, 6 June 2018 (case involving a woman with US nationality living in her country of origin and a man with Indian nationality, who moved to Italy after the celebration of their marriage. They met via Facebook and had no opportunity to reside in the same country before or after the marriage. One year after the celebration of the marriage the husband filed for divorce in Italy since the wife refused to live with him, in order to keep her job as a physician in the United States. Summary available at: <http://www2.ipr.uni-heidelberg.de/eufams/index.php?site=entscheidungsdatenbank&lang=en> EUFAMS code ITF20180606a).

about assuming that people prefer the legal system whose provisions are known or can be easily known at the moment of getting involved in a legal relationship. By resorting to the normal course of events it is possible to design a rule that assures an efficient allocation of the costs of internationality when spouses have never lived together. In this respect it is important to take into account that when establishing the cheapest-cost-avoider, it is necessary to consider not only the amount of the expenditure necessary to avert or mitigate the negative consequences of the occurrence of certain event; the eventual gains arising from the investment of the liable party should also be considered. Based on that, the application of the place of the first common residence of the spouses was put forward as prime connecting factor, even for situations where spouses live in different countries at the moment of the conclusion of their marriage. When they establish their first marital home in a country of residence of one of them, the acquired knowledge about the foreign law generates further gains, as this law applies to further relationships of a contractual and non-contractual nature concluded by the immigrating spouse in the new environment.

Finally, after comparing the main connecting factors used in more than 70 jurisdictions around the world, it was concluded that using the law of the place of celebration of the marriage is – from an economic perspective – the best option for a subsidiary connecting factor in situations where the spouses have never lived in the same place after their marriage. This connecting factor satisfies the formal attributes required to facilitate cooperation between two individuals in a context of legal pluralism: predictability, stability, precision, uniformity, consistency and simplicity.

CONCLUSION

Certainty, Precision, Coherence, and Simplicity in the Determination of the Applicable Law

The existence of multiple legal systems in the international arena is a major issue for married couples with distinct nationalities, owning property abroad or having resided in at least two countries. Any of these circumstances might cause significant changes in the rights and obligations derived from their marriage, as courts can use a variety of approaches to determine the legal system – or legal systems – applicable to legal disputes between them. Although there are national and international sets of rules dealing with this problem, their solution does not cope adequately with the challenges of legal pluralism in the current context. The international instruments promoted by the European Union are a good example of this. They not only restrict party autonomy unnecessarily and include dissimilar limits and conditions for the enforceability of choice of law agreements; they also use dissimilar approaches for the determination of the applicable law in the absence of a choice of law agreement. Furthermore, under certain circumstances, the default conflict rules undermine legal certainty significantly, and allow one spouse to manipulate the law governing their relationship unilaterally.

The aim of the book was to present a new approach to understanding marriage and marriage law that in turn serves as a corner-stone for building a conflict of laws system that prioritizes predictability and congruency in the determination of the applicable law. With this goal in mind, the book borrowed some ideas and concepts from economics to reframe the matrimonial dynamic from a different perspective and so tried to provide fresh and new answers to legal questions related to the determination of the applicable law. Against this background, marriage has been described as having the same objective as a contract, an instrument that builds trust between two individuals to enable exchanges of complementary and reciprocal efforts. Marriage is seen as a tool to obtain, through reciprocal cooperation, certain assets of monetary and non-monetary value that are otherwise impossible or very difficult to obtain alone. The function of marriage law is providing a framework that reinforces trust and removes obstacles hindering these cooperative dynamics. The book showed that quite a few sets of rules on marriage law in modern legal systems tend to reflect this logic. Although marriage is not expressly regarded as a mere economic instrument aimed at improving the initial situation of individuals, the legislation in force in a number of legal systems induces people to maximize the benefits from their joint cooperation in the household. In general, the law provides a substantive regulation fostering investments that increase the spouses' well-being through the surplus generated by a more intensive cooperation.

Based on those premises, the next step was identifying the particular problems experienced by individuals involved in a marital relationship with international connotations. In this vein, it was shown that the fragmentation of the world into sovereign states leads to a situation where the rights arising from the marriage as well as the obligations assumed by spouses become significantly blurred because their very content finally depends on the particular law chosen by the authority of the jurisdiction where the legal relationship will be eventually discussed. Private international law was then presented as the area of the law in charge of resolving this issue. Its main task is providing a method for determining the specific set of mandatory and default rules applicable to a dispute in order to identify the concrete rights and obligations arising from the relationship. Having a system of conflict of laws is essential to bolster the conclusion of cross-border arrangements, but its mere existence does not assure by itself the willingness of people to be involved in relationships with an international component. The capacity of a system of conflict rules to encourage cooperative cross-border dynamics depends on the presence of certain attributes in the way conflicts of laws are resolved. Conflict rules should strive to be precise, be of extended use, cover most aspects of the relationship, avoid unnecessary complexities in their wording, and seek to apply a law whose content is easy to access for the parties. The law appointed by the connecting factor should also be predictable by spouses as early as possible, as this allows them to plan their life prudently and take decisions that maximize the benefits of their relationship.

Party autonomy was presented as the key element in the system of conflict of laws, not only because both the possibility to accommodate the relationship to the specific needs and preferences of the spouses, and the legal certainty obtained *via* choice of law agreements encourage more people to be legally engaged with another person. The freedom of choice might also generate a positive dynamic comparable to competition in regular markets and lead to the improvement and innovation of the substantive law. The term "law market" was used to describe a situation where the wishes of individuals to choose a law triggers the desire of other actors to produce novel domestic laws or alter them in response to competitive pressure from other entrants. On the whole, the book suggested that the most salient advantages from the elimination of barriers to the spouses' party autonomy are: legal certainty; greater capacity to influence one's own well-being; safeguarding the rights of minorities; experimentation and innovation in law-making; the tendency towards convergence; and incentives for the formalization of the relationship. However, many individuals have neither the time nor the interest to agree on the applicable law to issues related to maintenance obligations, divorce and property regime. Many others might not even have thought about the problems arising from legal pluralism or not have known about the possibility to choose a governing law. For those cases, the place of the first common residence of the spouses was presented as the main connecting factor for the determination of the applicable law if spouses have not concluded a choice of law agreement. The suitability of this solution lies in the allocation of the costs of internationality to the spouse in the better position to bear them. The place of celebration of the marriage was put forward as a subsidiary connecting factor in situations where spouses have never lived together.

What does the thesis defended in the book entail? Major certainty, precision, coherence, and simplicity; in other words, interesting arguments for considering seriously the introduction of amendments in the current conflict of laws system. The adoption of the proposal presented here entails major congruency and predictability in the resolution of conflict of laws. Indeed, the book proves that regardless of how complex in terms of its multiple international connections a marriage might be, a clear, straightforward and – above all – solidly grounded answer to the question of the applicable law can be given. Following the introductory example:[962]

If María Isabel and Giovanni have not concluded a choice of law agreement, the law of a single country – Dutch law – applies to questions about their maintenance obligations, divorce and the division of their property. As simple as that.

---

962 See Introduction *in initio*.

BIBLIOGRAPHY

Abbott, Edith. "The History of Industrial Employment of Women in the United States: An Introductory Study". *Journal of Political Economy* 14.8 (1906), pp. 461–501. Available at: <www.jstor.org/stable/1817741>.

Achermann, Alberto; Achermann, Christin; D'Amato, Gianni; Kamm, Martina; Von Rütte, Barbara. *EUDO Citizenship Observatory: Country Report: Switzerland.* Robert Schuman Centre for Advanced Studies (2010). Available at: <https://core.ac.uk/download/pdf/45680124.pdf>.

Ackerman, David T. *International Business Contracts Survey – Snapshot Report* (September 12, 2011). Available at SSRN: <https://ssrn.com/abstract=1946552>.

Advisory Committee on the Framework Convention for the Protection of National Minorities. *The Framework Convention: A Key Tool to Managing Diversity Through Minority Rights – Thematic Commentary no. 4.* Council of Europe (2016).

Akerlof, George A. "The Market for 'Lemons': Quality Uncertainty and the Market Mechanism. *The Quarterly Journal of Economics* 84.3 (1970), pp. 488–500.

Albornoz, María Mercedes. "Mexico". In: Basedow, Jürgen; Rühl, Gisela; Ferrari, Franco; de Miguel Asensio, Pedro. *Encyclopedia of Private International Law*, vol. 3. Edward Elgar Publishing (2017), pp. 2333–2345.

All, Paula María. "Argentina". In: Girsberger, Daniel; Kadner Graziano, Thomas; Neels, Jan L. *Choice of Law in International Commercial Contracts – Global Perspectives on the Hague Principles.* Oxford University Press (2021), pp. 951–970.

Allen, Douglas W. "The Impact of Legal Reforms on Marriage and Divorce". In: Dnes, Antony W.; Rowthorn Robert (eds.). *The Law and Economics of Marriage and Divorce.* Cambridge University Press (2002).

Ancel, Bertrand; Lequette, Yves. *Les Grands Arrêts de la Jurisprudence Française de Droit International Privé*, 4th edn. Dalloz (2001).

Anderson, James E.; Van Wincoop, Eric. "Gravity with Gravitas: A Solution to the Border Puzzle". *American Economic Review* 93 (2003), pp. 170–192.

Andrae, Mariane. *Internationales Familienrecht*, 3rd edn. Nomos (2014).

—— "Haager Protokoll vom 23. November 2007 über das auf Unterhaltspflichten anzuwendende Recht". In: Rauscher, Thomas. *Europäisches Zivilprozess- und Kollisionsrecht, EuZPR/EuIPR*, 4th edn., vol. 4. Otto Schmidt (2006), pp. 629–769.

Antokolskaia, Masha. *Harmonisation of Family Law in Europe. A Historical Perspective.* Intersentia (2006).

—— "Harmonisation of Substantive Family Law in Europe: Myths and Reality". *Child and Family Law Quarterly* 22.4 (2010), pp. 397–421.

Applbaum, Kalman D. "Marriage with the Proper Stranger: Arranged Marriage in Metropolitan Japan". *Ethnology* 34.1 (1995), pp. 37–51.

Arruñada, Benito. "The Economics of Notaries". *European Journal of Law and Economics* 3.1 (1996), pp. 5–37.

Arshad, Raffia. *Islamic Family Law*. Sweet & Maxwell (2010).

Asoskov, Anton. "Russian Federation". In: Basedow, Jürgen; Rühl, Gisela; Ferrari, Franco; de Miguel Asensio Pedro. *Encyclopedia of Private International Law*, vol. 3. Edward Elgar Publishing (2017), pp. 2451–2462.

Assan, Dan. "Israel". In: Bergmann, Alexander; Ferid, Murad; Henrich, Dieter (eds.). *Internationales Ehe- und Kindschaftsrecht*. Verlag für Standesamtswesen (2012).

Atkinson, Hugh; Wade, Ros. *The Challenge of Sustainability: Linking Politics, Education and Learning*. Policy Press (2014).

Axelrod, Robert. *The Evolution of Cooperation*. Basic Books, Inc., Publishers (1984).

Ayres, Ian. "Default Rules for Incomplete Contracts". In: Newman, Peter. *The New Palgrave Dictionary of Economics and the Law*, vol. 2. Palgrave Macmillan (1998), pp. 585–589.

Ayres, Ian; Gertner, Robert. "Filling Gaps in Incomplete Contracts: An Economic Theory of Default Rules". *Yale Law Journal* 99 (1989), pp. 87–130.

Baarsma, Nynke Anna. *The Europeanisation of International Family Law. From Dutch to European Law: an Analysis on the Basis of the Choice of Law on Divorce and on the Termination of Registered Partnerships*. Ulrik Huber Institute for Private International Law Doctoral Series 11 (2010).

Backhouse, Roger E.; Medema, Steven G. "Retrospectives: On the Definition of Economics". *Journal of Economic Perspectives* 23.1 (2009a), pp. 221–233.

—— "Defining Economics: The Long Road to Acceptance of the Robbins Definition". *Economica* 76 (2009b), pp. 805–820.

Baetge, Dieter. "Habitual Residence". In: Basedow, Jürgen; Hopt, Klaus; Zimmermann; Stier, Andreas. *The Max Planck Encyclopedia of European Private Law*, vol. 1. Oxford University Press (2012), pp. 813–815.

Bahner, Christiane. "Iceland". In: Bergmann, Alexander; Ferid, Murad; Henrich, Dieter (ed.). *Internationales Ehe- und Kindschaftsrecht*. Verlag für Standesamtswesen (2014).

Baird, Douglas G.; Gertner, Robert; Picker, Randall. *Game Theory and the Law*. Harvard University Press (1994).

Baker, John Hamilton. *An Introduction to English Legal History*, 3rd edn. Butterworths (1990).

Bartl, Franziska. *Die Neuen Rechtsinstrumente zum IPR des Unterhalts auf Internationaler und Europäischer Ebene*. Mohr Siebeck (2012).

Basch, Norma. "The Emerging Legal History of Women in the United States: Property, Divorce, and the Constitution". *Signs* 12.1 (1986), pp. 97–117.

Basedow, Jurgen. "Communitarization of the Conflict of Laws under the Treaty of Amsterdam". *Common Market Law Review* 37 (2000), pp. 687–708.

—— "Lex Mercatoria and the Private International Law of Contracts in Economic Perspective". In: Basedow, Jürgen; Toshiyuki Kono. *An Economic Analysis of Private International Law* (2006a), pp. 57–71.

—— "Lex Mercatoria und internationales Schuldvertragsrecht – Eine Rechtsökonomische Skizze". In: Berger, Klaus Peter; Borges, Georg; Herrmann, Harald; Schlüter, Andreas; Wackerbarth, Ulrich. *Zivil- und Wirtschaftsrecht im Europäischen und Globalen Kontext. Festschrift für Norbert Horn zum 70. Geburtstag*. De Gruyter (2006b), pp. 229–247.

—— "The State's Private Law and the Economy - Commercial Law as an Amalgam of Public and Private Rule-Making". *The American Journal of Comparative Law* 56.3 (2008), pp. 703–722.

—— "El Derecho Privado Estatal y la Economía - el Derecho Comercial como una Amalgama de Legislación Pública y Privada". In: Basedow, Jürgen; Fernández Arroyo Diego P.; Moreno Rodríguez, José A. *¿Cómo se Codifica Hoy el Derecho Comercial Internacional?* FEDYE (2010), pp. 5–27.

—— *The law of Open Societies: Private Ordering and Public Regulation in the Conflict of Laws*. Brill (2015).

Basedow, Jürgen; Rühl, Gisela; Ferrari, Franco; de Miguel Asensio, Pedro. *Encyclopedia of Private International Law*, vol. 1–4. Edward Elgar Publishing (2017).

Bateman, Julia. Law Societies. Joint Brussels Office, Brussels Bulletin: the French EU Presidency 2008. International Family Law (2008), pp. 119 et seqq.

Bebchuk, Lucian A. "Federalism, and the Corporation: The Desirable Limits on State Competition in Corporate Law". *Harvard Law Review* 105 (1992), pp. 1437–1510.

Bebchuk, Lucian A.; Ferrell, Allen. "Federalism and Corporate Law: The Race to Protect Managers from Takeovers". *Columbia Law Review* 99 (1999), pp. 1168–1199.

Becker, Gary Stanley. "A Theory of Marriage: Part I". *Journal of Political Economy* 81.4 (1973), pp. 813–846.

—— "A Theory of Marriage: Part II". *Journal of Political Economy* 82.2 (1974), pp. 11–26.

—— "A Theory of Competition among Pressure Groups for Political Influence". *Quarterly Journal of Economics* 98.3 (1983), pp. 371–400.

—— *The Economic Approach to Human Behavior*. University of Chicago Press (1990).

Bentham, Jeremy. *The Works of Jeremy Bentham, vol. 3. Usury, Political Economy, Equity, Parliamentary Reform*. John Bowring (1843).

—— "Rationale of Judicial Evidence". In: *The Works of Jeremy Bentham, vol. 6, Rationale of Evidence, Rationale of Judicial Evidence* ([1843] 1962).

Berman, Harold Joseph. *Law and Revolution: The Formation of the Western Legal Tradition*. Harvard University Press (1983).

Bergmann, Alexander; Ferid, Murad; Henrich, Dieter (eds.). *Internationales Ehe- und Kindschaftsrecht*. Verlag für Standesamtswesen (1983–2021).

Bettman, J.R., Luce, M.F.; Payne, J.W. Constructive Consumer Choice Processes. *Journal of Consumer Research* 25 (1998), pp. 187–217.

Bishop, William. "Is He Married? Marriage as Information". *University of Toronto Law Journal* 34.3 (1984), pp. 245–262.

Biswas, Tushar Kumar. "India". In: Basedow, Jürgen; Rühl, Gisela; Ferrari, Franco; de Miguel Asensio, Pedro. *Encyclopedia of Private International Law*, vol. 3. Edward Elgar Publishing (2017), pp. 2155–2162.

Bix, Brian H. "Choice of Law and Marriage: A Proposal". *Family Law Quarterly* 36.2 (2002), pp. 255–271.

Blackstone, William. *Commentaries on the Laws of England: Book the First*. Clarendon Press (1765).

Blake, Nelson Manfred. *The Road to Reno: A History of Divorce in the United States*. Macmillan (1962).

Blom, Joost. "Canada". In: Basedow, Jürgen; Rühl, Gisela; Ferrari, Franco; de Miguel Asensio, Pedro. *Encyclopedia of Private International Law*, vol. 3. Edward Elgar Publishing (2017), pp. 1950–1959.

Boar, Bernard. "Planning Theory: Sun Tzu and Machiavelli On Strategy". *Journal of Business Strategy* 16.1 (1995), pp. 16–18.

Boele-Woelki, Katharina. "Artikel 8 Haager Unterhaltsübereinkommen Steht einer Rechtswahl nicht Entgegen". *IPRax* (1998), pp. 492–495.

—— (ed.). *Perspectives for the Unification and Harmonisation of Family Law in Europe*, vol. 4. Intersentia (2003).

—— (ed). *Common Core and Better Law in European Family Law*, vol. 10. Intersentia (2005).

—— "To Be, or not to Be: Enhanced Cooperation in International Divorce Law within the European Union". *Victoria University of Wellington Law Review* 39 (2008), pp. 779 et seqq.

Boele-Woelki, Katharina; Sverdrup Tone. *European Challenges in Contemporary Family Law*. Hart Publishing (2008).

Boele-Woelki, Katharina; Braat, Bente; Curry-Sumner, Ian. *European Family Law in Action*, vol. 3. Intersentia (2003).

—— *European Family Law in Action*, vol. 4. Intersentia (2009).

Boele-Woelki Katharina, Ferrand Frederique, Gonzalez Beilfuss Cristina, Jänterä-Jareborg, Maarit; Lowe Nigel; Martiny, Dieter; Pintens, Walter. *Principles of European Family Law Regarding Divorce and Maintenance between Former Spouses*. Intersentia (2004).

—— *Principles of European Family Law Regarding Property Relations between Spouses*. Intersentia (2013).

Bogdan M. "The EC Treaty and the Use of Nationality and Habitual Residence as Connnecting Factors in International Family Law". In: Johan Meeusen (ed.). *International Family Law for the European Union*. Intersentia (2007), pp. 303–317.

Bonomi, Andrea. *Explanatory Report, Protocol of 23 November 2007 on the Law Applicable to Maintenance Obligations*. Permanent Bureau of The Hague Conference. HCCH (2013).

—— "Regulations in Family and Succession Matters". In: Forner Delaygua, Joaquim; Santos, Alfredo. *Coherence of the Scope of Application – EU Private International Legal Instruments*, Publications of the Swiss Institute of Comparative Law. Schulthess Éditions Romandes (2020), pp. 27–41.

Bourreau-Dubois, Cécile; Doriat-Duban, Myriam. "Covering the Costs of Divorce: The Role of the Family, the State and the Market". *Population* 71:3 (2016), pp. 457–477.

Bratton, William; McCahery, Joseph A. "The New Economics of Jurisdictional Competition: Devolutionary Federalism in a Second Best World". *Georgetown Law Journal* 86 (1997), pp. 201–278.

Breiman, Leo; Friedman, Jerome, Olsen, R.A.; Stone, Charles. *Classification and Regression Trees*. Chapman & Hall (1993).

Brenton, Paul; Vancauteren, Marc. *The Extent of Economic Integration in Europe: Border Effects, Technical Barriers to Trade and Home Bias in Consumption*. Center for European Policy Studies, Working Document no. 171 (2001).

Brilmayer, Lea. *Conflict of Laws: Foundations and Future Directions*. Little Brown & Co. (1991).

Brinig, Margaret F.; Crafton, Steven M. "Marriage and opportunism". *The Journal of Legal Studies* 23.2 (1994), pp. 869–894.

Bröder, A. "Assessing the Empirical Validity of the 'Take the Best' Heuristic as a Model of Human Probabilistic Inference". *Journal of Experimental Psychology, Learning, Memory, Cognition* 26.5 (2000), pp. 1332–1346.

Brosch, Marlene. *Rechtswahl und Gerichtsstandsvereinbarung im internationalen Familien- und Erbrecht der EU*. Mohr Siebeck (2019).

Brown, Dee. *The gentle tamers: Women of the old wild west*. New York: Putnam (1958).

Brown, Jennifer Gerarda. "Competitive Federalism and the Legislative Incentives to Recognize Same-Sex Marriage". *Southern California Law Review* 68 (1994), pp. 745–840.

Browne, M. Neil; Biksacky Lauren. "Unconscionability and the contingent assumptions of contract theory". *Michigan State Law Review* (2013), pp. 211–255.

Buckley, Frank. H. *The Fall and Rise of Freedom of Contract*. Duke University Press (1999).

Buckley, Frank H.; Ribstein, Larry E. "Calling a Truce in the Marriage Wars". *University of Illinois Law Review* (2001), p. 561.

Buler, Marta.; Pustułka, Paula. "Gendered Family Practices and Cultural Diffusion in Binational Couples of Polish Migrant Women". *Studia Migracyjne – Przegląd Polonijny* 166.4 (2017), pp. 37–59.

Bundesnotarkammer; Bundesrechtsanwaltskammer; Deutscher Anwaltverein; Deutscher Notarverein; Deutscher Richterbund. *Law Made in Germany. Global – Effektiv – Kostengünstig* (2008). Available at: <http://www.gaccny.com/dienstleistungen/recht-steuern/law-made-in-germany/>.

Cachia Paul. "Malta". In: Basedow, Jürgen, Rühl Gisela; Ferrari Franco, de Miguel Asensio Pedro. *Encyclopedia of Private International Law*, vol. 3. Edward Elgar Publishing (2017), pp. 2326–2333.

Calabresi, Guido. *The Costs of Accidents*. Yale University Press (1970).

Calabresi, Guido; Melamed, A. Douglas. "Property Rules, Liability Rules, and Inalienability: One View of the Cathedral". *Harvard Law Review* 85.6 (1972), pp. 1089–1128.

Camerer, Colin; Lovallo, Dan. "Overconfidence and Excess Entry an Experimental Approach". In: Kahneman, Daniel; Tverky, Amos. *Choices, Values, and Frames*. Cambridge University Press (2009), pp. 414–423.

Campbell, David. "The Relational Constitution of Remedy: Co-operation as the Implicit Second Principle of Remedies for Breach of Contract". *Texas Wesleyan Law Review* 11 (2005), p. 455.

Caraballo-Arias, Yohama; Madrid, Jesús; Barrios, Marcial. "Working in Venezuela: How the Crisis has Affected the Labor Conditions". *Annals of Global Health* 84.3 (2018).

Carbonara, Emanuela; Parisi Francesco. "The Paradox of Legal Harmonization". *Public Choice* 132:3–4 (2007), pp. 367–400.

—— "Bargaining for Legal Harmonization: Jurisdictional Competition and Legal Obsolescence". In Eger, Thomas; Bigus, Jochen; Ott, Claus; vonWangenheim, Georg. *Internationalisierung des Rechts und seine ökonomische Analyse. Festschrift für Hans-Bernd Schäfer zum 65 Geburtstag*. Gabler (2008), pp. 339–352.

Carrascosa González, Javier. *Conflicto de Leyes y Teoría Económica*. Colex (2011).

Castilla Barea, Margarita. "La Disolución del Matrimonio". In: Cuena Casas, Matilde; Yzquierdo Tolsada, Mariano. *Tratado de Derecho de la Familia*, vol. 2. Thomson Reuters-Aranzadi (2011).

Castles, Stephen; De Haas, Hein; Miller, Mark J. *The Age of Migration: International Population Movements in the Modern World.* Palgrave Macmillan (2013).

Charny, David. "Competition among Jurisdictions in Formulating Corporate Law Rules: An American Perspective on the Race to the Bottom in the European Communities". *Harvard International Law Journal* 32 (1991), pp. 423–456.

Chen, Natalie. "Intra-national versus International Trade in the European Union: Why do National Borders Matter?". *Journal of International Economics* 63 (2004), pp. 93–118.

Chen, Weizuo. "China". In: Basedow, Jürgen, Rühl Gisela; Ferrari Franco, de Miguel Asensio Pedro. *Encyclopedia of Private International Law*, vol. 3. Edward Elgar Publishing (2017), pp. 1970–1980.

Chiappori, Pierre-Andre; Weiss, Yoram. "Divorce, Remarriage, and Child Support". *Journal of Labor Economics* 25.1 (2007), pp. 37–74.

Chou, Eileen Y.; Halevy, Nir; Murnighan, J. Keith. *The Relational Costs of Complete Contracts* (June 25, 2011). IACM 24th Annual Conference Paper. Available at: <https://ssrn.com/abstract=1872569>.

Cian, Giorgio; Trabucchi, Alberto; Abatangelo Chiara; Bolego, Giorgio. *Commentario Breve Al Codice Civile*, 12th edn. Wolters Kluwer (2016).

Cigno, Alessandro. "Marriage as a Commitment Device". *Review of Economics of the Household* 10.2 (2012), pp. 193–213.

CIJUL en Línea Centro de Informaci6n Jurídica en Linea. *La Sevicia como Causal de Divorcio y las Ofensas Graves.* (2006). Available at: <https://cijulenlinea.ucr.ac.cr/2006/la-sevicia-como-causal-de-divorcio-y-las-ofensas-graves-como-causal-de-separacion-judicial/>.

Coale, Ansley J. "Age Patterns of Marriage". *Population Studies* 25.2 (1971), pp. 193–214.

Coase, Ronald H. "The Problem of Social Cost". *Journal of Law & Economics* 3 (1960), pp. 1–44.

—— The new Institutional Economics. *American Economic Review* 88.2 (1998), pp. 72–74.

Coester-Waltjen, Dagmar. "Marriage". In: Basedow, Jürgen; Hopt, Klaus; Zimmermann, Reinhard; Stier, Andreas. *The Max Planck Encyclopedia of European Private Law*, vol. 2. Oxford University Press (2012).

—— Connecting Factors to Determine the Law Applicable to Matrimonial Property Regimes. In: Bonomi, Andrea; Romano, Gian Paolo. *Yearbook of Private International Law* 19 (2018), pp. 195–211.

Coester-Waltjen, Dagmar; Jacob, Dominique. "Irland". In: Bergmann, Alexander; Ferid, Murad; Henrich, Dieter (eds.). *Internationales Ehe- und Kindschaftsrecht.* Verlag für Standesamtswesen (1999).

Cohen, George M. "Implied Terms and Interpretation in Contract Law". In: Bouckaert, Boudewijn; De Geest, Gerit. *Encyclopedia of Law and Economics*, vol. 3. Edward Elgar Publishing (2000), pp. 78–99.

Cohen, Lloyd R. "Marriage: the Long-term Contract". In: Dnes, Antony W.; Rowthorn, Robert (eds.). *The Law and Economics of Marriage and Divorce.* Cambridge University Press (2002), pp. 10–34.

Coleman, Jules L.; Heckathorn, Douglas D.; Maser, Steven M. "Bargaining Theory Approach to Default Provisions and Disclosure Rules in Contract Law". *Harvard Journal of Law & Public Policy* 12 (1989), pp. 639–709.

Cooter Robert; Ulen, Thomas. *Law and Economics*, 6th edn. Berkeley Law Books (2016).
Copen, Casey; Daniels, Kimberly; Vespa, Jonathan; Mosher, William. *First Marriages in the United States: Data From the 2006–2010 National Survey of Family Growth*. National Center for Health and Statistics (2013).
Cordero-Moss, Giuditta. "Norway". In: Basedow, Jürgen; Rühl, Gisela; Ferrari, Franco; de Miguel Asensio, Pedro. *Encyclopedia of Private International Law*, vol. 3. Edward Elgar Publishing (2017), pp. 2386–2397.
Corneloup, Sabine. "Grundlagen der Rechtswahl im Familien- und Erbrecht". In: *Die Wahl Ausländischen Rechts im Familien- und Erbrecht*. Nomos (2013).
Coulson, Noel James. *A History of Islamic Law*. Edinburgh University Press (1964).
Cramton, Roger C. "Why Legal Services for the Poor". *American Bar Association Journal* 68.5 (1982), pp. 550–554.
Craswell, Richard. "Efficiency and Rational Bargaining in Contractual Settings". *Harvard Journal of Law & Public Policy* 15 (1992), pp. 805 et seqq.
—— "Contract Law: General Theories". In: Bouckaert, Boudewijn; De Geest, Gerit. *Encyclopedia of Law and Economics*, vol. 3. Edward Elgar Publishing (2000), pp. 1–24.
Cserne, Péter. "Duress in Contracts: An Economic Analysis". In: De Geest, Gerrit (ed.). *Encyclopedia of Law and Economics*, 2nd edn., vol. 6 (2011), pp. 57–79.
Cuena Casas, Matilde; Yzquierdo Tolsada, Mariano. *Tratado de Derecho de la Familia*, vol. 7. Thomson Reuters-Aranzadi (2011).
Cuniberti, Gilles. "The International Market for Contracts: the Most Attractive Contract Laws". *Northwestern Journal of International Law & Business* 34 (2013), pp. 455–517.
Czerlinski Jean; Gigerenzer, Gerd; Goldstein, Daniel. "How Good are Simple Heuristics?". In: Gigerenzer Gerd, Todd Peter; the ABC Research Group. *Simple Heuristics that Make US Smart*. Oxford University Press (1999), pp. 97–118.
Danilevich, Aliaksandr. "Belarus". In: Basedow, Jürgen; Rühl, Gisela; Ferrari, Franco; de Miguel Asensio, Pedro. *Encyclopedia of Private International Law*, vol. 3. Edward Elgar Publishing (2017), pp. 1894–1906.
de Chernatony, Leslie. "Brand Building". In: Baker, Michael (ed.). *The Marketing Book*. Butterworth Heinemann (2003), pp. 411–494.
—— "Adapting Brand Theory to the Context of Nation Branding". In: Dinnie, Keith. *Nation Branding: Concepts, Issues, Practice*. Butterworth-Heinemann (2008), pp. 16–22.
De Geest, Gerrit; De Moor, Bart; Depoorter, Ben. Misunderstandings between Contracting Parties: Towards an Optimally Simple Legal Doctrine. *Maastricht Journal of European and Comparative Law* 9.2 (2002), pp. 161–187.
De Groot, Gerard René. "Auf dem Wege zu einem Europäischen (Internationalen) Familienrecht". *Zeitschrift für Europäisches Privatrecht* (2001), pp. 617–627.
De Groot, David Armand Jacques Gérard. *The Many Faces of Civil Status Recognition – A Legal Analysis in the Light of EU Citizenship and the Case Law of the European Court of Justice and the European Court of Human Rights*. Proefschrift Maken (2021).
de Molina, Antonio García-Pablos. *Introducción al Derecho Penal: Instituciones, Fundamentos y Tendencias del Derecho Penal*. Editorial Universitaria Ramón Areces (2012).
Dee, Thomas S. "The Capitalization of Education Finance Reforms". *Journal of Law and Economics* 43.1 (2000), pp. 185–214.

DeLecce, Tara. "Sources of Conflict in Marriage". In: Weisfeld, Carol Cronin; Weisfeld Glenn; Dillon, Lisa M. *The Psychology of Marriage*. Lexington Books (2018), pp. 265–280.

Demsetz, Harold. "Information and Efficiency: Another Viewpoint". *Journal of Law and Economics* 12.1 (1969), pp. 1–22.

—— "When does the Rule of Liability Matter?". *Journal of Legal Studies* 1.1. (1972), pp. 13–28.

—— *Toward a Theory of Property Rights. Classic Papers in Natural Resource Economics*. Palgrave Macmillan (1974), pp. 163–177.

Depoorter, Ben W.F. "Regulation of Natural Monopoly". In: Bouckaert, Boudewijn; De Geest, Gerit. *Encyclopedia of Law and Economics*, vol. 3. Edward Elgar Publishing (2000).

Dethloff, Nina. "Arguments for the Unification and Harmonisation of Family Law in Europe". In: Boele-Woelki, Katharina (ed.). *Perspectives for the Unification and Harmonisation of Family Law in Europe*, vol. 4. Intersentia (2003), pp. 37–64.

Dickinson, Andrew. "United Kingdom". In: Basedow, Jürgen; Rühl, Gisela; Ferrari, Franco; de Miguel Asensio, Pedro. *Encyclopedia of Private International Law*, vol. 3. Edward Elgar Publishing (2017), pp. 2612–2626.

Dieckmann, Anja; Dippold, Katrin; Dietrich, Holger. "Compensatory versus Noncompensatory Models for Predicting Consumer Preferences". *Judgment and Decision Making* 4.3 (2009), pp. 200–213.

Dinnie, Keith. *Nation Branding: Concepts, Issues, Practice*. Elsevier (2008).

Dnes, Antony W. *Principles of Law and Economics*. Edward Elgar Publishing (2018).

Dnes, Antony W.; Rowthorn Robert (eds). *The law and Economics of Marriage and Divorce*. Cambridge University Press (2002).

D'Oliveira, Hans Ulrich Jessurun. "Characteristic Obligation in the Draft-EEC Obligation Convention". *American Journal of Comparative Law* 25 (1977), pp. 303–331.

Dreyzin de Klor, Adriana Silvia. "Argentina". In: Basedow, Jürgen; Rühl, Gisela; Ferrari, Franco; de Miguel Asensio, Pedro. *Encyclopedia of Private International Law*, vol. 3. Edward Elgar Publishing (2017), pp. 1867–1879.

Dutta, Anatol. "Domicile, Habitual Residence and Establishment". In: Basedow, Jürgen; Rühl, Gisela; Ferrari, Franco; de Miguel Asensio, Pedro. *Encyclopedia of Private International Law*, vol. 1. Edward Elgar Publishing (2017), pp. 555–561.

Earnest, David C. *Voting Rights for Resident Aliens: A comparison of 25 Democracies*. Annual Meeting of the Northeast Political Science Association and the International Studies Association-Northeast (2003).

Ehrlich, Isaac; Posner, Richard A. "An Economic Analysis of Legal Rulemaking". *Journal of Legal Studies* 3.1 (1974), pp. 257–286.

Eichel, Florian. Reference to Non-Unified Legal Systems. In: Leible, Stefan. *General Principles of European Private International Law*. Wolters Kluwer (2016), pp. 275–303.

Eidenmüller, Horst. "Recht als Produkt". *Juristenzeitung* 64 (2009), pp. 641–653.

Eisenberg, Theodore; Miller, Geoffrey. "The Flight to New York – An Empirical Study of Choice of Law and Choice of Forum Clauses in Publicly-Held Companies' Contracts". *Cardozo Law Review* 30 (2009), pp. 1475–1512.

Engel, Charles; Rogers, John H. "How Wide is the Border?" *American Economic Review* 86 (1996), pp. 1112–1125.

European Policy Evaluation Consortium (EPEC). *Study to Inform a Subsequent Impact Assessment on the Commission Proposal on Jurisdiction and Applicable law in Divorce Matters.* EU Publications (2006). Available at: <https://www.euromed-justice.eu/en/system/files/20090707140842_Studytoinform.ontheCommission proposalonjurisdictionandapplicablelawindivorcematters.pdf>.

—— *Impact Assessment Study on Community Instruments Concerning Matrimonial Property Regimes and Property of Unmarried Couples with Translational Elements.* EU Publications (2010). Available at: <https://op.europa.eu/en/publication-detail/-/publication/48820a62-4950-4ebb-a20c-d5bc9f35bd84/language-en>.

Epstein, Wendy Netter. "Facilitating Incomplete Contracts". *Case Western Reserve Law Review* 65:2 (2014), pp. 297–340.

Estin, Ann Laquer. "Love and Obligation: Family Law and the Romance of Economics". *William & Mary Law Review* 36 (1994), pp. 989–1087.

European Commission MEMO/11/175. *Clearer property rights for Europe's 16 Million International Couples – Frequently Asked Questions.* Brussels (2011). Available at: <http://europa.eu/rapid/press-release_MEMO-11-175_en.pdf>.

Evans, Carolyn L. "The Economic Significance of National Border Effects". *American Economic Review* 93 (2003), pp. 1291–1312.

Falconi, Federica. "Il Regolamento (UE) n. 1259/2010 sulla Legge Applicabile al Divorzio e alla Separazione Personale nella Recente Prassi Giurisprudenziale italiana". *Cuadernos de Derecho Transnacional* 10.1 (2018), pp. 568–580.

Fana, Marta; Milasi, Santo; Napierala, Joanna; Fernández-Macías, Enrique; González Vázquez, Ignacio. *Telework, Work Organisation and Job Quality During the COVID-19 Crisis: a Qualitative Study.* JRC Working Papers Series on Labour, Education and Technology, no. 2020/11 European Commission, Joint Research Centre (JRC). Seville (2020).

Felkey, Amanda J. "Will You Covenant Marry Me? A Preliminary Look at a New Type of Marriage". *Eastern Economic Journal* 37.3 (2011), pp. 367–389.

Ferrari, Franco. "Forum (and law) shopping". In: Basedow, Jürgen; Rühl, Gisela; Ferrari, Franco; de Miguel Asensio, Pedro. *Encyclopedia of Private International Law*, vol. 1. Edward Elgar Publishing (2017), pp. 789–797.

Fiorini, Aude. "Rome III – Choice of Law in Divorce: Is the Europeanization of Family Law Going Too Far?" *International Journal of Law, Policy and the Family* 22:8 (2008), pp. 178–205.

Fischel, W.A. *Public Goods and Property Rights: Of Coase, Tiebout, and Just Compensation.* Paper presented at the Economics and Law of Property Rights conference held at the Hoover Institution (2000).

Fogt, Morten M. "Denmark". In: Basedow, Jürgen; Rühl, Gisela; Ferrari, Franco; de Miguel Asensio, Pedro. *Encyclopedia of Private International Law*, vol. 3. Edward Elgar Publishing (2017), pp. 2019–2036.

Ford, J. Kevin.; Schmitt, Neal; Schechtman, Susan L.; Hults, Brian H.; Doherty, Mary L. "Process Tracing Methods: Contributions, Problems, and Neglected Research Questions". *Organizational Behavior and Decision Processes* 43 (1989), pp. 75–117.

Franq, Stéphanie. "Unilateralism". In: Basedow, Jürgen; Rühl, Gisela; Ferrari, Franco; de Miguel Asensio, Pedro. *Encyclopedia of Private International Law*, vol. 2. Edward Elgar Publishing (2017), pp. 1779–1791.

Franzina, Pietro. "The Law Applicable to Divorce and Legal Separation under Regulation (EU) no. 1259/2010 of 20 December 2010". *Cuadernos Derecho Transnacional* 3 (2011), p. 85.

—— "Applicable law in the Absence of a Choice by the Parties". In: Corneloup, Sabine. *The Rome III Regulation - A Commentary on the Law Applicable to Divorce and Legal Separation*. Edward Elgar Publishing (2020), pp. 92–112.

Fresnedo de Aguirre. "Uruguay". In: Girsberger, Daniel; Kadner Graziano, Thomas; Neels, Jan L. *Choice of Law in International Commercial Contracts - Global Perspectives on the Hague Principles*. Oxford University Press (2021), pp. 1123–1136.

Frey, Bruno; Eichenberger, Reiner. "Marriage Paradoxes". *Rationality and Society* 8.2 (1996), pp. 187–206.

Friedberg, Leora; Stern, Steven. "Marriage, Divorce, and Asymmetric Information". *International Economic Review* 55.4 (2014), pp. 1155–1199.

Friedländer, Saul. *Nazi Germany and the Jews, 1933–1945*. Harper Perennial (2009).

Friedman, David D. *Law's Order*. Princeton University Press (2000).

Friedman, Michael. "Austria - Federal Statute of 15 June 1978 on Private International Law". In: Basedow, Jürgen; Rühl, Gisela; Ferrari, Franco; de Miguel Asensio, Pedro. *Encyclopedia of Private International Law*, vol. 4. Edward Elgar Publishing (2017), pp. 2951–2957.

Friedman, Milton. *Capitalism and Freedom*. University of Chicago Press (1962).

Fulli-Lemaire, Samuel. "L'autonomie de la Volonté en Droit International Privé Européen de la Famille". In: Parra Lucán, María Angeles; Gaspar Lera, Silvia. *Límites a la Autonomía de la Voluntad* (2017), pp. 435–447.

Gabor, Barbara. *Regulatory Competition in the Internal Market: Comparing Models for Corporate Law, Securities Law and Competition Law*. Edward Elgar Publishing (2013).

Gaissmaier, Wolfgang; Marewski, Julian N. "Forecasting elections with mere recognition from small, lousy samples: A Comparison of Collective Recognition, Wisdom of Crowds, and Representative Polls". *Judgment and Decision Making* 6.1 (2011), pp. 73–88.

Gama, Lauro; Tiburcio, Carmen; Albuquerque, Felipe. "Brazil". In: Girsberger, Daniel; Kadner Graziano, Thomas; Neels, Jan L. *Choice of Law in International Commercial Contracts - Global Perspectives on the Hague Principles*. Oxford University Press (2021), pp. 984–999.

Gamillscheg, Franz. *Der Einfluss Dumoulins auf Die Entwicklung des Kollisionsrechts*. W. de Gruyter, J.C.B. Mohr (1955).

Garcimartín Alférez, Francisco J. "La Racionalidad Económica del Derecho Internacional Privado". *Cursos de Derecho Internacional y Relaciones Internacionales de Vitoria Gasteiz* 1 (2002), pp. 87–154.

—— "Harmonization, State of Origin or State of Destination: An Outline of the EU Legislator's Diemma from an Economic Standpoint". In: Audit, Mathias; Muir Watt, Horatia; Pataut, Étienne (eds.). *Conflits de Lois et Régulation Économique. L'expérience du Marché Intérieur*. LGDJ (2008), pp. 253–260.

Garoupa, Nuno; Liguerre, Carlos Gomez. "Efficiency of the Common Law". In: Faure, Michael G.; Smits, Jan (eds.). *Does Law Matter? On Law and Economic Growth*. Intersentia (2011), pp. 223–264.

Gatsios, Konstantine; Holmes, Peter. "Regulatory Competition". In: Newman, Peter (ed.). *The New Palgrave Dictionary of Economics and the Law*, vol. 3. Palgrave Macmillan (1998), pp. 271–275.

Gebauer, Martin; Huber, Stefan. *Gestaltungsfreiheit im Familienrecht*. Mohr Siebeck (2017).

Gerber Jenni, Regula. "Rechtshistorische Aspekte des Bernischen Emanzipationsgesetzes von 1847". In: Gerhard, Ute. *Frauen in der Geschichte des Rechts: von der frühen Neuzeit bis zur Gegenwart*. C.H. Beck (1997), pp. 480–493.

Gerber Jenni, Regula; Kaufmann, Claudia. "Frauenforderungen an das Schweizerische Zivilgesetzbuch". In: Caroni, Pio (ed.). *Eugen Huber (1849–1923). Akten des im Sommersemester 1992 Durchgeführten Seminars (mit bibliographischem Anhang)*. Universität Bern (1993), pp. 178–220.

Gerhard, Ute. "Die Rechtsstellung der Frau in der Bürgerlichen Gesellschaft des 19. Jahrhunderts: Frankreich und Deutschland im Vergleich". In: Jürgen Kocka (ed.). *Bürgertum im 19. Jahrhundert*, vol. 3. Deutscher Taschenbuch Verlag (1995), pp. 167–196.

—— "Die Frau als Rechtsperson - oder: Wie verschieden sind die Geschlechter? Einblicke in die Jurisprudenz des 19. Jahrhunderts". *Zeitschrift der Savigny-Stiftung für Rechtsgeschichte* 130 (2013), pp. 281–304.

Gerken, Lüder. "Institutional Competition: An Orientative Framework". In: Gerken, Lüder (ed.). *Competition among Institutions*. Palgrave Macmillan (1995), pp. 1–31.

Gigerenzer, Gerd. *Gut Feelings*. Penguin (2007).

Gigerenzer, Gerd; Goldstein, Daniel. G. "Reasoning the Fast and Frugal Way: Models of Bounded Rationality". *Psychological Review* 103.4 (1996), pp. 650–669.

—— "Betting on One Good Reason: The Take The Best Heuristic". In: Gigerenzer, Gerd; Todd, Peter; the ABC Research Group. *Simple Heuristics that Make Us Smart*. Oxford University Press (1999), pp. 75–98.

Gigerenzer Gerd; Engel, Christoph. *Heuristics and the Law*. MIT Press in cooperation with Dahlem University Press (2006).

Gigerenzer, Gerd; Gaissmaier, Wolfgang. "Heuristic Decision Making". *Annual Review of Psychology* 62 (2011), pp. 451–482.

Gigerenzer, Gerd; Hertwig, Ralph; Pachur, Thorsten. *Heuristics: The Foundations of Adaptive Behavior*. Oxford University Press (2011).

Gigerenzer, Gerd; Todd, Peter. "Fast and Frugal Heuristics the Adaptation Toolbox". In: Gigerenzer, Gerd; Todd, Peter; the ABC Research Group. *Simple Heuristics that Make Us Smart*. Oxford University Press (1999), pp. 3–34.

Gigerenzer, Gerd, Todd, Peter; the ABC Research Group. *Simple Heuristics that Make Us Smart*. Oxford University Press (1999).

Gilles, Stephen G. "Negligence, Strict Liability, and the Cheapest Cost Avoider". *Virginia Law Review* 78.6 (1992), pp. 1291–1375.

Gilovich Thomas; Griffin Dale; Kahneman Daniel. *Heuristic and Bias: The Psychology of Intuitive Judgment*. Cambridge University Press (2002).

Ginger, Ray. "Labor in a Massachusetts Cotton Mill, 1853–60". *The Business History Review* 28.1 (1954), pp. 67–91.

Girsberger, Daniel; Kadner Graziano, Thomas; Neels, Jan L. "General Comparative Report". In: Girsberger, Daniel; Kadner Graziano, Thomas; Neels, Jan L. *Choice of Law in International Commercial Contracts – Global Perspectives on the Hague Principles*. Oxford University Press (2021), pp. 3–128.

Gödker, Katrin; Hornuf, Lars. "Regulatory Competition". In: Marciano, Alain; Ramello, Giovanni (eds.). *Encyclopedia of Law and Economics*. Springer (2019), pp. 1787–1795.

Goetz, Charles J.; Scott, Robert E. "Liquidated Damages, Penalties and the Just Compensation Principle: Some Notes on an Enforcement Model and a Theory of Efficient Breach". *Columbia Law Review* 77.4 (1977), pp. 554–594.

Goldstein, Daniel G.; Gigerenzer, Gerd. "The Recognition Heuristic: How Ignorance Makes Us Smart". In: Gigerenzer, Gerd; Todd, Peter; the ABC Research Group. *Simple Heuristics that Make Us Smart*. Oxford University Press (1999), pp. 37–58.

González Beilfuss, Cristina. "Choice of applicable law by the parties". In: Corneloup, Sabine. *The Rome III Regulation – A Commentary on the Law Applicable to Divorce and Legal Separation*. Edward Elgar Publishing (2020a), pp. 65–78.

—— "The Choice of the Applicable Law in EU Family Law". In: Forner Delaygua, Joaquim; Santos, Alfredo. *Coherence of the Scope of Application – EU Private International Legal Instruments, Publications of the Swiss Institute of Comparative Law*. Schulthess Éditions Romandes (2020b), pp. 71–91.

Gray, Jacqueline. *Party Autonomy in EU Private International Law: Choice of Court and Choice of Law in Family Matters and Succession*. Intersentia (2021).

Gröteke, Friedrich. *Europäische Beihilfenkontrolle und Standortwettbewerb: eine Ökonomische Analyse*. Lucius & Lucius (2007).

Grossbard-Shechtman, Shoshana; Lemennicier, Bertrand. "Marriage Contracts and the Law-and-Economics of Marriage: an Austrian Perspective". *Journal of Socio-Economics* 28.6 (1999), pp. 665–690.

Gruber, Peter. "Rechtswahl in der Rom III-Verordnung". In: Roth, Andres. *Die Wahl ausländischen Rechts im Familien- und Erbrecht*. Nomos (2013).

Guadagni, Marco. Legal Pluralism. In: Newman, Peter. *The New Palgrave Dictionary of Economics and the Law*, vol. 2. Palgrave Macmillan (1998), pp. 542–544.

Gunst, Dirk. *Die Charakteristische Leistung: zur Funktionellen Anknüpfung im Internationalen Vertragsrecht Deutschlands, der Schweiz und der Europäischen Gemeinschaft*. Hartung-Gorre (1994).

Guzman, Andrew T. "Choice of Law: New Foundations". *Georgetown Law Journal* 90 (2001), pp. 883–940.

Guzman, Victoria R. "A Comparison of Surrogacy Laws of the US to Other Countries: Should There be a Uniform Federal Law Permitting Commercial Surrogacy?". *Houston Journal of International Law* 38 (2016), pp. 619 et seqq.

Haro Seijas, José Juan. "¿Periculum Est Dubitabilis? Algunas Precisiones sobre el Papel del Riesgo en la Contratación Privada". *Themis Revista de Derecho* 49 (2004), pp. 183–204.

Hartog, Hendrik. *Man and Wife in America*. Harvard University Press (2002).

Hatzis, Aristides N. "The Negative Externalities of Immorality: the Case of Same-Sex Marriage". *Skepsis* 17 (2006), pp. 52–65.

Hausheer, Heinz; Geiser, Thomas; Aebi-Müller, Regina E. *Das Familienrecht des Schweizerischen Zivilgesetzbuches*, 4th edn. Stämpfli (2010).

Hausmann, Rainer. *Internationales und Europäisches Familienrecht*, 2nd edn. C.H. Beck (2018).

Haussamen, Florence; Guitar Mary Anne. *The Divorce Handbook*. GP Putnam & Sons (1960).

Hayek, Friedrich August. "Economics and Knowledge". In: Hayek, Friedrich August. *Individualism and Economic Order*. University of Chicago Press (1948a), pp. 33–56.

—— "The Meaning of Competition". In: Hayek, Friedrich August. *Individualism and Economic Order*. University of Chicago Press (1948b), pp. 92–106.

—— "The Economic Conditions of interstate Federalism". In: Hayek, Friedrich August. *Individualism and Economic Order*. University of Chicago Press (1948c), pp. 255–272.

—— "Individualism: True or False". In: Hayek, Friedrich August. *Individualism and Economic Order*. University of Chicago Press (1948d), pp. 1–32.

—— "Der Wettbewerb als Entdeckungsverfahren". In: Hayek, Friedrich August. *Freiburger Studien*. Mohr (1969), pp. 249–165.

He, Qisheng. "China (Mainland)". In: Girsberger, Daniel; Kadner Graziano, Thomas; Neels, Jan L. *Choice of Law in International Commercial Contracts – Global Perspectives on the Hague Principles*. Oxford University Press (2021) 431–450.

Head, Keith. "Gravity for Beginners" (2000). available at: <http://www.econ.ubc.ca/nmalhotra/490/Articles/KHead%20on%20gravity.pdf>.

Head, Keith; Mayer, Thierry. "Non-Europe: The Magnitude and Causes of Market Segmentation in Europe". *Review of World Economics* 136 (2000), pp. 284–314.

Helliwell, John F., "National Borders, Trade and Migration". *Pacific Economic Review* 2 (1997), pp. 165–185.

—— *How Much do National Borders Matter?* Brookings Institution (1998).

Helmholz, Richard H. "Ockham's Razor in American Law". *Tulane European & Civil Law Forum* 21 (2006), pp. 109–123.

Helms, Tobias. "Verordnung (EU) des Rates vom 20. Dezember 2010 zur Durchführung einer Verstärkten Zusammenarbeit im Bereich des auf die Ehescheidung und Trennung ohne Auflösung des Ehebandes Anzuwendende Recht". In: Rauscher, Thomas. *Europäisches Zivilprozess- und Kollisionsrecht, EuZPR/EuIPR*, 4th edn., vol. 4. Otto Schmidt (2016), pp. 771–923.

Henrich, Dieter. "Rechtswahl im Unterhaltsrecht nach dem Haager Protokoll". In: Roth, Andreas (ed.). *Die Wahl Ausländischen Rechts im Familien- und Erbrecht*. Nomos (2013).

Herbei, Peter. "Paris Der internationale Unternehmensjurist – ein Vaterlandsloser Geselle?" In: Schwenzer, Ingeborg; Herbel, Peter; Schlechtriem, Peter. *Schuldrecht. Rechtsvergleichung und Rechtsvereinheitlichung an der Schwelle zum 21. Jahrhundert*. Mohr Siebeck (1999).

Hermalin, Benjamin E.; Katz, Avery W.; Craswell, Richard. "Contract Law". In: Polinsky, A. Mitchell; Shavell, Steven (eds.). *Handbook of Law and Economics*, vol. 1. North Holland (2007), pp. 3–138.

Hoens, Frank; Schols, F.W.J.M. "CNR-Huwelijksvoorwaardenonderzoek. Deel II: verrekenbedingen en bijzondere facetten". *Weekblad voor Privaatrecht*, Notariaat en Registratie 145.7002 (2014), pp. 33–43.

Hoffman, Philip T.; Postel-Vinay, Gilles; Rosenthal, Jean-Laurent. "What do notaries do? Overcoming Asymmetric Information in Financial Markets: The Case of Paris, 1751". *Journal of Institutional and Theoretical Economics* 154.3 (1998), pp. 449–530.

Hoxby CM. "The Productivity of Schools and Other Local Public Goods Producers. *Journal of Public Economics* 74.1 (1999), pp. 1–30.

Iriarte, Gonzalo Lorenzo. In: Basedow, Jürgen; Rühl, Gisela; Ferrari, Franco, de Miguel Asensio, Pedro. *Encyclopedia of Private International Law*, vol. 3. Edward Elgar Publishing (2017), pp. 2626–2637.

Jacobson, Paul Harold. *American Marriage and Divorce*. Rinehart (1959).

Jänterä-Jareborg, Maarit. "Jurisdiction and Applicable Law in Cross-Border Divorce Cases in Europe". In: Basedow, Jürgen; Baum, Hans; Nishitani, Yuko (eds.). *Japanese and European Private International Law in Comparative Perspective*. Mohr Siebeck (2008), pp. 317–343.

Jevons, W. Stanley. *Money and Mechanism of Exchange*. D. Appleton (1893).

Jolls, Christine; Sunstein, Cass R.; Thaler Richard. "A behavioral Approach to Law and Economics". In: Sunstein, Cass. *Behavioral Law & Economics*. Cambridge University Press (2000), pp. 13–57.

Joubert, Natalie. "Consent and Material Validity. In: Corneloup, Sabine. *The Rome III Regulation – A Commentary on the Law Applicable to Divorce and Legal Separation*. Edward Elgar Publishing (2020), pp. 79–86.

Juárez, Fátima; Palma, José Luis; Singh, Susheela; Bankole, Akinrinola. *Las Necesidades de Salud Sexual y Reproductiva de las Adolescentes en México: Retos y Oportunidades*. Nueva York Guttmacher Institute (2010).

Juenger, Friedrich. "The E.E.C. Convention on the Law Applicable to Contractual Obligations: an American Assessment". In: North, Peter Machin. *Contract Conflicts*. North-Holland Publishing Company (1982), pp. 295–322.

Kahneman, Daniel; Tverky, Amos. *Choices, Values, and Frames*. Cambridge University Press (2009).

Kaplow, Louis. "A model of the Optimal Complexity of Legal Rules". *Journal of Law, Economics, & Organization* 11 (1995), pp. 150–163.

Kaplow, Louis; Shapiro, Carl. "Antitrust". In: Polinsky, A. Mitchell; Shavell, Steven (eds.). *Handbook of Law and Economics*, vol. 2. Elsevier (2007).

Karayanidi, Milana. "Russia". In: Girsberger, Daniel; Kadner Graziano, Thomas; Neels Jan L. *Choice of Law in International Commercial Contracts – Global Perspectives on the Hague Principles*. Oxford University Press (2021), pp. 822–837.

Katz, Daniel Martin; Bommarito, Michael James. "Measuring the Complexity of the Law: the United States Code". *Artificial Intelligence and Law* 22.4 (2014), pp. 337–374.

Keeney, Ralph; Raiffa, Howard. *Decisions with Multiple Objectives*. Cambridge University Press (1993).

Kerber, Wolfgang. "Rechtseinheitlichkeit und Rechtsvielfalt aus Ökonomischer Sicht". In: Grundmann, Stefan (ed.). *Systembildung und Systemlücken in Kerngebieten des Europäischen Privatrechts*. Mohr Siebeck (2000), pp. 67–97.

Kerkmeester, Heico. "Methodology: General". In: Bouckaert, Boudewijn; De Geest Gerrit. *Encyclopedia of Law and Economics*, vol. 1. Edward Elgar (2010).

Kieninger, Eva-Maria. "Rechtsentwicklung im Wettbewerb der Rechtsordnungen". In: Ott, Claus; Schäfer, Hans-Bernd (eds.). *Vereinheitlichung und Diversität des Zivilrechts in Transnationalen Wirtschaftsräumen: Beiträge zum VIII: Travemünder Symposium zur ökonomischen Analyse des Rechts* (2002a), pp. 72–107.

—— "Wettbewerb der Privatrechtsordnungen im Europäischen Binnenmarkt". *Studien zur Privatrechtskoordinierung in der Europäischen Union auf den Gebieten des Gesellschafts- und Vertragsrechts*. Mohr Siebeck (2002b).

Kirchner, Christian. "Zur Ökonomik des Legislatorischen Wettbewerbs im Europäischen Gesellschaftsrecht". In: Fuchs, Andreas; Schwintowski, Hans-Peter; Zimmer, Daniel (eds.). *Wirtschafts- und Privatrecht im Spannungsfeld von Privatautonomie, Wettbewerb und Regulierung. Festschrift für Ulrich Immenga zum 70. Geburtstag*. Beck (2004), pp. 607–626.

—— "An Economic Analysis of Choice-of-Law and Choice-of-Forum Clauses". In: Basedow, Jürgen; Toshiyuki Kono. *An Economic Analysis of Private International Law*. Mohr Siebeck (2006), pp. 33–53.

Klerman, Daniel. "Jurisdictional Competition and the Evolution of the Common Law". *University of Chicago Law Review* 74.4 (2007) pp. 1179–1226. Available at: <https://chicagounbound.uchicago.edu/uclrev/vol74/iss4/2>.

Knetsch, Jack; Sinden, J.A. "Willingness to Pay and Compensation Demanded: Experimental Evidence of an Unexpected Disparity in Measures of Value". *Quarterly Journal of Economics* 99 (1984), pp. 507–521.

Kobayashi, Bruce H.; Ribstein, Larry E. "Law as Product and Byproduct". *Journal of Law, Economics & Policy* 9 (2013), pp. 521–567.

Korobkin, Russell. "The Endowment Effect and Legal Analysis". *Northwestern University Law Review* 97.3 (2002), pp. 1227–1291.

Kötz, Hein. "Rechtsvereinheitlichung–Nutzen, Kosten, Methoden, Ziele". *Rabels Zeitschrift für ausländisches und internationales Privatrecht/The Rabel Journal of Comparative and International Private Law* 50.1–2 (1986), pp. 1–18.

Kramer, Larry. "Rethinking Choice of Law". *Columbia Law Review* 90.2 (1990), pp. 277–345.

—— "On the Need for a Uniform Choice of Law Code". *Michigan Law Review* 89 (1991), pp. 2134–2149.

Kraus, Jody. "Hobbes and Contractarianism". In: Newman, Peter. *The New Palgrave Dictionary of Economics and the Law*, vol. 2. Palgrave Macmillan (1998).

Kren Kostkiewicz, Jolanta; Eichenberger, Michaela. "International Maintenance Law in Legal Relations between Switzerland and the EU". *Comparative Law Review* 20 (2015), pp. 13–31.

Kroll-Ludwigs, Kathrin. *Die Rolle der Parteiautonomie im Europäischen Kollisionsrecht*. Mohr Siebeck (2013).

Kronke, Herbert. „Ziele-Methoden, Kosten-Nutzen: Perspektiven der Privatrechtsharmonisierung nach 75 Jahren UNIDROIT". *Juristenzeitung* (2001), pp. 1149–1157.

Kronman, Anthony T. "Specific performance". *University of Chile Law Review* 45 (1977), pp. 351–382.

—— "Contract Law and Distributive Justice". *Yale Law Journal* 89 (1980), pp. 472–511.

—— "Paternalism and the Law of Contracts". *Yale Law Journal* 92.5 (1983), pp. 763–798.

—— "Contract Law and the State of Nature". *Journal of Law, Economics & Organization* 1 (1985), pp. 5–32.

Kronman, Anthony; Posner, Richard. *The Economics of Contract Law*. Little, Brown and Co. (1979).

Kropholler, Jan. *Internationales Privatrecht*. 6th edn. Mohr Siebeck, (2006).

Krüger, Hilmar. "Saudi Arabia". In: Basedow, Jürgen; Rühl, Gisela; Ferrari, Franco, de Miguel Asensio, Pedro. *Encyclopedia of Private International Law*, vol. 3. Edward Elgar Publishing (2017), pp. 2462–2469.

Kuper, Adam. "Incest, Cousin Marriage, and the Origin of the Human Sciences in Nineteenth-Century England". *Past & Present* 174 (2002), pp. 158–183.

Kurz-Milcke, Elke; Gigerenzer, Gerd. "Heuristic Decision Making". *Marketing: Journal of Research and Management* 3.1 (2007), pp. 48–56.

Landes, Elisabeth M. "Economics of Alimony". *Journal of Legal Studies* 7.1 (1978), pp. 35–63.

Langbein, Laura; Yost, Mark A. "Same-Sex Marriage and Negative Externalities". *Social Science Quarterly* 90.2 (2009), pp. 292–308.

Lass, Christiane. *Der Flüchtling im Deutschen Internationalen Privatrecht*. C.H. Beck (1995).

Law Society of England and Wales. *The Jurisdiction of Choice* (2008). Available at: <http://www.eversheds-sutherland.com/documents/LawSocietyEnglandAndWales JurisdictionOfChoice.pdf>.

Lee Badgett, Mary Virginia. "The Economic Value of Marriage for Same-Sex Couples". *Drake Law Review* 58 (2009), pp. 1081–1116.

Leib, Ethan J. "Contracts and Friendships". *Emory Law Journal* 59 (2009), pp. 649–726.

Levine, Robert; Sato, Suguru; Hashimoto, Tsukasa; Verma, Jyoti. "Love and Marriage in Eleven Cultures". *Journal of Cross-Cultural Psychology* 26. (1995), pp. 554–571.

Looschelders, Dirk. "Verordnung (EU) 2016/1103". In: *Münchener Kommentar zum Bürgerlichen Gesetzbuch: BGB*. 7th edn., vol. 11. Beck (2018), pp. 801–852.

Li, Rita Yi Man; Li, Yi Lut. "The Role of Competition Law: An Asian Perspective". *Asian Social Science* 9.7 (2014), pp. 47–53.

Lipstein, Kurt. "Characteristic Performance – A New Concept in the Conflict of Laws in Matters of Contract for the EEC". *Northwestern Journal of International Law & Business* 3 (1981), pp. 402–414.

Lemke, Jayme S. "Interjurisdictional Competition and the Married Women's Property Acts". *Public Choice* 166.3–4 (2016), pp. 291–313.

Lenton, Alison; Penke, Lars; Todd, Peter; Fasolo Barbara. "The Hart Has its Reasons: Social Rationality in Mate Choice". In: Hertwig, Ralf; Hoffrage, Uhrlich; ABC Research Group. *Simple Heuristics in a Social World*. Oxford University Press (2012), pp. 433–458.

Lima Marques, Claudia; Lixinski, Lucas; Marcello Baquero, Pablo. "Brazil". In: Basedow, Jürgen; Rühl, Gisela; Ferrari, Franco, de Miguel Asensio, Pedro. *Encyclopedia of Private International Law*, vol. 3. Edward Elgar Publishing (2017), pp. 1928–1939.

Macaulay, Stewart. "Renegotiations and Settlements: Dr. Pangloss's Notes on the Margins of David Campbell's Papers". *Cardozo Law Review* 29 (2007), p. 261.

Macey, Jonathan R.; Miller, Geoffrey. "Toward an Interest-Group Theory of Delaware Corporate Law". *Texas Law Review* 65 (1986), pp. 469–523.

Mackaay, Ejan. *Law and Economics for Civil Law Systems*. Edward Elgar Publishing (2013).

Magat, Wesley A. "Information Regulation". In: Newman, Peter. *The New Palgrave Dictionary of Economics and the Law*, vol. 2. Palgrave Macmillan (1998).

Magnus, Ulrich. Art. 4 Applicable Law in the Absence of Choice. In: Magnus, Ulrich; Mankowski Peter. *European Commentaries on Private International Law, ECPIL*, vol. 2. Otto Schmidt (2017), pp. 263–441.

Mak Vanessa. *Legal Pluralism in European Contract Law*. Oxford University Press (2020).

Makarov, A.N. *Quellen des Internationalen Privatsrecht*, 2nd edn. (1953).

Mangion, Ann Marie. *The Financial Aspect of Family Law*. Bank of Valletta in collaboration with the Economics Department of the University of Malta (2012), pp. 109–121.

Mankiw, Nicholas Gregory. *Principles of Microeconomics*. 6th edn. South-Western, Cengage Learning (2012).

Mankowski, Peter. "The principle of Characteristic Performance Revisited Yet Again". In: Boele-Woelki, Katharina; Einhorn, Talia; Girsberger, Daniel; Symeonides, Symeon. *Convergence and Divergence in Private International Law: Liber Amicorum Kurt Siehr*. Eleven International Publishing (2010), pp. 434–462.

—— *Haager Unterhaltsprotokoll (HUP), (Internationales Unterhaltsrecht). J. von Staudingers Kommentar zum Bürgerlichen Gesetzbuch: Staudinger BGB - EGBGB/IPR Einführungsgesetz zum Bürgerlichen Gesetzbuche/IPR Haager Unterhaltsprotokoll (Internationales Unterhalts- und Unterhaltsverfahrensrecht)*, vol. 7. Sellier-De Gruyter (2016).

—— "Article 3 Freedom of choice". In: Magnus, Ulrich; Mankowski, Peter. *European Commentaries on Private International Law (ECPIL)*, vol. 2. Schmidt (2007), pp. 87–263.

Mansel, Heinz-Peter. "Connecting Factor". In: Basedow, Jürgen, Rühl Gisela; Ferrari Franco, de Miguel Asensio Pedro. *Encyclopedia of Private International Law*, vol. 1. Edward Elgar Publishing (2017), pp. 441–452.

Marewski, J.N.; Schooler L.J. "Cognitive niches: An Ecological Model of Emergent Strategy Selection". *Psychological Review* 118.3 (2011), pp. 393–437.

Martignon, Laura; Hoffrage, Ulrich. "Why Does One-Reason Decision Making Work? A Case Study in Ecological Rationality". In: Gigerenzer, Gerd; Todd, Peter; the ABC Research Group. *Simple Heuristics that Make Us Smart*. Oxford University Press (1999), pp. 119–140.

—— "Fast, Frugal, and Fit: Simple Heuristics for Paired Comparisons". *Theory Decision* 52 (2002), pp. 29–71.

Martiny, Dieter. "Europäisches Familienrecht-Utopie oder Notwendigkeit?". *Rabels Zeitschrift für ausländisches und internationales Privatrecht/The Rabel Journal of Comparative and International Private Law* 3–4 (1995), pp. 419–453.

—— "Die Entwicklung des Europäischen Internationalen Familienrechts - ein Juristischer Hürdenlauf". *Familie. Partnerschaft und Recht (FPR)* (2008), pp. 187–192.

—— "Applicable Law in the Absence of Choice by the Parties". In: Viarengo, Ilaria; Franzina, Pietro. *The EU Regulations on the Property Regimes of International Couples - A Commentary*. Edward Elgar Publishing (2020) pp. 241–259.

Matouschek, Niko, and Imran Rasul. "The Economics of the Marriage Contract: Theories and Evidence". *Journal of Law and Economics* 51.1 (2008), pp. 59–110.

Maurer, Hans-Ulrich. "Grundsatz der eigenen Verantwortung". In: Franz Jürgen Säcker, and Jan Schürnbrand. *Münchener Kommentar Zum Bürgerlichen Gesetzbuch*, 7th edn., vol. 8. C.H. Beck (2017).

McCallum, John, "National Borders Matter: Canada-U.S. Regional Trade Barrier". *American Economic Review* 85 (1995), pp. 615–623.

Mechoulan, Stéphane. "Divorce Laws and the Structure of the American Family". *Journal of Legal Studies* 35.1 (2006), pp. 143–174.

Medema, Steven; Mercurio, Nicholas; Samuels, Warren. "Institutional Law and Economics". In: Bouckaert, Boudewijn; De Geest Gerrit. *Encyclopedia of Law and Economics*, vol. 1 (2010).

Merrill, Thomas W.; Henry E. Smith. "Optimal Standardization in the Law of Property: the Numerus Clausus Principle". *Yale Law Journal* 110.1 (2000), pp. 1–70.

Mertens, Hans-Joachim. "Nichtlegislatorische Rechtsvereinheitlichung durch Transnationales Wirtschaftsrecht und Rechtsbegriff". *Rabels Zeitschrift für ausländisches und internationales Privatrecht/The Rabel Journal of Comparative and International Private Law* 56.2 (1992), pp. 219–242.

Metzger, Axel. "Article 12 1951 Convention". In: Zimmermann, Andreas (ed.). *The 1951 Convention Relating to the Status of Refugees and its 1967 Protocol: A Commentary.* Oxford University Press (2011).

Meulders-Klein, Marie Therèse. "Towards a European Civil Code on Family Law?: Ends and Means". In: Boele-Woelki, Katharina (ed.). *Perspectives for the Unification and Harmonisation of Family Law in Europe*, vol. 4. Intersentia (2003), pp. 105–117.

—— "Towards a Uniform European Family Law? A Political Approach. General Conclusions". In: Antokolskaia, M. *Convergence and Divergence of Family Law in Europe*. Intersentia (2007).

Miceli, Thomas J. *The Economic Approach to Law*. Stanford University Press (2004).

Mill, John Stuart. *On Liberty*. Broadview Press ([1859] 1999).

Miller, Geoffrey; Eisenberg, Theodore. "The Market for Contracts". *Cardozo Law Review* 30.5 (2009).

Mills, Alex. "Australia". In: Basedow, Jürgen; Rühl, Gisela; Ferrari, Franco; de Miguel Asensio, Pedro. *Encyclopedia of Private International Law*, vol. 3. Edward Elgar Publishing (2017), pp. 1879–1885.

Ministry of Justice. *UK Legal Services on the International Stage: Underpinning growth and stability*. Available at: <https://www.justice.gov.uk/downloads/publications/corporate-reports/MoJ/legal-services-action-plan-0313.pdf>.

Molina, Juana; Espiau, Santiago; Raventós Lídia; Navas, Susana; Zaího, María Luisa; Ginebra, Maria. "Los Regímenes Económicos Matrimoniales en el Derecho Civil de Cataluña". In: Cuena Casas, Matilde; Yzquierdo Tolsada, Mariano. *Tratado de Derecho De La Familia*, vol. 7. Thomson Reuters-Aranzadi (2011).

Moore, Elena. "Delaying divorce: Pitfalls of Restrictive Divorce Requirements". *Journal of Family Issues* 37.16 (2016), pp. 2265–2293.

Moroney, John R.; Lovell C. A. K. The Relative Efficiencies of Market and Planned Economies. *Southern Economic Journal* (1997), pp. 1084–1093.

Muir Watt, Horatia. "Aspects Économiques du Droit International Privé. Réflexions sur L'mpact de la Globalisation économique sur les Fondements des Conflits de Lois et de Jurisdictions". *Recueil des Cours* 307 (2004), pp. 25–380.

—— "Private International Law beyond the Schism". *Transnational Legal Theory* 2.3 (2011), pp. 347–428.

Musgrave, Richard Abel. "The Voluntary Exchange Theory of Public Economy". *Quarterly Journal of Economics* 53.2 (1939), pp. 213–237.

Najm Kobeh, Marie-Claude. "Lebanon". In: Basedow, Jürgen; Rühl, Gisela; Ferrari, Franco; de Miguel Asensio, Pedro. *Encyclopedia of Private International Law*, vol. 3. Edward Elgar Publishing (2017), pp. 2264–2276.

Neuhaus, Paul Heinrich. "Legal Certainty versus Equity in the Conflict of Laws". *Law and Contemporary Problems* 28.4 (1963), pp. 795–807.

Neuhaus, Paul Heinrich; Kropholler Jan. "Rechtsvereinheitlichung–Rechtsverbesserung?" *Rabels Zeitschrift für ausländisches und internationales Privatrecht/The Rabel Journal of Comparative and International Private Law* 45.1–2 (1981), pp. 73–90.

Nishitani, Yuko. "Japan". In: Girsberger, Daniel; Kadner Graziano, Thomas; Neels, Jan L. *Choice of Law in International Commercial Contracts – Global Perspectives on the Hague Principles*. Oxford University Press (2021) pp. 537–555.

Nowicka, Ewa. "Transnational marriages in Poland: Cultural Contact and Cultural Capital in Binational Families". *Studia Migracyjne – Przegląd Polonijny* 166.4, (2017), pp. 113–142.

Nozick, Robert. *Anarchy, State and Utopia*. Basic Books (1974).

Oates, Wallace E. *Decentralization of the Public Sector: an Overview. Decentralization, Local Governments, and Markets*. Oxford University Press (1990), pp. 43–58.

—— "The Many Faces of the Tiebout Model". In: William A. Fischel (ed.). *The Tiebout Model at Fifty*. Lincoln Institute of Land Policy (2006), pp. 21–45.

Obstfeld, Maurice; Kenneth, Rogoff. *The Six Major Puzzles in International Macroeconomics: Is There a Common Cause?* National Bureau of Economic Research, Working Paper Series, Working Paper no. 7777 (2000).

OECD Family Database. Marriage and Divorce rates (SF 8) OECD – Social Policy Division – Directorate of Employment, Labour and Social Affairs (2008). Available at: <https://www.oecd.org/social/family/database.htm>.

O'Flaherty, Kathleen M.; Workman Eells, Laura. "Courtship Behavior of the Remarried". *Journal of Marriage and the Family* (1988), pp. 499–506.

Ogus, Anthony. "Law and Spontaneous Order: Hayek's Contribution to Legal Theory". *Journal of law in Society* 16 (1989), p. 393.

—— *Regulation: Legal form and Economic Theory*. Clarendon Press (1994).

—— "Competition between National Legal Systems: A Contribution of Economic Analysis to Comparative Law". *International and Comparative Law Quarterly* 48 (1999), pp. 405–418.

O'Hara, Erin Ann. "Opting Out of Regulation: A Public Choice Analysis of Contractual Choice of Law". *Vanderbilt Law Review* 53 (2000), pp. 1551–1604.

O'Hara, Erin A.; Ribstein, Larry E. "From politics to efficiency in Choice of Law". *University of Chicago Law Review* 67 (2000a), pp. 1151–1232.

—— "Conflict of Laws and Choice of Law". In: Bouckaert, Boudewijn; De Geest, Gerit. *Encyclopedia of Law and Economics*, vol. 5. Edward Elgar Publishing (2000b), pp. 631–660.

Olson, Mancur. *The Logic of Collective Action*. Harvard University Press (1971).

Oppong, Richard Frimpong. "Nigeria". In: Basedow, Jürgen, Rühl Gisela; Ferrari Franco, de Miguel Asensio Pedro. *Encyclopedia of Private International Law*, vol. 3. Edward Elgar Publishing (2017a), pp. 2378–2386.

—— "Ghana". In: Basedow, Jürgen; Rühl, Gisela; Ferrari, Franco; de Miguel Asensio, Pedro. *Encyclopedia of Private International Law*, vol. 3. Edward Elgar Publishing (2017b), pp. 2112–2118.

Orbuch, Terri L.; Veroff, Joseph; Holmberg, Diane. "Becoming a Married Couple: The Emergence of Meaning in the First Years of Marriage". *Journal of Marriage and the Family* (1993), pp. 815–826.

Ortmann, A.; Gigerenzer, G.; Borges, B.; Goldstein, D.G. "The Recognition Heuristic: a Fast and Frugal Way to Investment Choice?" In: Plott, Charles; Smith, Vernon (eds.). *Handbook of Experimental Economics Results* 1.28 (2008), pp. 993–1003.

Ostrowski, James. "The Moral and Practical Case for Drug Legalization". *Hofstra Law Review* 18.3 (1989), pp. 607–702.

Ostroy, Joseph M.; Starr Ross, M. "The Transactions Role of Money". *Handbook of Monetary Economics* 1 (1990), pp. 3–62.

Ota, Shozo. "Choice of Law and Economic analysis: a Methodological Introduction". In: Basedow, Jürgen; Toshiyuki Kono. *An Economic Analysis of Private International Law*. Mohr Siebeck (2006), pp. 3–14.

Ott, Claus; Schäfer, Hans-Bernd. *Die Vereinheitlichung des Europäischen Vertragsrechts: Ökonomische Notwendigkeit oder Akademisches Interesse? Vereinheitlichung und Diversität des Zivilrechts in Transnationalen Wirtschaftsräumen*. Mohr Siebeck (2002), pp. 203–236.

Owen, Bruce M.; Portillo, Jorge E. "Legal Reform, Externalities and Economic Development: Measuring the Impact of Legal Aid on Poor Women in Ecuador" (2003). Available at SSRN: <https://ssrn.com/abstract=406260>.

Palao Moreno, Gillermo. "Individual Employment Contracts". In: Magnus, Ulrich; Mankowski Peter. *European Commentaries On Private International Law, ECPIL*, vol. 2. Otto Schmidt (2017).

Parisi, Francesco. "Positive, Normative and Functional Schools in Law and Economics". *European Journal of Law and Economics* 18.3 (2004), pp. 259–272.

—— *Harmonization of European Private Law: An Economic Analysis*. Minnesota Legal Studies Research Paper no. 07-41 (2007). Available at SSRN: <https://ssrn.com/abstract=1014385>.

Parisi, Francesco; O'Hara, Erin A. "Conflict of Laws". In: Newman, Peter (ed.). *The New Palgrave Dictionary of Economics and the Law*, vol. 1. Palgrave Macmillan (1998), pp. 387–396.

Parisi, Francesco; Ribstein, Larry. "Choice of Law". In: Newman, Peter (ed.). *The New Palgrave Dictionary of Economics and the Law*, vol. 1. Palgrave Macmillan (1998), pp. 236–241.

Parisi, Francesco; Smith, Vernon. *The Law and Economics of Irrational Behavior*. Stanford University Press (2005).

Pellenbarg, P.H. *How to Calculate the Impact of University on the Regional Economy. A Case Study of the University of Groningen*. The Netherlands University of Groningen – Paper presented to the Conference on Knowledge and Regional Economic Development, organised by Regional Quantitative Analysis Research Group. University of Barcelona (2005).

Pérez Loose, Hernán. "Ecuador". In: Basedow, Jürgen; Rühl, Gisela; Ferrari, Franco; de Miguel Asensio, Pedro. *Encyclopedia of Private International Law*, vol. 3. Edward Elgar Publishing (2017), pp. 2043–2053.

Permanent Bureaus. Extracts from the Response to the Questionnaire on Maintenance Obligations, Preliminary Document no. 3 for the Attention of the Special Commission of April 1999 (1999).

Permanent Bureaus. Compilation of Responses to the 2002 Questionnaire Concerning a New Global Instrument on the International Recovery of Child Support and Other

Forms of Family Maintenance, Preliminary Document no. 2 of April 2003 for the Attention of the Special Commission of May 2003 on the international Recovery of Child Support and Other Forms of Family Maintenance (2003).

Pietsch, Peter. „Scheidung in Malta". *Zeitschrift für das gesamte Familienrecht* 59 (2012), pp. 426–427.

Planck, Max. *Wissenschaftliche Selbstbiographie*. Leipzig/Barth (1948).

Poling-Kempes, Lesley. *The Harvey Girls: Women who opened the West*. Paragon House (1989).

Polinsky, A. Mitchell. *An Introduction to Law and Economics*. Little, Brown & Co. (1983).

Polinsky, A. Mitchell; Shavell, Steven (eds.). *Handbook of Law and Economics*, vol. 2. Elsevier (2007).

Posner, Eric A. "There are no Penalty Default Rules in Contract Law". *Florida State University Law Review* 33 (2005), pp. 563–587.

Posner, Richard A. "Legislation and Its Interpretation: A Primer". *Nebraska Law Review* 68 (1989), pp. 431–453.

—— "The Law and Economics of Contract Interpretation". *Texas Law Review* 83 (2005), pp. 1581–1614.

—— *Economic Analysis of Law*, 9th edn. Wolters Kluwer (2014).

Posner, Richard A.; Rosenfield, Andrew M. "Impossibility and Related Doctrines in Contract Law: An Economic Analysis". *Journal of Legal Studies* 6.1 (1977), pp. 83–118.

Potz, Andrea; Runggaldier, Ulrich. "Employment Protection". In: Basedow, Jürgen; Hopt, Klaus; Zimmermann; Stier, Andreas. *The Max Planck Encyclopedia of European Private Law*, vol. 1. Oxford University Press (2012).

Rafeeq, Mona. Rethinking Islamic Law Arbitration Tribunals: Are They Compatible with Traditional American Notions of Justice. *Wisconsin International Law Journal* 28 (2010), pp. 108–139.

Rasul, Imran. Marriage Markets and Divorce Laws. *Journal of Law, Economics, and Organization* 22.1 (2005), pp. 30–69.

Raupach, Claudia. *Ehescheidung mit Auslandsbezug in der Europäischen Union*. Mohr Siebeck (2014).

Rauscher, Thomas. *Europäisches Zivilprozess- und Kollisionsrecht, EuZPR/EuIPR*. 4th edn. Otto Schmidt (2015–2016).

Regan, Milton C. *Family Law and the Pursuit of Intimacy*. New York University Press (1993).

Rehman, Javaid. "The Sharia, Islamic Family Laws and International Human Rights Law: Examining the Theory and Practice of Polygamy and Talaq". *International Journal of Law, Policy and the Family* 21.1 (2007), pp. 108–127.

Reimann, Mathias. *Conflict of laws in Western Europe: A Guide Through the Jungle*. Irvington Transnational Publishers (1995).

—— "Interest and Policy Analysis in Private International Law". In: Basedow, Jürgen; Rühl, Gisela; Ferrari, Franco; de Miguel Asensio, Pedro. *Encyclopedia of Private International Law*, vol. 2. Edward Elgar Publishing (2017), pp. 980–988.

Reimer, Torsten; Rieskamp, Jörg. "Fast and Frugal Heuristics". In Baumeister, R.F.; Vohs, K.D. (eds.). *Encyclopedia of Social Psychology*. Sage (2007), pp. 346–348.

Reinhartz, Barbara; Vlaardingerbroek, Paul. "Niederlande". In: Süß, Rembert; Ring, Gerdhard. *Eherecht in Europa*, 4th edn. (2021), pp. 873–933.

Requejo Isidro, Marta. "Lex Fori". In: Basedow, Jürgen; Rühl, Gisela; Ferrari, Franco; de Miguel Asensio, Pedro. *Encyclopedia of Private International Law*, vol. 1. Edward Elgar Publishing, (2017), pp. 1104–1113.

Reyes Lopéz, María José. *Comunidad de Bienes*. Tirant le Blach (2014).

Riaño, Yvonne. "Latin American Women Who Migrate for Love: Imagining European Men as Ideal Partners". In: Enguix, Begonya; Roca, Jordi (eds.). *Rethinking Romantic Love. Discussions, Mobilities and Practices*. Cambridge Scholars Publishing (2015), pp. 45–60.

Ribstein, Larry E. "Lawyers as Lawmakers: a Theory of Lawyer Licensing". *Missouri Law Review* 69 (2004), pp. 299–364.

Ribstein, Larry E.; O'Hara, Erin A. *The Law Market*. Oxford University Press (2009).

Rieskamp, Jörg; Hoffrage, Ulrich. "When Do People Use Simple Heuristics, and How Can We Tell?". In: Gigerenzer, Gerd; Todd, Peter M. *Simple Heuristics that Make Us Smart. Evolution and Cognition* Oxford University Press (1999), pp. 141–168.

Riley, Christopher A. "Designing Default Rules in Contract Law: Consent, Conventionalism, and Efficiency". *Oxford Journal of Legal Studies* 20.3 (2000), pp. 367–390.

Rinaldi, Manuela. *Assegno Divorzile e Nuovi Parametri dopo la Sentenza no. 11504/201*. Maggioli Editore (2017).

Robbins, Lionel C. *An Essay on the Nature and Significance of Economic Science*. Macmillan (1932).

—— *An Essay on the Nature and Significance of Economic Science*. Ludwig von Mises Institute (2007).

Robinson, Harriet. *Loom and Spindle, or Life among the Early Mill Girls*. Press Pacifica ([1898] 1976). Available at: <https://archive.org/details/loomspindleorlif00robi>.

Rodrik, Dani. "How Far Will International Integration Go?". *Journal of Economic Perspectives* 14 (2000), pp. 177–186.

—— "Globalization and Growth – Looking in the Wrong Places". *Journal of Policy Modeling* 26 (2004), pp. 513–517.

Romano, Roberta. "Law as a Product: Some Pieces of the Incorporation Puzzle". *Journal of Law, Economics, & Organization* 1 (1985), pp. 225–283.

Rösler, Hanes. Consumers and Consumer Protection law. In: Basedow, Jürgen; Hopt, Klaus; Zimmermann; Stier, Andreas. *The Max Planck Encyclopedia of European Private Law*, vol. 1. Oxford University Press (2012).

Roth, Wulf-Henning. *Internationales Versicherungsvertragsrecht: das Versicherungsverhältnis im Internationalen Vertragsrecht, Zugleich ein Beitrag zum Schutz des Schwächeren Vertragspartners im IPR und zur Dienstleistungsfreiheit in der Europäischen Gemeinschaft*. Mohr Siebeck (1985).

Rudden, Bernard. *Economic Theory v. Property Law: The numerus Clausus Problem*. Oxford Essays on Jurisprudence 3 (1987), pp. 254–256.

Rühl, Giesela. "Methods and Approaches in Choice of Law: an Economic Perspective". *Berkeley Journal of International Law* 24 (2006), pp. 801–841.

—— Die Kosten der Rechtswahlfreiheit: zur Anwendung Ausländischen Rechts durch Deutsche Gerichte. *Rabels Zeitschrift für ausländisches und internationales Privatrecht/The Rabel Journal of Comparative and International Private Law* 3 (2007a), pp. 559–596.

—— "Party Autonomy in the Private International Law of Contracts: Transatlantic Convergence and Economic Efficiency". In: Gottschalk, Eckart; Michaels, Ralf; Rühl Gisela; Von Hein, Jan. *Conflict of Laws in a Globalized World*. Cambridge University Press (2007b), pp. 153–183.

—— *Statut und Effizienz: Ökonomische Grundlagen des Internationalen Privatrechts*. Mohr Siebeck (2011).

—— "The Protection of Weaker Parties in the Private International Law of the European Union: a Portrait of Inconsistency and Conceptual Truancy". *Journal of Private International Law* 10.3 (2014a), pp. 335–358.

—— "Wettbewerb der Rechtsordnungen im Vertragsrecht - Wunsch oder Wirklichkeit?". In: Ehricke, Ulrich; Kaal, Wulf; Schmidt, Matthias; Schwartze, Andreas (eds.). *Festschrift für Christian Kirchner*. Mohr Siebeck (2014b), pp. 975–994.

—— "The Role of Private Economic Efficiency in European Private International Law". In: Leible, Stefan. *General Principles of European Private International Law*. Wolters Kluwer (2016).

—— "Regulatory Competition". In: Basedow, Jürgen; Rühl, Gisela; Ferrari, Franco; de Miguel Asensio, Pedro. *Encyclopedia of Private International Law*, vol. 2. Edward Elgar Publishing (2017), pp. 1515–1523.

Ryter, Annamarie. "Die Geschlechtsvormundschaft in der Schweiz: das Beispiel der Kanton Basel-Landschaft und Basel-Stadt". In: Gerhard, Ute. *Frauen in der Geschichte des Rechts: von der frühen Neuzeit bis zur Gegenwart*. C.H. Beck (1997), pp. 494–506.

Ryznar, Margaret; Stępień-Sporek, Anna. "The Harmonization of Matrimonial Property Law in the United States and European Union". *Issues in Contemporary International, European and Comparative Law* 9 (2011), pp. 35–53.

Sabean, David. Allianzen und Listen: Die Geschechtsvormundschaft im 18. und 19. Jahrhundert". In: Gerhard, Ute. *Frauen in der Geschichte des Rechts: von der Frühen Neuzeit bis zur Gegenwart*. C.H. Beck (1997), pp. 460–479.

Sacks, Stephen R. "Transaction Costs in Non-Market Economies". *Journal of Institutional and Theoretical Economics (JITE)/Zeitschrift für die gesamte Staatswissenschaft* 144.5 (1988), pp. 865–870.

Samuelson, Paul A. "The Pure Theory of Public Expenditure". *Review of Economics and Statistics* 36.4 (1954), pp. 387–389.

—— "Diagrammatic Exposition of a Theory of Public Expenditure". *Review of Economics and Statistics* (1955), pp. 350–356.

Sanchez, Laura; Nock, Steven L.; Wright, James D.; Pardee, Jessica W. "The Implementation of Covenant Marriage in Louisiana". *Virginia Journal of Social Policy & the Law* 9 (2001), pp. 192–223.

Sánchez Gassen, N.; Perelli-Harris, Briena. "The Increase in Cohabitation and the Role of Union Status in Family Policies: A Comparison of 12 European Countries". *Journal of European Social Policy* 25.4 (2015), pp. 431–449.

Sandmo, Agnar. "Gary Becker's Contributions to Economics". *The Scandinavian Journal of Economics* 95.1 (1993), pp. 7–23.

Schack, Heimo. "Das IPR - ein Buch mit Sieben Siegeln, Reif für das Moderne Antiquariat?". In: Krüger, Hilmar; Mansel, Heinz-Peter (eds.). *Liber Amicorum Gerhard Kegel*. C.H. Beck (2002), pp. 179–198.

Schäfer, Hans-Bernd. "Rule Based Legal Systems as a Substitute for Human Capital: Should Poor Countries Have a More Rule Based Legal System?" (2001). Available at SSRN: <https://ssrn.com/abstract=999863>.

Schäfer, Hans-Bernd; Lantermann, Katrin. "Choice of law from an Economic Perspective". In: Basedow, Jürgen; Toshiyuki, Kono. *An Economic Analysis of Private International Law*. Mohr Siebeck (2006), pp. 87–119.

Schäfer, Hans-Bernd; Ott, Claus. *The Economic Analysis of Civil Law*. Edward Elgar Publishing (2005a).

—— *Lehrbuch der Ökonomischen Analyse des Zivilrechts*, 4th edn. Springer (2005b).

—— *Lehrbuch der Ökonomischen Analyse des Zivilrechts*, 5th edn. Springer (2012).

Scheibehenne, Benjamin; Bröder, Arndt. "Predicting Wimbledon 2005 Tennis Results by Mere Player Name Recognition". *International Journal of Forecasting* 23.3 (2007), pp. 415–426.

Scherpe, Jens M. *Marital Agreements and Private Autonomy in Comparative Perspective*. Hart Publishing (2012a).

—— "Marital Agreements". In: Basedow, Jürgen; Hopt, Klaus; Zimmermann, Reinhard; Stier, Andreas. *The Max Planck Encyclopedia of European Private Law*, vol. 2. Oxford University Press (2012b).

—— *Marital Agreements and Private Autonomy in Comparative Perspective*. Hart Publishing (2012c).

—— *The Present and Future of European Family Law*, vol. 4. Edward Elgar Publishing (2016).

Schlegel, Stefan. *Der Entscheid über Migration als Verfügungsrecht*. Mohr Siebeck (2017).

Schmidt-Trenz, Hans-Jörg. *Außenhandel und Territorialität des Rechts. Grundlegung einer Neuen Institutionenökonomik des Außenhandels*. Nomos (1990).

Schmidt-Trenz, Hans-Jörg; Schmidtchen, Dieter. "Private International Law in the Shadow of the Territoriality of Law: Why Does It Work?" *Southern Economic Journal* 58 (1991), pp. 329–338.

Schmidtchen, Dieter. "Territorialität des Rechts, Internationales Privatrecht und die Privatautonome Regelung Internationaler Sachverhalte". *Rabels Zeitschrift für ausländisches und internationales Privatrecht/The Rabel Journal of Comparative and International Private Law* 59 (1995), pp. 56–112.

—— "Lex Mercatoria und die Evolution des Rechts". In: Ott, Claus; Schäfer, Hans-Bernd (eds.). *Vereinheitlichung und Diversität des Zivilrechts in Transnationalen Wirtschaftsräumen*. Mohr Siebeck (2002), pp. 1–31.

—— "Vereinheitlichung des Vertragsrechts in Europa – eine Lösung auf der Suche nach dem Problem? Die Sicht der Neuen Institutionenökonomik". In: Eger, Thomas; Schäfer, Hans-Bernd (eds.). *Ökonomische Analyse der Europäischen Zivilrechtsentwicklung*. Mohr Siebeck (2007), pp. 1–45.

Schmidtchen, Dieter; Schmidt-Trenz, Hans-Jörg. *Private Law, the World Production Possibility Frontier and the Need for an International "Private Law Community": German Theory of Order and Constitutional Economics at Work*, Liberty Fund Symposium on "German Ordnungstheorie and American Constitutional Economics", Bonn (1989).

—— "Territoriality of Law and the International Trade Game – Towards a New Institutional Economics of International Transactions". In: Bindseil, Ulrich; Haucap, Justus; Wey, Christian (eds.). *Institutions in Perspective. Festschrift in Honor of Rudolf Richter on the Occasion of his 80th Birthday*. Mohr Siebeck (2006), pp. 327–348.

Schmidtchen, Dieter; Koboldt, Christian; Monheim Helstroffer, Jenny; Will, Birgit E.; Haas, Georg. *The Internalisation of External Costs in Transport: From the Polluter Pays to the Cheapest Cost Avoider Principle*. Saarland University, CSLE–Center for the Study of Law and Economics (2007).

Schneider, Hildegard; Kortese, Lavinia; Mertens, Pim; Sivonen Susanne. *Cross-border mobility in times of COVID-19: Assessing COVID-19 Measures and their Effects on Cross-border Regions within the EU*. EU-CITIZEN: Academic Network on European Citizenship Rights (2021).

Schnitzer, Adolf F. *Handbuch des Internationalen Privatrechts*, 4th edn., vol. 1 Verlag für Recht und Gesellschaft (1957).

—— *Handbuch des Internationalen Privatrechts*, 4th edn., vol. 2. Verlag für Recht und Gesellschaft AG (1958).

—— "Die Zuordnung der Verträge im Internationalen Privatrecht". *Rabels Zeitschrift für ausländisches und internationales Privatrecht/The Rabel Journal of Comparative and International Private Law* (1969), pp. 17–29.

Schoeman, Elsabe. "New Zealand". In: Basedow, Jürgen; Rühl, Gisela; Ferrari, Franco;, de Miguel Asensio, Pedro. *Encyclopedia of Private International Law*, vol. 3. Edward Elgar Publishing (2017a), pp. 2339–2378.

—— "South Africa". In: Basedow, Jürgen; Rühl, Gisela; Ferrari, Franco; de Miguel Asensio, Pedro. *Encyclopedia of Private International Law*, vol. 3. Edward Elgar Publishing (2017b), pp. 2515–2523.

Schumpeter, Joseph. *Theorie der wirtschaftlichen Entwicklung*, 8th edn. Dunkler & Humblot ([1911] 1993).

Schwartz, Alan and Scott, Robert E. *Contract Theory and the Limits of Contract Law*. John M. Olin Center for Studies in Law, Economics, and Public Policy Working Papers. Paper 275 (2003).

Schwartz, Barry; Ward, Andrew; Monterosso John; Lyubomirsky, Sonja; White Katherine; Lehman, Darrin. "Maximizing versus Satisficing: Happiness is a Matter of Choice". *Journal of Personality and Social Psychology* 83.5 (2002), pp. 1178–1197.

Schwenzer, Ingeborg. *Model Family Code: from a Global Perspective*, vol. 12. Intersentia (2006).

Scott, Robert. "Conflict and Cooperation in Long-Term Contracts". *California Law Review* 75 (1987) pp. 2005–2054.

—— "A Relational Theory of Default Rules for Commercial Contracts". *Journal of Legal Studies* 19.2 (1990), pp. 597–616.

Scott, Elizabeth S. "Rational Decision-making about Marriage and Divorce". *Virginia Law Review* 76 (1990), pp. 9–94.

Scott, Elizabeth S.; Scott, Robert. "Marriage as Relational Contract". *Virginia Law Review* 84 (1998), pp. 1225–1334.

—— "A Contract Theory of Marriage". In: Buckley, F.H. *The Fall and Rise of Freedom of Contract*. Duke University Press (1999).

Serwe, S; Frings, C. "Who will win Wimbledon? The Recognition Heuristic in Predicting Sports Events". *Journal of Behavioral Decision Making* 19 (2006), pp. 321–332.

Shavell, Steven. *Foundations of Economic Analysis of Law*. Belknap Press of Harvard University Press (2004).

Shleifer, Andrei. "A Theory of Yardstick Competition". *Rand Journal of Economics* 16.3 (1985), pp. 319–327.

Shur-Ofry Michal; Tur-Sinai Ofer. "Constructive Ambiguity: IP Licenses as a Case Study". University of Michigan Journal of Law Reform 48 (2015), pp. 391–435.

Silberman, Linda. "(American) Conflict of laws Revolution". In: Basedow, Jürgen; Rühl, Gisela; Ferrari, Franco; de Miguel Asensio, Pedro. *Encyclopedia of Private International Law*, vol. 1. Edward Elgar Publishing (2017a), pp. 66–70.

—— "USA". In: Basedow, Jürgen; Rühl, Gisela; Ferrari, Franco; de Miguel Asensio, Pedro. *Encyclopedia of Private International Law*, vol. 3. Edward Elgar Publishing (2017b), pp. 2637–2647.

Silveri, Annamaria, Samayoa, Maria Faustina. "Beyond the Honeymoon: Physical Attraction and Its Role throughout Marriage". In: Weisfeld, Carol Cronin; Weisfeld, Glenn; Dillon, Lisa M. *The Psychology of Marriage*. Lexington Books (2018), pp. 211–222.

Simon, Herbert. "Invariants of Human Behavior". *Annual Review of Psychology* 41 (1990), pp. 1–19.

Skåtun, John Douglas. "Bargaining on your Spouse: Coasean and Non-Coasean Behaviour within Marriage". *Journal of Family and Economic Issues* 38.2 (2017), pp. 263–278.

Smith, Adam. *Lectures on Jurisprudence. R.L. Meek, D.D. Raphael, and Peter Stein*, Oxford ([1766] 1978).

—— *An Inquiry into the Nature and Causes of the Wealth of Nations*. Edwin Cannan ([1776] 1976).

Smith, Ian. "The Law and Economics of Marriage Contracts". *Journal of Economic Surveys* 17.2 (2003) pp. 201–226.

—— "12 European Divorce Laws, Divorce Rates, and their Consequences". In: Dnes, Antony W.; Rowthorn, Robert (eds.). *The Law and Economics of Marriage and Divorce*. Cambridge University Press (2002).

Smits, Jan M. "A European Private Law as a Mixed Legal System: Towards a Ius Commune through the Free Movement of Legal Rules". *Maastricht Journal of European and Comparative Law* 5.4 (1998), pp. 328–340.

—— "The Harmonisation of Private Law in Europe: Some Insights from Evolutionary Theory". *Georgia Journal of International & Comparative Law* 31 (2002), pp. 79–99.

Söhngen, Martin. *Das internationale Privatrecht von Peru*. Mohr Siebeck (2006).

Solomon, Dennis. "The Private International Law of Contracts in Europe: Advances and Retreats". *Tulane Law Review* 82 (2007), pp. 1709–1740.

Spence, Michael. "Job Market Signaling". *Quarterly Journal of Economics* 87.3 (1973), pp. 355–374.

—— "Signaling in retrospect and the informational structure of markets". *American Economic Review* 92.3 (2002), pp. 434–459.

Spier, Kathryn E. "Incomplete contracts and signalling". *Rand Journal of Economics* 23.3 (1992), pp. 432–443.

Sportel, Iris, "Because It's an Islamic Marriage" Conditions Upon Marriage and after Divorce in Transnational Dutch-Moroccan and Dutch-Egyptian Marriages. *Oñati Socio Legal Series* 3.6 (2013), pp. 1091–1110.

Stark, Johanna. *Law for Sale: A Philosophical Critique of Regulatory Competition*. Oxford University Press (2019).

Staudinger, Ansgar. "Protokol über das auf Unterhaltspflichten anzuwendende Recht". In: *Münchener Kommentar zum Bürgerlichen Gesetzbuch: BGB*, 7th edn., vol. 11. C.H. Beck (2018), pp. 1255–1353.

Stevenson, Betsey. "The impact of divorce laws on marriage-specific capital". *Journal of Labor Economics* 25.1 (2007), pp. 75–94.

Stevenson, Betsey; Wolfers, Justin. "Bargaining in the shadow of the law: Divorce laws and family distress". *The Quarterly Journal of Economics* 121.1 (2006), pp. 267–288.

Stigler, George. "The Economics of Information". *Journal of Political Economy* 69.3 (1961), pp. 213–222.

Stone, Peter. *Stone on Private International Law in the European Union*. 4. edn. Edward Elgar Publishing (2018).

Streit, Manfred E., "Das Wettbewerbskonzept der Ordnungstheorie". In: Streit, Manfred E. (ed.). *Freiburger Beiträge zur Ordnungsökonomik*. Mohr Siebeck (1995), pp. 57–70.

—— "Systemwettbewerb und Europäische Integration". In: Zimmermann, Felix A. (ed.). *Ordnungspolitische Aspekte der Europäischen Integration*. Nomos (1996), pp. 11–22.

Streit, Manfred E.; Mangels, Antje. *Privatautonomes Recht und Grenzüberschreitende Transaktionen*. Jena (1996), pp. 73–100.

Streit, Manfred E.; Mussler, Werner. "Wettbewerb der Systeme und das Binnenmarktprogramm der Europäischen Union. In: Gerken, Lüder (ed.). *Europa zwischen Ordnungswettbewerb und Harmonisierung. Europäische Ordnungspolitik im Zeichen der Subsidiarität*. Springer (1995), pp. 75–107.

Stuart, Charles. "Consumer Protection in Markets with Informationally Weak Buyers. *Bell Journal of Economics* (1981), pp. 562–573.

Stucke, Maurice E. "Is Competition Always Good?". *Journal of Antitrust Enforcement* 1.1 (2013), pp. 162–197.

Sunstein, Cass R. *Behavioral Law & Economics*. Cambridge University Press (2000).

—— "The Right to Marry". *Cardozo Law Review* 26 (2004) pp. 2081–2120.

Sunstein, Cass R.; Thaler, Richard. "Libertarian Paternalism is not an Oxymoron". *University of Chicago Law Review* (2003), pp. 1159–1202.

—— "Privatizing Marriage". *Monist* 91.3–4 (2008), pp. 377–387.

Swennen, Frederik. *Contractualisation of Family Law – Global Perspectives*. Springer International Publishing (2015).

Teitelbaum, Lee E. "Placing the Family in Context". *UC Davis Law Review* 22 (1988), pp. 801–827.

Thaler Richard. "Toward a positive Theory of Consumer Choice". *Journal of Economic Behavior and Organization* 1 (1980), pp. 39–60.

Thiel, Stuart E. "Choice of Law and the Home-Court Advantage: Evidence". *American Law and Economics Review* 2.2 (2000), pp. 291–317.

Thompson, Barton H. "People or Prairie Chickens: The Uncertain Search for Optimal Biodiversity". *Stanford Law Review* 51.5 (1999), pp. 1127–1185.

Tiebout, Charles M. "A Pure Theory of Local Expenditures". *Journal of Political Economy* 64.5 (1956), pp. 416–424.

Tjiong, Henri. "Breaking the Spell of Regulatory Competition: Reframing the Problem of Regulatory Exit". *Rabels Zeitschrift für ausländisches und internationales Privatrecht/ The Rabel Journal of Comparative and International Private Law* 1 (2002), pp. 66–96.

Todd, Peter; Miller, Geoffrey. "From Pride and Prejudice to Persuasion Satisficing in Mate Search". In: Gigerenzer, Gerd; Todd, Peter; the ABC Research Group. *Simple Heuristics that Make Us Smart*. Oxford University Press (1999), pp. 287–308

Toshiyuki, Kono. "Japan". In: Basedow, Jürgen; Rühl, Gisela; Ferrari, Franco; de Miguel Asensio, Pedro. *Encyclopedia of Private International Law*, vol. 3. Edward Elgar Publishing (2017), pp. 2219–2229.

Trachtman, Joel P. "Regulatory Competition and Regulatory Jurisdiction". *Journal of International Economic Law* 3.2 (2000), pp. 331–348.

Trebilcock, Michael J. *The Limits of Freedom of Contract*. 2nd edn. Harvard University Press (1997).

—— "Marriage as a Signal". In: Buckley, F.H. *The Fall and Rise of Freedom of Contract*. Duke University Press (1999).

Trebilcock, Michael J.; Keshvani, Rosemin. "The Role of Private Ordering in Family Law: a Law and Economics Perspective". *University of Toronto Law Journal* 41 (1991), pp. 533–590.

Trebilcock, Michael; Leng, Jing. "The Role of Formal Contract Law and Enforcement in Economic Development". *Virginia Law Review* 92 (2006), pp. 1517–1580.

Tuor, Peter; Rumo-Jungo, Alexandra; Schmid, Jörg; Schnyder, Bernhard. *Das Schweizerische Zivilgesetzbuch*, 14th edn. Schulthess (2015).

Turrini, Alessandro A.; Van Ypersele, Tanguy. *Legal Costs as Barriers to Trade* Center for Economic Policy Research, Discussion Paper no. 5751 (2006).

Ulen, Thomas. "Rational Choice in the Law and Economics". In: Bouckaert, Boudewijn; De Geest, Gerit. *Encyclopedia of Law and Economics*, vol. 1. Edward Elgar Publishing (2000).

UN High Commissioner for Refugees (UNHCR). *The Refugee Convention, 1951: The Travaux Préparatoires Analysed with a Commentary by Dr. Paul Weis*. UNHCR (1990). Available at: <http://www.refworld.org/docid/53e1dd114.html>.

—— *The "Essential Right" to Family Unity of Refugees and Others in Need of International Protection in the Context of Family Reunification*, 2nd edn. UNHCR (2018). Available at: <https://www.refworld.org/docid/5a902a9b4.html>.

Van den Bergh, Roger. "Subsidiarity as an Economic Demarcation Principle and the Emergence of European Private Law". *Maastricht Journal of European and Comparative Law* 5.2 (1998), pp. 129–152.

—— "Towards an Institutional Legal Framework for Regulatory Competition in Europe". *Kyklos* 53.4 (2000), pp. 435–466.

Vanberg, Viktor. "Wettbewerb in Markt und Politik". In: Zimmermann, Felix A. (ed.). *Ordnungspolitische Aspekte der Europäischen Integration*. Nomos (1996), pp. 85–100.

Veljanovski, Cento G. *Economic Principles of Law*. Cambridge University Press (2007).

Verwilghen, M. *Explanatory Report on the 1973 Hague Maintenance Conventions. Acts and Documents of the Twelfth Session*. HCCH (1975), pp. 384–465.

Viarengo, Ilaria. "The Rome III Regulation in Legal Practice: Case Law and Comments". *ERA Forum* 15.4 (2014).

Vihanto, Martti. "Competition between Local Governments as a Discovery Procedure". *Journal of Institutional and Theoretical Economics (JITE)/Zeitschrift für die gesamte Staatswissenschaft* (1992), pp. 411–436.

Vischer, Frank. *Internationales Vertragsrecht*. Stämpfli (1962).

—— "The Concept of the Characteristic Performance Reviewed". In: Borrás, Alegría; Bucher, Andreas; Struycken Teun; Verweilghen, Michel (eds.). *E Pluribus Unum: Liber Amicorum Georges A.L. Droz - on the Progressive Unification of Private International Law*. Martinus Nijhoff Publishers (1996), pp. 499-520.

Vlaardingerbroek, Paul. "Family Law". In: Chorus, Jeroen M.J.; Hondius, Ewoud H.; Voermans, Wim. *Introduction to Dutch Law*, 5th edn. Wolters Kluwer (2016).

Vogel, Ursula. "Patriarchale Herrschaft, Bürgerliches Recht, Bürgerliche Utopie: Eigentumsrechte der Frauen in Deutschland und England". In: Kocka, Jürgen (ed.). *Bürgertum im 19. Jahrhundert*, vol. 1. Deutscher Taschenbuch Verlag (1988), pp. 134–166.

Vogenauer, Stefan. "Regulatory Competition through Choice of Contract Law and Choice of Forum in Europe: Theory and Evidence". *European Review of Private Law* 21 (2013), pp. 13–78.

Vogenauer, Stefan; Hodges, Christopher. *Civil Justice Systems in Europe: Implications for Choice of Forum and Choice of Contract Law*. Hart Publishing Limited (2010). Available at: <https://www.fondation-droitcontinental.org/fr/wp-content/uploads/2013/12/oxford_civil_justice_survey_-_summary_of_results_final.pdf>.

Vogenauer, Stefan; Weatherill, Stephen. "The European Community's Competence to Pursue the Harmonisation of Contract Law – an Empirical Contribution to the Debate". In: Vogenauer, Stefan; Weatherill, Stephen (eds.). *The Harmonisation of European Contract Law*. Hart Publishing (2006), pp. 105–148.

Voigt, Stefan. "Are International Merchants Stupid? Their Choice of Law Sheds Doubt on the Legal Origin Theory". *Journal of Empirical Legal Studies* 5.1 (2008), pp. 1–20.

Von Overbeck, Alfred E. *Explanatory Report on the 1978 Hague Matrimonial Property Regimes Convention*. HCCH (1978).

Von Savigny, Friedrich C. *System des Heutigen Römischen Rechts*, vol. 8. Scientia Berlin ([1849] 1981).

Voltaire, *Dialogues Et Anecdotes Philosophiques. Introduction, Notes et Rapprochements par Raymond Naves*. Garnier (1966).

Waaldijk Kees. "Small Change: How the Road to Same-Sex Marriage Got Paved in the Netherlands". In: Robert, Wintemute; Mads Andenaes (eds.) *Legal Recognition of Same-Sex Partnerships – A Study of National, European and International Law*. Hart Publishing (2001), pp. 437–464.

Walther, Selma. Moral Hazard in Marriage: the Use of Domestic Labor as an Incentive Device. *Review of Economics of the Household* 15.2 (2017), pp. 357–382.

Wautelet, Patrick. "What's Wrong with Article 22? The Unsolved Mysteries of Choice of Law for Matrimonial Property". In: Bonomi, Andrea; Romano, Gian Paolo. *Yearbook of Private International Law*, vol. 19 (2018), pp. 213–231.

Weber, Albrecht. "Scheidung in der Ehe". In: Säcker, Franz Jürgen; Schürnbrand, Jan. *Münchener Kommentar Zum Bürgerlichen Gesetzbuch*. 7th edn., vol. 8. C.H. Beck (2017), pp. 2015–2018.

Weber-Will, Susanne. "Geschlechtsvormundschaft und Weibliche Rechtswohltaten im Privatrecht des Preußischen Allgemeinen Landrechts von 1794". In: Gerhard, Ute. *Frauen in der Geschichte des Rechts: von der Frühen Neuzeit bis zur Gegenwart*. C.H. Beck (1997), pp. 452–459.

Wedgwood, Ralph. "Is Civil Marriage Illiberal?". In: Brake, Elizabeth. *After marriage*. Oxford University Press (2016).

Wei, Shang-Jin. *Intra-National versus Inter-National Trade: How Stubborn are Nations in Global Integration?* National Bureau of Economic Research, Working Paper Series, Working Paper nr. 5531 (1996).

Weisfeld Glenn; Weisfeld, Carol Cronin. "The Mysteries of Marriage: Its Functions, Evolution, and Development". In: Weisfeld, Carol Cronin; Weisfeld, Glenn; Dillon, Lisa M. *The Psychology of Marriage*. Lexington Books (2018), pp. 3–24.
Weisfeld, Glenn E.; Weisfeld, Carol Cronin; Goetz, Stefan M.M. "Toward a Model of Marriage". In: Weisfeld, Carol Cronin; Weisfeld, Glenn; Dillon, Lisa M. *The Psychology of Marriage*. Lexington Books (2018), pp. 317–334.
Weiss, Yoram. "The Formation and Dissolution of Families: Why Marry? Who Marries Whom? And What Happens upon Divorce". *Handbook of Population and Family Economics* 1 (1997), pp. 81–123.
Welchman, Lynn. *Women and Muslim Family Laws in Arab States. A Comparative Overview of Textual Development and Advocacy*. Amsterdam University Press (2007).
Wennersbusch, Jasmin. *Rechtswahl im Spannungsfeld von Parteiautonomie und Kollisionsrechtlichem Schutz des Schwächeren*. Jenaer Wissenschaftliche Verlagsgesellschaft (2018).
Whincop, Michael J.; Keyes, Mary. *Policy and Pragmatism in the Conflict of Laws*. Routledge (2001).
White, Kimberly David. "Covenant Marriage: An Unnecessary Second Attempt a Fault-Based Divorce". *Alabama Law Review* 61 (2009), pp. 869–890.
Wiedemann, Anton; Pertot, Teresa. "Italien". In: Süß, Rembert; Ring, Gerdhard. *Eherecht in Europa*. 4th edn. Zerb Verlag (2021) pp. 683–756.
Wilderspin, Michael. "Consumer Contracts". In: Magnus, Ulrich; Mankowski Peter. *European Commentaries on Private International Law, ECPIL*, vol. 2. Otto Schmidt (2017).
Williams, Neil G. "What to Do When There's No I Do: A Model for Awarding Damages under Promissory Estoppel". *Washington Law Review* 70 (1995), pp. 1019.
Wittman, Donald. "General Structure of the Law". In: Bouckaert, Boudewijn; De Geest, Gerit. *Encyclopedia of Law and Economics*, vol. 1. Edward Elgar Publishing (2000).
Yassari, Nadjma. *Die Brautgabe im Familienvermögensrecht: Innerislamischer Rechtsvergleich und Integration in das Deutsche Recht*. Mohr Siebeck (2014).
—— "Iran". In: Basedow, Jürgen; Rühl, Gisela; Ferrari, Franco; de Miguel Asensio, Pedro. *Encyclopedia of Private International Law*, vol. 3. Edward Elgar Publishing (2017), pp. 2173–2182.
Yee, M.; Hauser, J.; Orlin, J.; Dahan, E. "Greedoid-Based Non-compensatory Inference". *Marketing Science* 26.4 (2007), pp. 532–549.
Yi, Kei-Mu. *Vertical Specialization and the Border Effect Puzzle* Federal Reserve Bank of Philadelphia Working Paper Series, Working Paper no. 24 (2005).
Yurko, Anna. *Costly Divorce and Marriage Rates*. University Library of Munich (2014).
Zelder, Martin. "For Better or for Worse? Is Bargaining in Marriage and Divorce Efficient?". In: Dnes, Antony W.; Rowthorn, Robert (eds.). *The Law and Economics of Marriage and Divorce*. Cambridge University Press (2002), pp. 157–170.
Zywicki, Todd J. "The Rise and Fall of Efficiency in the Common Law: a Supply-Side Analysis". *Northwestern University Law Review* 97 (2002), pp. 1551–1632.

INDEX

ABOUT THE AUTHOR

Rorick Tovar Galván is a Swiss-Peruvian specialist in private international law with extensive expertise in comparative law. After studying law in Peru, he obtained a law degree from the University of the Balearic Islands (Spain), completed an LL.M. degree with honors at the University of Bern, and undertook research stays in the Netherlands and Germany before obtaining his PhD in Switzerland. His doctoral thesis was awarded the distinction *summa cum laude* by the Faculty of Law at the University of Bern. He has been admitted to practice law in Spain and Switzerland. He currently works as a Research Associate and Lecturer at the University of Bern and as a lawyer in Bern. His research interests concern conflict of laws, economic analysis of law, contract law, and marriage law.

www.ingramcontent.com/pod-product-compliance
Ingram Content Group UK Ltd.
Pitfield, Milton Keynes, MK11 3LW, UK
UKHW051921100926
8556IPUK00021B/1293